Crafting State-Nations

Crafting State-Nations

India and Other Multinational Democracies

ALFRED STEPAN

JUAN J. LINZ

YOGENDRA YADAV

The Johns Hopkins University Press
Baltimore

The Johns Hopkins University Press
2715 North Charles Street
Baltimore, Maryland 21218-4363
www.press.jhu.edu

Library of Congress Cataloging-in-Publication Data

Stepan, Alfred C.
Crafting State-Nations : India and other multinational democracies /
Alfred Stepan, Juan J. Linz, and Yogendra Yadav.
p. cm.
Includes bibliographical references and index.
ISBN-13: 978-0-8018-9723-8 (hardcover : alk. paper)
ISBN-10: 0-8018-9723-8 (hardcover : alk. paper)
ISBN-13: 978-0-8018-9724-5 (pbk. : alk. paper)
ISBN-10: 0-8018-9724-6 (pbk. : alk. paper)
1. Multinational states—Case studies. 2. Democracy—Case studies.
I. Linz, Juan J. (Juan José), 1926– II. Yadav, Yogendra. III. Title.
JC311.S827 2010
321'.8—dc22   2010006887

A catalog record for this book is available from the British Library.

*Special discounts are available for bulk purchases of this book. For more
information, please contact Special Sales at 410-516-6936 or
specialsales@press.jhu.edu.*

The Johns Hopkins University Press uses environmentally friendly book
materials, including recycled text paper that is composed of at least 30
percent post-consumer waste, whenever possible. All of our book papers
are acid-free, and our jackets and covers are printed on paper with recycled
content.

Contents

List of Tables and Figures   vii

Preface   xi

1 Comparative Theory and Political Practice: *Do We Need a "State-Nation" Model as Well as a "Nation-State" Model?*   1

2 India as a State-Nation: *Shared Political Community amidst Deep Cultural Diversity*   39

3 Four Indian Cases That Challenge State-Nation Theory?   89

4 Tamils in India: *How State-Nation Policies Helped Construct Multiple but Complementary Identities*   116

5 Tamils in Sri Lanka: *How Nation-State Policies Helped Construct Polar and Conflictual Identities*   144

6 Ukraine: *State-Nation Policies in a Unitary State*   173

7 Federacy: *A Formula for Democratically Managing Multinational Societies in Unitary States*   201

8 The U.S. Federal Model and Multinational Societies: *Some Problems for Democratic Theory and Practice*   257

Bibliography   277

Index   297

Tables and Figures

TABLES

1.1 Two Ideal Types of Democratic States: "Nation-State" and "State-Nation" — 8

1.2 Multiple but Complementary Identity in Spain: Subjective National Identity in Spain, Catalonia, and Basque Country — 32

1.3 Multiple but Complementary Identity in Belgium: Subjective National Identity by Region — 33

1.4 State-Nations More Trusted than Nation-States: Average Trust Ranking in State Institutions in Longstanding Federal Democracies — 38

2.1 Comparative Indicators of India's Human and Income Poverty — 45

2.2 Pride in Nationality in the Eleven Longstanding Federal Democracies — 58

2.3 Pride in India for All Citizens and for Marginal Groups, 2005 — 59

2.4 Subjective National Identity and Religion in India — 61

2.5 Attitudes toward Democracy and Authoritarianism in India and Five Important "Third Wave" Democracies — 65

2.6 Support for Democracy in India by Four Disadvantaged Social Groups, 2004 — 66

2.7 Support for Democracy in India as a Whole and by Four Major Religions — 70

2.8 Relationship between Intensity of Religious Practice and Support for Political Institutions in India — 72

2.9 Citizen Trust in Six Major Institutions in Eleven Longstanding Federal Democracies — 76

2.10 Trust in Institutions in India — 77

2.11 Sense of Political Efficacy and Legitimacy of Democracy among Marginalized Groups in India, 1971–2004 — 79

2.12 Socioeconomic Status and Voting Turnout in the United States   80
      and India

3.1   Rejection of Pro-Khalistan Violence by the Sikh Community: 97
      Attitudes toward Methods Used by the Militants and Punjab
      Police in the Punjab by Religion, 1997

3.2   Persistent Alienation in the Kashmir Valley: Public Opinion on   114
      Solutions to the Kashmir Problem in the Kashmir Valley,
      2002–2008

4.1   Vote Share of Polity-wide Parties in Tamil Nadu State Assembly   135
      Elections, 1952–2001

4.2   Five-Point Scale of Identity in Tamil Nadu and the Rest of India,   136
      2005

4.3   Levels of Trust in Central Institutions and Satisfaction with   137
      Democracy, India and Tamil Nadu, 2005

4.4   Name Recognition and Evaluation of Some Major Political   139
      Figures, Tamil Nadu and the Rest of India, 2005

4.5   Self-identification of Americans within a Binary Ethnic Scale   141

4.6   Identity by Level of Trust in Central Government and   142
      Satisfaction with Democracy in India and Tamil Nadu, 2005

4.7   National and Regional Pride in India and Tamil Nadu, 2005   143

5.1   Perceptions of Discrimination by Community in Sri Lanka, 2005   162

5.2   Majoritarianism in Sri Lanka and India by Majority Religion,   163
      2005

5.3   Opinions on Measures to End the Present Conflict by Ethnicity   166
      in Sri Lanka, 2005

5.4   Opinions on Trust in the Army and Unequal Treatment in   167
      Sri Lanka and India, 2005

5.5   Contrasting Policies of India and Sri Lanka toward Their Tamil   170
      Minority Populations

6.1   Percentage of "Confident Democrats" in Ukraine, Russia, and   195
      Eight Central European Post-Communist Countries, 1996 and
      2005

6.2   Opinions on Democracy and Authoritarianism in Ukraine,   196
      Russia, and Selected Latin American Democracies

8.1   Overrepresentation in the Upper Houses of Eight Longstanding   260
      OECD Federal Democracies and India

8.2   Malapportionment in Burma's Proposed Upper Chamber   267

8.3 A Continuum of the Degree of Overrepresentation in the   268
     Proposed USA Territorial-style Seat Allocation of the
     Upper House in Burma in Comparison with the Upper Houses of
     the Entire Universe of the Eleven Longstanding Federal
     Democracies
8.4 Classification of the Number of Electorally Based Institutional   272
     Veto Players in the Universe of the Twenty-three Longstanding
     Advanced Economy OECD Democracies
8.5 Veto Players and Inequality in OECD Advanced Democracies   274
8.6 USA Inequality Indicators in Comparison to Other OECD   274
     Federal States and Entire OECD Set

FIGURES

1.1 Intensity of Political Activation of Multiple, Territorially   10
     Concentrated, Sociocultural "National" Identities
2.1 In All Four of India's Major Religions, the Greater the Intensity of   71
     Religious Practice, the Greater the Support for Democracy
2.2 Institutions and Political Trust in India and Twenty Other   74
     Democracies, 1990–1993
2.3 Rise and Decline of BJP Seats in Lok Sabha, 1984–2009   86
3.1 Map of India with Contested Peripheral States   90
3.2 Annual Casualties in Terrorist-Related Violence in Punjab,   96
     1981–2009
5.1 Opposite Relationship between Intensity of Religious Practice   168
     and Support for Democracy by Majority Religion in India and
     Sri Lanka
8.1 Constitutional-Legal Arrangements of Entire Universe of the   264
     Eleven Federal Systems That Have Been Democracies since 1988

Preface

The territory of the world today is divided into 195 states; 192 of them are members of the United Nations, and their boundaries are internationally recognized by other states.[1] Such internationally recognized states are presumed to have the right to exercise authority over the population within their borders, whether the people are citizens, subjects, or even foreigners. In many cases, this authority has little to do with the population having a "we-feeling" as members of a community or as members of a nation, because the states were not created by a coherent nation, instead arising as the result of rulers successfully imposing themselves, often by wars or international settlements following wars. No new independent state was created by a national movement without some other existing states supporting it and without very important states, normally the international system of states, recognizing it. What we see as "nation-states" all have had a major component of being "constructed" by existing powers. A nation-state without a prior state helping construct it is inconceivable. The major functional alternative to a nation-state is what we will call a "state-nation." But note: both "nation-states" and "state-nations" are states, and must be states if they are to work.

This leads us to the major theme of this book, which is "state-nations." This may seem an awkward term. We have considered many alternatives, but we keep returning to "state-nations," because both the state and the nation are indispensible elements for modern democracies but stand in an opposite relationship to each other in our state-nation model than they do in the standard nation-state model.

Democracy entails the democratic management of a specific territorial state and its citizens. For too long, the normatively privileged model for a modern state

---

1. The Vatican is recognized as a state by many states but is a not a member of the United Nations. Kosovo is recognized by the United States, but it is still not a member of the United Nations. Taiwan is not a member state of the United Nations but even the divided states North Korea and South Korea are.

has been the nation-state. However, in some countries, more than one group thinks of itself as a nation and has leaders who strive for independence. In this book, we call such states "robustly politically multinational." We are convinced that in some circumstances, especially if a polity is "robustly multinational," a politics of nation-state-building is in conflict with a politics of inclusionary democracy and societal peace. In our judgment, therefore, the complexities, conflicts, and identities of citizens require the theoretical, normative, and political imagining of alternatives to the nation-state model.

In this book, our major alternative is what we call the state-nation model. In chapter 1, we present the core assumptions of the standard nation-state model in Weberian ideal-type terms and then create a normatively and institutionally coherent alternative ideal type, the state-nation model, and show how it stands in sharp contrast to the nation-state's core assumptions.[2] Since we are interested in realizable and observable political alternatives, we then propose a "nested set" of six policies that we believe are supportive of the crafting of state-nations.

We believe our model can, and should be, subject to empirical testing. We thus stipulate that if a polity is close to a state-nation ideal type—even if the state recognizes and supports numerous different languages, cultures, and indeed, nations within the polity—its citizens should have four empirically documentable characteristics. These four characteristics are: (1) a high degree of positive identification with the state; (2) multiple but complementary political identities; (3) a high level of trust in the state's institutions; (4) a high degree of positive support for democracy among all the extremely diverse groups of citizens in the country.[3]

A central claim of nation-state theorists is that only the nation-state can cultivate the trust and identification with the state that a functioning democracy requires. In an opening test of this hypothesis, we explore, using data from the World Values Survey, the degree of trust in six key political institutions found in the eleven longstanding federal democracies in the world. We divided these eleven longstanding federations into those closest to the state-nation pole (Switzerland, Canada, Belgium, Spain, and India) and those states closest to the nation-state pole (Germany, Austria, the United States, Australia, Argentina, and Brazil). We find that states closer to the state-nation pole actually score higher on trust than states closer to the nation-state pole. We also show that in Spain, even in regions like Catalonia, where Catalan and Spanish are official languages and where there

2. For the reader who would like to see these two ideal types side by side in one table before going further, please see table 1.1.
3. If a polity is close to what we call "pure multinational" because it has a series of virtual nation-states within its borders, these attitudes will not be found. See chapter 1, especially figure 1.1.

is some separatist sentiment, the prevailing self-identification is multiple but complementary, in this case, "equally Catalan and Spanish," using the question designed by Linz.

India would seem to present one of the most difficult tests for our argument that multiple but complementary identities and democratic state-nation loyalties are possible even in a polity with robustly multinational dimensions and a plethora of intense linguistic and religious differences. In chapter 2 we argue that such diversity could not have been molded into a nation-state peacefully and democratically. However, many of the founders of Indian democracy, such as Gandhi and Nehru, creatively reflected on this great diversity and conceived and crafted an inclusionary discourse, as well as an inclusionary set of political institutions, very close to what we call the state-nation model.

Was the "idea of India" described above confined merely to the high traditions of political theory and legal constitutional texts? Or did this idea find resonance among ordinary Indian citizens across different religions, regions, communities, and classes? Fortunately, we are able to explore this question in great detail through the data generated by the Lokniti Network of survey analysts. Yogendra Yadav, one of the authors of this book, was its founder-director.

CSDS regularly conducts what may be the largest census-based surveys in the world in India; on occasion Yadav and Lokniti also conduct surveys in Sri Lanka, Pakistan, Bangladesh, and Nepal. Lokniti's most recent survey, the Indian National Election Study in 2009, had over 36,000 respondents. Because Lokniti's surveys are census-based stratified random samples, all significant marginalized groups are included and in the correct proportion. These groups include Muslims, Scheduled Castes, Scheduled Tribes, socioeconomic groups identified as "very poor" and "poor," and most ethnic linguistic groups, some of which see themselves as nations.[4] The results of these surveys, many of whose questions were designed by the three coauthors in order to explore the salient questions raised in this book, show strikingly high support for India's political institutions.[5] For example, 71% of Hindus and 71% of Muslims say that democracy is the best form of government for India. These surveys allow us to examine whether our hypothesis that citizens are capable of multiple but complementary identities is borne out.

---

4. CSDS uses booster samples in its nationwide surveys to ensure sufficient respondents from smaller states (e.g., Mizoram) or social groups. They also do surveys devoted to a single state such as Kashmir or Punjab.

5. The major exception to this is Kashmir, where respondents in the last decade have twice indicated a preference for an independent state.

In chapter 3, we attempt to submit our hypothesis about the relative success of state-nation policies in India by exploring four cases that many would consider "inconvenient facts" for our argument: the insurgencies for independence in the Punjab, Mizoram, Nagaland, and Kashmir.

In chapters 4 and 5 we create a "matched pair" between two different approaches to minority populations, those in post-Independence India and in Sri Lanka. We analyze how India treated its Tamils, and how Ceylon (today Sri Lanka) has treated its Tamil population. What is interesting in this matched pair is that Sri Lanka started in a somewhat more favorable position vis-à-vis its Tamil population than India. For example, in the hundred years before independence in Sri Lanka, there had been no riots between Sinhalese/Buddhists and Tamil/Hindus.[6] In contrast, Dravidian leaders, in what is now Tamil Nadu in India, burned the Indian flag at Independence and burned the constitution upon its publication. Yet within a quarter-century of independence, the issue of Tamil independence had become a non-issue in India, while in Sri Lanka the one-time non-issue of Tamil secessionism had become the source of a civil war that eroded democracy and almost disintegrated the state. Why? A major constitutive ingredient of peaceful integration in India is the creative utilization of all six of the "nested" policies we argue in chapter 1 would be useful for creating state-nations. In sharp contrast, in Sri Lanka, aggressive nation-state policies were a constitutive part of the Tamil-Sinhalese civil war that led to more than a hundred thousand deaths.

The goal of this book is not to extol state-nations over nation-states but rather to expand our collective political imaginations about what is feasible, and unfeasible, in different contexts. We document how there are some cases where neither full nation-state nor state-nation policies are feasible. We have explored alternative formulas for dealing with robust multinationalism beyond either of these two ideal types.

In chapter 6 we analyze the case of Ukraine, where territorially based federalism, a core policy normally associated with state-nations, was, for geopolitical reasons, risky. Because of the possibility of Russian irredentism, a unitary state was more prudent. The questions we explore are how to utilize many state-nation policies *within* a unitary state, and whether a *mixture* of state-nation and nation-state policies can enhance inclusionary democracy and ethnic peace.

In chapter 7, we turn to the question of whether there can be a political

---

6. Sri Lanka also began its democratic experiment with greater per capita income and greater literacy than India.

formula that allows a unitary nation-state to respond to the demands of a potentially secessionist, territorially concentrated minority by creating constitutionally
embedded federal guarantees. We propose a strongly revised theory of "federacy"
to address this situation. In this chapter, we empirically examine how federacies
have actually been used to democratically manage "robust multinational" problems by the otherwise unitary nation-states of Finland (with the Åland Islands)
and Denmark (with both Greenland and the Faroe Islands). We also show that the
"scope value" of federacy arrangements can extend to the postwar reconstruction
of Italy (with its once-separatist 86% German speaking population of South Tyrol)
and to Portugal's 1975 response toward the emerging secessionist movement in
the Azores. We show how it was also of use in negotiating the Helsinki Agreement
that brought a relatively consensual, peaceful, and inclusionary end to the civil
war in Aceh in Indonesia in October 2005. We argue that if China were ever to
become democratic, a federacy formula could conceivably be of use in Tibet,
Hong Kong, and possibly even in Taiwan. But what is the relationship between
our concept of state-nation and our concept of federacy? In a federacy, the unitary
nation-state follows nation-state policies everywhere in the state *except for the
federacy itself*, where it employs state-nation policies.

We conclude our book in chapter 8 with a discussion of the extremely influential federal model of the United States. We question the very common assumption
that U.S.-style federalism is the most authentic type of federalism, the "best" for
any type of diverse democracy. In this chapter we identify seven core components
of U.S. federalism and demonstrate how *each* of these components—by themselves, and more especially when combined—create obstacles for managing democracy in robust multinational contexts. Indeed, our conclusion is that the U.S.
model of federalism, if attempted in robust multinational settings, would produce
close to the worst possible set of constraints for a democratization effort.

We have not aspired to write a "cookbook" for policy-makers or constitution-
makers. Although some countries have roughly similar characteristics and similar problems, the policies adopted to solve these problems must inevitably deal
with a range of historical, social, cultural, and geopolitical specificities that will
have a great impact on the policies' appropriateness or inappropriateness, their
relative success or failure. We can perhaps be more certain of what might be
possible, improbable, or very difficult to achieve. Social scientists and policy-
makers should not deceive themselves that all problems are solvable. However, we
should also be aware that more appropriate, more timely actions might prevent
some solvable problems from *becoming* unsolvable. The timely imagining of alternatives is crucial.

One problem that the present work has left out as a central concern, except for our small final chapter on the United States, is the complex relationships between federalism and democracy, between federalism and fraternity, and especially between federalism and equality. This problem cannot be studied without comparativists addressing why the United States has some of the highest rates of inequality in the democratic world. Inequality in the United States deserves monographic study. Indeed, the great difficulty of passing fundamental welfare legislation like health reform in the United States would seem to make this a major subject for further work by us and other scholars and practitioners.

A final comment here on the long genesis of this book is in order. In 1995, when Juan Linz and Alfred Stepan were completing their book *Problems of Democratic Transition and Consolidation: Southern Europe, South America, and Post-Communist Europe,* they had already turned their attention to their next book, on federalism, democracy, and nationalism.

Linz and Stepan had been drawn to this theme because they were aware of the relative success of federalism in the case of Spain, on the one hand, and the much less successful post-Soviet and Yugoslav experiences, on the other. Linz and Stepan were also uneasy with the standard treatments of federalism in the literature and felt that they should aim at a new and more general theory.[7] Linz and Stepan agreed that one of the major theoretical and political problems of our time was to conceptualize and realize political arrangements whereby deeply diverse cultures, even different "nations," can peacefully and democratically coexist within one state.

One of the most interesting cases of the successful solving of this problem appeared to be India, and Stepan began to make almost yearly research visits to that country starting in the late 1990s. During these visits, Stepan began to work with Yadav, the founder and convener of the Lokniti Network. Yadav invited Linz and Stepan to work with him in drafting questions for CSDS surveys.

As a result of the exciting findings that began to emerge from this process, Linz and Stepan decided to abandon their idea of writing a theoretical and comparative book that would have covered the entire world in a necessarily abstract way in favor of a more focused, comparative analysis of key countries, situations, and models, that could be empirically richer and based on their own original research.

7. Linz, as a social scientist and as a citizen of Spain, has been drawn to issues of nationalism since the late 1960s. Indeed, the second volume of his seven volume collected works is devoted entirely to nationalism and to federalism. See Juan J. Linz, "Obras Escogidas," in *Nación, Estado y Lengua,* ed. José Ramón Montero and Thomas Jeffrey Miley (Madrid: Centro De Estudios Políticos y Constitutionales, 2008).

Linz and Stepan found the exchanges with Yadav, which opened up such rich and often quite counterintuitive findings, so intellectually exciting that they eagerly invited Yadav to join them in the writing of what has become this book. The long and very collaborative process, which we hope has been fruitful for the book, has certainly been fruitful for us.

This book has only been possible because of the support of dozens of colleagues, students, and organizations in many countries. Let us begin with our students and colleagues. Stepan is fortunate to have had at Columbia a number of brilliant Ph.D. candidates who shared his passion for examining many of the puzzles in this book and who provided invaluable research assistance and intellectual partnership. In particular he wants to recognize the contributions of Neelanjan Sircar, Pavithra Suryanarayan, Israel Marquez, and Enrique Ochoa Reza. Thomas Jeffrey Miley, the author of an important book on nationalism, *Nacionalismo y política lingüística: el caso de Cataluña*, who is now on the faculty at Cambridge University in the United Kingdom, helped all of us, particularly Juan Linz, in developing the foundations of this book. While Miley was working on his dissertation at Yale, he was involved in virtually all of the early discussions of this book.

We thank the World Values Survey for opening their datasets to us. We are grateful to the extraordinary scholars in the Lokniti Network whose support we continuously drew upon, including Sanjay Kumar, Dhananjai Joshi, Sanjeer Alam, and Himanshu Bhattacharya and Kanchan Malhotra of the CSDS Data Unit for their help in accessing and analyzing the vast datasets at the CSDS. We thank Rekha Chowdhary of the University of Jammu and G. K. Prasad of the University of Madras for sharing their ideas and data to help us understand the politics of their states. Suhas Palshikar, of the University of Pune, and Peter deSouza, director of the Indian Institute of Advanced Study, were two of the principal investigators of the State of Democracy in South Asia study, and we thank them for sharing their insights and data with us. Yadav also thanks the Wissenschaftskolleg zu Berlin, where he was a fellow and had an opportunity to work on the final drafts of this book.

Many of the ideas in this book were presented to large groups of theorists and practitioners, including at the United Nations Development Program where we helped to conceptualize and write *Human Development Report 2004: Cultural Liberty in Today's Diverse World*, working closely with Amartya Sen.

The first joint article of Stepan, Linz, and Yadav was produced for a volume edited by Ambassador Shankar Bajpai, titled *Democracy and Diversity: India and the American Experience*. Bajpai brought together, over the course of a decade, many theoreticians interested in comparative approaches to the questions of democracy and deep diversity. We also thank Sudipta Kaviraj for his thoughtful critique of an early version of this book at the Centre d'Études et de Recherches Internationales (CERI) in Paris at a special session arranged for us by its director Christophe Jaffrelot and the founder of the Network on South Asian Politics and Political Economy (NETSAPPE), Ashutosh Varshney.

We would not have had the temerity to write a book like this if not for the special help from experts on many of the countries we discuss in this book and whose help and publications are cited in the relevant chapters.

We would like to explicitly acknowledge the late Neelan Thiruchelvam and the late Laksman Kadirgamer for sharing their vision of a pluralist Sri Lanka, which cost them their lives. In addition, we want to acknowledge Philip Oldenburg for sharing his insights into Indian politics with Stepan and Yadav, Harish Puri and Pramod Kumar for discussing the Punjab crisis with the authors, Ved Marwaha for discussing the situation in India's northeast with Stepan and for inviting him to Manipur when he was the governor of the state, and N. Ram, editor-in-chief of *The Hindu,* for discussing Tamil Nadu politics with Stepan and allowing him to use the newspaper's archives.

We would also like to thank the Ford Foundation for funding the convening of a conference at All Souls College, Oxford, and for generously supporting, through a grant on Federalism, Multinationalism, and Governance in the Modern World, Stepan's multiple research visits to India, Sri Lanka, Russia, Ukraine, Indonesia, and even to the borders of Burma to speak with political and military leaders from seven nationality groups. The Ford Foundation also supported the Lokniti Programme for Comparative Democracy at CSDS by funding their 2005 survey that was published as *The State of Democracy in South Asia.* This 2005 survey of India, Sri Lanka, Pakistan, Bangladesh, and Nepal would not have been possible without additional funding from the EU-India Cross Cultural Program and the International Institute of Democracy and Electoral Assistance. Stepan received grants from the Carnegie Corporation of New York, which allowed him to carry out research in many countries and to bring key scholars for meetings at Columbia University and for meetings with Linz and Yadav.

Stepan would also like to acknowledge the generous support of the Henry R. Luce Initiative on Religion and International Affairs, whose support allowed Columbia to create the Center for the Study of Democracy, Toleration, and Religion. He would also like to acknowledge Mark Kingdon, who gave a major endowment that allowed the creation of the Institute for Religion, Culture, and Public Life at Columbia University. Working together, these two organizations allowed us to explore in much greater depth than we otherwise could have, the relationship of religions, democracies, and state-nations.

We dedicate this book to Rocío de Terán, Madhulika Banerjee, and Nancy Leys Stepan, all of whom have their own projects but who always inspired and helped us in our attempts to imagine better futures.

Crafting State-Nations

CHAPTER ONE

Comparative Theory and Political Practice

Do We Need a "State-Nation" Model as Well as a "Nation-State" Model?

One of the most urgent conceptual, normative, and political tasks of our day is to think anew about how polities that aspire to be democracies can accommodate great sociocultural, even multinational, diversity within one state. The need to think anew arises from a mismatch between the political realities of the world we live in and the old political wisdom that we have inherited. The old wisdom holds that the territorial boundaries of a state must coincide with the perceived cultural boundaries of a nation. This understanding requires that every state must contain within itself one and not more than one culturally homogeneous nation, that *every* state should be a nation, and that *every* nation should be a state. Given the reality of sociocultural diversity in many of the polities of the world, this widespread belief seems to us to be misguided, indeed dangerous, since, as we shall argue, many states in the world today do not conform to this expectation.

While all independent democratic states have a degree of cultural diversity, for comparative purposes we can say that, at any given time, states may be divided analytically into three different categories:

1. States that have deep cultural diversity, some of which is territorially based and politically articulated by significant groups that, in the name of nationalism and self-determination, advance claims of independence;

2. States that are culturally quite diverse, but whose diversity is nowhere organized by territorially based politically significant groups mobilizing nationalist claims for independence; and

3. States in which a community, culturally homogeneous enough to con-

sider itself a nation, dominates the state and no other significant group articulates similar claims.

In this book, we will call countries, part of whose territory falls into the first category, "robustly multinational" societies. Canada (owing to Quebec), Spain (Basque Country and Catalonia), and Belgium (Flanders) are "robustly multinational." India, due to the Kashmir Valley alone, merits classification in this category. Furthermore, at various times the Mizo and Naga struggle for independence in northeast India, the Khalistan movement in the Punjab, the once-separatist Dravidian movement in southern India, and other secessionist movements have also given a robust multinational dimension to Indian politics.

Switzerland and the United States are both sociologically diverse and multicultural. However, since neither country has significant territorially based groups mobilizing claims for independence, both countries clearly fall into the second and not the first category.

Finally, countries such as Japan, Portugal, and most of the Scandinavian countries fall into the third category. It is not that these countries are devoid of ethnic minorities and regional differences, but as of now these differences are politically not very salient.

What political implications do these three very different situations have for reconciling democracy with diversity? For us a major implication is that, if at the time of the inauguration of competitive elections, a polity has only one significant group that sees itself as a nation and there exists a relatively common sense of history and religion and a shared language throughout the territory, nation-state building and democracy building can be mutually reinforcing logics.

However, if competitive elections are inaugurated under conditions that are already "politically robustly multinational," nation-state building and democracy building are conflicting logics. This is so because only one of a given polity's "nations" would be privileged in the nation-state-building effort, and the others would not be recognized or would even be marginalized. But before examining alternatives to the nation-state, we first need to explain the normative and political power of the nation-state.

STATE-NATION CONTRASTED WITH NATION-STATE

The belief that every state should be a nation is perhaps the most widely accepted normative vision of a modern democratic state, that is, the nation-state. After the French Revolution, especially in the late nineteenth century, many policies were deployed to create a unitary nation-state in France in which all French citizens had only one cultural and political identity. These policies included a package of incentives and disincentives to ensure that French would become the only acceptable language in the state. Political mechanisms to allow the recognition and expression of regional cultural differences were so unacceptable to French nation-state builders that advocacy of federalism was at one time a capital offense. Throughout France, state schools at any given hour were famously teaching the same curriculum with identical syllabi in schoolrooms led by teachers who had been trained and certified by the same Ministry of Education. Numerous other state institutions, such as universal conscription, were designed to create a common French identity and a country that was robustly assimilative.[1]

Some very successful democracies, such as contemporary Sweden, Japan, and Portugal, are close to the ideal type of a unitary nation-state. Some federal states, such as Germany and Australia, have also become nation-states. In our view, in a polity where sociocultural differences have not acquired great political salience, and most of its politicized citizens have a strong sense of shared history, the aspiration to create a nation-state should not create problems for the achievement of an inclusive democracy. In fact, the creation of such a national identity and relative homogeneity in the nineteenth century was identified with democratization and was possible in consolidated states.

In the twentieth century, however, attempts to create a nation-state by state policies encountered growing difficulties, even in an old state like Spain. In our judgment, in the last century virtually no new nation-states have been created, except as the result of international decisions, wars, violence, oppression, and secession.[2] Few or no new nation-states have been created as a result of public democratic decisions.

Thus, if a polity has significant politically-salient cultural or linguistic diversity —and a large number of polities do—we will argue that political leaders in such a

1. For a classic book on these policies, see Eugen Weber, *Peasants into Frenchman: The Modernization of Rural France, 1870–1914* (Stanford: Stanford University Press, 1976). Most nineteenth-century progressives and democrats, particularly those associated with the French Revolution, were profoundly opposed to federalism. On the normative advocacy of a unified, homogeneous, nation-state, see the entries on "Federalism," "Federation," "Nation," and "Departement" in the extremely illustrative but not widely known François Furet and Mora Ozouf, eds., *A Critical Dictionary of the French Revolution* (Cambridge: Belknap Press, 1989), pp. 54–64, 65–73, and 742–753.

2. See Juan J. Linz, "State Building and Nation Building," *European Review* 1 (1993), pp. 355–369; and Juan J. Linz and Alfred Stepan, *Problems of Democratic Transition and Consolidation: Southern Europe, South America, and Post-Communist Europe* (Baltimore: Johns Hopkins University Press, 1996), ch. 2. Also see Alain Fenet, "Difference Rights and Language in France," in *Language, Nation, and State: Identity Politics in a Multilingual Age*, ed. Tony Judt and Denis Lacorne (New York: Palgrave Macmillan, 2004), pp. 19–62.

polity need to think about, craft, and normatively legitimate a type of polity with characteristics of a "state-nation."

Linz and Stepan first introduced this concept in 1996, but only in a paragraph (and one figure): "We . . . believe some conceptual, political, and normative attention should be given to the possibility of state nations. The states we would like to call state nations are multicultural, and sometimes even have significant multinational components, which nonetheless still manage to engender strong identification and loyalty from their citizens, an identification and loyalty that proponents of homogeneous nation states perceive that only nation states can engender." They went on to say that neither Switzerland nor India were, in the French sense, "strictly speaking a nation state, but we believe both can now be called state nations. Under Jawaharlal Nehru, India made significant gains in managing multinational tensions through skillful and consensual usage of numerous consociational practices. Through this process India became in the 1950s and the early 1960s a democratic state nation."[3]

Nation-state policies stand for a political-institutional approach that attempts to match the political boundaries of the state with the presumed cultural boundaries of the nation, or vice versa. Needless to say, the cultural boundaries are far from obvious in most cases; thus, the creation of nation-state involves privileging *one* sociocultural identity over other potential or actual sociocultural cleavages that can be politically mobilized. Nation-state policies have been pursued historically by following a variety of routes, from relatively soft to downright brutal: (1) by creating or arousing a special kind of allegiance or common cultural identity among those living in a state; (2) by encouraging the voluntary assimilation of those who do not share that initial allegiance or cultural identity into the nation state's identity; (3) by using various forms of social pressure and coercion to achieve this and to prevent the emergence of alternative cultural identities or to erode them, should they exist; and (4) by resorting to coercion that might, in the extreme, involve ethnic cleansing.

By contrast, state-nation policies stand for a political-institutional approach that respects and protects *multiple but complementary* sociocultural identities. State-nation policies recognize the legitimate public and even political expression of active sociocultural cleavages, and they include mechanisms to accommodate competing or conflicting claims made on behalf of those divisions without imposing or privileging, in a discriminatory way, any one claim. State-nation policies

3. See the chapter titled "Stateness, Nationalism, and Democratization," in Linz and Stepan, *Problems of Democratic Transition and Consolidation*, esp. p. 34 and figure 2.1.

involve crafting a sense of belonging (or "we-feeling") with respect to the state-wide political community, while simultaneously creating institutional safeguards for respecting and protecting politically salient sociocultural diversities. The "we-feeling" may take the form of defining a tradition, history, and shared culture in an inclusive manner, with attachment to common symbols of the state, or of inculcating some form of "constitutional patriotism."

In democratic societies, the institutional safeguards constitutive of state-nation policies most likely take the form of federalism, often specifically *asymmetrical* federalism, or consociational practices.[4] Virtually every longstanding and relatively peaceful contemporary democracy in the world whose polity has more than one territorially concentrated, politically mobilized, linguistic-cultural group that is a majority in some significant part of the territory is not only federal but also "asymmetrically federal" (Belgium, Canada, and India).[5] This means that, up to a certain point, these polities, in order to "hold together" their great diversity in one democratic system, had to embed in the constitution special cultural and historical prerogatives for some of the member units, prerogatives that respond to their somewhat different linguistic or cultural aspirations, demands, and historical identities.

We believe that had political leaders in India, Belgium, Spain, and Canada attempted to impose one language and culture on their countries and insisted on imposing a homogenizing nineteenth-century French-style unitary nation-state model, the causes of social peace, inclusionary democracy, and individual rights would not have been served in any of these four longstanding democratic states. This was so because more than one territorially based linguistic-cultural cleavage had already been activated in each of these four countries. The strategic question, therefore, was whether to attempt to *repress* or *accommodate* this preexisting politically activated diversity.

We will also argue that the application of majoritarian nation-state policies after 1956 in the then-peaceful multicultural democracy of Ceylon eventually contributed directly to the civil war that beset the country from the early 1980s to

4. We accept Robert Dahl's definition of federalism as "a system in which some matters are exclusively *within* the competence of certain local units—cantons, states, provinces—and are constitutionally *beyond* the scope of the authority of the national government; and where certain other matters are constitutionally outside the scope of the authority of the smaller units." See "Federalism and the Democratic Process," in his *Democracy, Liberty, and Equality* (Oslo: Norwegian University Press, 1986), p. 114.

5. Sri Lanka, from independence in 1948 until the civil war about Tamil independence which began in the early 1980s, was an exception. The United Kingdom is a multinational society with Scottish, Irish, and Welsh assemblies, but English is spoken by the vast majority of the population in all three areas.

2009. Further, we will argue that if Burma or China ever were to attempt a democratic transition, it would be very useful for them to have other models in mind than just the nation-state model. For example, Ukraine correctly considered some variance of the full nation-state model, especially concerning the imposition of Ukrainian as the only language throughout the state. As another example, Indonesia is exploring the role of a "federacy" in Aceh, of the sort used in Denmark in relation to Greenland and the Faroe Islands, and in Finland to the Åland Islands. In short, one of our major political and theoretical efforts in this book is to expand our imaginations beyond the nation-state model and to document that, in all the above cases, the state-nation model was, and can be, extremely useful for political practice and for the theory of comparative politics.

Asymmetrical federalism historically emerged in Belgium, Spain, Canada, and India as a policy response aimed at accommodation. We therefore think that, as a normative concept, an institutional framework, and a set of historical experiences, "asymmetrical federalism" should be strongly considered, by theoreticians and political leaders alike, as a possible approach to democracy in polities such as Burma that have at least two territorially based and politically activated linguistic-cultural cleavages within the existing state.[6] At the same time, federalism is neither sufficient nor necessary for the establishment of a state-nation. The creation and maintenance of a state-nation requires a number of diversity-sustaining measures that are not exhausted by federal instruments. For the same reason, it is possible for a unitary state, where diversities are not geographically concentrated, to institute many multicultural practices that may lead to a pattern closer to a state-nation than a nation-state.[7]

In sum, then, the idea of the nation associated with the nation-state approach implies creating one common culture within the state, while the idea of the nation associated with the state-nation approach can contain more than one politically-salient culture but nonetheless encourages and requires respect for the

6. On "asymmetrical federalism," see Klaus von Beyme, "Die Asymmetrisierung des Postmodernen Föderalismus," in *Die Reformierbarkeit der Demokratie: Innovationen und Blockaden*, ed. Renate Mayntz and Wolfgang Streeck (Frankfurt/Main: Campus, 2003), pp. 239–258; and Rainer Bauböck, "United in Misunderstanding: Asymmetry in Multinational Federations," *ICE Working Paper Series*, Austrian Academy of Sciences, No. 26 (May 2002), Vienna, Austria.

7. For example, Luxembourg is a unitary state but a state-nation. Ukraine, even though it is a unitary state, is following many state-nation policies because most political elites, both ethnic Ukrainian and ethnic Russian, were worried that strong ethnic Ukrainian nation-state policies would generate conflicts with the Russophone population, especially in the eastern regions bordering Russia, where 90% of the Ukrainian citizens speak Russian. Also, given the above and irredentist sentiments in Russia, a policy of decentralization but not necessarily federalization might be prudent. See chapter 6 in this volume.

common institutions of the state and for existing sociocultural diversities. The analytical distinction between nation-state and state-nation, as the terms imply, involves an affinity—since both include the term *nation*; certainly, for some theorists of nationalism, both terms would fit under their conception of a nation. There is also of course an affinity of both terms with the great importance of the state.

Thus, *state-nation* is a term introduced to distinguish democratic states that do not, and can not, fit well into the classic French-style nation-state model based on a "we-feeling" resulting from an existing or forged homogeneity. For the difference between nation-state and state-nation as ideal types, see table 1.1.

Our advocacy of the term *state-nation* is also based on our recognition that in some countries, cultural groups are not territorially concentrated but instead are so diffusely located that even "asymmetrical federalism" is not an option. However, given the robustness of these different politically salient cultural groups, a classic French-style nation-state may not, in our times, be an option for a peaceful democracy without a costly and most likely nondemocratic period of state-imposed assimilation efforts and possibly even ethnic cleansing. Nonetheless, in the same cultural context, a state-nation may prove to be the most viable democratic model to pursue.

Our introduction of the term *state-nation* is intended both to establish a normative standard to which multinational democracies can aspire and to introduce a set of observable empirical sociopolitical realities that a polity, if it is a state-nation, will manifest.

Although nation-state and state-nation at one level are analytic ideal-type distinctions, they can be operationalized using a range of indicators. State-nations can manage, and have managed, to create powerful and positive citizen identification with the institutions and symbols of the state, such as a constitution, inclusive democratic institutions and procedures, and guarantees of basic freedoms.

We expect a diverse polity, if it has become a state-nation, to have the following four empirically verifiable patterns. First, despite multiple cultural identities among the citizens of the polity, there will be at the same time a high degree of *positive identification* with the state and pride in being citizens of that state. Second, citizens of the state will have *multiple but complementary* political identities and loyalties. Third, there will be a high degree of *institutional trust* in the most important constitutional, legal, and administrative components of the state. Fourth, by world democratic standards, there will be a comparatively high degree of positive *support for democracy* across all of the diverse groups of citizens in the country as well as for the specific state-wide democratic institutions through

TABLE 1.1

Two Ideal Types of Democratic States: "Nation-State" and "State-Nation"

	Nation-state	State-nation
Preexisting conditions: Sense of belonging/"we-feeling"	Awareness of, and attachment to, one major cultural civilizational tradition. With minor exceptions, this cultural identity corresponds to existing state boundaries.	Awareness of, and attachment to, more than one cultural civilizational tradition within the existing boundaries. However, these attachments do not preclude identification with a common state.
State policy: Cultural policies	Homogenizing attempts to foster one core cultural identity, particularly one official language; non-recognition of multiplicity of cultures. Unity in oneness.	Recognition and support of more than one cultural identity (particularly recognition of more than one official language), even more than one cultural nation, all within a frame of some common polity-wide symbols. Unity in diversity.
Institutions: Territorial division of power	Unitary states or symmetrical federations.	Federal system. Often de jure or de facto asymmetrical. Can even be a unitary state if aggressive nation-state policies are not pursued and de facto state multilingual areas are accepted. Federacies possible.
Politics		
Ethno-cultural or territorial cleavages	Not very salient.	Salient and recognized and democratically managed.
Autonomist and/or secessionist parties	Autonomist parties are normally not "coalitionable." Secessionist parties are outlawed or marginalized in democratic electoral politics.	Autonomist parties can govern in federal units and are "coalitionable" at the center. Nonviolent secessionist parties can sometimes participate in the democratic political process.
Citizen orientation		
Political identity	Single identity as citizens of the state and overwhelmingly as members of the same cultural nation.	Multiple but complementary identities.
Obedience/loyalty	Obedience to the state and loyalty to the nation.	Obedience to the state and identification with institutions, neither based on a single national identity.

which the multicultural and possibly multinational polity is governed. To be sure, these patterns do not simply exist right from the beginning. "State-nation" is not a matter of recognizing a preexisting reality. We argue that "state-nation" is all about crafting and is very much an outcome of deliberate policies and designs.

This takes us to some vital questions: in what political contexts is a democratic nation-state or a democratic state-nation most probable and most improbable? Are there some circumstances in which neither ideal type is probable? Obviously, neither is possible if there is no useable state. However, theory and empirical experience both indicate that "context matters" in deciding what general state institutional arrangements are appropriate, or even possible, given different intensities of ethno-cultural mobilization. In terms of ethno-mobilization and its relationship to state structures, there can be three sharply different contexts.

The first is a context of near absence or low intensity of politically activated and territorially concentrated sociocultural diversities. If, for example, only one significant, territorially concentrated, politically activated sociocultural identity exists, democratic nation-state crafting is possible. State structures can be unitary (for example, France and Japan in the nineteenth century) or symmetrically federal (Australia in the early twentieth century and the German Federal Republic after World War II). This context does not require policies and institutional designs that we have characterized as "state-nation."

Second is a context of bounded plurality characterized by moderate to intense sociocultural identities that are territorially concentrated and politically activated. If more than one significant mobilized sociocultural identity exists in the polity, democratic state-nation crafting is possible, but nation-state crafting will probably be quite conflictual. For most polities in a multilingual context, for example, the least conflictual state structure would be asymmetrical federalism, in which some cultural prerogatives are constitutionally embedded for sub-units with salient and mobilized territorial cultural identities (for instance, India, Spain, Canada, and Belgium). Such a context is best suited to and requires the "state-nation" model.

Third is a context of unbounded plurality or what we may call a *pure multinational* context. If almost no loyalty to central state authorities and common symbols exists, if almost all of the functions of the central state have been transferred or acquired by national sub-units, if most citizens in sub-units of the state primarily identify with "national" aspirations within these units and see these units as nation-states *in potentia*, then political identities will tend to be singular and conflictual. Crafting a democratic, federal, "pure multinational" polity in one territory is extremely improbable in such a context, due to interacting, probably violent conflicts between secessionist attempts and possible re-centralization efforts (for example, Yugoslavia in the late 1980s). These three radically different contexts are depicted visually in figure 1.1 below.

The circle in the upper right-hand side space in figure 1.1, representing what we call "pure multinationalism," has a noncontinuous and faint border to indicate

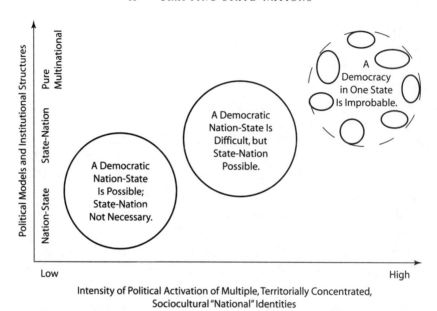

Figure 1.1. Democratically Probable and Improbable Relationships between Activated, Territorially Concentrated, Sociocultural Identities and Political-Institutional Strategies

that the polity is more porous, and has a substantially lesser degree of "stateness," than either a nation-state or a state-nation.[8] The numerous small circles and ovals within this space indicate that there is really a cluster of emergent nation-states within this weak state. The situation depicted in the upper right-hand corner is inherently unstable as a single democratic state. The two most likely reequilibrations are: (1) the aspirant nation-states become independent states and the previous single state fragments or is reduced to a rump; or (2) there is an attempt at authoritarian re-centralization by a major ethno-political military component of the threatened state.

In the late 1980s the ethno-federal states of the former U.S.S.R. and Yugoslavia could analytically be said to have occupied space in the upper-right corner of figure 1.1. At last count, twenty-five near–nation-states have emerged, often with substantial bloodshed and repression, out of these two ethno-federal states. But is it right to assert, as many have done, that all ethno-federal arrangements are "state-subverting"?

8. For a discussion of the concept of "stateness," see Linz and Stepan, *Problems of Democratic Transition and Consolidation,* ch. 2. See also the seminal article by J. P. Nettl, "The State as a Conceptual Variable," *World Politics* 20 (July 1968), pp. 559–592.

Such a deduction is a dangerous half-truth, one more example of the "tyranny of the last instance." A federal state can be a state-nation (Spain, India) or a nation-state (Austria, Germany) but not a multinational state in the sense of being composed of units, each of which considers itself to be a nation-state or aims to be an independent nation-state because there will be no identification with the larger state. Thus, as the title of our book implies, states can be multinational *societies* but not multinational *states*. It is significant that no democratic federal state is the result of the voluntary unification of independent nation-states. In fact, countries that should have, according to Riker's condition of security incentives, created a federation during the interwar years, like the Scandinavian countries (Sweden, Denmark, Norway) or the Baltic Republics (Estonia, Latvia, Lithuania), never seriously considered voluntarily subsuming their identities into one federal state. A confederation or some other form of association such as the European Union can be formed by nation-states—but *not* a fully democratic federation.

Therefore, our concept of state-nation must be radically differentiated from the model of pure multinationalism depicted in the upper right-hand corner of figure 1.1. In this book we are investigating patterns of politics that facilitate, in multinational societies, democracies and peace within the territory of one state. In our judgment, "pure multinationalism" is not such a model. Before developing our alternative model in greater detail, let us analyze this major normative and political competitor to our model of "state-nation."

"STATE-NATION" DISTINGUISHED FROM "PURE MULTINATIONALISM"

A pure multinational model is one in which a nationalist vocabulary is used by groups who conceive of their nationalities as nation-states *in potentia* and aim at reducing the state to a basic minimum, with the result, intended or not, of bringing about an extremely weak "we-feeling"—if any.

The leaders of nationalities—or nations—in a pure multinational state may reject being part of a state-nation; they may define themselves as nations living under a state (not "part of" or "in" a state) and commit themselves to a nation-building project against the state, with the goal of achieving statehood at the first opportunity, whether by peaceful or violent means. Obviously, many advocates of such a "pure" (or what we consider extreme) multinational state do not express themselves so bluntly. Some of them demand that the whole state become multinational "all the way down," doing away with as many symbols and practices supporting the idea of a common state as possible. They may advocate a state that is a sum of nations, each with its own exclusive identity, symbols, and laws, in which the state becomes an empty shell and the citizens of the state have nothing important to say about common institutions—except to the extent that in international relations and organizations, the states and their citizens have a say.

It is crucial to understand the differences between a state-nation, even when it contains important multinational components, and a "pure" multinational state composed of nations, in which the state would be reduced almost to an "empty shell," or at the most a confederation, rather than a federation.

In a relatively early formulation (unpublished, but dating from 2000), Linz argued: "It is difficult to define the difference between a multinational state and a state nation. It could be argued that any stable multinational state would also be a state nation since it requires some sense of identification, of loyalty, to the state rather than wishing its disintegration."[9] Elsewhere in the same essay, Linz also stressed that the kind of affective attachment that the state-nation inspires in its citizens is something that cannot be fully captured by Habermas's overly rationalistic conception of "constitutional patriotism" alone. Linz argued: "Although the *Verfassungspatriotismus*—the commitment to be a liberal-democratic-social constitutionalism—is one of the elements of the legitimation of state nations, I do not believe that it is the only or a sufficient one. The construction of a state nation requires other elements of symbolic and emotional nature we still do not know well."[10]

Since this earlier formulation, we have become more acquainted with a series of theoretical arguments for "multinational federalism" that have recently proliferated among Catalan nationalist intellectuals in the Spanish context (perhaps most prominently exemplified by the work of Ferran Requejo and Miquel Caminal).[11] What strikes us about these accounts is that, despite the language

9. Juan J. Linz, "Democratic States, Nation States, State Nations, and Multinational States," unpublished. Quotation from pp. 12–13.

10. Ibid., p. 35.

11. See, for example, Miquel Caminal, *El federalismo pluralista: del federalismo nacional al federalismo plurinacional* (Barcelona: Paidós, 2002); and Ferran Requejo, *Federalisme, per a què?* (Valencia: L'hora del present, 1998). Quite strikingly, a section of the Indian left has often advocated a multinational state along similar lines. See, for example, Prakash Karat, "Theoretical Aspects of the National Question" and Irfan Habib, "Emergence of Nationalities," both in a special edition of *Social Scientist* titled "The National Question in India," no. 37 (August 1975). Karat is now the general secretary of the Communist Party of India (Marxist) [CPI(M)], India's largest Communist party. However, in practice, the Indian Communist parties no longer support the hollowing out of the state by different "nationalities."

they use, they seem to be arguing not for a truly federal state at all but rather for a model of confederation between multiple nation-states. In particular, their hostility to the Habermasian conception of "constitutional patriotism" and even to the related concept of *Bundestreue* (roughly, "loyalty to the federation")—for allegedly being unfriendly to diversity itself—alarms us. For our sense is that commitment to Habermas's conception of "constitutional patriotism" alone cannot provide a sufficient basis for any state to be perceived as legitimate—that something more is necessary; yet, to our dismay, we have found that these other theorists of "multinational federalism" object to Habermas's conception on the opposite grounds. For them, a state that demands "constitutional patriotism" from all of its citizens is demanding too much. This has led us to suspect that these intellectuals are in fact using the conceptualization of "multinational federalism" as a mere tactic for legitimating the hollowing-out of the state altogether, for chipping away at its sovereignty, even as they attempt to legitimate projects of piecemeal nation-state building at the periphery. Hence the shift in emphasis in this chapter from the position taken earlier by Linz. We think it urgent to underscore the necessity for some form of basic loyalty to the institutions of the state, some form of symbolic attachment to it and identification with it, some form of "we-feeling" even though it makes the project of demonstrating the utility of state-nations more difficult.

That said, we need to keep in mind the fact that the concept of state-nation, like that of the nation-state, is an ideal type that only imperfectly corresponds to any given empirical case. We also need to keep in mind the fluidity of empirical reality—that is, that cases that once fit closer to the model of the nation-state can and have evolved into something closer to state-nations (witness Spain and the UK) and vice versa (witness Austria). With these caveats already in mind, we have formulated our concept of the state-nation and its partial distinction from both the nation-state and the "pure" multinational state.

Again, though, these are analytical distinctions that can be operationalized using a range of indicators. What is more, the distinctions themselves are fluid; some theorists of nationalism would include in their definitions of nation-states our state-nations. This, however, would obscure crucial differentiating facts and have the dangerous political implication of creating demands on citizens based on the ideals of a nation-state.

Multinationalism is more a sociological conceptualization than a particular type of political institutionalization. Multinational societies cannot be nation-states (in a specific sense of the term) but can be either state-nations *or* the basis for conceptualizations aiming at a *confederation* rather than a federation in one state. Relatively stable democratic federal states are either nation-states or state-nations but not mere aggregates of multiple nation-states (that is, confederations of multiple nation-states). When the "we-feeling" is only or predominantly centered on a nation and the state is identified with only one of the nation-states or is seen as an alien, if not as an oppressor, the construction of a state-nation becomes difficult, if not impossible. Democracies are stable in multinational societies only if an effort is made to legitimate the state by those who could also bring about its disintegration.

Normatively and empirically, we believe in the possibility of multiple but complementary identities in a multinational society, which serve as the support for the construction of affective attachment and loyalty to the state.[12] Indeed, later in this chapter we will document that the modal self-identification in Spain and Belgium, for example, is a dual identity. It is also clear to us that if, in a federal state, the citizens in all the sub-units define their primary loyalty as being exclusively to their respective sub-units, and if they have little loyalty or identification with the state, not only that federal system but that state as well is prone to disintegration—Yugoslavia by the late 1980s being the clearest case in point.

Let us now turn to the relationship between the two axes, one representing activated sociocultural diversities and the other representing institutional responses and political strategies. As we have suggested, a key question here is the relation between state-nations and pure multinationalism (such as Yugoslavia in the late 1980s), in which all the nationalities are conceived of as nation-states *in potentia* and in which the leaders aim at reducing the common state to a basic minimum. The result of this process can be the generation of a very weak "we-feeling" among the citizens of the state. In the case of Yugoslavia, by the early 1990s, most politicians and probably most citizens of the state felt that they were "Croatian," "Slovenian," "Serbian," "Bosnian," or "Macedonian," and very few felt that they were also "Yugoslavian" in any serious way. Dual but complementary political identities and loyalties had virtually disappeared, as "multinational" Yugoslavia had increasingly become merely a composite of hostile, aspirant nation-states with very little or no "we-feeling." Multinational societies (even those that tolerate and indeed manifest dual identities and much "we-feeling," like Spain) cannot be complete nation-states in the classic French sense of the term. However, and this

---

12. Here we differ substantially with Ernest Gellner. On this point, see Alfred Stepan, "Modern Multinational Democracies: Transcending a Gellnerian Oxymoron," in his *Arguing Comparative Politics* (Oxford: Oxford University Press, 2001), pp. 181–199.

is crucial, multinational and multicultural societies can be, or can become, state-nations with much "we-feeling," if *complementary* as well as *multiple* cultural and political identities exist, are nurtured, or even are generated.

Another issue concerns the relation between multicultural societies and the competing conceptions of the nation-state and the state-nation. Our conception of state-nation derives from our belief, based on historical case studies and analysis, that democracy is possible in polities that are sociologically and politically multicultural and even partly (but not exclusively) multinational, *if* an effort is made to legitimate the state by those minorities and majorities who could conceivably aim at its disintegration.

At this point, we need to address what many may see as a powerful argument from the opposite end against our idea of a state-nation. After the bloody disintegration of Yugoslavia and parts of the Soviet Union, many analysts have begun to reject wholesale all political and institutional frameworks that grant any form of prerogatives to territorially concentrated sociocultural groups—arrangements they call "ethno-federal" or "national federal." These scholars criticize "ethno-federal" arrangements because they believe that such arrangements privilege "subnational" sociocultural identities at the expense of identification with common symbols, institutions, and individual rights. This privileging, they claim, is likely to foster the activation of conflictual, *as opposed to complementary*, identities and, in some cases, violence and fragmentation.[13]

These critics ignore, however, that nearly all successful democratic states with more than one politically activated, territorially concentrated, linguistic-cultural majority have institutional frameworks that include a substantial (but absolutely

13. Even though in her book, *Subversive Institutions: The Design and Destruction of Socialism and the State* (New York: Cambridge University Press, 1999), Valerie Bunce does not explicitly argue this point, many scholars who read her book have employed its analysis of the Yugoslavian and Soviet experiences to make the case that "ethno-federal" institutions *in and of themselves* are "subversive" institutions for stateness and peace. See for example David John Meyer, "Ethnic Territorial Autonomy and Post-Soviet Ethnic Political Mobilization," unpublished Ph.D. dissertation, Department of Political Science, Columbia University, 2007. For a related argument, see Jack Snyder, *From Voting to Violence: Democratization and Nationalist Conflict* (New York: Norton, 2000). For her part, Bunce refers to "national federalism" as one of the most important "subversive institutions." She argues that national federalism helped "produce over time a 'disintegration' of the Soviet, Yugoslav, and Czechoslovak states along republican lines" and that "with the expanded opportunities for major change in the 1980s, 'disintegration' in all three instances translated into actual disintegration, and the state and the regime departed from Europe in virtual tandem" (p. 102). Likewise, she maintains that "national federalism worked to build nations (or reinforce such processes, if nations were already formed), along with protostates at the republican level" (p. 136) and that this "contributed not just to homogeneity *within* republics, but also to diversity *among* republics, and that it was the latter that made a single-state project untenable, especially in turbulent times" (p. 140).

not, as in Yugoslavia, a virtually exclusive) ethno-federal dimension. In successful state-nations, group rights do not, and should not ever, violate the rights of individuals who come to them as members of the state. Witness the institutional frameworks of the states that we consider to be exemplary state-nations—namely, Belgium, Canada, Spain, and India. The institutional frameworks of all of these contain an element of ethno-federalism. Nevertheless, none of these states can be classified as purely ethno-federal either, since in these states recognition of the legitimate public and political expression of active "national" sociocultural cleavages is balanced by constitutionally sanctioned respect for common symbols, institutions, and individual rights, thus facilitating the maintenance and nurturing of *multiple but complementary*, as opposed to *singular and conflictual*, identities.

For Yugoslavia in particular, Bunce specifically states that after Tito's death in 1980, "new institutions were introduced that created full political equality among the republics and provinces, that allocated to them *all* the decision-making powers vested in the party and the government and that, as a result, encouraged republican party elites to go in very different economic and political directions."[14] However, we would like to note that such devolution of "*all* decision-making powers" goes beyond the Dahlian definition of federalism as consisting of "multiple jurisdictions" and "shared sovereignty," so that, even when we bracket the important issue of democracy, to describe the Yugoslav state from the mid-1980s onward as "federal," rather than "confederal," as some do, would be completely inconsistent with Dahl's, and our own, definition of federalism or even with our definition of asymmetrical federalism. Furthermore, for our purposes, we insist that none of the countries that we consider state-nations have reduced the central state to an "empty shell" remotely analogous to the Yugoslav case, even though they all have introduced a significant ethno-federal dimension.

Whereas the model of pure multinationalism does in fact lead to the disintegration of a single state and, often, after substantial bloodshed or ethnic cleansing, to the emergence of multiple nation-states, the model of the state-nation does not. Instead, as we will analytically argue and empirically demonstrate, the state-nation model can help contribute to the maintenance of state integration.

Thus, we believe that it would be a grave error to discard the state-nation approach simply because the institutional framework associated with it tends to contain a significant ethno-federal dimension. In our judgment, in order for a variety of states (such as Burma or Sri Lanka) that are not peaceful or democratic at this point to achieve a consolidated democracy, they would have to strive to

14. Ibid., p. 88.

become state-nations. This means, quite simply, that for consolidated democracy to be viable, these states would have to craft institutional frameworks that contain both (a) a substantial ethno-federal dimension and (b) mechanisms facilitating identification with common symbols and institutions. If, in the process of democratization, leaders of these states were to pursue either a pure nation-state model or a pure ethno-federal model of the sort we label "pure multinationalism" in figure 1.1, the result would almost certainly be continued armed struggle and failure to achieve democratic consolidation.

Let us not allow a reading of the Yugoslavian and Soviet experiences to destroy the legitimacy of all institutional arrangements containing an ethno-federal dimension; to do so would require giving up on the middle ground of the state-nation—a model that has proven valuable in the important but extremely difficult task of reconciling cultural inclusiveness with democratic stability in states containing more than one politically activated, territorially concentrated "national" sociocultural group.

However, if we argue that ethno-federal arrangements in the state-nation ideal type are not necessarily state-subverting mechanisms, it is incumbent upon us to explicate a well-argued alternative. What are the identifications, norms, practices, and institutions that can facilitate the construction of a democratic polity close to a state-nation ideal type, even in a politically robust multinational society? This takes us to the interlinked set of policies that help craft successful "state-nations."

THE NESTED POLICY GRAMMAR OF STATE-NATIONS

On theoretical and empirical grounds we would like to make the case that there are arrangements that cohere in an unusual, almost counterintuitive, "nested policy grammar" that may facilitate the emergence and persistence of a state-nation.[15] By nested, we mean that each of the seven policies mentioned below is most likely to be implemented, or facilitated, if the previous policy in the sequence has already been adopted. Seven phrases are an intrinsic part of this grammar:

1. An asymmetrical federal state *but not* a symmetrical federal state or a unitary state;
2. Individual rights *and* collective recognition;
3. A parliamentary *instead of* a presidential or semi-presidential system;

15. The Oxford English Dictionary defines *grammar* as a "means of indicating the relations of words."

4. Polity-wide *and* "centric-regional" parties and careers;
5. Politically integrated *but not* culturally assimilated populations;
6. Cultural nationalists *versus* secessionist nationalists; and
7. A pattern of multiple *but* complementary identities.

Again, these policies are "nested": the second policy, "group recognition," is normally nested within the first, federalism (especially asymmetrical federalism); the fourth policy, involving the coalitionability of what we call centric-regional parties, is greatly facilitated if the choice of the third policy has been parliamentarianism because the executive is a sharable good; and successful achievement of complementary identities depends heavily on the success of the previous six policies.

1. *Why an asymmetrical federal state?* A federal state, rather than a unitary state, is part of the nested grammar of a state-nation because federal state structures allow a large territorially concentrated cultural group with serious nationalist aspirations and possibly a language with its own script to attain self-governance within that territory. Why asymmetrical? In a symmetrical federal system, all units must have identical rights and obligations. It is politically possible, however, that some territorially concentrated and culturally diverse groups have in their history acquired prerogatives that they desire to retain or reacquire, and it is also possible that some tribal groups that control a large territory (such as the Mizos in India) would only agree to remain in or join the federation if some of their laws pertaining to such matters as land use or education, found nowhere else in the polity, were respected. Bargains and compromises on these issues, which might be necessary for peace, and voluntary membership in the political community are negotiable in an asymmetrical system but are normally unacceptable in a symmetrical system.

2. *Why both individual rights and collective recognition?* The polity would not be democratic unless *throughout* the polity individual rights are constitutionally inviolable and state-protected. This necessary function of the center cannot be devolved. But in Charles Taylor's sense, some territorially concentrated cultural groups, even nations, may need some collective recognition for rights beyond classic liberal rights (or what Michael Walzer calls "Liberalism 2") for members of some groups to thrive culturally or even possibly to exercise fully their classic individual liberal rights.[16] Walzer argues that Liberalism 2 "allows for a state

16. See Charles Taylor, "The Politics of Recognition," in *Multiculturalism*, ed. Amy Gutmann (Princeton: Princeton University Press, 1994). An elegant development of a variant of this argument in found in Joseph Raz, *The Morality of Freedom* (Oxford: Oxford University Press, 1986), esp. chs. 8

committed to the survival and flourishing of . . . a (limited) set of nations, cultures and religions—so long as the basic rights of citizens who have different commitments or no such commitments are protected."[17] There may well be concrete moments in the crafting of a democracy in which individuals cannot develop and exercise their full rights until they are active members of a group that struggles and wins some collective goods common to most members of the group. These collective, group-specific rights might be most easily nested in asymmetrical federalism. For example, if a large territorially concentrated cultural group speaks a different language with its own script, some official recognition of the privileged right of that language to be used in self-government and in schools, radio, and television might be necessary to enable the individual rights of the members of this unit to be realized. Furthermore, in a state-nation, individuals in their ethno-federal units may not be able to participate fully in the overall federal polity, if in addition to their right of self-government in their own language, some polity-wide lingua franca is not maintained.

If there are territorially concentrated minority religions in the polity, the identification of the practitioners of such religions with the center may very well be reduced if the majority religion is the only established religion throughout the territory. In such cases, it may encourage identity with the state-nation if instead *all* religions are recognized and possibly even financially supported. The financial support of religions, majority and minority, is of course a violation of classical U.S. or French separation of church and state doctrines, but it is not a violation of any person's individual human rights.[18] Finally, if the polity contains citizens with sharply different historically constructed inequalities, some type of collective recognition of this problem and corrective group-specific affirmative action might be necessary.

---

and 10, and his *Ethics in the Public Domain: Essays in the Morality of Law and Politics* (Oxford: Clarendon Press, 1994), esp. preface and chs. 1, 6, and 8.

17. The quotation from Michael Walzer is from his "Comment" in *Multiculturalism*, ed. Guttman, p. 99. For a somewhat different approach to group recognition, see Will Kymlicka's discussion of "group specific rights" in his *Multicultural Citizenship: A Liberal Theory of Minority Rights* (Oxford: Clarendon Press, 1995), esp. ch. 4.

18. See Alfred Stepan, "The World's Religious Systems and Democracy: Crafting the 'Twin Tolerations,'" in his *Arguing Comparative Politics*, pp. 213–254. Also see Alfred Stepan, "The Multiple Secularisms of Modern Democratic and Non-Democratic Regimes," in *Rethinking Secularism*, ed. Mark Juergensmeyer, Craig Calhoun, and Jonathan Van Antwerpen (New York: Oxford University Press, forthcoming). For an authoritative analysis of India's pioneering "principled distance" form of secularism, see Rajeev Bhargava, "What is Secularism For?" in *Secularism and Its Critics*, ed. Bhargava (Delhi and Oxford: Oxford University Press, 2004), pp. 486–542. Also see his "Political Secularism" in *The Oxford Handbook of Political Theory*, ed. John S. Dryzek, Bonnie Honig, and Anne Phillips (Oxford: Oxford University Press, 2006), pp. 636–655.

3. *Why a parliamentary instead of a presidential or semi-presidential system?*
The elected executive in a presidential or a semi-presidential system is an "indivisible good"—it is necessarily occupied by one person, from one nationality, for a
fixed term. However, a parliamentary system more easily creates the possibility of
a "sharable good." That is, there is a possibility of other parties, composed of other
nationalities, helping constitute the ruling coalition. For example, if no single
party has a majority or support from "the outside" by a party or parties that can give
it a majority, parliamentarianism is *coalition-requiring.* Also, because the government can collapse unless it constantly bargains to retain the support of its coalition partners, it often has *coalition-sustaining* qualities. The working of parliamentary democracy in India, especially since 1996, illustrates the coalition-requiring
and coalition-sustaining features in this system. These "sharable" and "coalitionable" aspects of a parliamentary executive might be useful in a politically robust
multinational society.

4. *Why polity-wide and "centric-regional" parties and careers?* If almost all
the parties in the polity get the overwhelming majority of their votes from their
own ethno-territorial units, trust and identity with the center will necessarily
remain low. Many analysts would call such parties "regional-secessionist." Political life in a polity dominated by such regional-secessionist parties would approximate the upper right-hand space depicted in figure 1.1. We call this space "pure
multinationalism."

However, if the polity contains some major polity-wide parties that regularly
need allies from regional parties to help them form a government at the center,
and if the polity-wide parties often help their regional party allies to form a
majority in their own ethno-federal units, then the logic of incentives at work
makes these purported "regional-secessionist" parties in fact "centric-regional"
parties because they regularly co-rule at the center. This coalitional pattern is
most feasible if both the polity-wide and the regional parties are nested in a federal
and a parliamentary system. There can, of course, be party coalitions in a presidential system, but their characteristics and implications are different since the
members of the coalitional government are not necessarily responsible to their
parties and especially since they are often appointed by the president who can
dismiss them.

What about "polity-wide careers"? If some polity-wide lingua franca, such
as English in India and Sri Lanka, is created or maintained, many university-
educated members of a regional nationality group who may not speak the majority-
language in the country (say, Hindi in India or Sinhalese in Sri Lanka) can still
successfully pursue polity-wide careers in the civil service, law, communications,

and business. Furthermore, if citizens can pursue such public and private polity-wide careers, the incentives to "exit" from these polity-wide networks will be weaker.[19]

5. *Why politically integrated but not culturally assimilated?* In a state-nation, many cultural and especially ethno-national groups will be educated and self-governing in their own language. They will thus probably never be fully assimilated to the dominant culture in the polity. Indeed, any attempt to assimilate these groups would invite resentment, resistance, and perhaps rejection of the system. This is a reality of state-nations, which distinguishes them from nation-states, where cultural assimilation is a possibility and very often a reality.

The absence of cultural assimilation does not preclude the possibility of political integration. If the ethno-federal group sees the polity-wide state as having helped put a "roof of rights" over its head, and if the "centric-regional" parties are "coalitionable" with polity-wide parties and regularly help form government at the center and many individuals from the ethno-federal group also participate in, and feel they benefit from, polity-wide careers, then they are politically integratable into the polity-wide state-nation.

6. *Why cultural nationalists versus secessionist nationalists?* Ernest Gellner forcefully articulated the position of many nation-state theorists when he famously asserted, "Nationalism is primarily a political principle, which holds that the political and the national unit should be congruent. . . . Nationalist *sentiment* is the feeling of anger aroused by the violation of the principle. . . . A nationalist *movement* is one actuated by a sentiment of this kind."[20] Similarly, we are constantly admonished not to advocate state-nation policies because all nationalism inevitably becomes "secessionist nationalism" with eventual demands for independence.

However, we can have a situation in which a "cultural-nationalist" movement, nested within asymmetrical federal and parliamentary systems, wins democratic political control of a component unit of a federation; governs and educates the citizens of its territory in the language, culture, and history of its nation; and is also coalitionable at the center. If such a group is challenged by secessionist nationalists who use, or threaten to use, violence in order to become independent, the ruling nationalist group would risk losing the treasured resources they have acquired. Given that, it is entirely possible that the cultural nationalists would use

19. However, the systematic effort by an ethno-cultural group to monopolize access to careers, even in their ethno-federal unit, runs counter to the nurturing and preservation of a state-nation.

20. All quotations are from the influential opening paragraphs of Ernest Gellner's *Nations and Nationalism* (Oxford: Oxford University Press, 1983), p. 1, emphasis in original.

the political and security resources now under their control *against* the secessionist nationalists.[21]

7. *Why not only multiple identities but also complementary identities?* In the
non-zero-sum polity-wide system produced by the six nested policies and norms
we have just discussed, it is likely that citizens in the multinational society would
strongly identify with, and remain loyal to, both their culturally powerful ethno-
federal unit *and* the polity-wide center. Most citizens would have such complementary identities because the center has recognized and defended many of their
cultural demands and, in addition, helped structure and protect their full participation in the overall politics of the polity. Such citizens are also likely to have
strong trust in the center because they see the center, and the institutions historically associated with it, as helping to deliver some valued collective goods such as
independence from a colonial power, security from threatening neighbors, and
participation in a large common market. Thus the pattern of complementary and
multiple identities that is likely to obtain is not just an accident; this outcome
would have been earned through the deliberate crafting of policies.

SUITABILITY OF "HOLDING TOGETHER" FEDERALISM FOR STATE-NATIONS

We have already referred to asymmetrical federalism as a part of the nested policy
grammar of institutions and practices that work best for state-nations. Since most
discussions about accommodating deep diversities within democratic states revolve around the institutional form of federalism, we need to reflect on some of
the foundational issues associated with federalism. That a number of the oldest
and most successful states were nation-states led many to think that all states
should be coterminous with nations; that states should be nation-builders, as
France was in the nineteenth century; and that all nations should become states,
as the Wilsonian ideology of self-determination implies. This of course evaded the
question of federalism altogether.

However, a large number of states do not fit into the classical conception of the
nation-state and in fact have significant multinational components. One example
is Spain, one of the oldest states in Europe, a country whose borders have not
changed since the mid-seventeenth century. Linz, writing in 1970 before the

---

21. However, it cannot be denied that if there is a conflict between secessionist nationalists and
the central state apparatus over the use of force, there might be a convergence on some issues in the
dispute between cultural nationalists and the secessionist nationalists.

transition to a federal type of state after the death of Franco, asserted that Spain is a state for all Spanish citizens, a nation-state for a large part of the population, and only a state but not a nation for important minorities. Also, he added, there is a small minority that contests or rejects that state and seeks independence.[22]

In the Spanish case, like that of quite a few other countries, would-be nation-builders who sought to create a unique shared sense of identity based on language, history, and culture following the French model ultimately failed. We would argue that such efforts in the twentieth century were often not fully successful; in the twenty-first century, they might well backfire and arouse the latent sense of national identity of significant minorities.[23] In 1993, in a paper titled "State Building and Nation Building," Linz cogently formulated some of the main reasons why we feel this is the case. He stressed in particular how in today's world, sensibilities have emerged within the "international community" that act as an effective pressure against it:

> We are living in an era in which the liberal democratic principles of legitimacy, the institutions of the Rechtsstaat, are being loudly proclaimed by everyone, even when they might be constantly violated. That legitimacy formula makes it impossible in many countries needing the respect of the world community to pursue oppressive and discriminatory policies against those asserting primordial identities, cultural and linguistic rights, and also the articulation of nationalist sentiments, even of extreme nationalists. This is a reality that modern states cannot ignore except by turning to authoritarianism, a choice that often is also not legitimate for those who do not share sympathy with, or tolerance for, the nationalists questioning the idea of nation state building by the state. In this context, it is necessary to turn to different and new methods of state integration other than those based on nation building.[24]

Complementary to Linz's point about the international zeitgeist, Stepan has also stressed interconnected technological and normative developments that have led to a certain "de-territorialization" of conceptions of individual identity, thus rendering the chances of successfully pursuing classical models of nation-state building increasingly unlikely in contexts where a significant percentage of the

22. Juan J. Linz, "Early State-Building and Late Peripheral Nationalisms against the State: The Case of Spain," in *Building States and Nations: Analyses by Region*, vol. 2, ed. S. N. Eisenstadt and Stein Rokkan (Beverly Hills, CA: Sage Publications, 1973), pp. 32–116.

23. In India the term *minority* normally refers only to a religious minority. However, in this book we follow standard social science vocabulary when we use the word *minority* to include linguistic, tribal, ethnic, and religious minorities.

24. Linz, "State Building and Nation Building."

permanent residents are first- or second-generation immigrants (or, originally, guest workers) and have different cultures. In an article titled "Modern Multinational Democracies: Transcending a Gellnerian Oxymoron," first published in 1998, he argued:

> Given the significant technological changes that have occurred since the late nineteenth century state-induced homogenization processes so well described by Eugen Weber, and the analytically distinct but related emergence of what Charles Taylor calls "the politics of recognition," there are grounds for thinking such processes are now less available. Most of the world's minorities can keep in cultural contact with their home cultures via radio, cassettes, and cheap air travel to a vastly greater extent than was possible a hundred years ago. Also, due to advances in literacy and communications, more minority communities have semiprofessional "cultural carriers," in the Weberian sense of *Träger*, than a hundred years ago. Normative changes in the form of increased desire for cultural autonomy in some minority (especially Muslim) communities—contested by rising antiforeign sentiments in the majority cultures that reduces the integrating capacity that in theory the majority culture would like—probably have contributed to greater cultural will, and greater cultural capacity, for minorities to resist cultural assimilation.[25]

Given all of these developments, we think it necessary to issue a warning to would-be nation-state builders in contexts with a significant degree of politically salient cultural and linguistic diversity: specifically, that their strategy is likely to be ineffectual at best and most likely will end up being radically counterproductive. Put simply, the pursuit of nation-state-building policies will probably provoke the very kind of fragmentation that adherents of the nation-state model most deeply fear. In the process, it will frequently engender significant levels of resistance—resistance that can often only be countered effectively by descent into authoritarian styles of rule. As such, it seems clear that in many parts of the contemporary world, nobody with a genuine commitment to democratic governance should support the pursuit of the nation-state model in contexts where there are already politically salient issues that revolve around deep, especially territorially based, cultural differences.

Any minority today has articulated leadership and structures, has intellectuals who formulate their national aspirations, and finds support among those con-

25. Stepan, "Modern Multinational Democracies," in his *Arguing Comparative Politics*, pp. 187–188.

cerned with their rights as a culture. This makes the assimilating policies of the successful nineteenth-century nation-builders, aimed at erasing such distinct identities, as in France, extremely costly. However, paradoxically, the minority that has gained control of ethno-cultural political institutions can often pursue nation building or exclusionary policies that large states—the center—cannot pursue without being sanctioned.

In our view, as we shall show in chapter 2, India at certain times has been and is, like Spain, Belgium, and Canada, to mention three democratic federal states with multinational components, a nation-state for most citizens, a state to which they owe allegiance but not a nation in the classical sense for significant minorities, and a state that is contested by some minorities in the periphery of the state.[26]

This brings us to a basic distinction among federal states between those federations that are largely "coming together" in their origin versus those that are largely "holding together" in their origin.[27] "Coming together" federations are formed by a process in which relatively autonomous separate units, often sharing much of the same political culture, sometimes a common enemy, jointly arrive at an agreement to pool part of their previous sovereignty in order to gain the advantages of creating a new federal state. This was the case of the United States, when the thirteen colonies got together to achieve a more perfect union as an independent state. The history of Australia fits that same pattern, as does even multicultural Switzerland in the course of its long history. This is the standard theory of how federal states are created.[28]

But there is another quite different process for the emergence of new federal states. Old states, governed as unitary states and originally conceived as future nation-states, when confronted with rising peripheral nationalisms, with new identities based on language, culture, or history that threaten their unity, can turn

26. For a typology of democratic states that takes into account both whether they are unitary or federal ones and whether they are mononational or multinational, see Juan J. Linz, "Para un mapa conceptual de las democracias," *Politeia*, no. 26 (2001), pp. 25–46.

27. A more detailed discussion of the necessary distinction between "coming together" federalism and "holding together" federalism can be found in Alfred Stepan, "Toward a New Comparative Politics of Federalism, (Multi)Nationalism, and Democracy: Beyond Rikerian Federalism," in his *Arguing Comparative Politics*, pp. 315–361.

28. The classic statement of what we call "coming together" federations is found in William Riker, *The Development of American Federalism* (Boston: Kluwer Academic Publishers, 1987), pp. 17–42. See also his "Federalism" in *Handbook of Political Science*, vol. 5, ed. Fred Greenstein and Nelson W. Polsby (Reading, MA: Addison-Wesley, 1975), pp. 93–172. Riker implies that autonomous political units who come to believe that their security and economy will be enhanced if they create a federation often tend to do so. However, we want to note that *no* country, once it was an established nation-state, has ever created a "coming together" federation. Certainly, on security grounds in the interwar years, the Baltic states and the Scandinavian nation-states had significant reasons to create federations but did not.

to federalism to continue to "hold together" the people in a common state. This was the origin of the long process of the transition in Belgium since independence in the 1830s from what was supposed to be a unitary nation-state to a new federal state. A similar process occurred in Spain in the 1970s. There are great differences between the federations formed by a "coming together" of separate units, like the United States and Australia, where the pre-federal units retained considerable power and sometimes a sense of identity and are zealous of their rights with respect to the center, and those "holding together" federations created on the basis of an existing state, particularly a unitary state, that devolves power to units to satisfy their emerging demands.[29]

The "coming together" process of federation formation tends to create constitutionally symmetrical federations in which all full constituent members of the federation have identical prerogatives and obligations, whereas federations that are "holding together" in their origins and intentions tend to have important asymmetrical characteristics in which some cultural prerogatives are constitutionally embedded for sub-units with salient territorial identities.

Obviously, some countries do not fit neatly into this typology. Occasionally the reality involves elements of both processes.[30] This was the case in Canada where, in 1867, asymmetrical federalism was used to "hold together" French-speaking Quebec and English-speaking Canada, but Canadian federalism also served to incorporate the Maritime Provinces that, after important incentives were arranged, wanted to "come together" and join the new federation.[31]

In the case of India, the entry of Sikkim, facilitated by Article 2 of the constitution, which allows for the possibility of other political units to join the republic, reflected some "coming together" elements, as did the social reality of the Indian

---

29. It is possible that if the princely states in India had coincided with cultural, linguistic, and other social characteristics and the federation had been created, as was sometimes discussed in the 1930s by the princely states retaining their identities and acceding to a federation, India could have been a case of a "coming together" federation. For many reasons we shall not discuss here, this did not happen. For the atmosphere of the debate in the 1930s, see N. D. Varadachariar, *Indian States in the Federation* (Calcutta: Oxford University Press, 1936).

30. In the case of the Soviet Union, especially in 1919 to 1923, there was actually a third pattern that Stepan calls "putting together" federalism. See his "Russian Federalism in Comparative Perspective," *Post-Soviet Affairs*, no. 16 (April–June 2000), pp. 133–176.

31. For an overview of the constitutional impasse in Canada, see Richard Simeon, "Canada: Federalism, Language and Regional Conflict" in *Federalism and Territorial Cleavages*, ed. Ugo M. Amoretti and Nancy Bermeo (Baltimore: Johns Hopkins University Press, 2004), pp. 93–122; and Simeon, "Debating Secession Peacefully and Democratically: The Case of Canada," in *Democracies in Danger*, ed. Alfred Stepan (Baltimore: Johns Hopkins University Press, 2009), pp. 41–56. On the evolution of Québécois nationalism, see Maurice Pinard, "Les quatre phases du mouvement indépedantiste québécois," in *Combat Inachevé*, ed. Robert Bernier, Vincent Lemieux, and Maurice Pinard (Sainte-Foy, Quebec: Presses de l'Université du Quebec, 1997).

Independence movement itself. German federalism in the nineteenth century served the processes of nation building, giving the nation the roof of the common state, although formally it was the "coming together" of kingdoms, duchies, and city states under Prussian hegemony.

Some federal states are based on a strong national identity in practically all its citizens. They are relatively homogeneous in their culture, language, and sense of history and can be seen as nation-states. The state and the nation are one. Germany, after giving up claims to Alsace-Lorraine and losing the eastern territories inhabited by large numbers of Poles, is now a nation-state with tiny minorities enjoying a special status, like the Danes on the northern border and the Sorbs to the east. However, with the Cold War division between the *Bundesrepublik* and the German Democratic Republic, there were two states and one nation. Each state sought to legitimate its rule, in West Germany by what was called the *Verfassungspatriotismus*, the loyalty to the democratic liberal state and its market institutions, and in East Germany by the construction of a socialist state.[32]

The first Austrian republic was founded in 1918 and in its constitution defined itself as part of the German nation; it was committed to joining the German Federal Republic. Only after the Second World War did Austria acquire an identity of its own as a state, though not for a long time as a nation.[33]

Most of the social scientists writing about Switzerland do not see it as a nation-state but as a voluntary state, close to our state-nation. With its linguistic heterogeneity of largely monolingual German, French, and Italian (Raeto-Romansch-speaking) cantons, Switzerland is a unique federation. Given that none of its linguistic regions, none of its religious communities, and none of its cantons considers itself a nation, as many Basques and Catalans consider their autonomous communities in Spain, it would be wrong to consider Switzerland a multinational state. The Swiss confederation enjoys a legitimacy, felt by all its multicultural and largely canton-focused citizens, that is unique and provides the ideal type of what

32. For the original formulation of the concept of "constitutional patriotism," see Dolf Stern-berger, *Verfassungspatriotismus* (Frankfurt am Main: Insel-Verlag, 1990). For Jürgen Habermas's development of the concept, see his *Einbeziehung des Anderen: Studien zur politschen Theorie* (Frankfurt am Main: Suhrkamp, 1996). For a recent elaboration on the theme (in English) and adaptation of it to contexts outside of Germany, see Habermas, "Citizenship and National Identity," in *Between Facts and Norms* (Cambridge, MA: MIT Press, 1998), pp. 491–515.

33. On the recent emergence of national consciousness in Austria, see T. Bluhm, *Building an Austrian Nation: The Political Integration of a Western State* (New Haven: Yale University Press, 1973), esp. pp. 220–241. On the same theme, see also the excellent piece by Fritz Plasser and Peter A. Ulram, "Politisch-Kulturell Wandel in Österreich," in *Staatsbürger oder Untertanen? Politische Kultur Deutschlands, Österreichs und Schweiz im Vergleich*, ed. Plasser and Ulram (New York: P. Lang, 1991), pp. 157–245.

28   CRAFTING STATE-NATIONS

we call a state-nation, where the institutions of the state, with its distinctive political culture, are the basis of a particular type of identification of its citizens.[34]

In contrast to the ideal-type state-nation of Switzerland, in state-nations with important multinational components, such as Spain, Belgium, or Canada, many citizens, who may constitute a significant proportion of the population of federal units, identify with a distinctive territorially based culture that some influential members of the community see as a nation, with its own language, history, rights, and grievances against the state in which they live. The federal state-nation is a nightmare to those who originally conceived of the state as a nation-state; a nightmare to those who want to nationalize the whole population in the process of nation building, of which the French Republic would be the historically most successful model; a nightmare to those nation builders for whom federalism would be conceived, at the most, as a form of decentralization for purposes of administrative efficiency. It is also a nightmare to nationalists who want to create a separate nation-state.

EVIDENCE ON IDENTITY AND TRUST IN STATE-NATIONS

There are those who think that the multinational federal state is inevitably condemned to break up, who see federalism in those states as only a step toward disintegration and who therefore want to limit the federal constitution and engage in a process of more or less aggressive nation building. For complex reasons we have already noted, such efforts are likely to fail, producing a backlash that will lead to the opposite result from the one that their proponents pursue. However, intelligent political engineering, constructive political leadership, and some favorable contextual factors can serve to overcome the tension inherent in multinational societies. A federal state that is multinational can become a successful state-nation. Unfortunately, we have few systematic studies of how this has been

34. A fine overview of the Swiss case can be found in Lidija Basta, "Minority and Legitimacy of a Federal State," in *Federalism and Multiethnic States: The Case of Switzerland*, ed. L. Basta and Thomas Fleiner (Fribourg, Switzerland: Institute of Federalism, 1996), pp. 41–69. For another treatment that deals extensively with language policy in Switzerland, see Kenneth D. McRae, *Conflict and Compromise in Multilingual Societies*, vol. 1 (Ontario, Canada: Wilfred Laurier University Press, 1986). For an earlier formulation of the concept of the state-nation, and its distinctiveness from both the nation-state and the multinational state, see Juan J. Linz, "Democratic States, Nation States, State Nations, and Multinational States." A shortened version of this article was published in German as "Nationalstaaten, Staatsnationen und multinationale Staaten," in *Staat, Nation, Demokratie. Traditionen und Perspektiven moderner Gesellschaften. Festschrift für Hans-Jürgen Puhle*, ed. Marcus Gräser, Christian Lammert, and Söhnke Schreyer (Göttigen, Germany: Vandenhoeck und Ruprecht, 2001), 27–38. See also Juan J. Linz, "Democracia, multinacionalismo y federalismo," in *Revista Española de Ciencia Política* 1 (October 1999), pp. 7–40.

achieved. That is why we believe that our study of the Republic of India and its history and institutions can make an important contribution to this important task for social scientists and policy-makers. Before we turn to a detailed study of the crafting of a state-nation in India in chapter 2, we first take on the suspicion that multinational federations cannot draw positive identification from its citizens and then get them to posit trust in its institutions. We consider some evidence from Spain and Belgium with regard to multiple but complimentary identities before turning to a comparative dataset for the level of citizen trust in some of the key institutions in eleven federal democracies.

It might seem natural for our task to draw on evidence and justification from the proponents of multiculturalism. Unfortunately, the brilliant theorizing about multiculturalism of recent years, particularly in the United States and, to a lesser extent, Europe, is only partly relevant to this task.[35] Multiculturalism in the way that we find it discussed in that literature is not distinctive to federal states. The literature is equally relevant to unitary states like France, with its increasingly important Muslim immigrant population.[36] The literature on multiculturalism is especially relevant to cultural minorities, particularly immigrants claiming a range of rights as individuals and communities without rising to the level of territorially based autochthonous communities with an articulated or latent national identity.

Multiculturalism represents a different dimension of social and political reality that we can find in nation-states, state-nations, and multinational societies. Also, multiculturalism certainly can be found in India as a whole and within the states of the Indian federation.

Most of the literature on nationalism treats national identities as if they were mutually exclusive. The literature is plagued with the use of expressions like "the

35. The literature on multiculturalism is of course extensive, and we refer here only to some of the most basic works, written from a variety of perspectives. These include: Brian Barry, *Culture and Equality: An Egalitarian Critique of Multiculturalism* (Cambridge, MA: Polity Press, 2001); Seyla Benhabib, *The Claims of Culture: Equality and Diversity in the Global Era* (Princeton: Princeton University Press, 2002); Will Kymlicka, *Liberalism, Community, and Culture* (New York: Oxford University Press, 1989) as well as his more recent contribution, *Multicultural Citizenship: A Liberal Theory of Minority Rights* (New York: Clarendon Press, 1995); Bikhu Parekh, *Rethinking Multiculturalism: Cultural Diversity and Political Theory* (Basingstoke, UK: Macmillan, 2000); Taylor, "Politics of Recognition"; James Tully, *Strange Multiplicity: Constitutionalism in an Age of Diversity* (New York: Cambridge University Press, 1995); and Iris Marion Young, *Justice and the Politics of Difference* (Princeton: Princeton University Press, 1990).

36. There is a growing selection of high-quality literature on precisely this point. See, for example, Ahmet Kuru, "Secularism, State Policies, and Muslims in Europe: Analyzing French Exceptionalism," *Comparative Politics* 4 (2008), pp. 1–19; and John R. Bowen, *Why the French Don't Like Headscarves: Islam, the State, and Public Space* (Princeton: Princeton University Press, 2006).

Catalans" or "the Flemish" and their opposites, "the Spanish" and "the Belgians." However, such expressions are a gross oversimplification. Though nationalists on both sides reject the idea of dual identities as a form of bigamy, in fact, in all more or less multinational societies, most citizens tend to have dual but often complementary, or at least not exclusive, identities.

Identities in Spain

The region of Catalonia, in Spain, provides a case in point. Since the late nineteenth century and particularly in the twentieth century, there has been a growing interest in cultural and, increasingly, *national* identities among people in bilingual regions in certain parts of Spain—most acutely, in Catalonia and the Basque Country.[37] At the turn of the century, nationalist parties emerged in both of these regions and began to articulate these identities. In the decades following the Spanish Civil War, such identities gained strength as a reaction to the Franco regime, since that regime pursued an aggressive policy against peripheral nationalist movements, including discriminatory language policies. By the end of the Franco era, the democratic opposition had come to sympathize with the peripheral nationalist movements and even to demand that their aspirations be at least partly recognized. In the transition to democracy, the drafters of the 1978 constitution did just that; they agreed to accommodate linguistic, cultural, and national differences by organizing the state as an "*estado de autonomías*," a type of federal political system.[38]

37. For a useful bibliography on the historiographical debates about the rise of peripheral nationalisms in Spain, see Xosé-M. Núñez, "Historical Research on Regionalism and Peripheral Nationalism in Spain: A Reappraisal," published as a working paper by the European University Institute in Florence as ECS no. 92/6 (1992). For Linz's contribution to this debate, see Juan J. Linz, "Early State-Building and Late Peripheral Nationalisms against the State: The Case of Spain," in *Building States and Nations*, vol. 2, ed. Eisenstadt and Rokkan, pp. 32–116.

38. On the process of devolution to a federal state in Spain, see Juan J. Linz, "Spanish Democracy and the Estado de las Autonomías," in *Forging Unity Out of Diversity*, ed. Robert A. Goldwin, Art Kaufman, and William A. Schambra (Washington, DC: American Enterprise Institute for Public Policy Research, 1989), pp. 260–303. On electoral results in and public opinion about the Estado de las Autonomías during the first fifteen years of democracy, see Juan J. Linz, "De la crisis de un estado unitario al Estado de las Autonomías," in *La España de las Autonomías*, ed. Fernando Fernández Rodríguez (Madrid: Instituto de Estudios de Administración Local, 1985), pp. 527–672. See also Linz for the five alternative questions on national identity. On the continuing conflict in the Basque Country, see Juan J. Linz, *Conflicto en Euskadi* (Madrid: Espasa Calpe, 1986). Also see Francisco J. Llera, *Los Vascos y la Política. El proceso político vasco: elecciones, partidos, opinión pública y legitimación en el País Vasco, 1977–1992* (Bilbao: Servicio Editorial Universidad del País Vasco, 1994). On public opinion in the Basque Country, see *Euskalherria en la encuesta Europea de valores* (Bilbao: Universidad de Deusto, 1992). Also see the series of *Euskobarometro*, directed by Francisco Llera (Bilbao: Servicio Editorial Universidad del País Vasco). For public opinion in

Since the transition to democracy in Spain, a number of questions about national identity have been asked in opinion polls—all of which reveal the predominance of multiple but complementary identities. Exclusive and competing identities turn out to be the exception, not the rule. For example, when asked, "Which of the following sentences would you identify with most: I feel only Spanish, I feel more Spanish than Basque/Catalan/etc., I feel as Spanish as Basque/Catalan/etc., I feel more Basque/Catalan/etc. than Spanish, or I feel only Basque/Catalan/etc.," only 13% of the Spanish population chooses an exclusive Spanish identity. Multiple identifications are dominant. Indeed, in Catalonia, the modal self-identification was multiple and complimentary; that is, "as Spanish as Catalan," 41%. Only a small minority of the population in Catalonia registers an exclusive identity. To be exact, in Catalonia a mere 16% of the population identify themselves as exclusively Catalan, while another 9% identify themselves as exclusively Spanish. The rest—fully three-quarters of the population—report some kind of dual identification.

Even in the Basque Country, the modal category chosen was "as Spanish as Basque," at 34%. Even though the Basque Country is the region of Spain where identification with the Spanish nation is weakest, those who self-identify as "only Basque" barely exceed a quarter of the population (see table 1.2).

Identities in Belgium

Nor is Spain an exception in this regard; for the same is true in the case of Belgium. Belgium was founded in 1830 as an independent unitary parliamentary monarchy. In the course of a complex process marked by considerable conflict, it evolved in the twentieth century into a federal, basically bi-national and bilingual federal democracy.[39] In Belgium, a number of relevant questions about national identity have been asked in opinion polls too, distinguishing among those who speak Dutch, those who speak French, and the inhabitants of Brussels. All of these again reveal the predominance of multiple but complementary identities. For

---

Catalonia, see the yearly surveys published by the Institut de Ciències Polítiques i Socials (Barcelona: Universitat Autònoma de Barcelona); and Francisco Andrés Orizo and Maria-Àngels Roque, *Cataluña 2001: Los catalanes en la encuesta Europea de valores* (Madrid: La Fundación Santa María, 2001). See also Thomas Jeffrey Miley, *Nacionalismo y política lingüística: el caso de Cataluña* (Madrid: CEPC, 2006).

39. For a good synthesis of this historical process and an extended discussion of language policy there, see McRae, *Conflict and Compromise in Multilingual Societies*, vol. 1, ch. 1. For a study that focuses on linguistic conflict in the metropolitan region of Brussels, the only place where significant numbers of French-speakers and Flemish-speakers live side by side, see Jan de Volder, "Le FN Brade Bruxelles," in *Revue Française de Geopolitique*, no. 6 (May 1998).

TABLE 1.2
Multiple but Complementary Identity in Spain:
Subjective National Identity in Spain, Catalonia, and Basque Country

Identity	All of Spain	Catalonia	Basque Country
Only Spanish	13	9	6
More Spanish than Cat/Basque/other	8	4	6
As Spanish as Cat/Basque/other	56	41	34
More Cat/Basque/other than Spanish	14	27	23
Only Cat/Basque/other	6	16	27
Do not know/no answer	4	3	4
(N)	(10,476)	(1,200)	(1,800)

Sources: For the Basque Country, Catalonia, and Galicia, *Sondeo de opinión del Observatorio Político Autonómico: 2003* (Barcelona: ICPS, 2004); for the rest of Spain and all of Spain, CIS study no. 2455 (2002). These five alternative questions were designed by Linz in 1979 and have been used in many surveys in Spain and by other scholars.

Note: All figures in column percentages may not add up to 100 due to rounding. N, number of respondents in each column.

example, in Flanders, which many analysts see as moving towards secession, the following question was asked: "Which of the following statements applies most to you: 'I consider myself only as a Belgian,' 'I feel more Belgian than Flemish,' 'I feel as Belgian as Flemish,' 'I feel more Flemish than Belgian,' or 'I feel only Flemish?'" What is most surprising about the poll is that only 4% of the Flemish population self-identified as "only Flemish." Indeed, in 1995 the modal form of self-identification in Flanders was the multiple but complementary identity "as Belgian as Flemish."[40]

Nonetheless, many analysts still predicted that an "only Flanders" sense of identity would grow steadily and imperil the unity of Belgium. What trends in identity, if any, seem to be occurring in Belgium? In surveys, the three-year average for 1980, 1981, and 1982 of Flemish respondents who said their strongest "feeling of belonging" was with Flanders was 47%. However, far from increasing, the three-year average for the same question for the years 1997, 1999, and 2003 had *dropped twenty points*, to 27%.[41] Furthermore, younger respondents were more

40. The data we use for Belgium in this survey are based on the 1995 *General Election Study*, conducted by the Interuniversitair Politieke-Opinieonderzoek, K. U. Leuven, and the Point d'appui Interuniversitaire sur l'Opinion publique et la Politique, U. C. Louvain, results published in 1998.
41. See Jaak Billiet, Bart Maddens, and André-Paul Frognier, "Does Belgium (Still) Exist? Differences in Political Culture between Flemings and Walloons," *West European Politics* 29, no. 5 (2006), pp. 912–932.

TABLE 1.3
Multiple but Complementary Identity in Belgium:
Subjective National Identity by Region

Identity	All of Belgium	Flanders	Wallonia	Brussels
Only Belgian	14	11	18	24
More Belgian than Flemish/Walloon	21	17	25	27
As Belgian as Flemish/Walloon	43	45	44	32
More Flemish/Walloon than Belgian	17	23	10	11
Only Flemish/Walloon	3	4	2	3
Do not know/no answer	2	1	2	5
(N)	(3,651)	(2,099)	(1,258)	(311)

Source: *1995 Belgian General Election Study.* See footnote 40.
    Note: All figures in column percentages have been rounded off. N, number of respondents in each column.

inclined to identify with Belgium than older respondents. In 1999 only 12% of Flemish respondents supported Flemish independence.[42]

Among the French-speaking Walloons, who at the time of the founding of the state lived in the more prosperous state-building community, identification with the Belgian nation is somewhat stronger than it is for the whole of the population: 18% of them identify themselves as "only Belgian"; 25% identify themselves as "more Belgian than Walloon"; and 44% consider themselves "as Walloon as Belgian." A mere 10% identify themselves as "more Walloon than Belgian"; and a miniscule 2% feel "only Walloon." In the capital city of Brussels, the only place in the country where significant numbers of French-speakers and Dutch-speakers live side by side, 24% identify themselves as "only Belgian"; 26% identify themselves as "more Belgian than Flemish/Walloon"; 31% report an equal dual identity; 11% identify themselves as "more Flemish/Walloon than Belgian"; and only 3% fail to mention the Belgian identity. In fact, only 15% of the population of Brussels speak Flemish. So a movement for an independent Flanders would run the risk of weakening or severing valued ties with Brussels for Flemish-speakers, because the citizens of Brussels would certainly not vote, given the chance, to leave Belgium to join a new state of Flanders (see table 1.3).

What's more, not only do the overwhelming majority of citizens in Belgium, regardless of the territory from which they hail, identify themselves at least some-

42. Wilfred Swenden and Marten Theo Jans, "Will It Stay or Will It Go? Federalism and the Sustainability of Belgium," *West European Politics* 29, no. 5 (2006), pp. 877–894.

times as Belgians, they also register a very high degree of affective attachment to an important common state institution—specifically, the monarchy. Such attachment is evident in the responses of Belgian citizens to a question about how much they trust their king—for fully 54% of them claim to trust him either "very much" or "a lot" (13% and 41%, respectively); while a mere 11% of them claim to trust him "only a little" or "very little" (6% and 5%, respectively).[43]

We understand this kind of affective attachment to a set of common institutions, symbols, and places such as Brussels to be indispensable for the legitimacy, and therefore stability, of any state with a high level of cultural, linguistic, and even national heterogeneity. This is why we stress the importance of not only multiple but complementary identities within a multinational, federal, democratic framework. Of course, as we have already suggested, there are two intimately related difficulties with this framework: first, that centralists often dream of doing away with the fact of *multiple* identities; and second, that peripheral nationalists often seek to undermine the fact of *complementary* identities. But, at least in the Belgian case, neither of these difficulties seems to be unmanageable. Belgium is certainly adopting more and more confederal policies, which many argue are decreasing overall state efficiency, but we do not share the skepticism of some other commentators, who feel that Belgium is falling apart.[44] Both the overwhelming preponderance of dual identities and, especially, the high level of affective attachment to common symbols and institutions justify our sense of optimism. Were such affective attachment to common symbols and institutions lacking, there would be reason for pessimism. Late in the history of Yugoslavia as a federal state, for example, it is highly doubtful that any Yugoslavian institution had a high level of trust shared by most of the citizens of the country. Fortunately, however, the Belgian case is quite different from that of Yugoslavia.

Yugoslavia's "pure multinationalism," as Bunce has shown, led to the hollowing out of almost all authoritative state-wide functions and to increasingly polarized and conflictual identities. In sharp contrast, Belgium's "holding together" federalization and other state-nation-building processes from 1970 to 1993 did neither. Liesbet Hooghe, in her detailed article on Belgium's "holding together" federalization since 1970, brilliantly documents what has happened, and what has not, to identities, ethnic conflicts, and central state functions.

Concerning identities, Hooghe argues that "from the mid-1980s, Belgian iden-

---

43. See 1995 Belgian General Election Study.
44. For an excellent assessment of the mix of statewide, regional, cultural community and confederal policies, see Swenden and Jans, "Will It Stay or Will It Go?"

tity has gained ground on regional and local identities. The development of regional governance institutions in Belgium has not gone hand in hand with a deepening of regional identity. The data show, instead, that a system of multilevel governance may encourage the development of complementary multiple identities. . . . The survey results also confirm that, like in Spain and the European Union (EU), regional and national identities are not exclusive, but complementary." Analyzing Walloon-Flemish conflicts and protests, Hooghe concludes that "disruptive, non-violent territorial protest became widespread in the 1950s and 1960s. It topped in the late 1970s, and it has declined since. Through much of the postwar period Flemish and Walloon identities gained strength at the expense of a Belgian identity, but in the 1990s Belgian and regional identities appear to have become more inclusive. The ebbing of disruptive, territorial protest and of exclusive identities coincides with the transformation from a unitary to a federal state in 1993." Regarding the polity-wide functions of the new "holding together" federal state, Hooghe correctly notes that in the process of moving from a unitary to a federal state, Belgium saw a significant transfer of functions to the sub-units; she even uses the phrase "Hollowing the Center" as her subtitle. However, in great contrast to Yugoslavia, many of the core attributes found in democratic federal states in the world still remain under the control of the Belgian federal center. As Hooghe stresses, "The list of exclusive federal competencies is . . . substantial: defense, justice, security, social security, fiscal and monetary policy." She also notes that central "federal institutions remain the prime venue for the resolution of much horizontal Flemish-Francophone conflict, and here the familiar consociational mechanisms are unchanged."[45]

Thus, in terms of our analytic categories, Belgium's often overlooked *reintegration* since the 1970s has come about largely because it has adopted ethno-conflict–ameliorating state-nation policies, such as "holding together" federalism. In complete contrast, from 1970 to 1991 Yugoslavia increasingly adopted ethno-conflict–intensifying, *disintegrative* "pure multinational" policies.

By all means, nationalists would like the question formulated not as, "Are you *more* Flemish *than* Belgian?" or "Are you *more* Catalan *than* Spanish?" but rather as, "Are you *either* Flemish *or* Belgian?" or "Are you *either* Catalan *or* Spanish?"— despite the ubiquity of multiple but complementary identities in settings that are more or less multinational. And inevitably, both those who speak of self-

45. Liesbet Hooghe, "Belgium: Hollowing the Center," in *Federalism and Territorial Cleavages,* ed. Ugo M. Amoretti and Nancy Bermeo (Baltimore: Johns Hopkins University Press, 2004), pp. 55, 65, 74.

determination, that is, the right of every nation to become an independent state, and those who favor total national integration into a single cultural or linguistic community reject the very idea of dual identities.

This is the main reason (and there are many) why democratic plebiscites are normally such an undesirable solution. People have to make one choice or another, like the one of defining the territorial units for which the decision should be binding. The quorum necessary to reverse such a decision is totally different from a normal election since it cannot be reversed four or five years hence. A plebiscite might be the only solution in certain extreme situations where the polarization created by violent conflict has destroyed any dual identity. But in those cases, it will mean a loss of rights and equal citizenship among those not supporting the majoritarian choice.

The state-nation concept would seem to have some utility for advanced democracies and the democratic management of a modest number of language groups. But what is the "scope value" of the concept? Is it appropriate in much poorer countries, in countries with much greater diversity? For this we turn to India, the poorest, the most diverse (and the most populous) democracy of long standing in the world in the next chapter.

We would like to conclude with a cautionary note, however. The attitudes documented in table 1.3 indeed support a state-nation, but we must acknowledge that we do not rule out political leaders acting in ways not congruent with the attitudes of their constituents and constantly pushing for autonomist or secessionist policies. We also do not rule out that a majority of people in Brussels and Wallonia might end up wishing that Flanders would exit Belgium. However, the reality is that, despite tensions, it is not clear that a majority within Flanders would be eager to embrace a political formula where they would politically and economically lose Brussels, the de facto capital of Europe.

TRUST IN STATE-NATIONS VERSUS NATION-STATES

A major claim of nation-state theorists and advocates is that only a nation-state can generate the necessary degree of trust in the major institutions of the state that a modern democracy needs to function well.

Let us do a simple empirical test of this claim by examining comparative trust in the entire universe of federal systems that have been democratic for at least twenty-five continuous years. In our judgment, there are eleven such countries; in alphabetical order, they are Australia, Argentina, Austria, Belgium, Brazil, Canada, Germany, India, Spain, Switzerland, and the United States.

Fortunately, the World Values Survey was carried out in all eleven of the countries.[46] We thus have data for the degree of trust for six key political institutions for all eleven countries. These key institutions are: the central government, the legislature, the legal system, the civil service, political parties, and the police. All of the data are presented in table 2.9, but we are interested here in a summary measure.

To proceed with our test, let us now divide our eleven countries into those countries that fit the nation-state ideal type in that they are (1) symmetrically federal; (2) have no constitutionally embedded ethno-federal dimensions; and (3) are not multilingual as a matter of law. These countries are Austria, Germany, Australia, the United States, Brazil, and Argentina.

Those countries in our country set that fit the state-nation ideal type in that they are (1) asymmetrically federal; (2) have constitutionally embedded ethno-federal features; and (3) are constitutionally multilingual are Belgium, Canada, Spain, and India. We will add Switzerland to this set because, even though it is symmetrically federal, Switzerland is much closer to a state-nation type than a nation-state type, based on the attributes detailed in table 1.1.

When we examine the average country trust scores for the six key political institutions for each of these polities, we get very surprising results (see table 1.4).

The "closer to the nation-state, the greater the trust" claim is obviously not supported by these data. If we look at the average ranking of trust (the lower the number the greater the trust), state-nations receive an average ranking of 4.8, whereas nation-states score much worse, with an average ranking of 7.0. The conclusion remains the same if we replace the crude measure of average ranking for a more precise average of percentages, as state-nations record an average of 47% trust in their institutions, whereas nation-states have an average of 39% trust. The same pattern obtains even if we throw out Argentina, which scores significantly lower on trust than the other countries and is something of an outlier. The nation-state set still has a trust average of 43%, four points lower than the state-nation set.[47]

The claim that "any use of ethno-federal devices is subversive of the state" is also obviously not supported by these data because *all* of the countries close to the state-nation pole have some ethno-federal features *as well as* strong polity-wide trust.

---

46. Five waves of this survey have been done since it began in 1981. These five waves have been carried out in 97 societies. The World Values Survey is under the overall supervision of Ronald Inglehart, the program director for the Institute of Social Research at the University of Michigan. For a discussion of these surveys, see appendix A in Pippa Norris and Ronald Inglehart, *Sacred and Secular: Religion and Politics Worldwide* (Cambridge: Cambridge University Press, 2004), pp. 243–246.

47. All figures computed from the data in table 2.9.

TABLE 1.4
State-Nations More Trusted than Nation-States:
Average Trust Ranking in State Institutions in Longstanding Federal Democracies

	Average trust ranking (the lower the number, the greater the trust)
States closest to fitting state-nation model	
India	3.0
Switzerland	3.7
Canada	4.0
Belgium	6.3
Spain	7.2
States closest to fitting nation-state model	
Brazil	4.6
Austria	5.0
United States	5.9
Germany	7.6
Australia	8.0
Argentina	10.6
State-nation average	4.8
Nation-state average	7.0

Source: World Values Survey. For a more extensive discussion of these sources, see the lengthy footnote to table 2.9.

Note: Average trust ranking was arrived at by ranking the world's eleven longstanding federal democracies by level of citizen trust in each of six institutions (the country with the highest level of trust in that institution was ranked 1, and so on) and then averaging the six ranks for each country. The data from which the ranks were derived is reported in table 2.9.

Advocates of the inherent superiority of nation-states also base their arguments on their assumption that *only* a nation-state can generate the necessary degree of strong identity and pride in membership in the state that is best for a democracy. However, when we tested the average World Values Survey scores for "strong pride" in being a member of one's country, we found that the results are statistically indistinguishable between nation-states and state-nations, with the latter actually having marginally more pride. In the survey, 82.8% of the respondents in the nation-state set expressed "strong pride" in being a member of their countries, but in the multilingual, multicultural polities closest to the state-nation ideal type, 84.4% expressed "strong pride."[48]

48. For disaggregated data on pride for all eleven countries, see table 2.2.

CHAPTER TWO

India as a State-Nation

*Shared Political Community amidst
Deep Cultural Diversity*

India would appear to be one of the most difficult cases for our argument that multiple but complementary identities and democratic state-nation loyalties are possible even in a polity with significant "robust multinational" dimensions as well as intense linguistic and religious differences. For many of its citizens, India is a nation-state; for others, it is what we call a state-nation. However, as we discussed in chapter 1, India also has some unmistakable dimensions of a multinational society. Think of the popular, enduring sentiment for "freedom" in the Kashmir Valley, the short-lived militant Sikh-led Khalistan movement in the Punjab, the longer armed rebellion in Mizoram and Nagaland, and the potentially secessionist Dravidian movement in the south, among others.[1] In addition, Indians have

---

1. Chapters 3 and 4 contain extensive analysis and documentation of each of these cases of "robust multinationalism" involving some separatist movements. At this point, let us simply say, if we divide Jammu and Kashmir into its three regions (Kashmir, Ladakh, and Jammu), the Kashmir region meets our definition of being "robustly multinational." The Kashmir Valley is a territorially concentrated linguistic-cultural majority of Muslims who speak Kashmiri. Also, significant armed groups with overt and covert support from Pakistan and varying degrees of support from the people in Kashmir Valley have waged a battle for "Azadi," or freedom. For the conflicts concerning the national and international status of Kashmir and its independence, see *Perspectives on Kashmir: The Roots of the Conflict in South Asia*, ed. Raju G. C. Thomas (Boulder, CO: Westview Press, 1992); and Sumantra Bose, *The Challenge in Kashmir* (London: Sage, 1997). On independence movements and secessionist wars in the Northeast, see Sanjoy Hazarika, *Strangers of the Mist: Tales of War and Peace from India's Northeast* (London: Penguin, 1994); and Ved Marwah, *Uncivil Wars: Pathology of Terrorism in India* (New Delhi: Harper Collins, 1995). On the Khalistan Independence Movement in the Punjab, see Surinder S. Jodhka, "Looking Back at the Khalistan Movement: Some Recent Researches on its Rise and Decline," *Economic and Political Weekly* 36, no. 16, April 21–27, 2001, pp. 1311–1318. On short-lived pro-Dravidistan separatist movements, see Eugene Irschick, *Politics and Social Conflict in South India: The Non-Brahmin Movement and Tamil Separatism,*

had to nurture, defend, and deepen democracy in a social and political context in which this multinational dimension interacts with more linguistic and religious diversity, and greater poverty, than found in any other longstanding democracy in the world. While all of this makes our task difficult, these difficulties enhance the scope value of India for building an analytical as well as a normative case for state-nation. Let us first attend to some of the complexities and specificities of India.

INDIA AND THE BROAD SCOPE VALUE
OF "STATE-NATION" THEORY

One of the greatest points of conflict in multicultural and multinational societies, federal or not, is language. In India, at Independence, ten different languages were spoken by at least thirteen million people, many of them with mutually unintelligible alphabets. In descending order of number of speakers (excluding Hindi), Telugu, Bengali, Marathi, Tamil, Urdu, Gujarati, Kannada, Malayalam, and Oriya were all spoken by between thirty-two and thirteen million inhabitants of India.[2] In addition, another seventeen languages were spoken by at least one million people.[3] The largest language, Hindi, according to the 1961 census of India, was only spoken by 30.37% of the total population. The proportion has gradually risen to 41.03% in the 2001 census, but is still short of anything like a majority.[4] What would John Stuart Mill have said in 1947 about India's chances of building a democracy under such conditions?[5] How has this "Millsian" problem been managed democratically?

India's democracy should also be of particular interest to contemporary com-

1916–1929 (Berkeley and Los Angeles: University of California Press, 1969); and Narendra Subramanian, *Ethnicity and Populist Mobilization: Political Parties, Citizens, and Democracy in Southern India* (Oxford: Oxford University Press, 1999).

2. For an analytic discussion of these figures, see Jyotirindra Das Gupta, *Language Conflict and National Development: Group Politics and National Language Policy in India* (Berkeley: University of California Press, 1970), pp. 31–68.

3. Ibid.

4. *Census of India*, 2001, Office of The Registrar General of Census, Statement 6, available at http://censusindia.gov.in/Census_Data_2001/Census_Data_Online/Language/Statement6.htm, accessed March 29, 2010.

5. His oft-cited judgment about the impossibility of having more than one important functioning language and significant nationality in a democratic polity was "free institutions are next to impossible in a country made up of different nationalities. Among a people without fellow-feelings, especially if they read and speak different languages, the united public opinion necessary to the working of representative institutions cannot exist." See Mill, *Considerations on Representative Government* (1861), in *Utilitarianism, On Liberty, Considerations on Representative Government*, ed. Geraint Williams (London: Everyman, 1993), p. 393.

parativists because it has been developed in the context of great religious diversity. Indian society has large communities of almost every major world religion— Hindu, Islamic, Buddhist, Sikh, and Christian. Even after Partition in 1947, India had a large Islamic population. In 2009, India's Muslim population constituted a "minority" of approximately 161 million people, which made it the third-largest Islamic population in any country in the world, exceeded only by Indonesia's 203 million and Pakistan's 174 million.[6] At a time when many scholars and political activists worry about the "clash of civilizations," and some see Islamic society as being in deep cultural conflict with democracy, we find it very useful to document and analyze that the world's largest Islamic community with extensive democratic experience is in multicultural, multinational, federal, and consociational India. India pioneered in the democratic world a form of secularism that gave "equal support and equal respect" to *all* of India's religions; in part due to this formula, citizens from all religions have shown a very high degree of support for Indian democracy and trust in the Indian state.[7]

Conceptually and comparatively, India's poverty raises important intellectual challenges, especially for those who might posit that state-nation norms are a luxury reserved for wealthy countries. One of the most enduring propositions in social science is Seymour Martin Lipset's formulation that democracy correlates very strongly with overall socioeconomic development.[8] Arend Lijphart did not

6. Pew Forum on Religion in Public Life, "Mapping the Global Muslim Population: A Report on the Size and Distribution of the World's Muslim Population," October 2009, p. 14, available at www.pewforum.org.

7. Numerous tables based on various national representative surveys by CSDS to follow in chapters 2, 3, and 4 document this assertion. An essential book on India's model of secularism, with important contributions by Rajeev Bhargava, Amartya Sen, Akeel Bilgrami, Charles Taylor, and Ashis Nandy, is Rajeev Bhargava, ed., *Secularism and Its Critics* (Delhi and Oxford: Oxford University Press, 2004). For Muslims, see the important work by Mushirul Hasan, *Legacy of a Divided Nation: India's Muslims since Independence* (Delhi: Oxford University Press, 1997). For Hindu fundamentalism, the standard text is Christophe Jaffrelot, *The Hindu Nationalist Movement in India* (London: Hurst, 1996). On India's model of secularism in comparative perspective, see Alfred Stepan, "The Multiple Secularisms of Modern Democratic and Non-Democratic Regimes," in *Rethinking Secularism*, ed. Mark Juergensmeyer, Craig Calhoun, and Jonathan Van Antwerpen (New York: Oxford University Press, forthcoming).

8. The classic initial formulation of this argument is Seymour Martin Lipset, "Some Social Requisites of Democracy: Economic Development and Political Legitimacy," *American Political Science Review* 53 (March 1959), pp. 69–105. Larry Diamond reviewed three decades of literature relevant to the development/democracy debate and concluded that the evidence broadly supports the Lipset proposition; see Diamond, "Economic Development and Democracy Reconsidered," in *Re-Examining Democracy*, ed. Gary Marks and Larry Diamond (Newbury Park, CA: Sage, 1992), pp. 93–139. Linz and Stepan discuss Lipset's proposition in their *Problems of Democratic Transition and Consolidation: Southern Europe, South America, and Post-Communist Europe* (Baltimore: Johns Hopkins University Press, 1996), p. 77. Yadav put together evidence to show that socioeconomic

include India in his list of the twenty-one continuously democratic countries in the world from 1945 through 1980 because of Indira Gandhi's imposition of a state of emergency from June 1975 to March 1977.[9] However, in a later book, Lijphart admitted that he considers India a democracy—and now believes that he should have done so in the original volume.[10] For purposes of comparison, if Lijphart had included India as a longstanding democracy in his 1984 book, it would have represented an extraordinary exception to Lipset's proposition. For example, India in 1985 had a per capita income that was 8.7 *times lower* than Ireland, the poorest longstanding democracy that actually made Lijphart's list of countries, and 14.2 times poorer than the average country.[11] India does not of course disprove Lipset's proposition, which is probabilistic, but from the perspective of Lipset's overall framework, India is one of the most overperforming democracies in the world.

India's comparative poverty also enhances the "scope value" of the state-nation concept, because it is applicable not only to rich but also to very poor countries. Of the four longstanding multinational federal democracies in the world—Spain, Canada, Belgium, and India—India is the only country that is not an advanced industrial economy. The 2008 per capita income (PPP, current prices) of the four multinational federal systems was, in descending order, Canada $36,220, Belgium $34,760, Spain $31,130, and India $2,960.[12]

Of course, the Indian case would be significant for a student of diversity and democracy on population grounds alone. With its population of slightly over 1.1 billion, it is almost *four times* as populous as any other democracy in the

status and electoral participation do not correlate positively in India. See his "Understanding the Second Democratic Upsurge: Trends of Bahujan Participation in Electoral Politics in the 1990s," in *Transforming India: Social and Political Dynamics of Democracy*, ed. Francine R. Frankel, Zoya Hasan, Rajeeva Bhargava, and Balveer Arora (Delhi: Oxford University Press, 2000), pp. 120–145.

9. For the list of the twenty-one countries, see Arend Lijphart's classic *Democracies: Patterns of Majoritarian and Consensus Government in Twenty-One Countries* (New Haven: Yale University Press, 1984), p. 38.

10. Arend Lijphart, *Patterns of Democracy: Government Forms and Performance in Thirty-Six Countries* (New Haven: Yale University Press, 1999), table 4.1. Also see Lijphart's article, "Democratic Institutions and Ethnic/Religious Pluralism: Can India and the United States Learn from Each Other—and from the Smaller Democracies?" in *Democracy and Diversity: India and the American Experience*, ed. K. Shankar Bajpai (Oxford: Oxford University Press, 2007), pp. 14–49.

11. Calculated using GDP per capita in 1985 at Purchasing Power Parity (PPP) and current international prices. India's GDP per capita in that year was US$919, in extremely sharp contrast to average GDP per capita of the other twenty countries (US$13,093). Data are from World Bank, *World Development Indicators: 2006* (Washington, DC: International Bank for Reconstruction and Development/World Bank, 2006).

12. All data from World Bank, *World Development Indicators: 2008* (Washington, DC: International Bank for Reconstruction and Development/World Bank, 2008). Figures are given in GDP per capita using current international purchasing power parity dollars (PPP).

world.[13] The next most populous democracy is the United States, with a population of 300 million. The combined population in 2006 of the only other long-standing multinational federal democracies—Spain, Canada, and Belgium—was less than 85 million, less than half the population of Uttar Pradesh, the most populous of India's twenty-eight states.

A final reason why the study of Indian democracy should be of particular interest to comparativists is precisely the exclusion of the Indian experience, or even Indian scholars, from the mainstream democratization literature. This absence has impoverished comparative politics and, more important, our imaginations of politically possible alternatives for democracies.[14]

Given its extraordinary diversity, the project of creating a democratic nation-

13. India is set to surpass China as the most populous country in the world by 2040, according to the 2004 revision of *World Population Prospects* by the Population Division of the United Nations.

14. The founding literature in democratization studies neglects India nearly entirely. Because of its focus on Latin America and southern Europe, there are no chapters on India in the pioneering four-volume series on democratization edited by Guillermo O'Donnell, Philippe Schmitter, and Laurence Whitehead, *Transitions from Authoritarian Rule* (Baltimore: Johns Hopkins University Press, 1986). Because of Linz and Stepan's focus on postcommunist Europe, southern Europe, and Latin America, they too never discuss India. There are, of course, many excellent books on Indian politics with important implications for democratization theory. Rajni Kothari's classic *Politics in India* (Boston: Little Brown, 1970) remains almost untapped for its larger implications. The only partial exception to this neglect was Myron Weiner, a comparativist by instinct and training, who wrote several essays spelling out the comparative insights from his work on India. See Gabriel A. Almond, "Myron Weiner on India and the Theory of Democratization," in *India and the Politics of Developing Countries: Essays in Memory of Myron Weiner*, ed. Ashutosh Varshney (New Delhi: Sage, 2004). The distinguished Indian scholar of the politics of language, Jyotirindra Das Gupta, wrote the chapter on India in the three-volume work edited by Larry Diamond, Juan J. Linz, and Seymour Martin Lipset, *Democracy in Developing Countries* (Boulder, CO: Lynne Rienner, 1989). In the main, Indian scholars' best-known work on politics has been on such themes as caste, nationalism, colonialism, and on the politics of the "subalterns" rather than on the interaction between political processes and democratic institutions. Three excellent critical reviews and bibliographies on Indian, and non-Indian, scholarly writings about politics in India can be found in Partha Chatterjee, ed., *State and Politics in India* (Delhi: Oxford University Press, 1997), pp. 566–576; Sudipta Kaviraj, ed., *Politics in India* (Oxford: Oxford University Press, 1997), pp. 1–36; and Sunil Khilnani, *The Idea of India* (London: Hamish Hamilton, 1997), pp. 217–242. For more recent contributions with wider implications, see, for example, Atul Kohli, ed., *The Success of India's Democracy* (Cambridge: Cambridge University Press, 2001); Pranab Bardhan, *The Political Economy of Development in India* (New Delhi: Oxford University Press, expanded edition 1998); Ashutosh Varshney, *Ethnic Conflict and Civic Life: Hindus and Muslims in India* (New Haven: Yale University Press, 2002); Pradeep Chhibber and Ken Kollman, *The Formation of National Party Systems: Federalism and Party Competition in Britain, Canada, India, and the U.S.* (Princeton: Princeton University Press, 2004); Kanchan Chandra, *Why Ethnic Parties Succeed: Patronage and Ethnic Head Counts in India* (Cambridge: Cambridge University Press, 2004); Steven I. Wilkinson, *Votes and Violence: Electoral Competition and Ethnic Riots in India* (Cambridge: Cambridge University Press, 2006); Partha Chatterjee, *The Politics of the Governed: Reflections on Popular Politics in Most of the World* (New York: Columbia University Press, 2004); SDSA Team, *State of Democracy in South Asia* (Delhi: Oxford University Press, 2008); and Paul Brass, *Ethnicity and Nationalism: Theory and Comparison* (London: Sage, 1991).

state is unviable in India in the foreseeable future. Nevertheless, we consider that India has already managed to create a democratic state-nation, supported, as we shall document in this chapter, by all religious communities, all socio-economic groups, and most, but not all, of the citizens of its once potentially secessionist states.

The analysis of democratic federalism in the multinational, multicultural society that is India thus presents an extraordinary challenge—and opportunity—for deepening our understanding of democracy in the modern world. Indeed, perhaps more than any country in the world, India has rich lessons to offer about democracy and diversity.[15]

INDIA'S SPECIFICITY

At this stage we need to take on three common, if unstated, beliefs that have prevented the Indian experience from being treated as appropriate material for larger generalizations about democracy and diversity. First, there is general unease about the socioeconomic record of democratic governance in India, giving rise to a suspicion that India's success on diversity and democracy may be too good to be true. Second, there is a tendency to view any example of federalism and diversity through the prism of the political system of the United States; it appears thus that India is too different to be relevant for comparative theorization. Finally, from a very different vantage point, India's success may appear to be too unique to allow general lessons. In one way or another, these three beliefs see India as a case that defies generalization. We examine these beliefs and suggest that while great attention must be paid to India's specificity—indeed, "specificity matters" is an important point this book makes about every single country—this does not render India so special that it rules her out as a source of general insights.

We are very aware of India's continuing problems with poverty and with low levels of literacy, nutrition, basic sanitation, Maoist-style violence (by the "Naxal-ites," named after Naxalbari, the place where Maoist militancy in India was born), violation of human rights and periodic communal riots. Table 2.1 makes some of these comparative problems abundantly clear. We also recognize that these facts are very relevant to an overall assessment of the quality of democratic governance

15. John Keane's recent global history of democracy, *The Life and Death of Democracy* (London: Simon and Schuster, 2009) recognizes the significance of the Indian experience to the global narrative; see pp. 585–647.

TABLE 2.1
Comparative Indicators of India's Human and Income Poverty

Average GDP per capita in purchasing power parity (PPP) in 2000 U.S. dollars among Arend Lijphart's universe of the thirty-six continuous democracies of the world from at least 1977 to 1996	$20,252
India's GDP per capita in PPP in 2007 U.S. dollars	$2,753
India's human development index (HDI) ranking among the 173 countries of the world ranked by the United Nations Development Programme (UNDP)	134th out of 182
India's HDI ranking among Arend Lijphart's thirty-six continuous democracies	34th out of 36
India's human poverty index (HPI-1) ranking among 135 ranked states	88th out of 135
Adult female literacy rate in India	54.5%
Percentage of underweight children in India at age 5	46.0%
"Great Poverty" Level	
All India	22.7%
Muslims	31.0%
States with more than 20 deaths due to Naxalite violence in 2008	6 (18%)

Sources: UNDP, *Human Development Report 2009: Overcoming Barriers: Human Mobility and Development* (New York: Palgrave Macmillan, 2009), pp. 173, 177, and 181–184; Government of India, Prime Minister's High Level Committee (Sachar Committee), "Social, Economic, and Educational Status of the Muslim Community of India," November 2006; and Arend Lijphart, *Patterns of Democracy: Government Forms and Performance in Thirty-Six Countries* (New Haven: Yale University Press, 1999)—table 4.1 shows Lijphart's universe of the thirty-six countries in the world, including India, that were continuous democracies in his judgment from at least 1977 to 1996. For information on Naxalite violence in India, see Ministry of Home Affairs, Government of India, Naxal Management Division, available at http://mha.nic.in/uniquepage.asp?ID_PK=540.

in India and believe that policies and outcomes in these areas should be, and could be, substantially improved.

However, this book is not about democracy and its links to development; we focus here only on how democratic political arrangements of the kind that we analyze below serve as mechanisms for handling societal diversity and potential conflict. It is quite clear to any student of democracy and democratization or of nationalism, multinationalism, and diversity and extreme crises of "stateness," as in the U.S.S.R. and Yugoslavia, that India began its democratic experiment with greater diversity than any longstanding democracy that ever existed. It is also evident to any analyst of survey data about contemporary India that democracy is increasingly supported by the overwhelming majority of these diverse groups in India. This pattern is not sufficiently recognized, much less analyzed, by general readers or even by most specialist scholars, so one of our major tasks in this chapter is to attempt to document and explain these phenomena. We do not see how the facts acknowledged above render this task useless.

We believe that this task requires placing India's experience in comparative perspective for us to gain greater insights into the Indian experience of dealing with diversity. Since some basic characteristics of Indian society and polity are clearly distinct from those of the United States, the experience of the American democracy is not always relevant—indeed, at times can be quite misleading—for our understanding of India. For example, as we shall show, while both India and the United States are federal, the origins of their federations—"holding together" federalism in India and "coming together" federalism in the United States—are radically different, as are the consequences of these origins. India shares many characteristics with a number of other democracies, particularly the eleven long-standing federal democracies of the world, and a comparison of this set should allow us to understand better its problems, successes, and failures.[16]

India houses substantially greater and more intensely politicized diversity involving culture, language, and religion than the United States. There is no numerically preponderant "ethnos" that might dominate democratic politics to the exclusion of the rest. Looked at in pure religious terms, it might appear that there is a dominant community, as, according to the 2001 census, the Hindus constituted 80.4% of the population. But this apparent homogeneity breaks down if one looks at regional and linguistic diversity. The speakers of the largest language, Hindi, comprise only 40.2%, even if we include populations who speak the various "dialects" of Hindi that may be mutually incomprehensible. In regional terms, the dominant "Hindi Belt," a broad stripe comprising nine states of the union and two "union territories" stretching across northern India, has 43.8% of the country's population. But if one looks for the signs of a dominant "ethnos" that shares religion, region, and language—those who are Hindus, are Hindi-speakers, and reside in the Hindi Belt—the proportion is only a little over a third, 34.7% to be precise.[17] A group of this size is not in a position to dominate the country's politics. Besides, it could be argued that this group of barely more than one-third

16. The eleven federal countries that have been functioning democracies for at least the last twenty years are India, the United States, Switzerland, Germany, Austria, Belgium, Spain, Australia, Brazil, Argentina, and Canada. Belgium's long transformation from a unitary to a federal state was only completed in 1993, but it had increasingly functioned as a federal system since the 1970s.

17. All calculations based on the population figures of the Census of India 2001. It should be noted that while the Census provides the exact breakdown of language and religion for each state, it does not provide a breakdown combining the two. This has been estimated here by assuming that all the Urdu-speakers in the Hindi heartland states are Muslims and that the rest of the language speakers are evenly distributed across religions.

of the population is too heterogeneous to constitute a unified political community. In fact only 38% of India's Hindus self-identify as being a member of "the majority."[18] For example, Dalits (ex-untouchables) and Adivasis (indigenous communities), both theoretically members of this group, articulate their political identities in terms of caste and community in some conflict with the aims of the general Hindu group. Members of both of these groups identify themselves more as minority than as majority.[19]

Furthermore, as we have seen, longstanding separatist struggles for national independence in some parts of the Republic of India introduce a multinational dimension into the Indian polity. Thus, India's federal structures, to a large extent, reflect a territorially based pluralism. In contrast, the United States, in spite of its multicultural setting, is more homogeneous than India, its pluralism has little territorial basis, and federalism does not reflect that pluralism directly in part because, unlike India, Canada, Spain, and Belgium, the United States does not have a politically salient multinational dimension. The distinct nature of India's diversity also means that the large body of theory and analysis of multiculturalism in the United States and Europe, the result of large-scale immigration from other societies in recent decades, is only partially relevant to India. This is so because in India the multicultural characteristics are the result of a long history and have a distinctive territorial basis, to which Indian federalism has been a response. Witness the creation of the new linguistic states in the 1950s and the process of creating new states that continues to this day. It should be noted that although the creation of three states (Uttarakhand, Jharkhand, and Chhattisgarh) in 2001 was not based on language, it did reflect the logic of political representation of diversities, for these states gave better representation to tribal populations (Jharkhand, Chhattisgarh) or otherwise socioculturally different groups (Uttarakhand). All this sets India apart from the United States but brings it closer, and thus more relevant, to the real-life experience of most of the existing and potential multinational democracies.

Finally, let us turn to some of the specificities of the institutional and contextual features of the Indian state that facilitated the accommodation of great cultural diversities. India, in contrast to many countries in the developing world, has a relatively strong and usable state with a government, a bureaucracy, an army, a judiciary, and, above all, democratic institutions that enjoy considerable legiti-

18. Findings based on a five-country survey reported in SDSA Team, *State of Democracy in South Asia*, p. 73.
19. Ibid., p. 263.

macy and are able to exercise their authority over most of its population and territory. As we shall document, the overwhelming majority of Indian citizens respect the Indian state and generally expect it to serve the collective interests of its citizens.

In analyzing the Indian experience, one cannot overlook the external aspects, specifically that the exit options were effectively closed. It is true that the struggle for independence and the democratic institutions created at that time legitimated a sense of Indian nationhood and a conception of the nation open to its pluralism. This makes it unlikely that major political forces, parties, and intellectuals would favor whatever secessionist demands might appear in the periphery (with the possible exception of Kashmir). Even the two main communist parties, the Communist Party of India and the Communist Party of India (Marxist), have on balance sided with the project of preserving the boundaries of the Indian nation-state, even if by selective use of coercive state apparatus.[20] This consensus on the overriding importance of the Indian nation, and on the Indian state-nation, lends weight to the provisions in the constitution that allow the government to act in defense of the Republic of India. We must remember that in India, as in many other federal constitutions, there are provisions to defend the constitution and the unity of the state, if necessary by coercive means. The awareness of that possibility, and the actual record of using those resources in Kashmir, Nagaland, Mizoram, and the Punjab has left those who might question the state in a "no exit" position, one that forces the search for negotiated compromise within the context of the federal institutions of the state.[21]

20. A case in point was the support by the communist parties for the suppression of Khalistani secessionism in the Punjab. Unlike, say, the communists in Sri Lanka, the Indian communists did not extend any support in this instance to the demand of separation from the Indian state. The communist workers were among the prime targets of the pro-Khalistan militants. A veteran leader of the Communist Party of India, Satyapal Dang, offers a defense of this stance in his *Genesis of Terrorism: Analytical Study of Punjab Terrorists* (New Delhi: Patriot Publishers, 1988). A statement by the Punjab state committee of the Communist Party of India (Marxist), issued a decade after terrorism had subsided, still "expressed deep concern over the increasing activities of Sikh fundamentalists and extremists in the state and felt that they posed a threat to the hard-earned peace in the state and also to the unity and integrity of the country." See *People's Democracy*, vol. 29, no. 35, August 28, 2005.

21. Various human rights groups within and outside India have documented the denial of basic civil rights guaranteed by the Indian constitution and law and the use of brutal repressive measures by security forces in the conflicts mentioned above. See the various annual reports and other India related material of Amnesty International at http://web.amnesty.org/library/eng-ind/index. Various human rights groups within the country have also extensively documented these violations. See the various publications of the reputable and independent Peoples' Union for Civil Liberties (PUCL) at www.pucl.org, especially its report "Kashmir: A Report to the Nation," 1993, published by PUCL and CFD. An academic compilation of these reports can be found in A. R. Desai, ed., *Violation of Democratic Rights in India* (Bombay: Popular Prakashan, 1986). For some recent reports, see Ram

Besides, India is not very vulnerable to "international" opinion when confronting secessionist threats, due to its longstanding democracy, its demonstrated atomic capability, large mobile combat forces, and its geo-political location in the world. Also, it so happens that most of the states (with the exception of the Punjab) where secessionist tendencies might have been strong are numerically too small, geographically peripheral, and weak in terms of resources to sustain aspirations to independent statehood without external support.[22] This, again, is not the case in some other federal multinational states, such as Spain or Canada. Geography is also a favorable factor, since there is a continuity of territory that does not exist in, for example, Indonesia on its more than two thousand inhabited islands. That India has a strong state with legitimate longstanding democratic institutions, a functioning if overburdened legal system, and loyal armed forces makes it very different from most other states in the developing world. Federalism and the flexible provisions for inclusion of new member states, the asymmetrical status of different states, and the multi-tier federalism in some of the states—all are essential elements of the building of India as a state-nation.

All this goes to show that India's experiment is rooted in its specific history and institutional context. India's success cannot be turned into a cookbook that can be used in every place and time. This book argues against a cookbook approach to crafting political institutions. At the same time, none of the elements of India's specificity is by itself unique to India. Therefore a study of India can shed light on other similar contexts. We also believe that putting the Indian experience into a comparative perspective can also contribute to our understanding of India. In India, as in other federal democracies like Spain or Canada, the institutionalization of an asymmetrical federalism creates tension and hostility. Once we enlarge our scope of analysis, we will see that many of the problems that scholars working on India see as unique and threatening may be found in one way or another in other federal multicultural, multilingual, or multinational societies in which there is no shared conception of the nation or a state-nation. At the

---

Narayan Kumar, Amrik Singh, Ashok Agrwaal, and Jaskaran Kaur, *Reduced to Ashes: The Insurgency and Human Rights in Punjab* (New Delhi: South Asia Forum for Human Rights, 2003), available at www.punjabjustice.org; and *Kashmir: An Enquiry into the Healing Touch*, a report by AFDR, HRF and OPDR, Hyderabad, 2003.

22. According to the Census of India 2001, the population of Nagaland was 1.9 million, about 0.19% of the Indian population. Mizoram's population was 890,000 and accounted for about 0.086%. Jammu and Kashmir's population was 10.1 million. With this absolute number, Jammu and Kashmir had about 0.99% of the total population of the country (of this, 5.7 million, or 0.56% of the Indian population lived in the Kashmir Valley, the heart of political alienation). Of these states, only Punjab has a national population share of more than 1%. Census of India-2001, Primary Census Abstract, Series 1 & 2: Registrar General of India, New Delhi.

same time, the comparison will show that India and its democratic institutions enjoy legitimacy among the citizens equal to, if not greater than, the institutions in other longstanding democratic federal pluralistic societies. It should be noted that in no political system do all the citizens grant to the state, its institutions and democratic processes, a unanimous legitimacy or allegiance. It is only the size of India and its multitudes that make these problems somewhat more significant than in some other countries, once we translate the proportions into absolute numbers of citizens.

IMAGINING A STATE-NATION

There is another, deeper reason to turn to India in our attempt to expand the imagination of how democracies can deal with diversities. An expansion of the kind advocated in this book cannot merely be a matter of designing or redesigning institutions; an expansion of democratic imagination must deal directly with ideas, ideals, and images. We need to engage with contestations around the difficult relationship between ideas of nationhood and the realities of complex diversities. Arguably, India has been the most fertile nursery of this kind of ideological contestation. We believe that democratic theory should draw on and reconstruct the rich discursive contestations that have taken place in India in the last two centuries.

The building of a state-nation in India was not an accident of history or an afterthought. We suggest that the state-nation model was implicit in the idea of India forged by modern Indian political thinkers, nurtured by the freedom movement, eventually enshrined in the Indian constitution, sustained by the first generation of post-Independence leadership, and institutionalized in competitive politics thereafter. In that sense our state-nation model is best seen as a new analytic ideal type as well as a theoretical defense of what political thinkers and practitioners in India have known for the better part of a century.

This is no doubt a tribute to the foresight and creativity of the leaders of India's freedom struggle. But it is equally important to acknowledge that this creativity itself was in a large measure the outcome of these leaders' reflections on the historical situation in which the anticolonial struggle found itself. British colonial rule produced a body of knowledge about India that denied her an identity except as a colonial subject. Modern Indian political thinkers found themselves pitted against this indictment by John Strachey, a British administrator and author of a very influential book entitled *India*, published in 1888: "This is the first and the most essential thing to learn about India—that there is not, and never was an

India, or even any country of India, possessing, according to European ideas, any sort of unity, physical, political, social or religious. . . . That men of the Punjab, Bengal, the North-Western Provinces, and Madras, should ever feel they belong to one great nation, is impossible."[23]

The colonial subject could respond to this in many ways. They could accept the characterization and agree that the very idea of Indian nationalism was incoherent; this line of reasoning led to collaboration with the colonial regime. Alternatively, they could argue that India was not one but many nations that warranted more than one nation-state; this line logically required the partition of the country and acceptance of British arbitration until it could be effected. These two responses did have some followers in the nineteenth and the twentieth centuries, but most of the Indian political thinkers began to question this colonial reading of India.

Thus started the search for the unity of India. This search was initially rather tentative and defensive but gradually turned more confident and even aggressive. This search took many forms. History writing and historical novels were the most popular forms of what Sudipta Kaviraj calls "the imaginary institution of India," but this search also took the form of sociological or philosophical arguments and political tracts.[24]

The colonial reading often encouraged simple counterarguments. One anti-colonial argument was that India was indeed a nation-state in the European sense of the term, that it was based on a unity of culture, race, religion, and language. This argument stressing cultural homogeneity tended to draw exclusively on the "great tradition" of Hindu heritage and to exclude the vast resource of non-Hindu and "little traditions" of India. This line of reasoning was adopted by some leading Hindu nationalist ideologues and organizations that stood on the fringes

23. John Strachey, *India* (London: Kegan Paul, 1888), pp. 5–8, cited in Ainslie Embree, *India's Search for National Identity* (Delhi: Chanakya Publications, 1980), p. 17. This was not an isolated statement but a sharp articulation of a very common view of the empire and its defenders. In making the above categorical assertion, Strachey seems not to appreciate fully that the United Kingdom, itself created only in 1707, has not always been "one great nation" but had robust territories and identities occupied by Scots, Welsh, Irish, and English. See, for example, Linda Colley, *Britons: Forging the Nation, 1707–1837* (New Haven: Yale University Press, 1992).

24. Sudipta Kaviraj, "The Imaginary Institution of India," *Subaltern Studies* 7, ed. Partha Chatterjee and Gyananendra Pandey (Delhi: Oxford University Press, 1993), pp. 1–39. For a detailed analysis of the imaginary histories produced in nineteenth-century Bengal, see Sudipta Kaviraj, *The Unhappy Consciousness: Bankimchandra Chattopadhyay and the Formation of Nationalist Discourse in India* (Delhi: Oxford University Press, 1995), pp. 107–157. For a scholarly critique of the idea that the unity of India was a gift of the British Empire, see Radha Kumud Mookerji, *The Fundamental Unity of India* (1914; repr. New Delhi: Bharatiya Vidya Bhavan/Chronicle Books, 2003). Partha Chatterjee's *Nationalist Thought and the Colonial World: A Derivative Discourse?* (Delhi: Oxford University Press, 1986) explores the complexities and contradictions that characterize the nationalist response to colonial constructions.

of the freedom struggle. M. S. Golwalkar, the head of Rashtriya Swayamsevak Sangh (RSS), a militant Hindu organization, famously articulated this position just before Independence. In essence he argued that India was actually close to a French-style nation-state and must use policies of cultural homogenization to get even closer to it: "We believe that our [Indian] notions today about the Nation concept are erroneous. They are not in conformity with those of the Western Political Scientists we think we are imitating. It is but proper, therefore, at this stage to understand what the Western Scholars state as the Universal Nation-idea and correct ourselves. With this end in view, we shall now proceed with stating and analyzing the World's accepted Nation-concept. . . . The idea contained in the word Nation is the compound of five distinct factors fused into one indissoluble whole." These five unities, according to Golwalkar, were geographical, racial, religious, cultural, and linguistic.[25]

Not surprisingly, the most powerful currents of the freedom struggle—the nationalist movement led by the Congress, popular movements led by socialists and communists, and other subaltern struggles—were not attracted to this way of looking for India's unity. The political, social, and moral cost of such a line of reasoning would have excluded over a third of undivided India's population. They also noticed how much this form of mirror-image nation-state nationalism depended on the colonial world view that they sought to oppose.

Rabindranath Tagore, poet, novelist, Nobel laureate, had already written, during World War I, a brilliant attack on the dangers of mono-culture nation-state worship for Europe. He simply calls such a nation-state "Nation"; in his most famous work on nationalism, he argues that "Nation" is a universal threat and that it plays no positive role in human development: "Neither the colorless vagueness of cosmopolitanism, nor the fierce self-idolatry of nation-worship, is the goal of humanity. . . . When this organization of politics and commerce, whose other name, the Nation, becomes all powerful at the cost of the harmony of the higher social life, then it is an evil day for humanity."[26]

Gandhi had a more complex attitude toward nationalism. Like Tagore, he disliked many versions of cultural nationalism and acknowledged that India's great diversity of peoples, languages, and religions was a reality that must be

25. M. S. Golwalkar, We, or Our Nationhood Defined, original edition 1939, 4th ed. 1947, cited in Christophe Jaffrelot, ed., Hindu Nationalism: A Reader (Princeton: Princeton University Press, 2007), pp. 98–99. This volume provides a useful introduction and selections to the ideas of the leaders of Hindu nationalist organizations such as Hindu Mahasabha, RSS, and the BJP.

26. Rabindranath Tagore, Nationalism (1917; repr. London: MacMillan, 1950), pp. 5, 12. For an elaboration of Tagore's critique of nationalism, see Ashis Nandy's iconoclastic reading, Illegitimacy of Nationalism: Rabindranath Tagore and the Politics of Self (Delhi: Oxford University Press, 1994).

recognized and supported. But he also felt that the Independence movement was mobilizing Indian nationalism into a positive force for India and the world: "Violent nationalism, otherwise known as imperialism is the curse. Non-violent nationalism is a necessary condition of . . . civilized life." He saw the multinational, multilinguistic nationalism of the Independence movement as "India's contribution to peace."[27] In many of his writings, he insisted that Indian nationalism must be inclusive and not based on any religion or language: "If the Hindus believe that India should be peopled only by Hindus they are living in a dream-land. The Hindus, the Mohammedans, the Parsis and the Christians, who have made India their country, are fellow countrymen and they will have to live in unity, if only for their own interest. In no part of the world are one nationality and one religion synonymous terms: nor has it ever been so."[28]

Thus modern Indian political thinkers and leaders were forced to look for unity of India in terms other than religious or linguistic unity. The starting point of such a search for unity was a frank acknowledgment of the various forms of diversity. Addressing the fifth meeting of the Indian National Congress held in Bombay in 1890, Ferozeshah Mehta expressed a fairly common sentiment at that time: "Despite social and religious differences, we have all begun earnestly to realize that we are fairly on the way to a common national existence, united and bound together by the common political ties."[29]

Insofar as the model of the nation-state was rooted in unease with diversity, Indian nationalism could not but be deeply uneasy with this model. It could not but reject images of essential unity drawn from a homogeneous cultural and religious community. Writing just before Independence, Jawaharlal Nehru summed up the nationalist thinking on Indian unity: "It was absurd, of course, to think of India or any country as a kind of anthropomorphic entity. I did not do so. I was also fully aware of the diversities and divisions of Indian life, of classes, castes, religions, races, different degrees of cultural development. Yet I think that a country with a long cultural background and a common outlook on life develops a spirit that is peculiar to it and that is impressed on all its children, however much they may differ among themselves."[30]

27. Ibid., p. 8.
28. M. K. Gandhi, *Collected Works*, vol. 10 (New Delhi: Publications Division, Government of India, 1969), p. 23.
29. Extract of the speech in R. V. Ramachandrasekhara Rao, ed., *Indian Unity: A Symposium* (New Delhi: Publication Division, Government of India, 1969), p. 21. This valuable official collection of extracts from the writings of a wide range of nationalist leaders reflects an anxiety on this score that extended well into the postcolonial period.
30. Jawaharlal Nehru, *Discovery of India* (Delhi: Oxford University Press, 1981), p. 59.

The state-nation model is rooted in this creative engagement of the Indian national movement with the fact of sociocultural diversity of a kind that nationalism had not faced before it. Their refusal to accept the colonial insinuation that they did not deserve self rule or to take the path of civil war and division of the country led them to be pioneers in the search for a democratic political model that could accommodate wide diversity. The search was not always successful, nor was the entire leadership consistently committed to this model. At one crucial moment, the project of building a diverse state-nation nearly failed, when the leadership of the national movement reluctantly accepted the idea of Pakistan, which involved a bloody Partition of the Muslim majority provinces from the rest of the country. Yet even this failure did not result from an intellectual acceptance of the nation-state model of one country, one culture, one language, one religion. The experience of Partition did strengthen the voices for greater power for federal government, but it did not weaken the project of building a diverse India.

FROM IDEAS TO INSTITUTIONS

Imagining a state-nation is necessary but not sufficient for crafting a viable state-nation. This imagination needs to be translated into a set of robust political institutions. Here again we encounter a specificity of the Indian experience: the would-be crafters of the Indian constitution deliberated and reflected on the institutional frame of independent India for nearly half a century. The search for appropriate political arrangements for accommodation of diversities began long before the Constituent Assembly met in 1946. In the very early days, the Indian National Congress, institutional embodiment of the anticolonial struggle and the dominant political party after independence, agreed on a consociational formula for decision-making that gave Hindu and Muslim delegates a veto over every major decision.[31] Although the Congress Party rejected the colonial provision of a separate electorate for the Muslims provided in the Government of India Act of 1909, it had already accepted the principle of special protection of minorities. By the middle of the 1920s the Congress began detailed studies about the future political set up of an independent India. The Congress Party rejected a British-drafted Simon Commission Report and appointed its own committee under the leadership of Motilal Nehru, the father of Jawaharlal Nehru, to suggest an outline of a constitution for free India. The Nehru Report of 1928 foreshadowed many

---

31. See S. R. Bakshi, *Dadabhai Naoroji: The Grand Old Man* (Delhi: Anmol Publications, 1991), p. 105.

provisions of the Indian constitution. It shows that the critique of the colonial definition of nationalism had already prepared the nationalist leadership in India for some key elements of what we describe as the state-nation model. The exact nature of these provisions were debated for the next two decades, but the core elements of the state-nation structure were already articulated in the Nehru Report, which was approved by the All Parties Conference in Lucknow in 1928.[32]

The definition of citizenship in the Nehru Report was very state-nation-friendly in that it was absolutely inclusive and territorial: "the word 'citizen' wherever it occurs in this constitution means every person who was born, or whose father was either born or naturalized, within the territorial limits of the commonwealth" (article 3). It also laid down the propositions that the system of independent India would be parliamentary (article 5) and bicameral and federal (articles 8–9). We should note that a parliamentary federal system is the most supportive combination for the emergence of "centric-regional" parties that may be a useful alternative to "exit" for parties with many different linguistic majorities. The radical linguistic reorganization and reconfiguration of India that allowed each Indian state to decide to govern itself in its local majority language did not fully occur until 1957, but it was strongly supported at the 1921 Congress meeting in Madras and endorsed in the Nehru Report: "The redistribution of provinces should take place on a linguistic basis on the demand of the majority of the population of the area concerned" (article 86). This is a classic state-nation "holding together" federal decision, unthinkable in a U.S.-style "coming together" federation. Also supportive of a relatively strong "holding together" federalism was the provision for the Supreme Court of the Union (unlike the "coming together" federalism of the United States) to have "original jurisdiction" in almost all matters (article 49). On the all-important question of religion too, the Nehru Report also supported state-nation policies. In the section on "Fundamental Rights," it clearly ruled out an established religion, supported a religiously impartial state but, unlike the U.S. Constitution, implied the admissibility of some state aid for religious educational establishments (article 4).

Thus, when the Constituent Assembly formally set about its tasks in 1946, there was little doubt about the provisions for protection of linguistic, cultural, and religious diversity. The institutional structures the Constituent Assembly established provided for a robust state-nation. In this sense, India's constitution inher-

32. All Parties Conference (India). Nehru Committee, *The Nehru Report: An Anti-Separatist Manifesto/The Committee Appointed by the All Parties Conference, 1928* (New Delhi: Michiko and Panjathan, 1975).

ited the intellectual legacy of modern Indian political thought. In chapters 2 through 4 we shall repeatedly come back to some of these institutional features that facilitated the crafting of a state-nation. Here we may in passing recall the first three features of what we called the "nested grammar" of state-nation in the first chapter, features that can and need to be incorporated in the constitution. These three principles are:

1. An asymmetrical federal state *but not* a symmetrical federal state or a unitary state;
2. Individual rights *and* collective recognition; and
3. A parliamentary *instead of* a presidential or semi-presidential system

Yet the constitution was not sufficient to put India firmly on the path to building a state-nation. As Sunil Khilnani notes, the role of political leadership was crucial: "The Indianness outlined in the two decades after 1947 was an extemporised performance, trying to hold together divergent nationalism that resists summary in clear or simple doctrinal statements. It tried to accommodate within the form of a new nation-state significant internal diversities; to resist bending to the democratic pressures of religion; and to look outwards. This experimental response to the question of how to be Indian was not a victory of theoretical consistency. It was a contingent acquisition, based on a coherent if disputable picture of India. It did not reassure itself by relying on a settled image of the culture, nor did it impose one. That was its most important trait: it did not monopolize or simplify the definition of Indianness."[33]

NATIONAL PRIDE AND IDENTITY IN INDIA

In the next two chapters we go into the details of how this constitutional design and political approach was deployed in specific situations involving some of the most serious challenges to the Indian state. Let us begin here by asking: Was this

33. Khilnani, *Idea of India*, p. 179. A recognition that Indian leadership was following an unusual approach to "nation-building" was quite widespread among perceptive analysts of Indian politics. Rajni Kothari argued that the Indian model of "nation building," involving recognition and political articulation of diversities, was relevant to many postcolonial societies. See his introduction to Rajni Kothari, ed., *State and Nation Building: A Third World Perspective* (Bombay: Allied, 1976). Rasheeduddin Khan argued that Indian federalism was unique, for the political institutions of federalism were superimposed on a federal society. See his "Federalism in India: A Quest for New Identity," in *Rethinking Indian Federalism*, ed. Rasheeduddin Khan, ed. (Shimla: Indian Institute of Advanced Study, 1997). Ravinder Kumar, a leading historian of modern India, contends that India was a civilization-state rather than a nation-state. Kumar, "India: A 'nation-state' or 'civilisation-state'?" in *Journal of South Asian Studies* 25, no. 2 (2002), pp. 13–32.

"idea of India" described above confined to the high traditions of political theory and legal constitutional texts? Did this idea find resonance across different religions, regions, communities, and classes among ordinary Indian citizens? Or did it remain an unrealized aspiration? To find out, we draw on empirical evidence in the form of available surveys of political opinion, attitudes, and values.

One important indicator of identification of a citizen with the society and the state is the sense of pride, in this case the pride in being Indian. Fortunately, a comparable question has been asked in all the longstanding federal democracies we are assessing and is continuously asked in the member states of the European Union by the Eurobarometer surveys.

The pride question has been asked in the widely used *World Values Survey* under the direction of Ronald Inglehart and his colleagues at the University of Michigan. We have used here three of the five rounds of these surveys available for our comparative analysis, 1990–93, 1995–97, and 1999–2001. The first round covered 42 independent countries, the second 53, the third 75. India has been included in all of these rounds. This set of surveys is particularly interesting for comparativists, because respondents in each country are asked mostly the same questions and many of the questions have been used in all of the rounds.[34] We have from the World Values Survey three fairly similar readings on the pride question for India. In all three waves, about two-thirds of the respondents said they were "very proud" to be an Indian. About 20% to 25% said they were "proud," thus pushing the proportion of "very proud" and "proud" to between 85% and 90%. In each of these waves, the proportion of those who said they were "not proud" or "not at all proud" was recorded at less than 10%. This can be confirmed with a report based on a major survey carried out by the Centre for the Study of Developing Societies that has a larger and more representative sample.[35] Better representation of rural and uneducated voters in the CSDS survey has led to a slightly higher proportion of "do not know" responses, but the basic pattern of response is the same as reported by the World Values Survey. We can thus be confident that Indians on the whole are highly proud of their national identity.

The World Values Survey allows us to place these figures in comparative

34. See Pippa Norris and Ronald Inglehart, *Sacred and Secular: Religion and Politics Worldwide* (Cambridge: Cambridge University Press, 2004), appendix A, pp. 243–246.

35. The survey, called State of Democracy in South Asia (SDSA), was carried out in the five countries of South Asia: India, Sri Lanka, Pakistan, Bangladesh, and Nepal. Yadav was the co-principal investigator Stepan and Linz served on the advisory board and, working with Yadav, created a number of new questions that were particularly relevant to the inquiry into state-nation, such as multiple and complementary identities and religion and politics. For a summary of results from the survey, see SDSA Team, *State of Democracy in South Asia*.

TABLE 2.2

Pride in Nationality in the Eleven Longstanding Federal Democracies

Democracy	Very proud	Quite	Not very	Not at all	Do not know/ not applicable
United States	71%	23%	4%	0%	2%
Australia	70	23	2	0	5
India	67	21	5	2	5
Canada	65	28	3	2	2
Argentina	65	24	4	3	5
Brazil	64	19	14	2	1
Spain	51	36	6	3	4
Austria	50	37	6	2	5
Belgium	20	46	15	7	11
Switzerland	23	47	16	7	7
Germany	15	46	22	7	9

Source: Data for all countries are from responses to the question "How proud are you to be [nationality]?" Ronald Inglehart et al., eds., *Human Beliefs and Values: A Cross-Cultural Sourcebook Based on the 1999–2002 Values Survey* (Mexico D.F.: Siglo XXI Editores, 2004).

Note: Percentages may not add up to 100 due to rounding.

perspective. Table 2.2 presents responses to the pride question across eleven long-standing federal democracies from the latest wave of the World Values Survey. This wave of World Values Survey (1999–2002, held in India in 2001) showed that only in the United States (71%) and Australia (70%) was the proportion of those who feel "very proud" even marginally higher than in India (67%). The proportion of those who felt "very proud" was lower in Argentina (65%), lower in Brazil (64%), lower still in Spain (51%), much lower yet in Germany (15%), and surprisingly low in Switzerland (23%).[36] Those saying "not very proud" or "not at all proud" add up to 7% in India, certainly more than the United States (4%) and Australia (2%), but lower than the other federal democracies, particularly Germany (29%), and sur-prisingly again, Switzerland (23%). In the case of Germany, the Nazi period and the Holocaust legacy represent a heavy burden, making it difficult for its citizens to feel fully proud of their nation.[37] Those who feel an exclusive identity with another nation and reject the state in which they live are also not likely to feel proud of the state or the nation and its heritage. Some of the variations across

36. On Switzerland, as the reader will see in table 2.9, consistent with our idea of state-nation, of the eleven longstanding federal democracies, Switzerland has the highest percentage of people with confidence in the government and the second-highest percentage of people with confidence in the legal system. So while they may not have inordinate pride in being Swiss *as such*, they nevertheless have great pride in their Swiss institutions.

37. On the complex issue of pride (or lack thereof) in the German nation, see Elisabeth Noelle-Neumann, "Nationalgefühl und Glück," in Noelle-Neumann and Renate Köcher, *Die verletzte Nation* (Stuttgart: Deutsche Verlags-Anstalt, 1987), 17–74.

TABLE 2.3
Pride in India for All Citizens and for Marginal Groups, 2005

	All of India	Muslim	Scheduled Caste	Scheduled Tribe	Nonliterate
Very proud	60%	57%	56%	44%	44%
Proud	29	31	29	37	34
Not proud	2	1	3	2	3
Not at all proud	1	2	2	1	2
Do not know/no answer	8	9	10	15	17
(N)	5,227	636	901	427	1,964

Source: *State of Democracy in South Asia: A Report* (Delhi: Oxford University Press, 2008).
    Note: Percentages may not add up to 100 due to rounding.

countries reflect these different attitudes. Thus, whether seen in its own terms, over a period of time, or in comparison with other countries, Indian citizens' sense of pride in their nationality is quite impressive.

Aggregate figures are not, however, very instructive in dealing with question of subjective identity. While it is important to understand the views of the citizens as a whole, it is equally important to look at the views of any significant minorities that may vary from this response. Therefore it is important to ask if the conclusion about the high level of national pride holds across the different sections of society. In order to find out, we need a disaggregated picture of national pride for some of most salient marginal groups in India: Muslims (the largest and most disadvantaged religious minority), Scheduled Castes or Dalits (the ex-untouchable community that has historically suffered social exclusion), Scheduled Tribes (forest-dwelling indigenous communities that have remained on the periphery of modern development), and nonliterates.

As table 2.3 makes clear, responses from the Muslim community and the Scheduled Castes are no different than the average national response on this question. The respondents from Scheduled Tribes and those without any formal education do report lower levels of pride, partly because a larger proportion of these groups fails to understand the question (itself a reflection of the uneven dissemination of the idea of nationalism in modern India) and partly because they are genuinely less enthusiastic about Indian nationalism. Yet this lower level of enthusiasm does not lead to any significant rejection of the national identity: in none of these groups does the proportion of those who do not feel proud at all exceed 2%. Thus, notwithstanding the variations in the reception of and enthusiasm for the national identity, there is no noticeable rejection of the national identity in any minority group for which we have information.

SUBJECTIVE NATIONAL IDENTITIES

The sense of pride in nationality is a useful but limited vantage point to understand the nature of cultural and political identities in any country. By posing the alternatives in terms of pride or lack of pride, the question limits our ability to find out much about the content of this pride or its absence. Citizens may attach very different meanings to the India that they take pride in. For most Indian citizens, India is a nation, so they see the Republic of India as a nation, though there are divergent visions of that nationhood, some which would exclude from the nation people that feel they are Indian without having to share an exclusivist conception of the nation.[38] There are many people who feel other identities, sometimes equally strong, sometimes somewhat stronger than the Indian national identity. With the data available to us, it is not easy to define how many people feel an Indian identity, and even less easy to define those who have different conceptions of the Indian nation. It is more difficult than in the case of Spain, since the matter of language, so important in that case, is less hegemonic and defining in India. The linguistic states recognize and allow for a certain identification with a distinctive language and culture, and we quickly see that many Indians have a dual identity, that of being Indian and that of belonging to their state. We discover that some of them feel an identity with their state that may actually be a linguistic cultural identification, without explicitly seeing themselves as Indian. It is not easy to say if that identity is similar to that of a national identity in multinational societies.

While it is imperative to recognize areas of alienation in India, we also should look at aggregate data on subjective political identities in India. Survey evidence gathered by the CSDS allows us to examine the question of political identities in contemporary India in an empirical manner. A question about subjective national identity was asked in the Indian component of the *State of Democracy in South Asia Survey: 2005*. Unlike both Spain and Belgium, the modal response category in India is "only Indian." Nearly half the respondents privilege their Indian identity over identities of their respective states, which in most cases also happen to be linguistic identities.[39] Even when asked about the in-between category of "more

38. On visions of the nation in India, see Ashutosh Varshney, "Contested Meanings: India's National Identity, Hindu Nationalism, and the Politics of Anxiety," in *Daedalus* 122 (Summer 1993), pp. 227–261.

39. While there is a great deal of overlap between the linguistic divisions of India and the boundaries of the various states of the Indian union, it is not a perfect match. Most of the states have significant linguistic minorities. The largest language, Hindi, is the official language of nine states of the Indian union in addition to two Union Territories. Most of the large languages are internally divided among various dialects that vary considerably.

TABLE 2.4
Subjective National Identity and Religion in India

	Hindu	Muslim	Christian	Sikh	All of India
Only Indian	34%	43%	30%	44%	35%
More Indian than state identity	12	11	16	9	12
As Indian as state identity	19	16	16	13	19
More state identity than Indian	10	7	18	17	10
Only state identity	12	10	13	16	12
Do not know/no answer	13	13	7	1	12
(N)	(4,274)	(636)	(152)	(87)	(5,385)

Source: *State of Democracy in South Asia Survey*, 2005, CSDS.

Indian than state identity," as many as 35% of all respondents chose "only Indian" to describe their identity, with 12% opting for the new category. To recall, only 13% of Belgians and 14% of Spanish respondents opted for only national identity in response to the same question. This reflects the depth of nationalist sentiment in a country where nationalism emerged from intense anticolonial struggle. At the same time, this response does not rule out significant reservations: about a fifth of the respondents privileged their state identity over their Indian identity. Even with the in-between option of "more state identity than Indian," the proportion of those who opted for "only state" identity was a little higher than in Belgium or Spain. Less than one-fifth of Indians opted for the middle category of "equally Indian and state identity," compared to about half of the respondents in Spain and Belgium who had equal and dual identities. Table 2.4 presents data from the 2005 State of Democracy in South Asia (SDSA) survey for the whole of India and also for major religious communities.

The implications about religion are quite clear: more Muslims—the largest and the most disadvantaged religious minority in the country—identify themselves as "only Indian" than do the majority Hindu community. This is largely because, except for the Kashmir Valley, India's 161 million Muslims are exceptionally territorially dispersed and, again excepting Jammu and Kashmir, are not a majority in any state of the union. Conceptually and politically, this means two things. First, the great territorial dispersion of Muslims means that the vast majority of Muslims cannot be accommodated by the mechanism of asymmetrical federalism alone, meaning that other diversity-accommodating policies, such as the equal support of all religions and some consociational devices, must contribute to engendering a state-nation. Second, Muslims self-identify more with their Indian than their state identity.

The Christians, on the other hand, are more concentrated in certain pockets of southern and northeastern India and constitute a majority in several small hill states in the northeast (Meghalaya, Mizoram, and Nagaland). The Sikhs are split into those who live in the Punjab and see themselves as primarily Punjabis and those who live outside the Punjab and identify more with India. Here again, as in analysis of pride by social groups, the central point is that notwithstanding differences among groups, there are no signs of serious disaffection with the political community of India.

SUPPORT FOR DEMOCRACY

We would like to argue that democracy, and with it democratic political institutions and processes, are an essential component of the viability and stability of multicultural, multilingual, multinational state-nations. Democracy makes possible the identification with the state for many of its citizens who might have different identities, who might question a nation-state, but are neverthe less ready to be loyal citizens of the state. Authoritarianism might serve to impose a nation-state model on the society, as was the case of Spain under the authoritarian regime of Franco. But, as the data for Spain show, the result ultimately was a backlash of resurgent and, in the Basque Country, violent extreme nationalism.

Democracy, and more concretely federal democracy, can serve to integrate such a society. The *Verfassungspatriotismus* ("constitutional patriotism") of Dolf Sternberger, developed by Jürgen Habermas in the German Federal Republic, is an important component for heterogeneous societies. It is not the only component of support for a state-nation but certainly one of the most important ones. It is for that reason that a more detailed discussion of the attitude of Indians and of the various groups within Indian society toward democracy and democratic institutions is vital to our interpretation of the politics of diversity.

In analyzing the attitudes of citizens toward the democratic institutions—beginning with democracy, compared to authoritarian alternatives, and ending with political parties—there are some serious problems with the indicators used. There is sufficient evidence from many countries that we need to distinguish the belief in the need for certain institutions and their desirability and legitimacy from the attitudes about the way those institutions actually perform. People in principle might support democracy, but they may often have serious misgivings about how their particular democracy is actually functioning. The distinction between the "legitimacy of institutions" and the "efficacy of institutions" is therefore crucial.[40] Citizens may believe that democracy is the best form of government for a country like theirs, but when asked if democracy is able to solve the problems of their society, they might be less enthusiastic. When that question is followed by "How is democracy working in our country?," in many circumstances the answers might be quite negative. The negative response to the actual performance of democratic institutions in the long run is likely to erode the belief in the need for those institutions, but many studies show that these are different dimensions. The same is true, even more so, with political parties. In many democratic countries, people agree on the need for parties to articulate their interests and demands, but at the same time, a large number of people have little trust in actual political parties. There are many and complex reasons for this distrust in practically all democracies, a distrust that is not translated into rejection of political parties in principle as necessary institutions in a democracy, even less so of democracy itself.[41] Nor does it necessarily translate into declining levels of identification with actual political parties. The same is true to an even greater extent concerning attitudes toward the incumbents of many offices in democratic systems. The use of one or another indicator alone may capture different dimensions and sometimes leads to pessimistic perceptions about the stability of democracy.

The question that has been asked in many countries is "With which of the following phrases are you most in agreement?" Allowable answers include: "Democracy is preferable to any other form of government," "In some circumstances an authoritarian government can be preferable to a democratic government," "For someone like me a democratic or non-democratic regime makes no difference," in addition to allowing for non-answers and "do not know." This question has been asked in India in two waves of the National Election Study held in 1999 and 2004 by CSDS. Table 2.5 reports the findings of both of these surveys with those of some other important countries that figure prominently in the democratization literature, such as Spain, Korea, Uruguay, Brazil, and Chile. The level of support for democracy in India varies from 60% in the 1999 survey to 70% in the 2004 survey. This is substantially higher than ex-authoritarian regimes like Chile,

40. This is a theme developed in Juan J. Linz, "Crisis, Breakdown, and Reequilibration," in *The Breakdown of Democratic Regimes*, ed. Linz and Stepan (Baltimore: Johns Hopkins University Press, 1978).

41. For an elaboration on this theme, see Juan J. Linz, "Parties in Contemporary Democracies: Problems and Paradoxes," in *Political Parties: Old Concepts and New Challenges*, ed. Richard Gunther, José Ramón Montero, and Juan J. Linz (New York: Oxford University Press, 2002), pp. 291–317.

Brazil, and Korea but clearly behind Spain and Uruguay. Another interesting fact from table 2.5 is that the proportion of Indians who support authoritarianism (6% and 4% in 1999 and 2004, respectively) or are indifferent to this choice (7% and 6%) is very small, even when compared to Spain and Uruguay. The unusually large proportion of the "do not know" response (27% and 20%), the highest recorded in any country for this question, accounts for the rest.

Given the strong relationship between a low level of education and saying "do not know" to this question, it is reasonable to assume that the "do not know" response is more a function of an inability to comprehend words like *democracy* and *authoritarianism* rather than unarticulated reservations about democratic political systems.[42]

Given this strong "do not know" effect and its correlation with education, a robust comparison of the Indian data with other countries would require neutralizing this effect. The figures in parentheses in the row for support for democracy achieve this by looking at the percentage of the support for democracy among those who give a valid response; the "do not know" response is treated as missing data in this calculation, a common practice in statistical analysis. Thus the level of support for democracy was 83% and 88%, respectively, in the 1999 and 2004 surveys, about the same as Uruguay and Spain, if we take only valid responses into account. In sharp contrast, Brazil, Chile, and Korea, among valid responses, range between 41% and 58%.

In Brazil, those clearly preferring democracy are only 41%, with a substantial proportion expressing potential support for an authoritarian alternative or no preference, a much less favorable response than we find in India. The figures for Spain, a relatively new democracy, are very similar to those we find in India. The Spanish data have been consistently within this range over a long period of time and are very similar to those we find in the other southern European democracies. Of the twenty countries of Latin America, only Uruguay is regularly more supportive of democracy than India, although Costa Rica sometimes places high as well. Even in Chile, after the painful experience of authoritarianism, democracy is endorsed by only 52%, with a large proportion of those who are indifferent. In Korea, 27% of respondents, in contrast to 4% in India, agreed with the statement, "In some circumstances an authoritarian government can be preferable to a

---

42. In 2004 the overall proportion of the respondents who said "do not know" to this question in India was 20%. The proportion was 4% among those who had completed graduation or a higher degree, 9% among those who had completed high school, 19% among those who managed to complete primary education, and 37% among those who had no formal education.

TABLE 2.5
*Attitudes toward Democracy and Authoritarianism in India and
Five Important "Third Wave" Democracies*

Attitude	Uruguay	Spain	India (2004)	India (1999)	Korea	Chile	Brazil
"Democracy is preferable to any other form of government."	80%	78%	70%	60%	58%	52%	41%
(Percentage of valid responses excluding Do not know/no answer)	(85)	(83)	(88)	(83)	(62)	(54)	(48)
"In some circumstances an authoritarian government can be preferable to a democratic government."	8	9	4	6	27	18	21
"For someone like me, a democratic or a non-democratic regime makes no difference."	6	7	6	7	8	25	23
Do not know/no answer	6	6	20	27	7	4	15
(N)	(1,213)	(1,000)	(27,148)	(8,133)	(1,037)	(1,200)	(1,240)

Sources: Data for India are from *National Election Study, 1999 and 2004,* Center for the Study of Developing Societies, Delhi. Data for Uruguay, Brazil, and Chile are from *Latino Barometer 1996,* directed by Marta Lagos. Data from Spain are from *Eurobarometer 37* (1992). Data from Korea are from *Korea Democracy Barometer, 2004,* directed by Doh Chull Shin.

democratic government."[43] In summary, in an international comparative perspective the support for democracy in India is very high (see table 2.5).

We immediately have to ask ourselves whether, in the heterogeneous Indian population, commitment to democracy is limited to one or another segment of the society. In particular it is crucial to find out if the support for democracy is

43. The much greater openness to nondemocratic solutions expressed by respondents in Korea, Chile, and Brazil in contrast to India needs more research and reflection. However, a hypothesis worth particular study is previous experience with and perception of nondemocratic and democratic regimes. For a significant section of the Chilean voters, the center right, the Pinochet military experience is associated with providing greater economic growth and more personal security. In Korea, the military authoritarian rule is associated with high economic growth. In Brazil, for many poor people, the most popular president was probably Getúlio Vargas, whose periods of rule were often marked by a more "inclusionary corporatist" style of populist authoritarianism than democracy per se. Independent India, in contrast, has never had a military regime, so it is not seen as an acceptable or desired alternative. The low support for nondemocratic alternatives in Uruguay may also be partly because the military is not associated with any successful and popular period of rule and they had no "inclusionary corporatist" figure comparable to Vargas.

TABLE 2.6
Support for Democracy in India by Four Disadvantaged Social Groups, 2004

Attitude	All of India	Scheduled Caste	Scheduled Tribe	Poor	Very poor
"Democracy is always preferable."	70%	65%	61%	71%	61%
(Percentage of valid responses excluding Do not know/no answer)	(88)	(87)	(81)	(88)	(87)
"Sometimes authoritarianism is preferable."	4	3	5	4	3
No difference	6	6	8	6	6
Do not know/no answer	20	25	26	19	30
(N)	27,145	4,967	2,356	9,409	8,117

Source: *National Election Study* [India] 2004, CSDS, Delhi.
 Note: Percentages may not add up to 100 due to rounding.

weaker among the marginalized sections of society. Table 2.6 offers this necessary disaggregation for four major disadvantaged social groups (the ex-untouchables of the Hindu social order or the "Scheduled Castes," the indigenous people or the "Scheduled Tribes") and the two poorest socioeconomic groups.

The most striking thing about the data in this table is that there is not a single exception to the national norm of very high support for a democratic political system. In no group does the support for democracy fall below the 60% mark, and nowhere does the support for authoritarianism reach double digits. At first sight, some groups appear to deviate slightly from the national norm: the support for democracy among the Scheduled Caste, the Scheduled Tribes, and the Very Poor is about five to ten percentage points lower than the national average. But much of this is a function of larger proportion of "do not know" among these groups, which is directly associated with lower levels of educational attainment. Once we control for "do not know" responses—by examining the valid percentages after treating "do not know" as missing data—most of the apparent, even if minor, differences among various groups and states disappear. On average, 88% of those respondents who gave valid responses support democracy; all but one group (the Scheduled Tribes, which register 81% valid responses for democracy) fall within five percentage points of this national average.

RELIGION AND DEMOCRACY

When we examine all of India's major religions, do we find comparable consensual support for democracy? Or is it an area of great dissensus and polarization, as the "clash of civilizations" literature would suggest? India has traditionally been a country with high levels of religious heterogeneity, coupled with high levels of religious practice and belief. According to the 2001 census, India had approximately 805 million Hindus, 138 million Muslims, 2.3 million Christians (about 60% Catholic and 40% Protestant), 800,000 Buddhists, 400,000 Jains, 600,000 "other religions," and only 100,000 people who did not state a religion.[44] India also has some of the highest levels of religious belief and practice in the world; 93% of the population describe themselves as believing in God, and 87% as being "very" or "somewhat" religious, 53% as praying daily; almost half (at least 400 million people) say that they have gone on a pilgrimage or traveled to another place for religious purposes within the last ten years. Finally, against this very high base, nearly four times as many respondents say that in the last ten years their "family's engagement in religious activities" has *increased* as say that they have *decreased*.[45] In recent decades, contrary to classic modernization theories, India has combined steadily increasing levels of education and urban living with sharply increasing self-reported levels of religious practice, especially among the more urbanized and better educated. For example, 46% of villagers say they pray daily, whereas 65% of those in towns and 77% of city-dwellers say they pray daily. The same trend is visible in education: 44% of nonliterates say they pray daily, but 56% of university graduates say they do, and whereas 18% of nonliterates were classified as "high participants" in public religious activities, 24% of university graduates were so classified.[46]

In such a context, what choices concerning the state's policies toward religion might have seemed most, and least, attractive to members of the India Constituent Assembly if they were interested in social peace, some social reform, and enlisting the support of the vast majority of this heterogeneous population for a democracy?

A small group of Hindu nationalists wanted to impose Hinduism as the established religion in India. An established church is not necessarily undemocratic. Arguably, for the last sixty years of the twentieth century, the countries in the

44. *Census of India, 2001.* Since these data are already old, we have in this book occasionally used more recent estimates from other sources, especially for the population of Muslims.

45. The above percentages concerning religious beliefs and practices are from the *State of the Nation Survey*, carried out by the CSDS in January 2007. The survey used a national representative sample of 15,373 respondents. Figures reported here are for questions B5, B3, B11, B6 and B17, respectively, and are sourced from the Data Unit, CSDS, Delhi.

46. Ibid. For a rich analysis of the data in this report, see Sanjay Kumar, "Religious Practices among Hindus: Does This Influence Their Political Choices?" CSDS Working Paper, Delhi, June 2008, pp. 3–9.

world with the highest quality of democracy, welfare, equality, and political stability were the Scandinavian countries. But we must remember that every single one of these high quality democracies had an established religion—Evangelical Lutheranism—during this entire period.

What conditions helped make such establishment socially and religiously acceptable? Such establishment was almost certainly facilitated by Scandinavia's combination of high religious homogeneity (in Denmark, for example, as late as 1990 more than 96% of the population were Lutherans) with a low intensity of religious practice (in Denmark, for more than forty years only about 5% of the population reported going to church once a week). In contrast, none of the West European countries that are substantially more religiously heterogeneous than Scandinavia, such as modern Germany, Belgium, Holland, or Switzerland, has an established religion.[47]

In sharp contrast to Scandinavia, precisely the opposite conditions existed in India's polity, which features low religious homogeneity and high religious practice. Less propitious still, in the post-Independence conditions of Partition between India and Pakistan, where even conservative estimates indicate that a half a million people were killed, Muslims would have felt very threatened if India had established Hinduism.

The French model of secularism, especially during the Third Republic (1870–1940) in its 1905 laïcité form, was driven by an animus against the Catholic Church, which many French secularists saw as a part of the ancien regime, and indeed by their religiously hostile desire to make the French state "free from religion."[48] For many Indians—this included Gandhi and his followers—a religiously hostile secularism would not have helped generate deep and sustained support for the new democracy. The U.S. version of the wall of separation between church and state would have made it difficult for the new democracy to give financial aid to impoverished religious facilities such as those once supported by the heads of the 565 princely states, which lost their political and financial autonomy once they "acceded" to the union after Independence and which had

47. See Stepan, "Multiple Secularisms." For a pioneering discussion of Europe's "historic mono-confessional belts" versus "multi-confessional belts" and the political consequences of these differences, see John T. S. Madeley, "A Framework for the Comparative Analysis of Church-State Relations in Europe," *West European Politics* 26, no. 1 (January 2003), pp. 23–50.

48. See Ahmet Kuru, *Secularism and State Policies toward Religions: The United States, France, and Turkey* (Cambridge: Cambridge University Press, 2009), esp. chs. 1, 4, and 5. Also see his "Secularism, State Policies, and Muslims in Europe: Analyzing French Exceptionalism," *Comparative Politics* 4 (2008).

been a part of Indian tradition for thousands of years. In any case, many Indian leaders were not attracted by an aspect of the U.S. model, which is the opposite of the French model in that it appears to be driven by a desire to attain "freedom of religion from the state."[49] For example, the chair of the drafting committee of the constitution for the Constituent Assembly, the ex-untouchable B. R Ambedkar, along with many others, felt that if some religious bodies were violating the rights of the citizens, say by forbidding the ex-untouchables from entering temples, then the new democracy should not have a "wall of separation from religion" but must be allowed to help expand citizens' liberties and dignity in cases of egregious denial by religious authorities. The major theorist of Indian secularism, Rajeev Bhargava, calls the Indian model of action vis-à-vis religions "principled distance" in that it is a "multi-value secularism" that respects all religions but does not rule out the use of the democratic state to protect its citizens against some undemocratic religious practices being imposed on them.[50]

In this historical and normative context, the model of state religion relations crafted by the Indian Constituent Assembly and developed later was a highly original model with strong affinities to our state-nation model. All religious communities were recognized and respected by the state. All religious communities could, for example, run schools, organizations, and charities eligible for state financial support. The norms and practices of this model are so pervasively accepted that the Hindu nationalist Bharatiya Janata Party (BJP) did not dare, when it was the head of the ruling coalition, not to honor the tradition of giving extensive state subsidies to help Muslim citizens make the hajj to Mecca.

We do not want to make the case that the Indian model of secularism, by itself, created the attitudinal and behavioral patterns we are about to present, but we do believe that the state-nation-like policies and values of India's secular model helped Indians address their great religious heterogeneity and their great intensity of religious practice and helped bring about the remarkable consensus among all religions concerning democracy that we will document.

The first point we would like to stress is that the percentage of members of *all* four of the major religions in India who self-identify as having a "preference for democracy as opposed to any other system" is very high by world standards; Muslims (87%), Hindus (88%), Sikhs, (88%) and Christians (91%). The Muslims,

---

49. Stepan, "Multiple Secularisms."
50. On Indian secularism, see his articles cited in chapter 1, as well as his "The Distinctiveness of Indian Secularism," in *The Future Of Secularism*, ed. T. N. Srinivasan (Oxford: Oxford University Press, 2007), pp. 20–53.

TABLE 2.7
Support for Democracy in India as a Whole and by Four Major Religions

Attitude	All of India	Hindu	Muslim	Christian	Sikh
"Democracy is always preferable."	70%	71%	71%	74%	71%
(Percentage of valid responses excluding Do not know/no answer)	(88)	(88)	(87)	(91)	(88)
"Sometimes authoritarianism is preferable."	4	4	4	3	4
No difference	6	6	7	5	6
Do not know/no answer	20	19	18	18	19
(N)	(27,145)	(21,626)	(3,103)	(838)	(687)

Sources: National Election Study [India] *2004*, CSDS, Delhi.
    Note: According to a Pearson's chi-square test, the findings for all religious communities are statistically significant (p-value < .001). Thus, the probability of this occurring by chance is less than 1 in 1,000.

the largest and the most disadvantaged religious community in India, thus have about the same figures as the national norm for all four of the categories concerning democracy (see table 2.7).

Given the self-reported increase in religious practice in India noted previously, we constructed an "intensity of religious practice index" ranging from "low" to "high" to see if the trend toward growing intensity of religious practice correlated with growing undemocratic attitudes and practices, as some had feared. Based on the data in figure 2.1, the exact opposite trend has occurred. For *all* four major religions in India, a steady counterintuitive trend is discernable; for each increase in the intensity of religious practice, there is an increase in support for democracy.

In the State of Democracy in South Asia survey, we constructed a battery of questions exploring the relationship between religion and democracy. Unfortunately, our sample size (5,387, compared with 27,189 for the National Election Study, 2004) only permits us to do a detailed comparative study of the two largest religions in India, Hinduism and Islam. The sample size for other minority religions is too small for a robust analysis. A key question we wanted to explore was the relationship of increased levels of "intensity of religious practice," our independent variable, to four critical components of democratic political society, which will be our dependent variables: "political efficacy," "overall trust in political institutions," "satisfaction with the way democracy works in this country," and "voting ratios." As table 2.8 makes clear, again counterintuitively when set against much of the literature, on all eight observations (Hindus and Muslims on each of the four variables) the group with "high religiosity" has higher scores on each of the four variables than does those the group with "low religiosity."

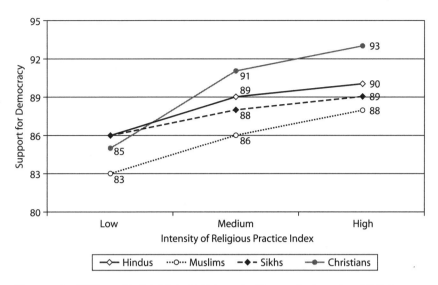

Figure 2.1. In All Four of India's Major Religions, the Greater the Intensity of Religious Practice, the Greater the Support for Democracy

Notes: The analysis is based on valid answers in the *National Election Study—2004* [India] (total n = 27,189). Valid responses for the table are: Hindus = 17,261; Muslims = 2,549; Sikhs = 544; and Christians = 697. The findings for Hindus are statistically significant (Pearson's chi square <0.001), which means that the probability of the findings occurring by chance are less than 1 per 1,000. The findings for Muslims are also statistically significant (Pearson's chi square <0.050), which means that the probability of the findings occurring by chance are less than 1 in 20. The findings for Sikhs and Christians are also positive but not statistically significant. Valid answers exclude "Do Not Know" and "No Opinion" from the analysis for reasons we have already explained. "Support for democracy" (Q23) is as measured in table 2.7. The "intensity of religious practice index" was computed by adding the self-reported frequency of praying (Q34a), visiting a religious place (Q34b), participating in religious meetings (Q35a), making donations to religious organizations (Q35b), and fasting (Q35c). In the index, 50% of the weight is given to frequency of praying, as it is the highest in all religions. Participating in religious meetings and fasting are given 20% weight each, as both these activities are high among all the four major religious groups in India but are much lower compared to the frequency of praying. Going to a place of worship and making donations have been given 5% weight each because making donations depends on the economic class of the respondent and because many Muslim women do not go to mosques. To further analyze the effect of the intensity of religious practice on support for democracy, we made a binary logistic regression model. In addition to the intensity of religious practice, we added as control variables efficacy of vote (q21), membership in organizations other than caste or religious organization (Q19), whether the respondent voted in the 2004 parliamentary election (Q3), gender, respondent's education (B4), monthly household income (B19), and level of urbanity (B10). The coefficient on the index of religiosity is 0.138. Thus, we can say that a one-unit increase in the index of religiosity (controlling for other factors) predicts approximately a 3.5% increase in the probability of support for democracy.

TABLE 2.8

Relationship between Intensity of Religious Practice and Support for Political Institutions in India

	Religious group	Support (%)			
		Low intensity	Medium intensity	High intensity	Net gain from low to high
Trust in public institutions: respondents	Hindus	31	35	38	+7
who reported a high degree of trust in public institutions	Muslims	39	40	48	+9
Satisfaction with "the way democracy	Hindus	76	82	80	+4
works in India": respondents who reported that they are "very satisfied" or "satisfied"	Muslims	71	83	84	+13
Political efficacy: respondents who	Hindus	76	81	81	+5
agreed that "your vote has an effect on how things are run in this country"	Muslims	75	80	77	+2
Frequency of voting: respondents who	Hindus	64	76	79	+15
reported that they had "voted in every election since they became eligible for voting"	Muslims	60	72	86	+26

Sources: The analysis is based on the *State of Democracy in South Asia* survey conducted in 2005 for "trust" (Question C-13 battery), voting (Question C-8), and "satisfaction" (Question C-12). "Efficacy" (Question 21) is based on *National Election Study* [India], 2004.

Note: The findings for "efficacy" and "trust," among both Hindus and Muslims, are statistically significant using a Pearson's chi-square test (p-value < .001), which means that the possibility of the findings occurring by chance are less than 1 in 1,000. "Trust in public institutions" is an index created by adding the responses to the frequency of self-reported trust in "Central government" (C-13a), "Provincial government" (C-13b), "Local government" (C-13c), "Civil service" (C-13d), "Police" (C-13e), "Army" (C-13f), "Courts" (C-13g), "Parliament" (C-13h), "Political parties" (C-13i), "Election Commission" (C-13j). The findings for "voting" are statistically significant for Hindus (p-value < .001) and for Muslims (p-value < .050). The findings for "satisfaction" for Hindus are statistically significant (p-value < .001), while the findings for Muslims are positive but not statistically significant.

The findings indicate that the followers of all four major religions in the state-nation of India do not see any contradiction between their practice of religion and their practice of democracy. It is fair to say that both democracy and religion are integral and valued aspects of Indian citizens' public and private lives.

TRUST IN INSTITUTIONS

Although we will turn later to the problem of the distrust in some institutions (particularly in political parties and the police), it is important to note how much the average Indian agrees with the need for some of the key political institutions necessary for a democracy. The CSDS has been using a somewhat different question to tap the legitimacy of the Indian democratic polity: "Suppose there were no parties or assemblies and elections were not held, do you think that the government in this country could be run better?" The percentage of valid respondents saying "no" increased from 74% in 1971 to 91% in 2004. This question is valuable for double-checking the conclusions drawn above: it has the advantage of measuring popular attitudes to democracy (without using the "D-word" itself) and also of avoiding a lazy "yes" by requiring the supporters of democracy to disagree with the statement.

Since political parties are one of the key democratic institutions, it is also useful to examine the level of party identification in India through the CSDS surveys over the last four decades (1971, 1996, and 2004). A similar movement across time can be observed in levels of party identification. Notwithstanding widespread popular disenchantment with political parties, the proportion of those who felt "close to a political party" in 2004 was quite high by global standards and up from the level recorded in 1971. While the global trend is in the direction of disengagement from political parties, the Indian data suggest otherwise.

Let us try to go beyond the overall question of support for the principle of democracy to *trust* in the functioning of the existing institutions of the Indian state. The study of trust has been a major research area in policy analysis and social science research for the last twenty years or so. Pippa Norris attempted to bring this research together so as to be able to make comparative judgments about trust in institutions.[51] Using the World Values Survey 1990–93 round, she constructed a composite index of trust by measuring expressed trust in six major institutions she felt were important for a democratic state: parliament, the legal system, civil service, the judiciary, police, and the military. She did this for twenty-one democracies, one of which was India. India's composite score for citizen's institutional trust was the highest among the twenty-one democracies, decisively ahead of its closest competitor, Norway (see figure 2.2).

One has to exercise caution in interpreting a composite index based on measurement at one point in time. In order to see if India's very high comparative standing concerning trust in institutions held up in a later survey, we checked the data on trust in institutions for the eleven longstanding federal democracies based on the 1995–97 round of the World Values Survey. If we combine the total percentages of respondents who answered that they had a "great deal of trust" or

51. Pippa Norris, *Critical Citizens: Global Support for Democratic Governance* (Oxford: Oxford University Press, 1999), esp. p. 229.

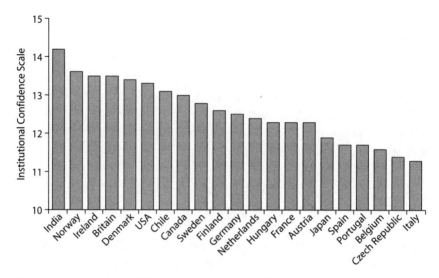

Figure 2.2. Institutions and Political Trust in India and Twenty Other Democracies, 1990–1993
Source: Pippa Norris, *Critical Citizens: Global Support for Democratic Governance* (Oxford: Oxford University Press, 1999), figure 11.2, p. 229.

"quite a lot of trust" in an institution, India ranks first or second out of the eleven longstanding federal democracies in five of the six categories. The only exception was, unsurprisingly, the trust in the police, where India ranks second-last, above only Argentina. For a poor and diverse country in which over a third of the citizens are not literate and over a quarter live below the poverty line, such a low level of trust in police is very disturbing. It suggests an unequal access to the rule of law that compromises the quality of democratic governance the citizens can enjoy. This lack of trust in police becomes critical for minorities and other marginalized groups in situations of group violence; the Indian police have often been accused, not without substance, of inaction and complicity during times of violence against minorities and marginal groups.[52] Despite this low trust in the Indian police, Indian citizens, in contrast to Pakistani citizens, to our surprise, still see the police as part of a "useable state." In the State of Democracy in South Asia survey, in answer to the question: "If you had a problem that needed police help, would you

52. Some of these instances are the massacre of Sikhs in Delhi and rest of the country following the assassination of Indira Gandhi in 1984, the large-scale killings of Muslims in Meerut, Uttar Pradesh, in 1987 and the massacre of Muslims in Gujarat in 2002. In all these instances, the police force was either a silent spectator to mass killings or was complicit in the crime. These and other lapses on the part of the police are extensively documented by human rights organizations and groups such as those found in footnote 21 in this chapter.

go to the police?" 82% of Indian respondents answered "yes," whereas only 27% of Pakistani respondents answered "yes."[53] From the perspective of trust, or lack of trust, in the state security apparatus, we should note that the lack of trust in the regular police force is not reflected in the case of the armed forces. The Indian Army, which exceptionally in the developing world has never deposed a government in a coup or ruled the country, is one of the most trusted institutions in India.[54]

With the exception of the police, the next institution the Indians trust least is political parties. But, this abstract disaffection does not prevent them from identifying with specific political parties in greater numbers than elsewhere. Besides, Indians trust political parties more than citizens in any other longstanding federal democracy do (see table 2.9).

We can conclude our discussion on trust here except for one technical aspect. The conclusions so far are drawn from the World Values Survey data. The Indian sample within the World Values Survey underrepresented nonliterates and rural dwellers in the rounds we have used and was only carried out in eight of the country's then fifteen official languages. Therefore we need to double-check these conclusions with the help of a national representative sample such as those carried out by the CSDS to measure trust with greater confidence. It is important to check if the inclusion in the sample of more nonliterates and more rural dwellers presents a somewhat different picture than that presented by the World Values Survey. Table 2.10 presents a comparison of the responses on trust in institutions from the World Values Survey of 2001 with the SDSA survey carried out by the CSDS in 2005. While the level of trust recorded in the latter is a little higher than that in the World Values Survey, the internal order of the five institutions is more or less the same: police and political parties finish at the bottom of the heap in both surveys, and the central government is at the top of both surveys. The data from the survey carried out by the CSDS have the advantage of expanding the range of institutions about which we have information. It shows that two of the most trusted institutions in India are the judiciary and the Election Com-

53. State of Democracy in South Asia survey, Question 38, data sourced from Data Unit, CSDS.

54. For example, in Pakistan only 38% expressed "great trust" in the military, in Sri Lanka only 31% did so, whereas in India 55% affirmed "great trust." See SDSA Team, *State of Democracy in South Asia*, pp. 250–251. One should also note that India is exceptional among developing countries. Since World War II, 18 of the 20 countries in Latin America have experienced direct military rule. In sub-Saharan Africa, more than 30 newly independent countries have had major military involvement in their governments. In South and Southeast Asia, Indonesia, Korea, the Philippines, Pakistan, Thailand, Bangladesh, and arguably Taiwan have had long periods of military rule. The military has governed Pakistan for about half the years since Independence.

TABLE 2.9

Citizen Trust in Six Major Institutions in Eleven Longstanding Federal Democracies

Institution	India (rank)	Switzer- land	Canada	Brazil	Austria	United States	Bel- gium	Spain	Ger- many	Aus- tralia	Argen- tina
Legal system	67% (1st)	65%	54%	55%	58%	36%	45%	45%	54%	35%	27%
Parliament	53 (1st)	41	38	33	41	30	43	35	28	31	16
Political parties	39 (1st)	25	n.a.	32	n.a.	21	n.a.	18	14	16	8
Central government	48 (2nd)	50	38	48	n.a.	31	n.a.	30	24	26	27
Civil service	53 (2nd)	43	50	59	42	52	43	40	47	38	8
Police	36 (10th)	67	84	45	68	71	51	61	70	76	23

Sources: Data for all countries but Austria, Belgium, and Canada are from Ronald Inglehart et al., *World Values Survey: 1995–97*, Inter-University Consortium for Political and Social Research, University of Michigan. Data for Germany are from the *Länder* of the former West Germany. Canada, Belgium, and Austria were not included in the 1995–97 survey. Data for these countries are from *World Values Survey: 1990–93*. For both the 1990–93 and 1995–97 surveys, the question numbers were 137 and 141 to 145. Question 143 was not asked in Canada. Questions 142 and 143 were not asked in Belgium and Austria.

Note: All figures in percentages, rounded to the nearest integer. Table entries refer to the sum of those who respond "A great deal" or "Quite" to the question "How much confidence you have in . . . ? (Great Deal, Quite, Not Very Much, None)." The countries are presented in the above table from left to right in descending order of average trust. Thus, India has the most trust, on average, and Argentina the least.

TABLE 2.10
Trust in Institutions in India

Institution	State of Democracy in South Asia, 2005	World Values Survey, 2001
Central government	62%	56%
Legal system	59	n.a.
Election commission	51	n.a.
Civil service	47	49
Parliament	43	55
Police	42	38
Political parties	36	34
(N)	(5,385)	(2,002)

Note: Table entries show percentage who responded that they had "a great deal" or "quite a lot" of trust in each of the institutions. The "N" value for the World Values Survey refers to the total number of cases, but the percentages are calculated from valid cases.

mission. The Election Commission of India, the independent and powerful federal institution, has the responsibility for supervising the fairness and efficiency of the entire electoral process.[55] That the Election Commission of India is a highly trusted institution helps give the democratic electoral process itself enhanced legitimacy. In comparative terms, even when we substitute the CSDS survey for the World Values Survey sample, India's relatively high trust ranking holds up.

LEGITIMACY AND EFFICACY

If these conclusions about trust in democratic institutions are robust, we would expect this to be reflected in citizens' perceptions regarding the legitimacy of the democratic system and citizens' feelings about the "efficacy" of their votes. A major thesis in U.S. political sociology literature is that there is a general decline in political participation in the democratic world; some hold that this decline is due to a decrease in what is called a sense of "efficacy" on the part of the voters. The U.S. political efficacy index (average of respondents who gave answers indicating they felt efficacious for the four consecutive observations) in 1952–64 was

55. The 2002 riots in Gujarat and the 2002 electoral outcome in Gujarat raised many disturbing questions. However, the Election Commission emerged stronger in one respect: against the ruling BJP desires, the Election Commission managed to postpone the timing of the Gujarat elections. The Election Commission also gained prestige due to the positive role it played in conducting reasonably fair elections in Kashmir in 2002.

69.7%. In four consecutive observations between 1994 and 2000, the average percentage of respondents who felt efficacious was only 39.7%.[56]

The National Election Study series in India uses a slightly different question for measuring political efficacy: "Do you think your vote has an effect on how things are run in this country or do you think your vote has no effect?" Unlike the data from the United States, we do not have a large number of data points, but the Indian NES offers three observation points—1971, 1996, and 2004—that allow us to discern a trend. The trend in India is quite the opposite of the United States: 48% of the respondents felt efficacious in India in 1971, 59% felt efficacious in 1996, and 68% felt efficacious in 2004. To be sure, efficacy is being measured here with reference to the value of the vote, and the significant changes in this respect partly reflect the growing competitiveness in India's electoral politics in the last fifteen years. Yet if a significantly greater proportion of citizens feels that their vote makes a difference, that is an undeniable positive for democracy and resonates well with the data on trust that we have examined.

Table 2.11 presents the data on changing levels of citizens' sense of efficacy and legitimacy of the Indian democratic system for some of the marginalized groups from 1971 to 2004. In 1971 the eight groups that expressed the lowest efficacy were Scheduled Tribes (ST), nonliterates, women, the lowest economic quintile (the "very poor"), Scheduled Castes (SC), the second-lowest economic quintile (the "poor"), the rural population, and Muslims. Since that time, *each* of these eight groups has reported a substantial increase in its level of efficacy.

This growing sense of efficacy could have expressed itself in a growing desire to be anti-system and with an increasing dissatisfaction with democracy. In India, however, what we see between 1971 and 2004, is a high correlation between the previously most marginal groups feeling more efficacious and expressing greater support for democracy. From 1971 to 2004, *every single one* of the eight groups that had scored the lowest on efficacy in 1971 increased its support for democracy by 27 to 35 points (see table 2.11). Once we control for the "do not know" effect, there are no noteworthy social differences in support for the democratic system.

Do these positive attitudes on trust, efficacy, and legitimacy translate in terms of behavior as well? There is a general presumption, especially in the U.S. socio-logical literature, that the lower the education level and the lower the income

56. See Virginia Sapiro, Steven J. Rosenstone, and National Election Study, Center for Political Studies, University of Michigan, *The American National Election Studies Cumulative Data File, 1948–2004.* The wording of the two key questions was: "People like me don't have any say about what the government does" (V613) and "I don't think public officials care much what people like me think" (V609).

TABLE 2.11
*Sense of Political Efficacy and Legitimacy of Democracy among
Marginalized Groups in India, 1971–2004*

Group	Political efficacy			Support for democracy		
	1971	1996	2004	1971	1996	2004
National average	48%	59%	68%	43%	69%	72%
Scheduled Tribe	31	48	59	41	66	68
Women	36	51	61	32	64	67
Nonliterates	36	47	55	31	62	61
Very poor	38	51	60	32	64	66
Scheduled Caste	42	60	65	38	67	69
Poor	43	55	68	37	68	71
Rural	44	57	66	39	69	70
Muslims	50	60	66	40	72	73

Source: *National Election Study* [India], 1971, 1996, and 2004, CSDS, Delhi.
   Note: The efficacy question was "Do you think your vote has effect on how things are run in this country or do you think your vote makes no difference?" The support for democracy question was "Do you think that the government in this country can be run better if there are no parties or assemblies or elections?"

level, the lower the voting participation rates and the lower the sense of personal political efficacy.[57] This is coupled with the belief that in the modern world, political trust in institutions has been declining for over three decades. Finally, there is Samuel Huntington's famous axiom that if participation increases faster than institutionalization, there can be a crisis of governability. Most of these assumptions and worries are true for the United States. Some are true for Western Europe. None is true for India.

In the United States this assertion (the lower the socioeconomic status, the lower the voting turnout) holds true with brutal regularity. Table 2.12 presents some of this evidence for the United States and India. If we divide levels of U.S. income into five quintiles, for each quintile that income decreases, there is a monotonic decline in voter turnout: 77%, 67%, 59%, 52%, 43%. The same holds true, even more sharply, for the six levels of education; the percentage of post-graduate voters is 84%, then for each descending level of education the percentages are 79%, 66%, 57%, 43%, 38%. Also, blacks and Latinos vote less than whites. In the nonpresidential year of 1994, 47% of whites voted, 37% of blacks voted, and 20% of Latinos voted.

In sharp contrast to the United States, voting rates in India do not decline as

57. See, for example, Sidney Verba and Norman H. Nie, *Participation in America: Political Democracy and Social Equality* (New York: Harper and Row, 1972), p. 97.

TABLE 2.12
Socioeconomic Status and Voting Turnout in the United States and India

United States (1988) (1998 turnout, 49%; 1988 turnout, 60%)		India (1998) (total turnout, 62%)	
Income		Income	
1) Lowest quintile	43%[a]	1) Lowest quintile	57.1%[b]
2)	52	2)	65.2
3)	59	3)	73.3
4)	67	4)	59.6
5) Highest quintile	77	5) Highest quintile	46.6
Education		Education	
No high school	38	Illiterate	56.5
Some high school	43	Up to middle school	82.6
High school graduate	57	College	56.5
Some college	66	Postgraduate	41.0
College graduate	79		
Postgraduate	84		

	% Voted				
Community	1994 (midterm year)	1996 (presidential year)	Community	1971	1998
White	47	56	Hindu (upper)	61.4	60.2
Black	37	50	Hindu (OBC)	45.3	58.4
Latino	20	27	Scheduled Caste	57.5	75.1
			Scheduled Tribe	35.9	59.0
			Muslim	87.9	69.6
			Sikh	84.6	89.4

Sources: For India, Yogendra Yadav, "Electoral Politics in Time of Change: India's Third Electoral System, 1989–99," *Economic and Political Weekly*, vol. 34, August 21–28, 1999, pp. 2393–99. For the United States, Jan E. Leighley and Jonathan Nagler, "Socioeconomic Bias in Turnout, 1964–1988: The Voters Remain the Same," *American Political Science Review* 86 (September 1992), pp. 725–736.

[a] U.S. turnout expressed as percentage of voting-age citizens.
[b] India's turnout expressed as percentage of the national electorate.

one goes down the social hierarchy. In the 1998 Lok Sabha election, for example, nonliterates had a higher turnout than did postgraduates, who in fact reported the lowest turnout rate. In terms of income, the two poorest quintiles voted at substantially higher rates than did the wealthiest quintile. The same pattern has been repeated in virtually every election in the recent past. In terms of ethnic or cultural communities, in 1998 the minority communities of Muslims, Sikhs, and Scheduled Castes all voted at higher rates than did upper-caste Hindus. This has not happened in every election, as the Muslim turnout dropped in one election after the Gujarat massacre of 2002. But the basic pattern holds: those at the top of the socioeconomic hierarchy are not at the top of voting turnout tables.[58] Thus we can conclude, from the tables just presented, that among previously marginalized groups there is growing participation, a growing sense of efficacy, and a growing commitment to Indian democracy as a way of managing diversity.

It is this spirit that has made for a smooth transition from the single-party rule on the national level in the 1980s to the extraordinary proliferation of "centric-regional" state parties that participate in the numerous state-nation ruling coalitions of the overall polity.[59] Indeed, India has far more parties that participate in ruling coalitions than any other democracy in the world. For example from 1945 to 1995, of the twenty-three OECD countries, the United States, Great Britain, and New Zealand never had more than one party in the government. The greatest number of parties that ever helped form a government at the center was eight, in Belgium in 1945 and in France in 1947. In sharp contrast, in 2003, near the completion of its five-year term, the BJP-led government had twenty-three parties in the ruling coalition. The Congress-led ruling coalition in 2008 had seventeen parties.[60]

As the above data indicate, the acceptance and use of this coalitional model is not confined to the centrist parties like the Congress; it cuts across the left-right divide as well as the "polity-wide" and "centric-regional" party divide. Even the right-wing BJP, which has questioned the consensus on the secular character of the Indian state, has accepted regional and linguistic diversity as one of the foundations of Indian governance.

INDIA AS A STATE-NATION:
PAST ACCOMPLISHMENTS AND POTENTIAL THREATS

In our opening chapter we argued that being a state-nation is an extremely important normative goal for culturally diverse democratic federations, especially those with a multinational dimension to their diversity. We also argued that the relative

58. Yogendra Yadav, "Understanding the Second Democratic Upsurge: Trends of Bahujan Participation in Electoral Politics in the 1990s," in *Transforming India: Social and Political Dynamics of Democracy*, ed. Francine R. Frankel, Zoya Hasan, Rajeev Bhargava, and Balveer Arora (Delhi: Oxford University Press, 2000), tables 14 and 15. It should also be said that the reverse pattern in India is of long standing. See Samuel Eldersveld and Bashiruddin Ahmed, *Citizens and Politics: Mass Political Behavior in India* (Chicago: University of Chicago Press, 1978), table 14.5, p. 195.
59. This transition has been described by Yogendra Yadav and Suhas Palshikar in "From Hegemony to Convergence: Party System and Electoral Politics in the Indian States, 1952–2002," *Journal of Indian Institute of Political Economy* 15, no. 1/2 (January–June 2003).
60. For data on all countries except India, see J. Lane, D. McKay, and K. Newton, *Political Data Handbook: OECD Countries*, 2nd ed. (Oxford: Oxford University Press, 1997), pp. 212–340.

presence or absence of a polity's state-nation characteristics could be empirically observed by focusing on three of the most politically important attributes: first, the degree of *pride* in citizens' identification with being members of the polity; second, the degree of citizens' *trust* in the most important state institutions, such as electoral procedures, the judiciary, and the civil service; and third, the degree of citizens' *support* for the democratic political system.

Notwithstanding the great linguistic, religious, ethnic, and caste differences within its diverse polity, India, as we have documented, is one of the world's democracies that scores most highly on these three state-nation indicators of country pride, institutional trust, and democratic support. We have seen that the evidence in this respect is quite robust. India also has extensive and rich patterns of multiple but complementary identities, which was our fourth indicator of a well-functioning democratic state-nation.

However, in a diverse polity, even if the average support for democracy is fairly high, low support for democracy within a major minority group can present a problem. Yet this is not the case in India concerning religious minorities because the largest religious minority group, the Muslims, supports democracy at virtually the same level as does the majority religious group, the Hindus. Of the major longstanding democracies in the world, India has by far the lowest per capita income. If the poorest segment of the population had a very low support for democracy in contrast to the rest of the population, this could also present a problem, but the very poor in India prefer democracy in about the same measure as everyone else. Finally, given India's caste system, it is significant that even among the Scheduled Castes (formerly called "untouchables"), the support for democracy is no different from that of other groups once we focus on valid responses. In comparative terms, therefore, the percentage of India's Muslims, of India's ex-untouchables, and of India's poorest strata who answer that "democracy is preferable to any other form of government" is about ten percentage points higher (for each of these potentially alienated antidemocratic groups) than the overall average of the people in Latin American countries for 2001. More important, the proportion of those who may prefer authoritarianism or who are indifferent to the choice between democracy or non-democracy is negligible across all marginal social groups.

Nonetheless, we must add a cautionary note. There is a significant element of "social construction" in politics. What has been socially constructed can, under some circumstances, be socially deconstructed. More than a quarter of a century ago, Linz and Stepan edited a volume on the breakdown of democracy in twelve West European and Latin American countries. One of their major conclusions was that "the independent contributions made to the breakdowns by political incumbents is a theme that emerges in almost all cases."[61] Linz and Stepan also concluded that virtually none of the breakdowns was inevitable.

The authors of this book have two major conclusions concerning India's political engagement with its sociocultural diversity. First, India is not a classic nation-state. Second, India has managed to create a functioning, democratic state-nation. In our judgment, the effort to attempt to forge in India a classic nation-state of the nineteenth-century French style would be extremely dangerous and ultimately unsuccessful and would almost certainly produce, at best, a lower-quality democracy, an eroded state-nation, and weaker attachments to the state. To the extent that the Indian state is not a classic nation-state and that India's federalism has historically recognized the diversity of people within the union, a nation-building campaign on the basis of a cultural, linguistic, or religious homogeneity and the marginalization of those not sharing in this sought-after homogeneity would create a threat to the Indian state. Many loyal segments of the population in India, many groups, many political administrative units can be part of a state-nation—but not part of a classical nation-state.

In the last twenty years, there has been an outpouring of speeches, articles, and books warning about the threat of the social deconstruction of India's relatively inclusive polity by Hindu fundamentalists. Hindu nationalist militias (such as the RSS, the VHP, and the Bajrang Dal), which are frequently—but not always—supported by the BJP, often use a discourse, and carry out actions, whose sociopolitical consequences, if their project for India were ever implemented, would make India sharply less inclusive.

A political project to create a majoritarian Hindu nation-state gained momentum in the 1990s. Four important events led to growing fears about the Indian model of democratically managing diversity. First, Hindu fundamentalists, mobilized by the BJP under the leadership of L. K. Advani (who later became the deputy prime minister in the BJP-led NDA government) destroyed the Babri mosque in Ayodhya in December 1992. Second, there was a steady growth over the course of five consecutive elections of the vote share of the BJP, from 7.8% in 1984 to 25.6% in 1998. This growth was accompanied by an expansion of the party in south and northeast India and also among less-privileged social groups. Third, the steep electoral ascent of the BJP greatly enhanced its legitimacy and attractiveness as the leader of a ruling coalition, the National Democratic Alliance (NDA),

61. See Linz and Stepan, eds., *Breakdown of Democratic Regimes: Europe* (Baltimore: Johns Hopkins University Press, 1978), ix.

that boasted twenty-two other parties at the end of its five-year term in 2004. Fourth, the anti-Muslim pogrom in February-March 2002 in Gujarat led to the killing of approximately fifteen hundred people, about 75% Muslim, and was followed by the electoral triumph of the BJP in the state under the leadership of Narendra Modi, widely believed to be strongly complicitous with the pogrom.

The question after Gujarat was whether its model would be the future for Indian politics and thus represent a fatal challenge to the state-nation model. After the Gujarat elections, Ashutosh Varshney wrote the following, which we will quote at length to give an indication of the worries that some important observers had about the threats to pluralism and inclusiveness in India:

> In effect, Gujarat's electorate has legitimized independent India's first unam-biguous pogrom, a pogrom much more vicious than the killings of the Sikhs in Delhi in 1984, a pogrom that came closest to the classic, anti-Jewish pogroms of Russia and Europe in the late 19th and the first half of the 20th century. The Congress Party, though deplorably involved in anti-Sikh violence in 1984, never had an anti-Sikh ideology. For purely electoral reasons, the Congress became contingently anti-Sikh for a while. In contrast, the VHP, the RSS and their stormtroopers, the Bajrang Dal, have an anti-Muslim ideological core.
>
> Therefore, the victory of Rajiv Gandhi's Congress in 1985 was basically a strategic phenomenon, cynically parasitic as the Congress campaign was on Mrs Gandhi's assassination by her Sikh bodyguards. The BJP's victory in Gu-jarat, on the contrary, is ideological. It is about a larger vision of the polity, in which minorities, as the RSS put it earlier this year, must seek protection in the goodwill of the majority community, not in the laws of the land. The massive legitimisation of an ideologically charged pogrom is a truly bruising embarrass-ment for all Indian liberals and a severe undermining of the pluralist national vision in Gujarat.[62]

Clearly, if the Gujarat model became a dominant model in India, this would bring about the sociopolitical destruction of India's state-nation. We hope that this will not occur, and we do not believe it is inevitable that it will.

In an article written in 2005, Linz, Stepan, and Yadav made the following argument as to why we believed the spread of the Gujarat model was unlikely:

> Let us briefly mention some reasons that make us more confident than many others that the "Gujarat model" is not bound to be successful in India's twenty-

---

62. Ashutosh Varshney, "Will the Stallion Baulk in Mid-Gallop?" *Outlook*, December 30, 2002.

seven other states. Gujarat has many features that make it exceptional in India. First, the Gujarat electoral model was aided by the fact that the BJP was
ruling in Gujarat without the actual, or at least potential, constraint of coalitional partners. . . . Second, Ashutosh Varshney presents data on deaths as
a result of communal violence per 1,000,000 of urban populations in seventeen
major states in India from 1950–1995. Gujarat, by far, had the highest death
rate.[63] Third, of the seventeen states for which we have survey data on support for democracy, the state that had the highest number of explicitly antidemocratic responses in 1998 was Gujarat. Fourth, Gujarat had emerged as the
safest electoral bastion for the BJP, and had witnessed the most intense Hindu-
fundamentalist mobilization of any state in the decade prior to the massacre.[64]
Fifth, the Godra incident in which 58 Hindus burned to death in a train returning from Ayodhya, one of the main symbols for Hindu fundamentalism, helped
ignite the massacres. Without great complicity by incumbents, and unprecedented terrorism by civil society groups (whether Muslim or Hindu), a Godra
type incident will be an extremely rare occurrence. More generally, we can say
that the leaders of the BJP as a political party (who were in a governing coalition
with twenty-three partners) for reasons of parliamentary, coalitional, electoral,
and even very important national and international investment imperatives,
might well want to distance themselves from full association or complicity with,
the projects of such groups as the RSS, VHP and the Bajrang Dal. Finally, a
non-BJP government at the center, might not allow this, not only out of a
commitment to value India's tradition of inclusiveness but also for reasons of
party competition. This would contribute to governability, a strong Indian state,
and wide-spread support for a state nation. Such a government at the center, in
all likelihood, would not tolerate an individual state leader's incitement of a
Gujarat type anti-inclusionary campaign and its attendant massacres.[65]

Events since then have made us even more confident in this judgment. In fact,
far from the Gujarat pogrom ushering in a new triumphal period of Hindu
nationalism and BJP growth, it may have helped set into motion countervailing
powers, many of them coming from state-nation values and practices. At the time
of the Gujarat pogrom, the BJP was heading a coalition of over twenty parties at
the center, including some of the minority parties like the Akali Dal and the

63. Varshney, *Ethnic Conflict and Civic Life* (New Haven: Yale University Press, 2003), p. 97.
64. See Yogendra Yadav, "The Patterns and Lessons," *Frontline* (India), January 3, 2003,
pp. 10–16.
65. Juan J. Linz, Alfred Stepan, Yogendra Yadav, " 'Nation State' or 'State Nation'? India in
Comparative Perspective," in *Democracy and Diversity*, ed. Bajpai, pp. 104–105.

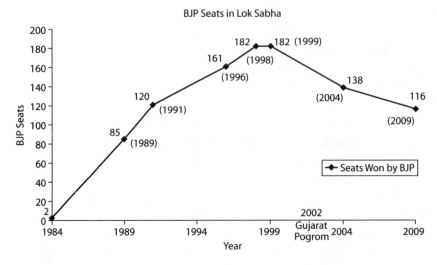

Figure 2.3. Rise and Decline of BJP Seats in Lok Sabha, 1984–2009
Source: Election Commission of India.

National Conference. Only one coalitional ally, Shiv Sena, shared its exclusionary and communal ideology, yet none registered an effective protest during or immediately after the pogrom. Some of the self-corrective mechanisms of democratic political competition did unfold, but very slowly. Once the BJP-led coalition, the NDA, lost the parliamentary election to the Congress-led UPA in the 2004 general elections, many of the BJP allies openly cited the Gujarat riots as a reason for the loss of Muslim votes and the defeat of the coalition. This consideration played an important role in the departure of some of the key NDA allies like the Telugu Desam Party in Andhra Pradesh, the All India Anna Dravid Munetra Kazhgam in Tamil Nadu, and the All India Trinamool Congress in West Bengal between 2004 and 2009. The BJP paid the price for Gujarat, but not inside Gujarat. The BJP's own vote share declined from its peak of 25.6% in 1998 to 18.8% in 2009, slipping below the 20% mark for the first time since 1989.

The outcome of the parliamentary election held in 2009 underscored that the BJP's defeat in 2004 was not a one-time setback. Figure 2.3 shows that the BJP's electoral fortunes declined consistently following its peak in the late 1990s. From the peak of 41.1% share of the national vote, the BJP-led alliance, the NDA, slipped to 35.9% in 2004 and more sharply to just 24.1% in 2009. The election was a serious setback for the BJP itself. Furthermore, not only did the BJP not succeed in coming back to power, but its seats and votes also plummeted to the lowest level since 1989, when its rise to power began. The BJP now faces the challenge of a long-term erosion, since its social base is threatening to come apart.

An analysis of long-term trends in the sociology of voting by Yadav and his coauthor, Suhas Palshikar, led them to conclude:

> Thus the shift that was discernible in 2004 appears to have been completed in 2009. The NDA's famous victory in 1999 represented the height of BJP's success in creating a "new social bloc." The core of this bloc comprised voters from the upper end of the social pyramid, a coalition of the privileged, which allowed the party to draw heavily from this smaller pool of potential voters. . . . It required ingenuous politics to convert ad hoc acquisitions of underprivileged into an enduring political bloc. And it required statesman-like leadership to sustain a coalition with allies who drew upon a very different social base that often included the Muslims. In retrospect it seems that the BJP simply could not rise up to this challenge. The story since 1999 is that of depolarization of this bloc: the core bloc of the privileged has started drifting away from the BJP to the Congress, demobilization appears to have set in for the social groups that had been stapled and the supplementary groups have simply walked away with the allies.[66]

It is important to remember that the elections of 2009 were held in the wake of the attack in Mumbai by Pakistani terrorists in late November 2008 that killed at least 170 people. The Indian response to the attack was a sign that many Indians— Hindus and Muslims alike—even in the face of grave provocation still support state-nation practices and values. Though the terrorists were Muslim, albeit from Pakistan, there were no anti-Muslim riots, either in the immediate aftermath of the attack in Mumbai or anywhere else in the rest of India. Muslim organizations were quick to condemn the attack in unequivocal terms and even refused to allow the burial of the perpetrators of the attack on the grounds that "people who committed this heinous act cannot be Muslim." The BJP did see this as an opportunity to exert pressure on the government and tried hard to turn it into a campaign issue for the parliamentary elections held a few months after the attack. This issue had little appeal in the election. The BJP and its ultra-chauvinist ally

---

66. See Yogendra Yadav and Suhas Palshikar, "Between 'Fortuna' and 'Virtu': Explaining the Congress' Ambiguous Victory in 2009," *Economic and Political Weekly*, vol. 44, September 26– October 2, 2009, pp. 33–51. This entire 206-page special issue is devoted to articles on *National Election Study 2009* and is an invaluable source for analysts.

Shiv Sena won *none* of the six parliamentary seats in Mumbai itself, where the attack took place.

It would be incorrect to infer from these findings that the BJP faces a terminal decline. Its status as the second-largest national political party and potentially the ruling party in a number of states does not seem to be threatened. Nor is there compelling evidence to show that the Gujarat pogrom was the most decisive factor that led to BJP's electoral reversals. The complex political process does not allow for such a mono-causal reading. But the electoral outcomes and political developments since 2002 provide strong evidence to negate the worry that Gujarat was going to be replicated across the country and thus be the beginning of the end of the state-nation enterprise in India. While Modi is still chief minister of Gujarat, as of this writing, in hindsight we know that fears of the "Gujarat model" being replicated all over the country were highly exaggerated. Indeed, instead of becoming the launching pad for BJP's rise to being a "natural party of governance," Gujarat proved to be a turning point for the BJP's political decline.

The anti-Muslim pogrom of 2002 in Gujarat reminds us that the success of a state-nation is contingent on continuous political practices. Creating a state-nation is not a one-shot affair but a continual effort. It also reminds us that what is made can also be unmade. As in the case of nation-states, a state-nation is also a politically imagined community that needs to be sustained through continuous contestation and re-creation in the realm of ideas, institutions, and political practices.

CHAPTER THREE

Four Indian Cases That Challenge State-Nation Theory?

In the last chapter we produced substantial aggregate evidence of public opinion that we believe supports the state-nation model. But have we neglected salient failures, which, if examined carefully, would present inconvenient facts for state-nation theory? We hope that others will submit our theory to full-blown analytic tests. Here, however, we want to meet this fair objection by taking a preliminary look at four of the most difficult cases that challenge the project of state-nation in India: the crisis that erupted in the state of Punjab in the 1980s; the insurgencies in the northeastern hill states of Mizoram and Nagaland, which had similar beginnings but ended very differently; and the well-known case of the ongoing separatist struggle in the Kashmir Valley. These cases also bring in different aspects of the difficulties encountered by the Indian state in reconciling its diversity: the Punjab crisis had a religious dimension, Nagaland and Mizoram involved communities that were not an integral part of the civilizational history invoked by the Indian state, and Kashmir is part of an international dispute. Each of these cases allows us to examine different aspects of our argument.

Let us begin by acknowledging some unpleasant facts. From 1980 to 1995, more than twenty thousand deaths occurred in the Punjab in the violence by and against Sikh militant groups demanding an independent country of Khalistan. In the northeast of India, the non-Hindi-speaking, Christian-majority tribal territories of Nagaland and Mizoram have witnessed protracted civil wars waged against the Indian state. The Mizos fought their own war of independence against India for twenty years before there was a lasting peace accord; in Nagaland,

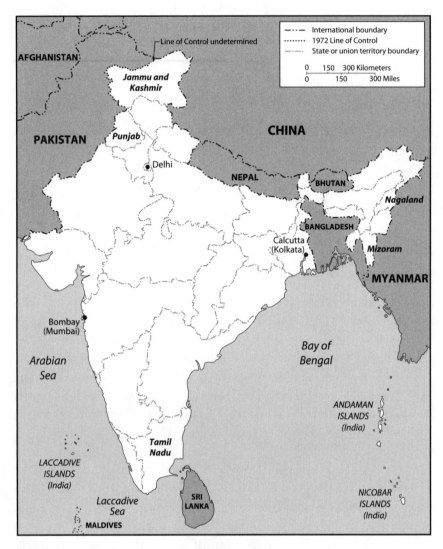

Figure 3.1. Map of India with Contested Peripheral States

insurgent groups have been fighting for independence for sixty years, with no victory or peace in sight. The presence of armed forces in the Valley of Kashmir, the heart of the state of Jammu and Kashmir, is one of the most embarrassing facts for any democrat in India. The stability of Jammu and Kashmir has been impeded by the unfulfilled UN Security Council resolution for a plebiscite to determine its status vis-à-vis conflicting Indian and Pakistani claims of sovereignty, long periods of formal and informal central government rule by Delhi, insurgencies, popular protests, and three wars between India and Pakistan. As the reader can see in figure 3.1, these four cases involve four states on the periphery of India.

This short chapter, of course, cannot do justice to the historical and socio-logical complexities of these cases. Our goal is much more limited. What do these cases tell us—or not tell us—about the limits of our state-nation model?

THE PUNJAB CRISIS:
WHY DEMOCRATIC BREAKDOWN? WHY REEQUILIBRATION?

The Punjab crisis presents us with the first challenge for our reading of India's democratic experience. Here the crisis refers to a series of political developments in the state of Punjab in the 1980s and 1990s that brought the constitutional order within the state to a standstill, gave rise to a powerful and violent secessionist movement, and complicated the relationship of the Sikh minority with the Indian union both inside and outside the state of the Punjab. The resolution of the crisis after 1996, as sudden and surprising as its onset in the 1980s, raises two sets of largely unanswered questions about what caused the disequilibrium and what led to the reequilibrium. First, did the Punjab crisis represent a failure of the state-nation model to accommodate diversity and democracy? How intractable were relations between Sikhs and the Indian political system in the late 1970s? Were state-nation policies increasingly being rejected by the 1970s? Second, was the reequilibrium after 1996 only the result of the effective application of the over-whelming coercive resources of the Indian state, a state to which the Sikhs are not reconciled? If the answer to one or both of these questions is yes, major reserva-tions about the state-nation model would seem legitimate. Let us find out.

By 1980 the Sikh community, a religious minority comprising less than 2% of the country's population but nearly a two-thirds majority within the state of the Punjab, had in many ways done well in independent India: Sikhs were economically better off than the rest of India, were educationally more advanced, enjoyed historical overrepresentation in the armed forces, and had a fair political representation.[1]

---

1. Indeed, Paul R. Brass, in his authoritative article written during the height of the Punjab crisis, argues that Sikh economic resentment toward the policies of the Indian federation was hard to see as a full explanation for the secessionist movement, because legitimate grievances of a federal nature concerning the location of the capital and the division of river waters notwithstanding, "on the great majority of aggregate economic indicators, Punjab is at the top of or very close to the top in comparison with all other Indian states. Moreover, per capita plan expenditures have been consis-tently higher in Punjab than in every other major Indian state for the last twenty years." See Brass, "Socioeconomic Aspects of the Punjab Crisis," in his *Ethnicity and Nationalism: Theory and Com-parison* (London: Sage, 1991), p. 229.

The overwhelming majority of Sikhs speak Punjabi. The massive transfer of population at the time of Partition meant that the Indian state of the Punjab became a Hindu-majority province with Sikhs as the major minority and virtually no Muslims. The Akali Dal, the major religio-political formation of the Sikhs since the 1920s, found itself at a permanent disadvantage vis-à-vis its main rival, the Congress Party, which drew its support from both communities. Citing the Indian federal principle of linguistic states accepted by the State Reorganisation Commission, the Sikh leadership increasingly mobilized for a Punjabi-speaking state, which would reduce the state in size and make it a Sikh-majority state. Nehru's prevarication on this issue—he suspected that the demand for "Punjabi suba" (a Punjabi-speaking state) was a ploy for carving out a Sikh religious majority state— delayed the formation of Punjabi-speaking state by a decade, while other linguistic states were formed earlier, leading to powerful and successful agitation and residual grievances among the Sikhs. The formation of the Punjabi-speaking and Sikh-majority state in 1966 assuaged the sense of hurt among the Sikhs and was consistent with the linguistic reorganization of India territory that was a part of the state-nation formula. This formula helped the Akali Dal to lead coalition governments in the Punjab three times before 1980.

The Akali Dal won a near-majority in the state legislative elections of 1977 and originally formed an "oversized" ruling coalition with two polity-wide parties, the Janata Party (dominated in the Punjab by the erstwhile Hindu right-wing party Jan Sangh) and the secular Communist Party of India (Marxist). The Akalis and the Janata Party were already partners in the first non-Congress government at the center, with Akali leader Prakash Singh Badal as the agricultural minister. Despite a history of intra-factional Sikh infighting, the Akali Dal was thus beginning to develop as a "centric-regional party" consistent with state-nation theory. The moderate and state-nation qualities of Sikh politics increased under the leadership of Prakash Singh Badal, who assumed the position of chief minister of the Punjab after the state assembly elections in 1977. His government was dismissed in 1980 when Indira Gandhi's Congress Party came back to power at the center following the collapse of Janata Party government. While this was done to most of the non-Congress governments, Indira Gandhi held a particular grudge against the Akalis, who had played a vital role in organizing resistance against the Emergency, the semi-authoritarian rule decreed by Indira Gandhi from June 1975 to March 1977.

It is important to reflect on this historical juncture, for this was the unlikely context of the rise of the Punjab crisis. In 1973 the Working Committee of the Akali Dal had passed the ambiguously worded Anandpur Sahib Resolution, which was interpreted by some, especially by Indira Gandhi and her close associates, as having secessionist overtones. However, Badal ensured that the original and controversial resolution was substantially diluted in 1978 by the full vote of a larger body, the 18th All India Akali Dal Conference. The 1978 version of the Anandpur Sahib Resolution, unlike the 1973 resolution, was actually approved by a vote of the full conference and was devoid of any secessionist overtones. It was a clear appeal for better federal relations in the context of the Indian constitution: "Akali Dal realizes that India is a federal and republican geographic entity of different languages, religions and cultures. To safeguard the fundamental rights of the religious and linguistic minorities to fulfill the demands of the democratic traditions and to pave the way for economic progress, it has become imperative that the Indian constitutional infrastructure should be given a real federal shape by redefining the Central and State relations and Rights on the lines of the aforesaid principles and objectives."[2]

Under Badal's leadership, the Akali Dal had contested, and won, the 1979 elections for the control of the most important and wealthy Sikh religious and social organization, the Shiromini Gurudwara Prabandhak Committee (SGPC), against some more militant Sikhs such as groups associated with Bhindranwale. Indeed, the Akali Dal claimed its victory to be "a verdict against the extremists who were trying to create communal tension in Punjab."[3]

Thus, immediately before the bloody crisis broke out in the Punjab, the two most representative political and religious organizations of the Sikhs in the Punjab, the Akali Dal and the SGPC, were firmly under the control of moderates, and the Punjab as a state in the Indian federation was functioning reasonably well in state-nation terms.

Why, then, was the Punjab in a bloody secessionist crisis within three years? In the judgment of Paul Brass, "Relentless centralization and ruthless, unprincipled intervention by the center in state politics have been the primary causes of the trouble in the Punjab . . . since Mrs. Gandhi's rise to power" in 1980.[4] Fair-minded academic histories of the period, such as that by Harish Puri et al., advance a similar argument. Immediately after discussing the growing triumphs of Badal's

2. The text of the Anandpur Sahib Resolution is reprinted as appendix 1 in Devinder Singh, *Akali Politics in Punjab (1964–1985)* (New Delhi: Anupreet Marwah Publishers, 1993), pp. 225–232. The above quotation is from Resolution One, p. 235.

3. Harish Puri, Paramjit Singh Judge, Jagrup Singh Sekhon, *Terrorism in Punjab: Understanding Grassroots Reality* (New Delhi, India: Har-Anand Publications, 1999), pp. 37–38, quotation from p. 8.

4. See the excellent chapter "The Punjab Crisis and the Unity of India" in his *Ethnicity and Nationalism*, quotation p. 210.

moderate form of Sikh politics, they assert that "the scales were, however, tilted against the Akali Dal after the return of Indira Gandhi's Congress to power at the Centre in 1980 [and] the immediate dismissal of the Badal government in Punjab (by a blatant abuse of Article 356)."[5] Direct rule by the center and the dismissal of a democratic majority government in a state with a minority population in themselves erode the multiple but complementary identities and state-nation sentiments.

Worse, there is substantial evidence that Indira Gandhi not only dismissed the moderate Akali government but also extended covert support to the extremist leadership represented by Sikh militant Sant Bhindranwale so as to divide and discredit moderate Sikh leaders and to prepare the way for political dominance by her Congress Party against the faction-ridden Akali Dal. Brass argues that "the involvement of Sanjay Gandhi in the recruitment of Bhindranwale also meant that that criminal actions, manipulation of the police and the judiciary, and the use of violence were considered acceptable tactics by Congressmen, by the police, and by its allies to defeat and discredit the Akali Dal."[6]

This is when the Punjab crisis erupted. Dislodged from power in 1980, the Akali Dal launched an agitation that combined routine regional demands like more power to states within the Indian union and a greater share of river water distribution with some religious demands of the Sikh community. Sensing an opportunity to disable their opponents for a long time to come, the Congress leadership actively encouraged a militant faction within Sikh politics so as to displace the moderate leadership of the Akali Dal. The game initiated by the ruling party soon took on a life of its own, and the militant faction took to arms. Thus ensued a deadly game of competitive extremism in Sikh politics, resulting in the rise of armed militant groups, many under the influence of Bhindranwale, who managed to take control of the most sacred Sikh holy shrine, the Golden Temple in Amritsar. The government of India responded in June 1984 with "Operation Bluestar," in which the army entered the Golden temple with tanks and eliminated the militants. This action was perceived by ordinary Sikhs as an attack on their faith. In a retaliatory action, the Sikh bodyguards of Prime Minister Indira Gandhi assassinated her in November 1984. The next few days saw a massacre of thousands of Sikhs in Delhi and some other cities, with the connivance of police

5. Puri et al., *Terrorism in Punjab*, p. 38.
6. Brass, "The Punjab Crisis and the Unity of India," p. 179. Among many other violations of democratic procedures by the democratic incumbents at the center was their interference in the judiciary process so as to inhibit the trial of Bhindranwale on a murder charge. See the well-documented section "Congress Support for Bhindranwale," ibid., pp. 190–193.

and state machinery at that time and an absence of any action against the guilty thereafter.[7]

This turn of events spawned a full-blown militancy. Ordinary Sikhs felt deeply alienated, and several militant and terrorist groups sprang up to demand the creation of Khalistan, which would be a Sikh homeland. The Khalistan movement did not enjoy great popular support but was powerful enough to split Akali Dal and sideline the moderate Sikh leadership, disrupt regular constitutional government, and render worthless a major agreement between the government of India and Sant Longowal, an important moderate Akali Dal leader, in 1985. Attempts to lodge a popularly elected Akali Dal government failed in the face of rising political violence in the state by the armed militants. The next five years saw the breakdown of constitutional order, an imposition of central rule in the state, large-scale terrorist violence, and an increasingly violent and undemocratic response by the armed forces.

As the battle between the militants and the state reached a stalemate, a Congress government was put in place in 1992 through a dubious election that was boycotted by the Akali Dal and a vast majority of Sikhs.[8] This "popular" government presided over some very heavy repression by the security forces, including a large number of extrajudicial killings of suspected militants. The militant movement could not stand this repression.[9]

This is when the Congress lost power at the center in the parliamentary elections held in 1996. The new political context encouraged the moderate Sikh leaders to participate in the next state assembly elections held in 1997, which produced an Akali-led government. By 1998 Punjabi politics seemed to have reequilibrated. At the height of the crisis, there were a thousand or more violent deaths every year for several years in a row. But from 1998 to 2008, according to figure 3.2, only thirty-one deaths occurred; indeed in seven of those years, there were zero violent deaths.

---

7. For a comprehensive documentation of the legal records concerning the massacre and the court proceedings, see Manoj Mitta and H. S. Phoolka, *When a Tree Shook Delhi: The 1984 Carnage and Its Aftermath* (New Delhi: Roli Books, 2007).

8. An analysis of the electoral turnout in this election by Yogendra Yadav confirmed that there was a direct and negative relationship between electoral turnout and the proportion of non-Dalit Sikhs among the electorate. See Yogendra Yadav, "Who Won in Punjab: Of the Real Contest," *Frontline* (India), vol. 10, April 1992, pp. 122–126.

9. This was meticulously documented by Ram Narayan Kumar, Amrik Singh, Ashok Agrwaal, and Jaskaran Kaur in *Reduced to Ashes: The Insurgency and Human Rights in Punjab* (New Delhi: South Asia Forum for Human Rights, 2003), available at www.punjabjustice.org. Interestingly, the Akali Dal–led government that came to power after reequilibration in the state refused to order a fair investigation into these gross violations of human rights under the Congress regime, much to the chagrin of human rights groups.

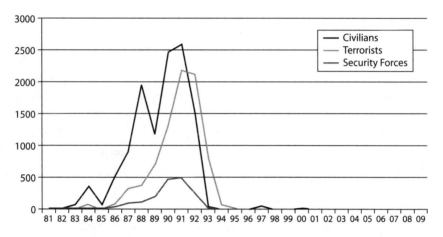

Figure 3.2. Annual Casualties in Terrorist-Related Violence in Punjab, 1981–2009
Source: The South Asia Intelligence Review's South Asia Terrorism Portal, available at
www.satp.org/satporgtp/countries/india/states/punjab/data_sheets/annual_casualties.htm.

The rapidity of the reequilibrium took everyone by surprise, just as the onset of crisis had about fifteen years earlier. This brings us to another of the major questions about the Punjab crisis. Why such rapid equilibrium? Was it a pyrrhic victory for Indian democracy? Certainly a crucial factor for the defeat of the Khalistan movement in the Punjab was India's useable state coercive apparatus. As we have argued, for most would-be separatists in India, in sharp contrast to the situation in the U.S.S.R. or Yugoslavia, the loyalty of the security forces to the central state and the state-nation is a given, as is the certainty that force will be met with greater force. Geopolitically speaking, there is no exit. The end of insurgency in the Punjab was no doubt made possible by massive, undemocratic, and often unconstitutional use of state repression. But the use of coercive apparatus succeeded in the Punjab in a way it did not in states like Nagaland, because the Indian state and its institutions enjoyed a certain legitimacy in the eyes of the people of the Punjab. This is why the Khalistan movement never enjoyed widespread popular support among the Sikhs. This is what made a return to normal politics so quick and complete.

The insurgents may have been defeated, but at what cost to the legitimacy of the Indian state? Do Sikhs believe that the methods used by the armed separatists were legitimate and that the tactics used by the Indian state, especially the Punjab police, were illegitimate? If so, there could still be a serious problem of political identities in the Punjab for India. The base for an insurgency, or at least a series of

TABLE 3.1

Rejection of Pro-Khalistan Violence by the Sikh Community: Attitudes toward Methods Used by the Militants and Punjab Police in the Punjab by Religion, 1997

Response	Opinion about the methods used by the Pro-Khalistan militants		Opinion about the methods used by Punjab police to suppress pro-Khalistan militants	
	Sikh	Hindu	Sikh	Hindu
"Justified"	5%	4%	27%	41%
"Somewhat justified"	21	12	33	36
"Not justified"	66	77	30	14
"Can't say/do not know"	8	7	10	10
(N)	(3,138)	(1,628)	(3,138)	(1,628)

Source: CSDS Data Unit, *Punjab State Assembly Elections Study, Exit Poll,* 1997.

Note: Responses to the following questions: "Do you believe that the means used by the Kharku [self-description of the pro-Khalistan militants] to fulfill their objectives were justified or not?" and "Do you believe that the means used by the Punjab Police to deal with the Kharku were justified or not?"

Four years after the poll referred to in this table, a similar battery of questions was asked after the Punjab State Assembly elections of 2002. The same pattern of responses was repeated—except for an even stronger rejection of the methods used by the pro-Khalistan militants. In the 1998 Indian NES "post-poll study," more respondents in Punjab than in any other state said that life and property were safer now than five years ago.

Percentages may not add up to 100 due to rounding.

disloyal violent activities that may weaken democracy in the future, might still be there.

Fortunately, we can begin to answer this fundamental question due to an unusually large exit poll with a sample of 4,950 randomly selected respondents for the Punjab State Assembly Elections of 1997. In answer to the question "Do you believe that the means used by the Kharku [a word coined by the Khalistan militants to describe themselves] to fulfill their objectives were justified or not?" for every Sikh who answered "justified" (5%) there were more than twelve (66%) among the Sikhs—whose independence was being sought, remember—who answered "not justified." Concerning the appropriateness of the (often quite violent) methods of the Punjab police to counter the Kharku, 27% of Sikhs said that the methods used by the police were "justified," 33% said "somewhat justified," and only 30% answered "not justified" (see table 3.1).

Was military victory alone the key to the reequilibration? Do Sikhs deeply distrust the center despite the "peace"? Or did the reestablishment of normal politics in the context of the unimpeded operation of state-nation mechanisms contribute to a democratic reequilibration?

The evidence seems to indicate that return of normal state-nation politics played an important role in itself. The assembly election of 1997 saw a very high popular turnout, 68.7% as compared to 23.8% in 1992; the moderate faction of Akali Dal swept the polls in alliance with the BJP, which represented the Hindu voters. Prakash Singh Badal, now an old but still a moderate Akali leader, again became chief minister of the state. Subsequent political developments have underlined the restoration of normal politics. Political (as opposed to ethnic) issues so dominated the 2002 elections that the Congress Party, which many thought would never hold office again in the Punjab, won control of the State Assembly, and the Congress Party leader in the Punjab became chief minister of the state. The Congress lost to the Akali Dal-BJP combination first in the parliamentary elections of 2004 and then in the 2007 assembly elections.[10] The trend was reversed again in the parliamentary elections in 2009, as the Congress rebounded in the state.

Since 2002, the political competition between the two rivals has become very close and intense, with no party assured of a unified vote from any social group. The Akali Dal has been a stable ally of the BJP-led National Democratic Alliance and participated in the BJP-led governments at the center from 1998 to 2004. Though it has continued with its anti-Congress and anti-center political rhetoric, any extreme posturing by the Akali Dal has been tempered by the identity, since 2004, of the prime minister of the Congress-led government at the center: Manmohan Singh, himself a Sikh. By successful participation in the fruits of Indian federal politics, both on the state level and at the center, the Akali Dal was clearly a "centric-regional party" as opposed to a regional party with separatist leanings. This has had a deep impact on the inter-religious conflict within the state. Hindu-Sikh strife has been pushed to the background, as the only notable religious strife in the Punjab now involves the mainstream Sikhs taking on certain heterodox *deras* (sects) within the Sikh religion.

Many analysts doubted that the Sikhs could ever trust the federal government at the center after the repressive policies undertaken during the crisis. To be sure, there are many bitter memories, accentuated by the absence of a serious trial for the perpetrators of the 1984 Sikh massacre in Delhi. However, the 2009 National

---

10. Various surveys by the CSDS show that Congress assembly election vote share among the Jat Sikhs, the community at the heart of Sikh militancy, went up steadily from 16% in 1997 to 23% in 2002 to 31% in 2007. The gap between the Akali and the Congress vote share among this community has steadily come down from 49 points in 1997 to only 24 points in 2007, thus indicating a decline in social polarization. Full details of these and other CSDS surveys are available at www.csds.in/questionnairebank.html#NES.

Election Study revealed that 63% of those polled in the Punjab expressed a "great deal" or "some" trust in the central government, which, as the reader will remember, is substantially above the average level of trust in central government among the eleven longstanding federations documented in table 2.9.

To conclude our discussion: Was the Punjab crisis evidence of the failure of the state-nation model in India? The evidence suggests that state-nation politics were functioning reasonably well until 1980. The Punjab crisis was akin to a "democratic breakdown" familiar to students of comparative democratic theory, except that it did not involve the entire system. This sub-system breakdown, like most democratic breakdowns, was neither inevitable nor irreversible.[11] This was one of the many instances in which a democratic regime subverts its own system. In the Punjab democratic incumbents at the center contributed to the collapse of the emerging state-nation democratic political game, which led to the loss of popular legitimacy in the Punjab. The cause of this state-induced crisis must be sought in politics itself, specifically in the failure of the political elite at the center to allow a moderate minority to rule peacefully. The breakdown in the Punjab was not due to the inability of state-nation policies to manage diversity democratically but rather to the central government's gross violation of state-nation policies. Indeed, in our introduction to the theory of state-nation, we argued that a fundamental principle necessary for the smooth functioning of a state-nation is what the Germans call *Bundestreue* (loyalty to the federation). The prime minister of India, Indira Gandhi, by her policies towards the Punjab, deeply violated *Bundestreue*.

The defeat of the insurgency was due to the overwhelming use of force by the center. But the democratic reequilibration we have just documented was made possible by a change in political context. State-nation politics were allowed to generate governments and policies, and state-nation principles and practices were re-embraced by former enemies with renewed commitment. The fifteen years of the Punjab crisis had taught the political leadership on both sides lessons in moderation: the tired Akali leaders were acutely aware of the costs of remaining outside the system, while the new generation of Congress leadership was less interventionist in non-Congress-led states. More important, the political climate in this "post-Congress polity" was more conducive to power-sharing. The Supreme Court had stepped in to prevent the frequent misuse of the emergency provisions of the constitution by the central government to dismiss inconvenient state governments. Congress was no longer the natural party of governance at the center—there

---

11. See Linz and Stepan, eds., *The Breakdown of Democratic Regimes* (Baltimore: Johns Hopkins University Press, 1978), preface, esp. p. ix.

was enough room in the new coalition arrangements for everyone. The Akalis entered into a stable coalition with the BJP both at the center and the state. Instead of the danger of permanently being in opposition, the Akali Dal is now quite regularly in power, either in the state or at the center. The critical elections of 1996, 1997, 2002, and 2007 were largely devoid of "ethnic outbidding"; indeed, Akali and Congress politicians alike frequently spoke of the need for "peace outbidding."

SEPARATIST INSURGENCY IN THE NORTHEAST: WHY PEACE IN MIZORAM AND NOT IN NAGALAND?

The history of separatist struggles in the two northeastern states of Mizoram and Nagaland offers an instructive contrast about the success of and limits to the state-nation policy followed in India.[12] Secessionism in Mizoram came to an end with an accord in 1986; today, the state is arguably the most peaceful state in the northeast. However, Naga insurgency has continued for more than sixty years. The contrast invites us to think about the conditions that led to the rise of the insurgency in both of these states and the factors that led to the resolution in Mizoram but not in Nagaland. Were these insurgencies linked to the failure of the state-nation model? Did this model contribute to the resolution in Mizoram? If so, why did it not work in Nagaland?

Mizoram and Nagaland are examples of politically activated, territorially concentrated sociocultural groupings of people that would seem extremely difficult to reconcile with membership in a nation-state community if the prevailing criterion was a common culture with India. Less than 3% of the population in Nagaland and less than 2% in Mizoram speak Hindi, the most common language in India. The population in both the states is predominantly Christian—87% in Mizoram and 90% in Nagaland. The Hindus, who comprise 81% of the rest of India's population, are a microscopic minority in both of these states. Scheduled Tribes in the rest of India represent only 8% of the population—but 95% of the population in Mizoram and 88% in Nagaland.[13]

Earlier in chapter 2 we documented that most Indians shared some civilizational identities despite significant cultural differences. Further, most parts of British India developed, via their involvement with the Congress-led Independence

12. For a detailed listing of all the insurgent groups operating in India's northeast, see South Asian Terrorism Portal at www.satp.org.

13. All demographic details are from *Census of India, 2001*, Office of The Registrar General of Census. Available at www.censusindia.gov.in/Census_Data_2001/Census_Data_Online/, accessed July 13, 2009.

movement, some identification with Indian political nationalism. But Mizoram and Nagaland did not really share civilizational identities or Congress-led anti-colonial experiences with the rest of India.

In historical, cultural, and political terms, both Mizoram and Nagaland had weak links with the rest of India. Both states constituted relatively isolated territories with limited contacts with India and Myanmar, and both were never fully integrated into any of the premodern empires.[14] They became a part of the Indian union essentially because these territories were annexed into British India toward the very end of the nineteenth century. Yet the colonial rulers, conscious of the difficulties of integrating these areas, imposed control very lightly, infrequently, and indirectly. The experience of limited franchise under the Government of India Act 1935 was denied to these areas, as these were "excluded areas" directly administered by the non-elected governor of Assam. Indeed, movement into these areas by India-wide organizations like the Congress Party was forbidden because of their "inner line" status, which in British colonial theory was supposed to leave these tribal societies untouched by outsiders. The anticolonial struggle thus had little resonance in these areas. A combination of demographic profile and political history ensured that the self-description of being an Indian did not come naturally to a Naga or a Mizo.[15] If anything, greater internal homogeneity and higher literacy in Mizoram made it a better candidate for successful separatism. Yet, since 1986 Mizoram has functioned as an integrated part of the Indian political community and accords legitimacy to Indian democracy. We will first examine how this happened for Mizoram and then attempt to analyze why this has not yet happened in Nagaland.

Mizoram

At Independence in 1947, the status of Mizoram was a subject of great confusion. The constitution assigned Mizoram to the state of Assam in India. However, aware that some tribal groups in the northeast might want to retain many of their

---

14. For an insider's account of Naga history, see M. Alemchiba, *A Brief Historical Account of Nagaland* (Kohima, India: Naga Institute of Culture, 1970). On Mizoram, see A. G. McCall, *Lushei Chrysalis* (London: Luzac, 1949).

15. Nehru acknowledged this in the case of Nagaland in a confidential letter to the chief minister of Assam: "I feel that we have not dealt with this question of the Nagas with wisdom in the past. We must not judge them as we would others who are undoubtedly part of India. The Nagas have no such background or sensation and we have to create that sensation among them by our goodwill and treatment." Secret and Personal Letter dated May 13, 1956, to B. R. Medhi, chief minister, Assam. Reproduced in Sanjoy Hazarika, *Strangers of the Mist: Tales of War and Peace from India's Northeast* (London: Penguin, 1994), p. 360.

traditional practices and norms, the drafters of the Indian constitution created from the beginning the possibility that some indigenous cultures within certain federal states would be allowed to make some special laws to protect their culture, such as not allowing nonmembers of the indigenous group to vote in local elections or to purchase land. The drafters were thus alive to the challenge of radical difference posed by areas such as Mizoram. The Constituent Assembly appointed a special subcommittee on the Tribal and Excluded Areas of the North East Frontier headed by G. N. Bordoloi, a Congress member from Assam who had empathy for and knowledge of the tribes in the northeast. This subcommittee drafted the special provisions of the Sixth Schedule of the constitution. As per the recommendations of the subcommittee, duly incorporated in the constitution, Mizoram was given the status of an Autonomous District within the state of Assam. This status granted a state a good deal of leeway in determining its own practices, especially in dealing with "customary" matters under the partially democratically elected district council.

Nonetheless, on Indian Independence Day, there was still much confusion about whether Mizos were free to join Pakistan or Burma—as well as ambivalence about what kind of relationship they would have with India if they became part of India. A resolution passed by a meeting of Lushei Hills (the older name for today's Mizoram) chieftains and other prominent citizens under the chairmanship of the district superintendent on August 14, 1947, urged the governor of Assam to inform them "whether the Lusheis are at this stage allowed the option of joining any other Dominion, i.e., Pakistan or Burma." In the event that they were to enter the Indian Union, the resolution demanded that "the Lusheis will be allowed to opt out of the Indian Union when they wish to do so subject to a minimum period of ten years."[16]

The turning point in the relationship between Mizoram and India came with the great famine of 1958–59 and the failure of the state of Assam and the government of India to respond properly.[17] The Mizo National Famine Front, initially a nonpolitical body formed in 1959 to provide relief and organize public action, was converted in 1962 into the Mizo National Front, a political party, as Pu Laldenga, a former government employee, rose to become its leader. After an inauspicious beginning in the 1962 elections, the MNF tasted success in the assembly by-

16. Cited in B. B. Goswami, *The Mizo Unrest: A Study of Politicisation of Culture* (Jaipur: Aalekh Publishers, 1979), pp. 134–135.

17. For a detailed account and critique of the official response first to the famine and then to the MNF-led insurgency in Mizoran, see Amritha Rangasami, "Mizoram: Tragedy of Our Own Making," *Economic and Political Weekly* 13, no. 15, April 15, 1978, pp. 653–662.

elections of 1963. Then followed a rapid turn of events: MNF demanded the dismissal of the district council leadership but did not succeed; a split within the MNF put pressure on the leadership to go for an openly secessionist plank, and the Assam Congress leaders tried to play the MNF against its electoral opponent for district council leadership, the Mizoram Union.[18] By the end of 1965, this sequence of events culminated in the MNF declaring the formation of a parallel government under the leadership of Pu Laldenga.

The Mizo insurgency began in 1965. With arms largely obtained in neighboring East Pakistan, "Laldenga stuck simultaneously at several places with Operation Jerico. Well-trained guerrillas overran Aizawl [the administrative center of Mizoram]: the Treasury, the radio station and the police station fell into their hands. Lungleh, the other major town was also swamped and the guerrillas had the run of the district."[19] The Indian Defense Ministry responded massively: "Air raids were ordered for the first time in free India's history" against domestic opponents.[20] Taking a page out of the U.S. "strategic hamlet" counterinsurgency tactics in Vietnam, the Home Ministry in Delhi "ordered the regrouping of villages into virtual concentration camps by security troops."[21] The Mizo National Army, the militant wing of the MNF, used guerrilla tactics in the hilly terrain to hold Indian armed forces but could not make dramatic advances, especially after it lost its secure base and source of supply in neighboring East Pakistan, when, with great help from India, East Pakistan seceded from Pakistan in 1971.[22] In 1975 and 1977 some key MNF fighters surrendered.

This was the time when formal negotiations with the government of India began but did not succeed. The legitimate political wing of the MNF split, yet the more unified underground organization controlled by Laldenga was still powerful enough to extract "taxes" and organize guerrilla raids. However, key actors in the MNF and the Indian government increasingly saw that the situation was what is now called in the literature a "mutually hurting stalemate"—that is, a situation in which neither side can be completely beaten, nor completely win.[23]

18. This period between the formation of MNF and the formation of parallel government in Mizoram's political history needs more research, for this could be another case of "democratic breakdown" within a sub-system. This account draws from evidence in Goswani (n. 16), pp. 139–156.

19. Hazarika, *Strangers of the Mist*, p. 113.

20. Ibid.

21. Ibid.

22. Ibid, p. 117.

23. See, for example, William I. Zartman, "The Timing of Peace Initiatives: Hurting Stalemates and Ripe Moments," *Global Review of Ethnopolitics* 1, no. 1 (2001), pp. 8–18. In chapter 7, where we offer a new theory of federacy, we document how a "hurting stalemate" played an important role in the 2005 federacy solution that ended a civil war in Aceh, Indonesia.

How and why did this "mutually hurting stalemate" end? Why did an enduring peace emerge? The historic Mizoram Accord of 1986 utilized almost every possible state-nation policy available and created some new ones. Both the Mizos and India fully accept and honor this agreement.

The long history of armed insurgency and state repression was brought to an end in the Mizoram Accord between the MNF, represented by Laldenga, and the government of India on June 30, 1986.[24] Negotiations between the two parties took well over a decade. There was an earlier accord in 1975 that involved a smaller faction of the MNF. Yet Laldenga and his band of loyal supporters remained underground. The government of India agreed to give Mizoram the status of a full-fledged state with a special provision to safeguard its autonomy. This special provision, later incorporated in the constitution as Article 371(g), stated: "Notwithstanding anything contained in the Constitution, no act of Parliament in respect of (a) Religion or Social practices of the Mizos, (b) Mizo customary Law or procedure, (c) Administration of Civil and Criminal Justice involving decisions according to Mizo customary Law, (d) Ownership and transfer of land, shall apply to the State of Mizoram unless the Legislative Assembly of Mizoram by a resolution so decides." The center also agreed not to amend or repeal "inner line" regulation without consulting the Mizoram government. There was also a co-signed written agreement five days *before* the accord between the Congress Party and the MNF that Congress, then in power in the state, would allow Laldenga to take over as interim chief minister pending a regular election.[25] For at least two years before this Mizoram Accord, the major civil society groups in Mizoram, especially the church groups, had been pressing Congress, MNF, and the government of India to reach a peace settlement. Thus, the two major groups in political society and the most important group in civil society, the church, were united behind ending the insurgency and crafting an enduring peace. The government of India did not concede any ground on the demand for unification of "Mizo-inhabited areas" in other states like Manipur, and the MNF agreed to shelve this issue.

In return, the MNF agreed to cease hostilities, to "bring out all the underground personnel of MNF with their arms, ammunitions and equipments," to stop supporting other insurgent groups in the northeast, to amend its own consti-

---

24. The text of the accord used here is from www.satp.org/satporgtp/countries/india/states/mizoram/documents/papers/mizoram_accord_1986.htm, accessed July 10, 2009

25. A copy of this agreement, dated July 25, 1986, was given to Stepan in January 2003 by Lal Thanhawla, the Congress chief minister at the time of the accord (he later stepped down but then became the chief minister of Mizoram again in 2008). Laldenga signed the agreement, which stated, "Sri Laldenga has pledged to bring the M.N.F. into the mainstream of the India polity and to irrevocably commit himself to strive for a strong and united India."

tution in accordance with the constitution of India, and to drop the demand for a separate sovereign state of Mizoram.

The Mizoram Accord was followed by an institutionalization of the routines of democratic politics—with surprising success. Within a few months of the accord, the necessary constitutional amendments were enacted. The incumbent chief minister from Congress, true to his word, stepped down to make way for Laldenga to become the interim chief minister. In 1987 Mizoram became a full state, and the MNF won the first election to the state legislative assembly. The MNF government did not survive long and lost to Congress in the midterm election of 1989. Since then, the state has had regular elections and transfers of power: Congress won in 1993; the MNF came back to power in 1998 and retained it in 2003 but lost to Congress again in 2008. Mizoram is one of the most peaceful places in the northeast, notwithstanding small insurgency groups representing the non-Mizo minorities within Mizoram. Laldenga passed away in 1980 and was succeeded as chief minister by his underground colleague Zoramthanga, once the number two in the underground chain of command, who headed two MNF governments and helped some of the neighboring states negotiate with their insurgents.

In an interview with Stepan, Zoramthanga recited, virtually from memory, key passages from the Mizo Accord and the Sixth Schedule. Zoramthanga remarked to Stepan that in effect, Mizoram had all of the benefits of being an independent state and all of the advantages of being a well-treated and well-subsidized member of the Indian federation.[26]

Zoramthanga's opinion is widely shared by his fellow Mizo citizens. CSDS carried out a survey of 1,116 randomly selected electors following the state assembly elections in Mizoram in 2003. The survey findings indicate a surprisingly high level of integration into India's federal democracy: as many as 84% expressed a preference for democracy. Despite the historical lack of a strong link to Indian culture or history, a majority of the respondents included India as constitutive of their identity: only 32% of the respondents identified themselves as "only Mizo." Two-thirds of those who had an opinion supported the Mizoram Accord of 1986, and 76% of those polled supported the special autonomy measures by which only Mizos can vote in local elections and only Mizos can buy land in Mizoram.[27]

But why does the insurgency in Nagaland continue? An analysis of the situa-

---

26. Interview of Stepan with Chief Minister Zoramthanga, Aizawl, January 2003.
27. Mizoram Assembly Election Study 2003, CSDS Data Unit, Center for the Study of Developing Societies, Delhi, India, 2003. Stepan also carried out interviews with both Congress and MNF political leaders in Mizoram in January 2003 and arrived at similar conclusions.

tion there can tell us much about the conditions in which state-nation policies can, and cannot, work. Before we turn to Nagaland, let us summarize the key points from the Mizoram story.

Insurgency and peace are relational concepts. There were five key relationships of Mizoram to the federal government of India involved in the MNF insurgency and the eventual peace. First, there was weak Mizo involvement and identification with the dominant religions and languages of India, together with almost no participation in the politics of pre-British India, British India, or the Congress-led Independence movement. Second, in independent India, major Mizo leaders and many of their followers came to see themselves as a nation that was not being treated well by the government of India and launched insurgency activities for complete independence. Third, the military conflict would have ended if either the government of India or the insurgents had won a decisive victory at any point. Neither outcome happened, so the "mutually hurting stalemate" ensued. Fourth, the government of India made an innovative offer for Mizoram to have a form of extreme asymmetrical federalism with large guarantees of cultural autonomy. Fifth, civil society and political society in Mizoram, led by a united armed underground leader, was sufficiently united to be able to arrive at a self-binding acceptance of the offer; normal state-nation politics rapidly ensued, and peace has endured.

Nagaland

For all intents and purposes, the relationship between Nagaland and India was very similar on the first four factors.[28] However, Nagaland was—and remains—extremely dissimilar on the fifth factor, so the mutually hurting stalemate continues, despite periodic ceasefires since 1997.

---

28. Five valuable sources for Nagaland with some Mizoram comparisons, particularly on the unity or disunity of the insurgent movements and its effect on peace, are: Sanjib Baruah, "Confronting Constructionism: Ending India's Naga War," *Journal of Peace Research* 40, no. 3 (2003), pp. 321–338; H. Srikanth and C. J. Thomas, "Naga Resistance Movement and the Peace Process in Northeast India," *Peace and Democracy in South Asia* 1, no. 2 (2005), pp. 57–87; Leanne C. Tyler, "Common Origins, Divergent Outcomes: A Comparative Analysis of India's Nagaland and Mizoram Wars of Secession," unpublished paper written at the Department of Political Science, Columbia University, May 8, 2009; the chapters on Nagaland and Mizoram in Ved Marwah, *Uncivil Wars: Pathology of Terrorism in India* (New Delhi: Harper Collins, 1995), pp. 224–286; and Hazarika, *Strangers of the Mist*. The most comprehensive and sympathetic, if dated, account of the violations of human rights in Nagaland is Luingam Luithi and Nandita Haksar, *Nagaland File: A Question of Human Rights* (New Delhi: Lancer, 1986). For a fairly detailed account and critique of the official response first to the famine and then to the MNF-led insurgency in Mizoram, see Amritha Rangasami, "Mizoram: Tragedy of Our Own Making," *Economic and Political Weekly*, vol. 13, no. 15, April 15, 1978, pp. 653–662.

Why the difference between successful accord in Mizoram and the continuing stalemate in Nagaland? The main answer is that the Naga leadership has never produced a united insurgent organization. Even dismissing smaller groups, there have always been between anywhere from two to four organizations speaking for the Nagas. In 2005 there were "four Naga militant groups—NNC (Adino), NNC (Panger), NSCN (IM) and NSCN (K)."[29] The NSCN (Isaac-Muivah) faction is the largest group, drawing some of its leaders from Tangkhul Naga tribe, largely based in the state of Manipur. This group is engaged in an internecine war with NSCM (Khaplang), led by Konya Nagas and mainly based in Myanmar. Another group, NSCN (Unification), has also become active since 2007. What this means is that whenever some organizations enter into peace talks with the government of India, a process of "outbidding" rapidly occurs. This occurred around Independence, when "moderate leaders like Aliba Imti and T. Sakhrie who were negotiating basically for greater autonomy within the Indian Union whereas leaders like Phizo gave the clarion call for independence."[30] In 1975 the Shillong Accord was signed by breakaway groups but this led to even greater division and conflict among the Nagas.[31] Inevitably, the insurgent group interested in peace is denounced by the others. In the language of international relations peace theory, Nagaland has multiple militarily credible "spoilers" to any negotiation. This contrasts sharply with the single united negotiator and the absence of "spoilers" in Mizoram.[32]

Why the Nagas are divided needs greater research, but some simple facts stand out: In 2001, 73% of the population in Mizoram spoke the Mizo language, whereas only 13% of the Nagas spoke Ao, the most common language in the state.[33] Furthermore, all of the Mizo military leaders came from the Lushei Hills, so their claims for a "greater Mizoram" to include all the Mizos in neighboring states were bargainable with the government of India.[34] In contrast, the home and base of the most important leader of NSCN (I-M), Th. Muivah, is the neighbor-

29. Srikanth and Thomas, "Naga Resistance Movement," p. 64.

30. Ibid., p. 77. By 1956 groups close to Phizo radically opposed, and were reported to have eventually killed, Sakhrie. This was political difference, not tribal competition. Phizo and Sakhrie were close relatives and both members of the same tribe.

31. Ibid., p. 68.

32. For two articles that discuss "spoilers" or "veto players" in negotiations, see Stephen Stedman, "Spoiler Problems in Peace Processes," *International Security* 22, no. 2 (1997), pp. 5–53; and David Cunningham, "Veto Players and Civil War Duration," *American Journal of Political Science* 50, no. 4 (2006), pp. 875–892.

33. Census of India 2001, www.censusindia.gov.in/Census_Data_2001/Census_Data_Online/, accessed July 13, 2009.

34. See Srikanth and Thomas, "Naga Resistance Movement"; and Baruah, "Confronting Constructionism."

ing state of Manipur. Nagas constitute a small proportion of the population of Manipur but are spread across vast hilly territory in the state, which Muivah claims as Naga homeland. Thus, the leadership is committed to a more rigid negotiating stance than what the population may want.[35] Baruah correctly argues that "the Naga desire for a homeland that would bring together all Nagas into one political unit can come into being only at expense of Manipur, as well as [the states] of Assam and Arunachal Pradesh."[36] Even the hint that the government might negotiate this demand set off prolonged rioting and destruction of state assembly and government offices in Imphal, the capital of Manipur.

In essence, the limits of the use of state-nation policies are that they cannot be utilized in a context that would violate prior state-nation agreements and practices entered into by the central state. The recognition of Naga homeland in Manipur and two other neighboring states would constitute such a violation and would have great costs for India's hard-won—and potentially vulnerable— state-nation gains in Assam and Manipur.

The combination of the "mutually hurting stalemate" and the vast repertoire of potential state-nation policies that might be helpful to the citizens and leaders of Nagaland may eventually yield a peace. However, unlike Mizoram, Nagaland's civil and political societies are divided among maximalists who want something the government of India cannot give without violating internal peace and its own state-nation agreements, and moderates who want the hurting stalemate to end via some agreement with India. A notable scholar of the nation-building process in India, Jyotirindra Dasgupta, reached similar conclusions with the help of a comparison of Assam and Mizoram: "The Northeastern cases actually suggest that proper institutional processing of ethnic demands, including violent ones, can transform 'dangerous enemies' into constructive contributors to the democratic process. However if the national or regional authorities use cynical, unscrupulous or simply unintelligent ways of manipulating ethnicity or insurgency, then the state itself can become an enemy of the democratic system."

35. The National Election Study 2004 by the CSDS included a sample of 522 randomly chosen respondents from Nagaland and was perhaps the first-ever survey of political opinions and attitudes in the state. The survey brought out an unwillingness to accept the Indian identity: about 57% of respondents identified themselves as "only Nagas" as againt 9% "only Indian" and 34 % "Indian and Naga." At the same time, the alienation did not affect attitudes to the peace process: 85% had heard about the negotiations, and two-thirds of those who had an opinion were optimistic of a positive outcome. The survey also revealed a lack of strong support for the hardline agenda of "greater Nagaland" that has blocked the negotiations.
36. For an excellent social science and political discussion of this issue, see Baruah, "Confronting Constructionism," esp. p. 333.

UNRESOLVED STATENESS IN JAMMU AND KASHMIR

In the preface to this book we argued, in effect, that relatively secure "stateness" is crucial for either a democratic nation-state or a democratic state-nation and that both "must be states if they are to work." In this fundamental sense, part of the, to date, unsolvable problem about Jammu and Kashmir is that its stateness has never been internationally recognized, nor peacefully settled between India and Pakistan.

The state of Jammu and Kashmir does not, by itself, present diversities that are any deeper or more challenging than, say, those of Mizoram and Nagaland. Geography, culture, and history tie this region to the rest of India in ways that are deep and well recognized.[37] A complex pattern of cultural ties yet distinctiveness vis-à-vis the rest of India combined with deep yet interconnected internal differences do not, by themselves, make Jammu and Kashmir a case apart from the rest of India, nor do these preexisting conditions, by themselves, account for the Kashmir problem as it stands today.

What makes the problem so very complicated is the complex political history of the state in the last century. Before India's independence, Jammu and Kashmir was a princely state with a Hindu ruler and an overwhelmingly Muslim population. The opposition to the princely rule was led by Sheikh Abdullah, a charismatic Kashmiri leader and a personal friend of Jawaharlal Nehru who transformed the Jammu and Kashmir Muslim Conference into a secular Jammu and Kashmir National Conference, an ally of the Indian National Congress.

In the Partition of India in 1947, Jammu and Kashmir emerged as an internationally disputed territory between India and Pakistan. The principle of accession in the more than five hundred principalities was that the princely ruler was free to decide whether to join India or Pakistan. Presumably, when a state had a Muslim majority and bordered Pakistan it would join that state. However, the

---

37. Jammu and Kashmir comprises three distinct regions—Kashmir, Jammu, and Ladakh—each with very different socio-religious composition. The Kashmir Valley, the largest region at the time of India's partition and at the heart of political alienation, is now almost entirely Muslim and Kashmiri speaking. Over the last three decades, the population of Kashmiri Hindus has come down from about 5% to just 2%. Kashmiri language and Kashmiri cultural identity binds the Muslims and the Hindus in the valley. A predominantly Sufi Islam distinguishes the form of Islam practiced in Kashmir from the rest of the subcontinent and outside. The Jammu region—now as populous as Kashmir—is majority Hindu and speaks many languages and dialects including Hindi. Ladakh is the third and the least known region in the state. A mountainous and scantily populated region with vast territory bordering China whose population at independence was largely Buddhist, Ladakh is now evenly split between Muslims and Buddhists. The region has its own languages, history, and culture.

ruling prince of Jammu and Kashmir, Maharaja Karan Singh, was a Hindu from Jammu and equivocated. But when insurgents with the support of Pakistan threatened his rule, he asked for Indian military support and agreed to accede to India in return. It is important that Sheikh Abdullah was against joining Pakistan. This emboldened the government of the prime minister of India, Jawaharlal Nehru, on December 31, 1947, to send a document to the UN Security Council asking it, in essence, to play a key role in determining the sovereignty of Jammu and Kashmir by holding and authoritatively supervising a plebiscite so that "its people would be free to decide their future by the recognized democratic method of plebiscite or referendum which, in order to ensure complete impartiality, might be held under international auspices." This offer was not totally unconditional. Nehru's offer stated that such a plebiscite should be held "after the soil of the State had been cleared of the invader and normal conditions restored."[38]

The plebiscite was never held by the United Nations, or any other organization, due to controversies and armed conflicts between Pakistan and India and geopolitical complications relating to the Cold War.[39] In this fundamental sense, internationally disputed territory of Jammu and Kashmir was not a state in the way we have defined it in the preface. Jammu and Kashmir was not like any other state in the Indian federation in that not only was the adjudication of its sovereignty in the hands of the United Nations but one third of its territory was also occupied by a neighboring state, Pakistan. Jammu and Kashmir, in relation to the Indian state-nation, from the beginning was therefore different and unique and critically did not conform to the requirements of a state-nation.

To compound the problems of the geopolitical conflict, the government of India again and again violated its own democratic procedures in the state of Jammu and Kashmir. State-nation policies can work only in democratic conditions. The absence of internationally recognized sovereignty constrained India

38. For three well-documented and somewhat different analyses of the international conditions surrounding this conflict over Kashmir and Nehru's invitation to the United Nations, see Gowher Rizvi, "India, Pakistan, and the Kashmir Problem, 1947–1972," Damodar R. Sardesai, "The Origins of Kashmir's International and Legal Status," and Ashutosh Varshney, "Three Compromised Nationalisms: Why Kashmir Has Been a Problem," all in *Perspectives on Kashmir: The Roots of the Conflict in South Asia*, ed. Raju G. C. Thomas (Boulder, CO: Westview Press, 1992), pp. 47–79, 80–92, and 191–234, respectively.

39. In the judgment of one of India's most experienced and distinguished diplomats a major opportunity to hold the plebiscite and possibly end the sovereignty dispute that has contributed to two more wars between India and Pakistan and killings and human rights violations by both countries in Kashmir was lost by the government of India when they insisted that a plebiscite could not be held unless India be allowed to have approximately ten thousand more Indian Army troops on the ground in Kashmir during the plebiscite to compensate for armed groups supported by the Government of Pakistan. Private conversation with Juan Linz and Alfred Stepan.

from exercising the full repertoire of state-nation policies; the absence of democratic conditions in the state for most of post-Independence India did not make for
a context where the citizens could respond to the limited state-nation policies that
were tried out. It is of course a counterfactual, but if India had had uncon-
tested sovereignty, some combination of the solutions applied to the Punjab and
Mizoram could have been applied, enhancing the "we-feeling" with India and
the geopolitical security of the Indian citizens of Kashmir, Jammu, and Ladakh.
Article 370 of the constitution, discussed below, already provided the framework
for a state-nation solution. Undisputed sovereignty and democratic context could
have led to an effective assertion of the autonomy of the state, while safeguarding
the autonomy of the three regions within the state. The Dogri-speaking region
of Jammu in the southern highlands with a Hindu majority and the Tibetan-
speaking region in the former Buddhist kingdom of Ladakh bordering China in
the north could have been given special linguistic and cultural autonomy within
Jammu and Kashmir, along the same lines as the tribal districts within the state of
Assam. If these three cultural regions of Jammu and Kashmir had felt that they
were all securely part of the state-nation of India and allowed to exercise their full
state-nation democratic and cultural prerogatives, the sixty-year tragedy that is the
"Kashmir crisis" may well not have occurred.

Some state-nation principles were nonetheless applied, at least in theory. On
paper, the institutional framework for division of power in India's constitution
appears appropriate for Jammu and Kashmir. Sensitive to the special political
history of the state and keen to retain the only Muslim-majority province in the
Indian union, the framers of India's constitution came up with Article 370, a
unique provision that carried the spirit of asymmetrical federalism to its limits
within the Indian constitutional order. This article, innocuously titled "Temporary provisions with respect to the State of Jammu and Kashmir," granted the state
a special status, different from any other state in the Indian union. It stipulated
that barring defense, communication, and foreign relations, the Indian parliament would not be able to make laws for this state on any subject without the
concurrence of the state government.[40] Jammu and Kashmir was the only Indian

40. The operational part of this article on "Temporary provisions with respect to the State of
Jammu and Kashmir" reads as follows:

(1) Notwithstanding anything in this Constitution,
. . .
(b) the power of Parliament to make laws for the said State shall be limited to,
(i) those matters in the Union List and the Concurrent List which, in consultation with the
Government of the State are declared by the President to correspond to matters specified in the
Instrument of Accession governing the accession of the State to the Dominion of India as the

state to be allowed its own separate constitution, citizenship, and titles of some officials. This provision was sharply opposed by Hindu nationalists; the abolition of Article 370 has remained on their political agenda ever since the constitution was promulgated. The only thing missing from the constitutional provisions was an arrangement to guarantee autonomy for the Jammu and Ladakh regions within the state.

The state-nation approach followed in India meant that there was no attempt to foster one language and one core cultural identity; this was as much true in Jammu and Kashmir as it was elsewhere in India. The Kashmiri language was included as one of the official languages of the Indian union, and in 2003 the Dogri language from the Jammu region was included as well. But the uncertain international status of Kashmir's sovereignty contributed to Nehru authorizing the arrest of Abdullah in 1953 to prevent him from leading a possible secessionist movement in Kashmir. With rare exceptions, Abdullah remained imprisoned until 1968.[41] Since 1953, for long periods of time, the requirements of relative political autonomy that are crucial for state-nation politics were arguably more violated by the center with respect to Jammu and Kashmir than they were for any other state in the Indian union. For more than two decades thereafter, Jammu and Kashmir was governed by puppets of the Congress government in Delhi, who enjoyed little popular legitimacy within the state. During this period, the state legislature ceded to the parliament most of the powers it enjoyed under Article 370. No less than forty-eight presidential orders were issued, with the concurrence of the state government, applying more and more provisions of the constitution to Jammu and Kashmir. The state still has its own citizenship, a requirement for holding land and other property, and its own constitution, but the special status conferred by the constitution, for all practical purposes, no longer exists because it has been so eroded by the central government.

Far from being a state with theoretically exceptional prerogatives and greater autonomy than the rest, Jammu and Kashmir (largely due to its unique status within the Indian federation as the only state subject to international dispute about its sovereignty) actually became *a specially disempowered state* that was practically run by the central government. The period between 1953 and 1974, between Sheikh Abdullah's arrest and his final release after a political settlement

---

matters with respect to which the Dominion Legislature may make laws far that State; and
(ii) such other matters in the said Lists as, with the concurrence of the Government of the State, the President may by order specify.

41. For an excellent account of the deterioration of the relations between Nehru and Abdullah, see Varshney, "Three Compromised Nationalisms," pp. 191–224.

with Indira Gandhi, witnessed a puppet government in Jammu and Kashmir and proxy government by the Congress Party and the central government characterized by pliable chief ministers, state governors functioning as agents of the center, restrictions on the operations of the National Conference, and attempts to break the party. After a partial and short-lived restoration of autonomy following an agreement between Sheikh Abdullah and Prime Minister Indira Gandhi in 1974, the old order was restored in 1983. The National Conference was left with no option but to ally with the Congress in the infamous 1987 election that was widely perceived to have been rigged against the candidates of the Muslim United Front, a coalition of pro-autonomy political forces. This was followed by a rise in militancy and an escalation in violence; the government of India then clamped down and suspended normal political activities and imposed "President's Rule," which means direct rule by the center.

This gross violation of political autonomy could take place only by denial of basic democratic norms and freedoms within the state. It is widely accepted that all of the elections that took place in the state between 1962 and 2002 were rigged, with the exception of the assembly elections held in 1977 and, to some extent, 1983. Electoral fraud in Kashmir took many forms: banning parties and organizations that were not "acceptable," not allowing opposition candidates to file nominations, rejecting their nominations on frivolous grounds, not allowing the opposition to campaign freely, intimidating voters, forcing nonvoters to the polling booths, encouraging multiple voting and mobile voters, stuffing ballots, and falsifying vote counts.[42] Since 1990 there has been an intermittent insurgency, making the Indian Army, backed up by the notorious Armed Forces Special Powers Act promulgated in the area that year, the most salient, and disliked, presence of the government of India in Kashmir.

In a 2009 CSDS survey in Mizoram and the Punjab (after both had been inclusive and peaceful state-nation polities for at least a decade), only 2% of respondents in Mizoram and only 15% in the Punjab said they had "no trust" in the central government. In sharp contrast, nearly two-thirds of the 1,118 people polled in the Kashmir Valley in 2002 said that they had "no trust" in the central government (88% said they had "no trust" in the Indian Army). In the same survey, virtually no one in the Kashmir Valley expressed a preference "to stay with India on present terms," only 8% expressed a preference for becoming "part of

42. For an account of how the 2002 elections in the state were an improvement over the past, see the book authored by former chief election commissioner James Lyngdoh, *The Chronicle of an Impossible Election: The Election Commission and the 2002 Jammu and Kashmir Assembly Elections* (Delhi: Viking India, 2004).

TABLE 3.2

Persistent Alienation in the Kashmir Valley: Public Opinion on Solutions to the Kashmir Problem in the Kashmir Valley, 2002–2008

In the present situation, which of the following is the most suitable option for Kashmir?	2002	2008
"Kashmir on both sides of the border should be merged and become an independent country."	79%	73%
"Kashmir should remain with India with maximum autonomy."	6	16
"Kashmir should remain with India as it is."	1	1
"Kashmir should become a part of Pakistan."	8	2
No opinion	6	8

Source: Jammu and Kashmir Assembly Election Study, 2002 and 2008, post-poll surveys (subsample from Kashmir Valley), CSDS, Delhi with Dept. of Political Science, Univ. of Jammu.

Note: That Jammu and Kashmir as a whole is not a state-nation polity with one overlapping and complementary identity is clear from the responses in the Jammu and Ladakh regions to the same question. In the 2002 survey only 7% of the respondents in the Jammu region and only 2% of the respondents in Ladakh supported the demand for merger of the two Kashmirs and none supported merger with Pakistan.

Pakistan," but a very strong 79% expressed a preference for Kashmir to become an "independent country" (see table 3.2).

The survey data in the Kashmir Valley in 2002 clearly indicate a picture of political alienation, absence of identification with India, and very low trust in some of the key institutions of India. We see this as a failure of international and transnational political processes and of many Indian politicians. However, we do not see this as evidence of the failure of state-nation politics, for two reasons.

First, the "scope conditions" for state-nation politics must be within the territory of an internationally accepted state. Only such a state has the authority to help create and legitimate state-nation structures, practices, and principles. Jammu and Kashmir has never been such a state, so from our theoretical perspective, it is outside the effective scope of the state-nation model.

Second, state-nation policies of the kind advocated here require a democratic political setting. Largely because of its unresolved international "stateness" problem, Jammu and Kashmir has not enjoyed democratic institutions and practices. The minimum conditions of relatively free and fair elections, civil and political rights, and respect for democratically elected state government, which can be taken for granted in the rest of the country, did not obtain in Jammu and Kashmir. Although it was supposed to be the most autonomous part of the Indian federation, as originally laid out in the constitution, Jammu and Kashmir has de facto been one of the least politically autonomous and one of the most centrally controlled states in the Indian federation. Thus, it is less analytically accurate to conclude that state-nation polities have "failed" in Jammu and Kashmir than it is to conclude that they could never be systematically applied because of largely unresolved stateness problems. In fact, Jammu and Kashmir allows us to reject any culturally essentialist argument about the success of the Indian experiment. India's extraordinary success in democratic accommodation of its diversities is a result of establishing institutions and following policies that we call state-nation; when it did not apply this model, the success could not be taken for granted.[43]

43. The case of Jammu and Kashmir also provides us with a temporal variation that can help us test our argument. The political context changed significantly in the state after the assembly election in 2002. This election was widely perceived to be the most free and fair election in the state since 1977. Since then two parliamentary elections and one assembly election have been held in the state, and the practice of largely free and fair elections appears to have been routinized. This has led to a subtle change in political alienation and a separatist mindset within the Kashmir Valley. The National Election Study 2004 records some of these changes. While nearly half of the sample of 954 respondents kept quiet on sensitive questions dealing with the fairness of the electoral process, an overwhelming majority of those who gave a response acknowledged marked improvement: 76% said that the 2004 parliamentary election saw virtually no rigging, 71% thought the level of electoral malpractice had gone down, and 90% felt either no fear or said the fear had decreased. A repeat post-poll survey in the state in 2008 recorded a sharp decline from 33% in 2002 to 22% in 2008 in respondents from the valley who suspected rigging in the state assembly elections. More importantly, those respondents in the Kashmir Valley who favored the valley's merger into Pakistan went down from 8% in 2002 to just 2% in 2008, while those who were for Kashmir staying with India but with greater autonomy went up from 6% to 16% during this period. However, the fragility of this achievement has been underscored by massive and popular anti-India protests in the valley in 2010. Between June and early October, more than one hundred civilians had been killed.

CHAPTER FOUR

Tamils in India

How State-Nation Policies Helped Construct
Multiple but Complementary Identities

There is an extremely long tradition in democratic social analysis that more or less argues that the term *multinational democracy* is an oxymoron.[1] In chapters 2 and 3 we presented compelling evidence to challenge that tradition, even in one of the world's most culturally diverse polities. Until now, except for our discussion of some of the most distinctive features of the Indian polity, we did not go very far in undertaking a theoretical and empirical inquiry into what helps increase or decrease the chances of democracy and social peace in polities with some multinational dimension to their political life. This is our primary task in this chapter.

We will attempt to carry out this task by analyzing how a potential problem of politically robust multinationalism with possible secessionist potential in South India, the Dravidian movement, especially in what is now the state of Tamil Nadu, became a non-problem.[2]

By Benedict Anderson's standards, there would appear to have been more than enough raw material for secessionist nationalists to "imagine a community" of

1. For a critical analysis of this political and intellectual tradition, see Stepan, "Modern Multinational Democracies: Transcending a Gellnerian Oxymoron," in his *Arguing Comparative Politics* (New York: Oxford University Press, 2001), pp. 181–199.

2. For one of the most cited books about the Tamil secession as a potential problem, see Eugene F. Irschick, *Politics and Social Conflict in South India: The Non-Brahmin Movement and Tamil Separatism, 1916–1929* (Berkeley: University of California Press, 1969). For two important reviews of the literature of the Dravidian movements, see M. S. S. Pandian, "Beyond Colonial Crumbs: Cambridge School, Identity Politics, and Dravidian Movement(s)," *Economic and Political Weekly*, February 18–25, 1995, pp. 385–391; and N. Ram, "Dravidian Movement in its Pre-Independence Phases," *Economic and Political Weekly*, vol. 14, no. 7/8 (February 1979), pp. 377–397.

their own that could be a separate independent nation in what is now South India.[3] Useable cleavages abounded.

A potentially useable cleavage grew out of religious-cultural differences. In the south, the Brahmins were seen as northern in origin. Nationalists in the south, particularly near the important city of Madras (now Chennai), argued that traditional Dravidian culture had been more socially egalitarian than the version of Hinduism imported and imposed upon Dravidians by northern Brahmins. The potential of caste to be a polarizing force was enhanced by the fact that under British rule Brahmins were accorded a new higher social status that in effect lowered the social status of some South Indian caste groups that had been socio-economically and religiously important.[4] For some analysts, since the two intermediate Hindu castes, Kshatriya and Vaishya, were virtually not present in South India, the South Indians therefore either belonged to the lowest category of caste Hindu—the Shudras—or were untouchables. This could have increased the social and political distance of southern Indians from northern ones.[5]

Modernity, à la Gellner, sharpened South Indians' sense of exclusion and contributed to the expanding anti-Brahmin movements. The emerging Dravidian nationalist movements in the early decades of the twentieth century gained adherents as they documented and dramatized job-related statistics aiming to prove that non-Brahmins were second-class citizens in South India. For example, the famous "Non-Brahmin Manifesto of 1916" argued that although Brahmins constituted less than 3% of the population in the major administrative sub-unit of South India, the Presidency (state) of Madras, all but one of the sixteen top civil service positions allocated to Indians in Madras were held by Brahmins, all four of the Hindu judges to the Madras Supreme Court were Brahmins, and the major gate-keeper of modern careers, the University of Madras, was effectively controlled by Brahmins.[6]

Language was a compounding factor that differentiated southern Indians from northern Indians. In the last decades of the British Raj, more than 90% of the

3. Benedict Anderson, *Imagined Communities: Reflections on the Origin and Spread of Nationalism* (London: Verso, 1983).

4. See Nicholas B. Dirks, *Castes of Mind: Colonialism and the Making of Modern India* (Princeton: Princeton University Press, 2001), esp. chs. 1 and 12.

5. For this argument, see Marguerite Ross Barnett, *The Politics of Cultural Nationalism in South India* (Princeton: Princeton University Press, 1976), pp. 46–47.

6. The manifesto is reproduced in its entirety in Irschick, *Politics and Social Conflict in South India: The Non-Brahmin Movement and Tamil Separatism, 1916–1929*, pp. 358–367. From 1901 to 1911, Brahmins received 71% of the degrees awarded by Madras University and controlled the key power center in the university, the Senate. See Barnett, *Politics of Cultural Nationalism*, p. 20.

population in South India spoke languages in the Dravidian family, each with a distinct script and unintelligible to users of the major language of the north, Hindi.[7] At Independence, the geographic, demographic, and imagined space of South India contained 88 million speakers of Dravidian languages. The four largest of these Dravidian languages in 1951 were Telugu (33 million), Tamil (27 million), Kannada (14 million), and Malayalam (13 million). The cultural capital of the Tamils was the city of Madras in what was then called the Madras Presidency, but the Dravidian movement also contained important advocates from the other three major Dravidian languages, some of whom also lived in the Madras Presidency.[8]

Would be secessionist nationalists had other valuable material. They could point out that they were economically more developed than the Hindi Belt of northern India, which they saw as politically dominant; that South India was geographically contained, in that two of its three borders were seas; and that it was populous enough to make one or more South Indian independent nations.

A leading scholar of India, Lloyd I. Rudolph, did extensive research in South India in the 1950s, graphically capturing how the different components of secessionist nationalism seemed to be accumulating at the time of Independence: "With the coming of independence, anti-Brahmanism was increasingly accompanied by an anti-North, Dravidian nationalist outlook. Opposition to Hindi as the national language, the destruction of the caste system, and threats of secession from the Indian Union became major political themes."[9]

In politics, facilitating *structures* normally do not become actualized realities without *agents*. There were powerful agents. One such agent was the charismatic, autocratic, Dravida nationalist leader Ramaswami Naicker (usually called "Periar" or "Periyar"), whom a leading specialist called "one of the most dynamic and colourful political leaders South India has ever produced."[10] A leading scholar of twentieth-century Tamil Nadu, Narendra Subramanian, asserts: "Periar called for the creation of a separate country in which the Dravidian-as-Sudra would enjoy primacy."[11] Another important agent was C. N. Annadurai, who broke with Periar

7. Jyotyrindra Das Gupta, *Language Conflict and National Development: Group Politics and National Language Policy in India* (University of California, Berkeley. Center for South and Southeast Asia Studies, 1970), pp. 46–47.

8. For the list of the major languages of India as of 1951, see ibid.

9. Lloyd I. Rudolph, "Urban Life and Populist Radicalism: Dravidian Politics in Madras," *Journal of Asian Studies* 20, no. 3 (May 1961), pp. 286–287.

10. See Robert L. Hardgrave Jr., "Religion, Politics, and the DMK" in *South Asian Politics and Religion*, ed. Donald Eugene Smith (Princeton: Princeton University Press, 1966), pp. 216, 223.

11. Narendra Subramanian, *Ethnicity and Populist Mobilization: Political Parties, Citizens, and Democracy in South India* (Oxford: Oxford University Press, 1999), p. 105.

in 1947 to form a political party. Subramanian comments that Annadurai "argued that the Dravidians were oppressed by the Brahmin, the Bania (a North Indian merchant caste) and the British, and that the departure of one of the oppressors could only be an occasion to rejoice. He wished to *continue the struggle for secession*, to free Tamil Nadu of the other two oppressors."[12]

As with any potential problem that becomes a non-problem, there is always a question about how severe the problem actually was, and this tendency may lead to a failure to examine *choices* that might have facilitated the management of the potential problem. It is true that the desire for secession never became a majority sentiment in South India, even at the height of the Dravidian movement from the 1920s to the 1940s, or even during the 1965 anti-Hindi language riots. It is also true that long after some Dravidian parties had abandoned their demands, or even possibly their desire for independence, they continued to deploy the language of separatism for purposes of voter mobilization in electoral politics.[13]

But as we have seen, one of the leaders of the interpretive movement that stresses the instrumental uses of separatist rhetoric in the 1950s and 1960s, Narendra Subramanian, acknowledges that the Dravidian movement had separatist dimensions. For example, he states that "the Dravidian movement in Tamil Nadu began during the 1910s by raising militant demands for secession and virulently opposed the upper Brahmin caste."[14] Elsewhere he writes that "Tamil Nadu was the first Indian state in which secessionist/autonomous impulses developed."[15]

If one accepts Subramanian's judgments as accurate, we must ask: Why did these articulations of separatist desires become a non-issue by the early 1970s? We particularly need to examine how politically strategic decisions and choices can ameliorate or aggravate potential multinational tensions. Since we believe that relatively successful federal democratic experiences in multinational polities have been underanalyzed, we propose to explore the South Indian case to see how the potential issues of "secessionist nationalism" and secession become non-issues. To explore these questions, we have to turn to the incentive systems that were developed as part of Indian federalism. To analyze this process, we will have to employ virtually the entire "nested policy grammar" that we laid out in chapter 1.[16]

---

12. Ibid., p. 122, emphasis added.

13. All of these positions are articulated by Subramanian in his careful and well-documented *Ethnicity and Populist Mobilization*, esp. pp. 15, 125, 131, and 313.

14. Ibid., p. 7.

15. Ibid., p. 131.

16. We will also use many of the distinctions concerning types of federalism such as "holding together" federalism and "demos-enabling" federalism that were described in great detail in Stepan's "Toward a New Comparative Politics of Federalism, (Multi)Nationalism, and Democracy: Beyond

INDIA'S CHOICE OF "HOLDING TOGETHER" AND "DEMOS-ENABLING" FEDERALISM

In terms of the analytic categories we have developed, India approaches the ideal type of a "holding together" and a "demos-enabling" federation that creatively and self-consciously differs from the "coming together" and "bargaining" modalities associated with the formation of federalism in the United States. In his address to the Constituent Assembly, the Chairman of the Constitution Drafting Committee, B. R. Ambedkar, explicitly made this distinction with the United States. He assumed that India was already a diverse polity with substantial unity and that to maintain this unity, under democratic conditions, a federation would be useful. Ambedkar told the members of the Assembly that "the use of the word Union is deliberate. . . . The Drafting Committee wanted to make it clear that though India was to be a federation, *the Federation was not the result of an agreement by the States to join in a Federation.*"[17]

Mohit Bhattacharya, in a careful review of the mindset of the founding fathers of India, argues that that the central motivation in the minds of the constitution drafters was to hold the center together: "What ultimately emerged was a 'devolutionary federation' as a fundamentally unitary state devolved powers on the units through a long process of evolution. . . . [Once] the problem of integration of the Princely States had disappeared after partition . . . The bargaining situation disappeared. . . . The architects of the Constitution were sensitive pragmatists. Their attention was focused on . . . the central authority that would *hold the nation together.*"[18] Let us again quote from Ambedkar to illustrate how this was to be achieved in the federation: "The . . . Constitution has sought to forge means and methods whereby India will have federation and at the same time will have uniformity in all basic matters which are essential to maintain the unity of the country. The means adopted by the Constitution are three: (1) a single judiciary,

---

Rikerian Federalism," in his *Arguing Comparative Politics*, and his "Federalism and Democracy: Beyond the U.S. Model," *Journal of Democracy* 10, no. 4 (1999), pp. 19–34.

17. Ambedkar, Address to the Constituent Assembly. Ambedkar's speech is found in its entirety in India, *Constituent Assembly Debates* (New Delhi, 1951), vol. 2, pp. 31–44, emphasis added.

18. Mohit Bhattacharya, "The Mind of the Founding Fathers," in *Federalism in India: Origins and Development*, ed. Nirmal Mukarji and Balveer Arora (New Delhi: Vikas, 1992), pp. 87–104, quotations from pp. 101–102. Bhattacharya's language concerning the function of the type of federalism adopted in India approaches our ideal type of "holding together" federalism.

(2) uniformity in fundamental laws, civil and criminal, and (3) a common All-India Civil Service to man important posts."[19]

In relation to the demos-constraining versus demos-enabling continuum, India chose one of the most demos-enabling formulas found in any democratic federation, be it mononational or multinational. The U.S. formula, which did grow out of a "coming together" bargaining process, gave each state equal representation in the upper house and gave the upper house somewhat greater legal competencies than the lower house. India's "holding together" federation was fundamentally different in both respects. The lower chamber, which was based on the principle of population, had the exclusive right to form the government and thus was vastly more important in legislative competence than the upper chamber, which represented the states. Furthermore, there was a significant degree of proportional representation in the upper chamber. The demos at the center, aided by the choice of a Westminster type of fused executive-legislative parliamentary model, was thus not nearly as constrained in independent India as was the demos at the center in the presidential and divided-government model chosen in the United States. In fact, as Stepan has documented, the United States has four electorally generated "veto players" in that the Senate, the House of Representatives, the president, and, in the matter of amendments, the states can all exercise powerful vetos. In contrast, India is like Austria in that the only veto player is the lower house of parliament.[20]

A major controversy in the Constituent Assembly was over the languages that would be used in the federation. Precisely because the members of the Constituent Assembly knew that the most controversial issue surrounding Indian unity in the future would be language policy and because there was a desire on the part of many delegates to reorganize the states at some point along linguistic lines, the language of the constitution was extremely demos-enabling for the lower house of the federal parliament, the Lok Sabha. Future parliaments were given the right to redraw state boundaries as they wished. Article 3 of the constitution is categorical on this point. With a simple majority, "Parliament may by law a) form a state by separation of territory from any state or by uniting two or more states . . . ; . . . c) diminish the area of any state . . . ; . . . e) alter the name of any state." In a "coming together" federation such as the United States, the sovereign states

---

19. Ambedkar, Address to the Constituent Assembly.

20. See Alfred Stepan, "Electorally Generated Veto Players in Unitary and Federal Systems," in *Federalism and Democracy in Latin America*, ed. Edward L. Gibson (Baltimore: Johns Hopkins University Press, 2004), pp. 323–362, esp. table 10.1.

would obviously have been able to bargain successfully for a much more demos-constraining constitution to protect states' rights.[21]

That the demos, as represented in the Constituent Assembly, gave the parliament the right to work with the numerous linguistic demoi of India to restructure the states turned out to play an important role in allowing the demos of India, and the demoi of India, to "hold together" in a multinational democratic federal system. We will not retell that story because it has been excellently analyzed by other writers.[22] The key point to stress here is that in 1955 a State Reorganization Commission was formed to suggest changes in state boundaries. As a result of that commission, eventually most of the units of the Indian federation were geographically and sociologically reconfigured to achieve greater congruence between languages and state boundaries. Each state was allowed to carry out its state administration in the dominant language of the state. This major constitutional change meant that a significant degree of politically legitimated linguistic and cultural nationalism had been achieved and recognized *inside* India's federal polity.[23]

Das Gupta's classic book on Indian national language policy concludes with an analysis of the integrative effects of India's recognition of the Tamil language as the language of self-government in the federal unit of Tamil Nadu:

> In Madras, most of the leaders of the DMK were once associated with the demand for a homeland for the Dravidians. But as soon as they discovered that they too were capable of winning the elections and capturing the political authority of the state, they gave up their secessionist associations. . . . [L]anguage politics has given a new meaning to the political community in India. It has indicated that a viable political community can be built in India on the basis of the recognition of the separate but related language communities. . . . [L]anguage politics has proved to be one of the most important positive democratic channels for pursuing political integration.[24]

21. See Stepan, "Federalism and Democracy: Beyond the U.S. Model," Indeed, it was precisely this feature of the Indian constitution that then led the leading theorist of federalism in the world, K. C. Wheare, to argue, "What makes one doubt that the Constitution of India is strictly and fully federal, however, are the powers of intervention in the affairs of the states given by the Constitution to the central government and parliament. To begin with, the parliament of India may form new states; it may increase or diminish the area of any state and it may alter the boundaries or name of any state." See K. C. Wheare, *Federal Government* (Oxford: Oxford University Press, 1963), p. 27.

22. See Das Gupta, *Language Conflict and National Development*, p. 33; and Paul Brass, *Language, Religion, and Politics in North India* (Cambridge: Cambridge University Press, 1974).

23. Any such restructuring of course creates some new linguistic minorities. In contrast to Spain and Belgium, the central government in India is mandated with the task of ensuring that these linguistic minorities have sufficient schools in their own language.

24. Das Gupta, *Language Conflict and National Development*, pp. 268, 269, and 270. Unlike

Clearly, the language policies that Das Gupta is describing here are *state-nation* policies nested inside India's "holding together" federalism. Let us now turn to another part of our nested grammar, one that concerns the role of polity-wide parties introducing multiple but complementary identities.

ROLE OF A "POLITY-WIDE" PARTY

In the immediate pre- and post-Independence era, what was the relationship between culturally nationalist "regional parties" or movements and a "polity-wide" party? In 1944 an offshoot of previous Dravidian movements, the Self-Respect Movement and the Justice Party, was renamed the Dravida Kazhagam (DK). According to Irschick, the DK had "as its primary aim the realisation of a separate non-Brahmin or Dravidian country."[25]

For our analytical purposes, it is important to note that this regional nationalist movement had to compete with the polity-wide party, the Indian National Congress. The Congress Party had an All-Indian institutional presence since its formation in 1885. This polity-wide party had acquired great legitimacy and experience owing to its leadership role in the Indian Independence movement and the mobilizing capacity of Mahatma Gandhi. However, the Congress Party originally made the mistake of recruiting most of its leaders in the Madras Presidency from the small and culturally alien Brahmin community.[26] Nonetheless, the regional nationalist movement led by Periar, the DK, never became a political party. In 1949 the DK lost some important followers when an equally charismatic but more democratic leader, C. N. Annadurai, left the DK to form a political party called the Dravida Munnetra Kazhagam. The DMK was not yet able to compete successfully with the Congress Party in the founding polity-wide elections. In the first post-Independence elections in 1952, the Congress Party won twelve of the fourteen seats for the parliament in Delhi from Madras but only a plurality, 152 of 375 seats, to the Madras state assembly. The DMK, even though it was a culturally nationalist party that still had not publicly renounced all secessionist possibilities, supported a United Democratic Front

---

Spain, where well over 90% of the population shares a mutually comprehensible language, Spanish, even if their first language might be Basque or Catalan, in India more than 50% of the population speaks neither Hindi nor English.

25. Irschick, *Politics and Social Conflict*, p. 347.

26. Indeed, the previously cited "Non-Brahmin Manifesto" explicitly laments that fourteen of the fifteen members of the Madras Congress Party Committee were Brahmins. See Irschick, *Politics and Social Conflict*, p. 361.

coalition of parties, some of which, the Communists and the Socialists, were polity-wide parties.

The original leader of the Congress-led government in Madras after the first post-Independence elections of 1952 was a Brahmin, C. Rajagopalachari, who was perceived to be insensitive to lower-caste and Tamil cultural aspirations. But in the new electoral context, which had become very competitive, Kamaraj Nadar, a lower-caste, Tamil-speaking, professional Congress Party organizer, became a crucial leader linking Tamils and the Congress Party. Kamaraj did not have the benefit of much formal education and did not speak Hindi or English, but he combined strong Indian nationalist *and* Tamil cultural-nationalist roots, making him a classic example of a state-nation political leader with multiple but complementary identities. Kamaraj, who was imprisoned six times by the British and had spent more than three thousand days in jail for his pro-Independence activities, emerged as the kingmaker in the Madras Congress Party. By 1954 he had become the chief minister of Madras. Significantly, there was not one Brahmin in his first cabinet.[27]

Jawaharlal Nehru employed a leadership style that, both as prime minister of the government and as president of the Congress Party, relied heavily on the consensual support of regional leaders. Nehru and Kamaraj related to each other in ways that prevented center-periphery relations from being a zero-sum game. As a major party regional boss, Kamaraj had political resources at the center. Indeed, Kamaraj became one of the five members of the group called "the syndicate" that co-ruled the Congress Party with Nehru. Moreover, after the death of Nehru, Kamaraj became the president of the Congress Party. Kamaraj was effective as a leader of a polity-wide party partly because his autonomy as a Tamil political and cultural leader won the respect of Nehru. Power for both leaders was thus non-zero-sum. Nehru, by ideological preference, would have preferred a strong Indian central government that generated an increasingly homogeneous nation-state culture. Politically, however, he knew that he had to depend on a core of Congress Party members who represented, and led, India's major regions with their diverse languages and cultures. In essence, Nehru followed a "strong centre, strong subunit" policy.

In this type of federal politics, Kamaraj was a regional leader in Tamil-speaking India who had sufficient strength and respect in the center for him to be allowed to deliver many cultural-nationalist demands. But as a regional boss of a large

27. See Duncan B. Forrester, "Kamaraj: A Study in Percolation of Style," *Modern Asian Studies* 4, no. 1 (1970), p. 49.

state, Kamaraj could also deliver valuable votes and support to the polity-wide party. Lloyd Rudolph summarizes Kamaraj's contribution to the strength, inside the state of Madras, of the polity-wide Congress Party: "Between 1952 and 1957 Congress increased its share of the popular vote from 35.5 percent to 45.3 percent largely by identifying itself more closely with the [Tamil] populist appeal. . . . The growth in Congress strength can be attributed largely to the leadership qualities of Mr. Kamaraj."[28]

In our discussion of the new "grammar" of federalism, we argued that it is necessary to analyze some important democratic federations such as Spain, Belgium, Canada, and India in their multinational context. Thus we stressed the importance of "multiple but complementary identities." We think this concept is valid, and indeed necessary, but perhaps our phrase does not quite capture the dual but nonetheless occasionally competing identities many nationalists might feel. Most Tamil-speakers were very interested in Tamil cultural-nationalist goals; from the 1930s on, many were members of parties or movements that periodically articulated separatist aspirations. However, many Tamils were *also* interested in the struggle for Indian independence. Since the most effective mass-based, pro-independence organization was the polity-wide Congress Party, many Tamil cultural nationalists identified with the Congress Party and never became secessionist nationalists.[29] As the chief minister of Madras, Kamaraj (and the Congress Party) received some cultural-nationalist credit for the creation of special quotas for lower-caste Tamils and for their support for the Tamil language. A leader like Kamaraj reduced the potential tension between polity-wide and the cultural-nationalist goals. But without a polity-wide party, he could not have played such a role.

That the three other major Dravidian-speaking areas of India had, by the late 1950s, also been given a state in which the language of the government was their own ended any possibility of a successful movement for an independent Dravidian country. This was so because by the late 1950s linguistic cultural-nationalist claims for the then 37 million Telegu speakers were organized and

28. Rudolph, "Urban Life and Populist Radicalism," p. 294. On the "cultural nationalist" and "polity-wide party" appeals of Kamaraj, see also Hardgrave, "Religion, Politics, and the DMK," pp. 226–227.

29. In electoral terms, in the 1920s the Congress Party, with its pan-Indian ideology, and the Dravidian cultural nationalist Justice Party would have seemed to be in a zero-sum relationship. However, the existential reality of people who simultaneously wanted to affirm support for cultural nationalism *and* pan-Indianism is beautifully shown by a quotation from Subramanian: "Congress was so popular that by 1927 the Justice Party was forced for reasons of survival to allow its members to have parallel membership in Congress." *Ethnicity and Populist Mobilization*, p. 125.

articulated by the state of Andhra Pradesh; for the 30 million speakers of Tamil by the state of Madras (which changed its name to Tamil Nadu in 1968); for the 17 million Kannada speakers by the state of Karnataka; and for the 17 million Malayalam speakers by the state of Kerala.[30]

But, if the States Reorganisation Commission Report effectively ended any chance of a united, separatist, Dravidian movement for a single country, there were still some advocates of a territorially independent country of Tamil Nadu. Why, then, did the Tamil cultural nationalists defeat the Tamil secessionist nationalists?[31]

FROM SECESSIONIST NATIONALISM TO CULTURAL
NATIONALISM TO POLITICAL INTEGRATION

The constitutional decision to make India a federation made it possible for political activists like Kamaraj to be a cultural-nationalist leader at the state level and an All India leader at the center. Furthermore, the decisions to craft a "demos enabling" and "asymmetrical" federation allowed the parliament at the center to go forward with the fundamental redrawing of the political boundaries of the federation to reflect the cultural-nationalist demands of language. And, of course, the political activity and organization of the Congress Party since 1885 allowed a polity-wide party to compete effectively in the elections against regional-cultural nationalists, even in the newly created linguistic states.

The creation of a Tamil-speaking state in a context where cultural nationalism was very strong gave the two Tamil nationalist political organizations, the DMK and the DK, an opportunity to win control of the state by waging cultural-nationalist campaigns. The DMK participated in the election for state and federal legislatures in 1957, but due to the popularity of Congress and Kamaraj, it did not do very well. The DK, which was not a party, did not compete in the election but continued with its formal demands for a sovereign and independent country.

In 1959, the DMK, with an adroit campaign focused on local government, finally won political control of Madras, the largest city and capital of the state of Madras.[32] After 1959 the Tamil nationalist DMK increasingly began to believe it could win control of the state assembly and the state government, and some of its

---

30. The number of speakers of these languages is from the Census of India, 1961, reproduced in Das Gupta, *Language Conflict and National Development*, p. 46.
31. Juan J. Linz, "From Primordialism to Nationalism," in *New Nationalisms of the Developed West*, ed. Edward A. Tiryakian and Ronald Rogowski (Boston: Allen and Unwin, 1985), pp. 203–253.
32. Barnett, *Politics of Cultural Nationalism*, p. 105.

leaders and followers even harbored ambitions for greater political autonomy. However, DMK parliamentarians in Delhi sent back warnings that separatist parties might be made illegal and that secessionist nationalist demands in the state of Madras were unfeasible and dangerous. The "no exit" dimension of Indian statehood we discussed previously was supported by the Indian Army, which, given its loyalty to the center and great size, was a completely credible coercive force.[33] Thus, not wanting to jeopardize their chances to win control of the state of Madras, top DMK leaders in 1960, in a closed private meeting, made a decision to drop their secessionist nationalist aspirations, implicitly but not explicitly.[34]

In the general election of 1962, the DMK emerged as the major opposition. In the 1962 campaign the DMK ran as a cultural-nationalist party that had not formally abandoned secessionist nationalism, but secessionist demands did not in fact figure prominently in its campaign. In 1967, the DMK defeated the Congress Party and won control of the state of Madras.[35] From 1967 on, the DMK never gave up its cultural nationalism, but it did become increasingly integrated into the politics and norms of the Indian federation.

LANGUAGE POLICIES AND CAREER OPPORTUNITIES

One of the elements that can help sustain complementary identities in a polity with some multinational dimensions is the role of material interests, especially accommodative language policies that enhance polity-wide career opportunities. In 1965 and 1970, there were two protest movements in Tamil-speaking India. Both were, in essence, struggles to maintain India-wide career opportunities. In one case there was a struggle against an expected change in official language policy of the central government for the whole country. In the other case, the struggle was against the excessive culturally nationalist language policies of the regional government. In both cases, some of the same activists participated.

The first protest movement was a response to the fifteenth anniversary of the constitution of India, which took place on January 26, 1965. The 1950 constitution

---

33. The "no exit" situation was made viable due to the absence of external state support for any secessionist movements and the probability that if the central government used force, it would not be subject to any significant international censure or sanctions.

34. Ibid., pp. 102–115.

35. For an account of the growing integration of Tamil politics into Indian federal politics by a leading specialist on Indian federalism, see Balveer Arora, *Specificite Ethnique, Conscience Regionale et Developpment National: Langues et Federalism en Inde* (Thèse pour le Doctorat de Recherches, Fondation Nationale des Sciences Politiques, Paris, 1972), esp. pp. 193–406. See also Subramanian, *Ethnicity and Populist Mobilization*, pp. 160–172.

stipulated that "it was the duty of the Union to promote the spread of the Hindi language, to develop it so that it may serve as a medium of expression for all elements of the composite culture of India."[36] Moreover, English was accepted as a useable "link language" of the federation for fifteen years, which were up in 1965. There were widespread demands in the northern Hindi heartland, even among the Socialists, to make Hindi the official language of the union. In the south, particularly among Tamil elites, there were intense fears that Hindi would become the only acceptable language for entrance examinations to the coveted and powerful Indian Administrative Service and for India's court system. A long-time observer of South Indian politics based in Madras in 1965 nicely captured elite and middle-class fears about career prospects in this period: "Students, lawyers, and businessmen, indeed the Madras middle class generally, see their interests as tied to the continuance of English as the medium for the Union Public Service Commission's competitive examinations. Northerners and Southerners start from the same point in English; the introduction of Hindi would impose a serious hardship on those for whom it is not their mother tongue."[37]

Faced with the threat of losing these polity-wide career opportunities, students, supported by lawyers and many other groups, waged for much of January and February 1965 the biggest protests in Madras since the anti-British "Quit India" protests of the 1940s. These protests rapidly became riots, and police and army troops opened fire in twenty-one towns in the state, arrested over ten thousand people, and reportedly killed over one hundred people.[38] The two Tamil-speaking ministers of the central government (for agriculture and petroleum) submitted their resignations.

To stop this growing crisis of the Indian state-nation, on February 11, 1965, Prime Minister Shastri announced a crucial decision on an India-wide broadcast: "For an indefinite period . . . I would have English an associate language . . . I do not wish the people of the non-Hindi areas to feel that certain doors of advancement are closed to them. . . . I would have [English] as an alternative language as

36. Constitution of India, Article 351.

37. Duncan B. Forrester, "The Madras Anti-Hindi Agitation, 1965: Political Protest and its Effect on Language Policy in India," *Pacific Affairs* (Spring–Summer 1966), p. 23. On the same page, Forrester gives a telling detail: From 1948 to 1962, the state of Madras won 23.3% of *all* positions allocated in the Indian Administrative Service, more than any other state in the Union. If English had been eliminated as a link langue for federal examinations, this figure would have been radically reduced, just as it was for Tamils in Sri Lanka when English was marginalized.

38. For much of these two months, the leading newspaper in Madras, *The Hindu*, carried two or three articles a day on these increasingly bloody and dramatic events, such as the self-immolation of a headmaster and others in defense of the Tamil language and also in defense of the use of English as well as Hindi for careers in the federal government.

long as people require it, and the decision [to maintain or revoke English as a link language] I would leave not to the Hindi-knowing people, but to the non-Hindi knowing people."[39] More than forty-five years later, Shastri's decision remains the de facto policy of the federal government. Both the protests and the center's reaction contributed to the maintenance of polity-wide careers that help undergird multiple but complementary identities in Tamil Nadu.

What if Hindi had been imposed as the only official language of the Indian federation in 1965? Stepan asked this question to C. Subramanian, one of the Tamil-speaking ministers who had submitted his resignation. Subramanian responded that the president of India virtually refused to accept his resignation and asked Shastri, "Do you want to lose Tamil Nadu from India? If not, kindly take back your recommendation."[40] Subramanian went on to speculate that if Hindi had been imposed and English had been eliminated as a link language, the protest movements would have been more virulent and the dormant secessionist movement would have suddenly become greatly reinvigorated and possibly have won.[41] It is impossible to say if C. Subramanian's speculations would have been borne out. However, the DMK, which, as we have seen, had become cultural-nationalist, might have faced increasing pressure to reintroduce a secessionist discourse so as not to lose control over Tamil nationalism. Significantly, Barnett notes that during the anti-Hindi mobilizations, the DMK, for the first time in many years, actually did lose control over the leadership of the most important Tamil and Dravidian protest movements and could not keep them within constitutional limits.[42] At the very least it would appear that the combination of Hindi imposition and the removal of English as a useable language for civil service examinations would have been a major blow, as in Sri Lanka, to the possibility of polity-wide careers and multiple but complementary identities that are so useful in maintaining peaceful and democratic federalism in multinational settings.

In 1967, the DMK won the provincial elections and became the first cultural-nationalist party to assume control of an Indian state. The question of career opportunities once again assumed great importance, but in this case students put pressure on the DMK's chief minister, C. N. Annadurai, not to close off their career paths in the Indian polity and market. Here the desire of a political party's

39. Cited in Barnett, *Politics of Cultural Nationalism*, p. 134. On the 1965 protests, see pp. 131–135 in Barnett's book as well as Richard L. Hardgrave Jr., "The Riots in Tamilnad: Problems and Prospects of India's Language Crisis," *Asia Survey* 5 (August 1965), pp. 399–407; and Forrester, "Madras Anti-Hindi Agitation, 1965."

40. Interview of Alfred Stepan with C. Subramanian, Chennai, Madras, April 1, 1998.

41. Ibid.

42. Barnett, *Politics of Cultural Nationalism*, pp. 132–135.

followers to maintain their access to polity-wide careers throughout the federation helped transform a potential exclusionary nationalist "regional party" into a more inclusionary "centric-regional" party that allowed dual identities.

Barnett's book *The Politics of Cultural Nationalism in South India* nicely shows how political struggle can be waged in the name of keeping open the possibility of multiple but complementary identities. Barnett argues that Annadurai's problems resulted from his proposed policy of progressively making Tamil the dominant, possibly the exclusive, medium of instruction in government colleges: "However, many students protested, demanding a free choice of medium of instruction. This caused colleges to close in late 1970 and early 1971. Many students were interested in high quality English medium instruction, believing it would improve their employment opportunities. They did not see this as a Tamil nationalist issue, and resented the DMK's efforts to define it as such."[43]

With elections on the horizon, and fearing damaging demonstrations, the chief minister of Tamil Nadu hastily set up a panel to respond to students' demands. A month and a half before the elections, the Chief Minister defused the situation by accepting the panel's recommendation that "the opportunity to choose the medium of instruction should be available to students."[44]

COALITIONAL INCENTIVES FOR BOTH "CENTRIC-REGIONAL" AND "POLITY-WIDE" PARTIES

Prime Minister Jawaharlal Nehru died in 1964 and closely fought elections became increasingly important after 1967. Indeed, the Congress Party lost power in what is now Tamil Nadu in 1967 and has never again formed the government by itself in that state. However, in the vast majority of states, India's combination of numerous political parties and a first-past-the-post, single-member-constituency electoral system means that since 1967 a single party running alone often loses to a candidate supported by a multi-party alliance, and a single party by itself normally does not get a majority in the provincial legislature, which would allow it to form a single-party government.

As long as the above conditions exist, nested *in a parliamentary context*, and as

---

43. Ibid., p. 291. For the tone of this conflict, which was shorter and less intense than that of 1965, see two front-page articles in *The Hindu*, January 1, 1971. In Spain, the policy effort of the Catalan government to impose a predominantly Catalan education system up to the university level does not generate an opposition of the large Spanish-speaking minority in metropolitan Barcelona because its members believe that the Spanish language is so present in their daily lives that it is not threatened as a language.

44. Ibid., p. 291.

long as state and federal elections are held and offices and appointments flow from electoral results, there will be *strong incentives to form multi-party electoral coalitions.*[45]

Surprisingly, this proposition holds even for coalitions that combine polity-wide parties and parties that would seem to be potentially separatist regional parties. But, and this is the crucial point, the mutual electoral benefit of coalitions can only be obtained if both the potentially separatist regional parties and the polity-wide parties adjust their behavior (and votes) to make the alliance possible.

The incentive system of this type of electoral bargaining works like this: A polity-wide party would be severely constrained against entering into an electoral alliance with a secessionist nationalist party, which articulates, or is widely believed to harbor, secessionist ambitions, because it would be attacked throughout the rest of India by polity-wide parties for contributing to the "disintegration" of India. For its part, a regional cultural-nationalist party would be severely constrained against entering into an alliance with any polity-wide party that voted in the federal legislature for the imposition of assimilationist policies, because it would fear losing votes to other culturally nationalist parties.

Tamil Nadu in 1971 illustrates the complex electoral and policy tradeoffs that can make an apparently cultural-nationalist "regional" party, in effect, "centric-regional," and a "polity-wide" party, in effect, supportive of regional cultural nationalism. Let us explore this complicated—but absolutely crucial—aspect of Indian federalism.

By the late 1960s the Congress Party had split into a Congress (R) faction led by Indira Gandhi and a Congress (O) faction. The Tamil cultural-nationalist parties had also divided into the DMK and another group that later became the Anna Dravida Munnetra Kazhagam (ADMK) in 1972. Congress (R) was primarily interested in how it did in the federal Lok Sabha elections, and the DMK was primarily interested in how it did in the Tamil Nadu state assembly elections. But both the Congress (R) and the DMK felt they would be greatly helped by forming a strong government in their respective spheres of greatest interest if they could work out

45. See E. Sridharan, "The Fragmentation of the Indian Party System, 1952–1999: Seven Competing Explanations," in *Parties and Politics in India*, ed. Zoya Hasan (Oxford: Oxford University Press, 2002). See also Balveer Arora, "Negotiating Differences: Federal Coalitions and National Cohesion," in *Transforming India*, ed. Francine Frankel, Zoya Hasan, Rajeev Bhargava, and Balveer Arora (Oxford and Delhi: Oxford University Press, 2000), pp. 176–206; and K. K. Kailash, "Coalitions in a Parliamentary Federal System: Parties and Governments in India," unpublished Ph.D. dissertation, Jawaharlal Nehru University, 2003. The major exception to this logic of incentives to form a coalition might be if a "regional secessionist" party controlling a government of a state was, for whatever reason, financially and politically independent of the center and did not want to enter a coalition at the center as a matter of principle.

an electoral alliance. Such arrangements were facilitated by the existence of real party leaderships who could decide candidates and retain the support of voters. This, in turn, was facilitated by regular elections at the provincial and central level and the absence of primaries.

Concerning Tamil Nadu State Assembly elections, Congress (R) agreed in 1971 not to compete against DMK in State Assembly races but to join a DMK-led coalition. Even though the DMK–Congress (R) coalition won 53% of the votes, they won an overwhelming 78% of the seats to the State Assembly. So the alliance meant that the DMK won strong control over the political arena most vital to *its* goals, the provincial legislative assembly.

In return, for elections to the all-important lower chamber of the federal parliament, the Lok Sabha, the DMK agreed to help the Congress (R) by not running against them—and urging their followers to vote for Congress(R)—in selected federal seat constituencies where Congress (R) could win with DMK support. Due to this noncompetition and mutual support coalitional agreement, the Congress (R)–DMK alliance won a total of 35 out of 39 Lok Sabha seats. The DMK won 25 seats and Congress (R) won the 10 constituencies in which the DMK agreed not to run a candidate. As per the coalitional agreement, in the federal lower chamber, the DMK lent its 25 votes to Congress (R) on all key issues such as bank nationalization and budgets as long as it did not hurt its power base back home in Tamil Nadu. So this alliance meant that the Congress (R) was significantly strengthened in *its* most important arena, the lower house of the Lok Sabha.[46]

Barnett succinctly captures the reinforcing incentives by which the leading cultural-nationalist party in Tamil Nadu—indeed then in all of India—became what we would call a "centric-regional" party deeply integrated into the federal political system.

Although the DMK alliance with Indira Gandhi's Congress (R) seems paradoxical, given previous DMK separatist tendencies, it is in fact consistent with DMK priorities and cultural nationalist orientation. In analyzing DMK political activities and policies on the national level, it is essential to remember that the primary party priority was consolidation of their state-level base.

After the November 1969 Congress party split, a unique opportunity was

---

46. The 1971 election was not an exception but a precedent. Since 1977 the DMK has had to compete with a spinoff party, the ADMK, later called AIADMK. In the vast majority of the elections since 1977, one or both of these once-Dravidian parties have been in alliances with non-Dravidian, polity-wide parties.

created for the DMK to enhance its national image, improve relations with the centre, and most importantly, consolidate its state support base by linking itself to the left-leaning economic and social policies of Indira Gandhi.

Since 1971 the DMK has been solidly "centric-regional." Given the coalitional incentive system we have just described, even the DMK's major cultural-nationalist competitor, the All India Anna Dravida Munnetra Kazhagam (AIADMK), routinely enters into alliances with polity-wide parties, so it, too, is subject to the same "centric-regional" incentive system.

POLITICAL INTEGRATION WITHOUT CULTURAL ASSIMILATION

By 1968, Tamil-speaking India controlled a major political entity of the Indian federation named after the Tamils (Tamil Nadu) and administered that state in Tamil. There has never been any cultural-nationalist assimilation into Hindi-speaking India in Gellnerian or Millsian terms. As we have seen, there is a strong intellectual and political body of opinion that is worried that such "cultural conquests" will proceed down the slippery slope toward "secessionist nationalism" and, eventually, violent demands for independence.

In the Tamil Nadu case, however, we have seen that many of the cultural nationalists, such as students and lawyers, who sparked off the 1965 anti-Hindi movement also had material interests in maintaining access to India-wide political, administrative, and legal careers.[47] Tamil businessmen also had an interest in continued access to the Indian common market. However, if their cultural-nationalist demands for a separate political state with its own language had been thwarted, if English had been eliminated as a link language for the Indian federation, and if Hindi had been imposed as the sole official language of the entire federation, cultural nationalism might easily have begun to tilt toward secessionist nationalism, as it did in Sri Lanka. Even as late as 1965, if the center had insisted on Hindi-only cultural assimilation, no provincial government of Tamil Nadu would have supported it because, in the words of the Madras-based observer Forrester, "No Madras government could in present circumstances make the study of Hindi in schools compulsory and survive."[48] But once the center clarified that it was not for Hindi dominance in the federation, English was accepted as a

47. Thus, Narendra Subramanian, writing about Tamil Nadu, correctly asserts that "the material interests of many core DMK supporters were not directly linked to secessionism." See his *Ethnicity and Populist Mobilization*, p. 313.

48. Forrester, "Madras Anti-Hindi Agitation, 1965," p. 34.

de facto permanent link language, and the Tamil language was secured as the language of regional power, virtually no key Tamil leaders ever again spent major resources on the goal of achieving independence and a separate independent country. In fact, in terms of the definitions advanced earlier, Tamil India remained deeply multicultural but was no longer "robustly multinational."

Barnett administered a poll in Tamil Nadu to DMK and Congress Party activists in 1968. Of the 459 local DMK party leaders who were asked the question "What do you consider the most important problem in your district?" only 2% mentioned issues of language as the first problem, and none mentioned independence. Of the thirty-eight members of the DMK General Council who were asked about their reasons for being active in the DMK movement, none mentioned Tamil Nadu separatism as the first reason, but 7.8% did mention Tamil language and culture, and 10.5% mentioned the two-language policy.[49]

In this context, worries about cultural nationalism or threats to integration were not salient even for the 120 state-level Congress Party leaders interviewed in Tamil Nadu. Indeed, in 1968 only 2.5% listed as their first worry threats to national integration.[50] The responses to these questions, by both the DMK "centric-regional parties" and the Congress "polity-wide" party activists, are further support for our overall argument that the potential issue of separatism in Tamil Nadu had, by the early 1970s, become a non-issue in India's state-nation.

EVIDENCE ON POLITICAL IDENTITY IN TAMIL NADU

When this chapter appeared in 2003 as a freestanding paper, it ended with the above discussion of the state of politics in Tamil Nadu in the late 1960s. However, since then, we have all participated in preparing some questions for the Indian *National Election Study, 2004*, and the five-country *State of Democracy in South Asia* survey. Since the original text stands (virtually) as written in 2003, the incorporation of these new survey results thus represents a postscript. The surveys are an invaluable source of information about opinions in Tamil Nadu toward India forty years after the events described in this chapter. We should also add that the three of us worked particularly hard to write questions that would shed light on our conceptual approach to state-nation politics and other issues that we consider central to our argument. Do these survey findings bolster or undermine our

49. Barnett, *Politics of Cultural Nationalism*, pp. 203–205.
50. Ibid.

TABLE 4.1
Vote Share of Polity-wide Parties in Tamil Nadu State Assembly Elections, 1952–2001

Election year	Vote share of polity-wide parties
1952	63.3%
1957	55.3
1962	63.9
1967	50.1
1971	43.2
1977	55.6
1980	29.7
1984	24.4
1989	26.5
1991	23.4
1996	13.0
2001	9.1

Source: CSDS Data Unit, Delhi, based on the official returns of the Election Commission of India.

Note: The table's identification of polity-wide parties follows the Election Commission of India's official classification of "recognised national" parties. This did not apply in the first general election of 1952. In that election, we have identified the following parties as "national": Indian National Congress, Communist Party of India, Socialist Party, Kisan Majdoor Praja Party, Bhartiya Jana Sangh, and Republican Party of India.

argument? On the basis of these survey results, which of our concepts, if any, might be tested and refined in further research?

Before we get to the survey results, we should note that in 1971, in the elections to the Tamil Nadu State Assembly, what we call "polity-wide" parties such as Congress, or the Communist Party of India, won 55.6% of the vote. However, in 2001 "polity-wide" parties only won 9.1% of the total Tamil Nadu State Assembly votes. Does this weaken our argument about "centric-regional" parties in state-nation parliamentary politics? For the thirty-year decline in Tamil Nadu State Assembly elections of polity-wide parties, see table 4.1.

Some of our survey results also demonstrate the continuing strength of the Tamil identity. The three authors agreed that we would like to replicate for India and Tamil Nadu the five-point scale of identity that we cited in chapter 1 for Catalonia in Spain and for Flanders in Belgium. The results to this question, taken by itself, would seem to refute some of our main arguments about the successful integration of Tamil Nadu into Indian politics. There is a much higher "only Tamil" response in Tamil Nadu (33.8%) than the "only Catalan" response in Catalonia (11.0%) or the "only Flemish" response in Flanders (3.5%) (see tables 1.2 and 1.3).

TABLE 4.2

Five-Point Scale of Identity in Tamil Nadu and the Rest of India, 2005

Identity	Tamil Nadu	Rest of India
Only regional	34	12
More regional than Indian	15	11
Equally Indian and regional	15	22
More Indian than regional	12	14
Only Indian	24	41

Source: SDSA 2005, India main dataset, weighted by state electorate, CSDS Data Unit, Delhi.

Note: "Do not know/no answer" responses are not included. The total number of respondents in Tamil Nadu is 391; for the rest of India, the total number of respondents is 4,811.

Question C-16: "When we ask people as to who they are, we get different answers. Some people say that they are only Indian, while others say they are more Indian and less regional (e.g., Tamil). Some people say they are only Indian, while others say they are as Indian as they are regional (e.g., Tamil). And others say they are more regional and less Indian, while others say they are only regional (e.g., Tamil). How do you identify yourself?"

Moreover, when we compared the Tamil Nadu responses with those in other Indian states, the percentage of respondents in Tamil Nadu who answered that they were "only Indian," was 17 points lower than the Indian average, and the "only regional" response was 22 points higher than the Indian average (see table 4.2).

Two questions emerge from tables 4.1 and 4.2. Given the seeming collapse of "polity-wide" parties in the elections for the Tamil Nadu State Assembly, the question must be asked: Are the Tamil parties no longer the "centric-regional" parties we showed they were in the 1971 elections? And further: if the "only Tamil" identity is so strong relative to other Indian states, were we wrong when we argued that multiple but complementary state-nation-type political identities were prominent in Tamil Nadu?

The first question is easier to answer. In 2004–2006, even though the polity-wide parties had won less than 10% of the State Assembly votes in the most recent elections, the DMK was more than ever engaged in highly rewarding "centric-regional" party politics in the context of India's parliamentary system. The DMK and two Dravidian allies—helped by their alliance with the polity-wide Congress Party—not only controlled the Tamil Nadu State Assembly but, in terms of seats, were the third-largest party in the Congress-led ruling coalition at the center. For this, they were rewarded with the crucial federal cabinet portfolio of the Ministry of Finance and five of the other twenty-seven cabinet posts.[51]

51. See E. Sridharan, "Electoral Coalitions in 2004 General Elections: Theory and Evidence," *Economic and Political Weekly*, vol. 39, December 18, 2004, pp. 5418–5425.

TABLE 4.3

Levels of Trust in Central Institutions and Satisfaction with Democracy,
India and Tamil Nadu, 2005

Level of trust	Tamil Nadu	Rest of India
Respondents saying that they had a "great deal of trust" in . . .		
. . . the central government	58%	30%
. . . the army	82	64
. . . the Election Commission	49	43
Respondents saying that they were "very satisfied" with the way democracy works in our country	35	23

Source: SDSA 2005, India main dataset, weighted by state electorate, CSDS Data Unit, Delhi.

Note: "Do not know/no answer" responses are not included. Total number of respondents in Tamil Nadu is 391; in the rest of India, 4,811. The exact N varies slightly for each question because of some missing cases.

Questions:

C-13a: "How much trust do you have in the Central Government?"

C-13f: "How much trust do you have in the Army?"

C-13j: "How much trust do you have in the Election Commission?"

C-12: "On the whole, how satisfied are you with the way democracy works in our country— very satisfied, somewhat satisfied, somewhat dissatisfied, totally dissatisfied?"

Indeed, a strong case can be made that for the last fifteen years, the state of Tamil Nadu has received more influential positions at the center than any other state in India.

The second question, about the implications of strong Tamil identity on the state-nation project, is more complicated. It is true that a much higher percentage of Tamils expressed an "only Tamil" identity than did respondents for comparable questions in Catalonia or Flanders. But the indicator value of the identity question is most useful to the analyst if it is part of a related bundle of questions, such as trust in the center, or trust in a major institutions of the state such as the military, or satisfaction with the overall quality of democracy within the polity. When we do this, we get a more accurate indication of multiple but complementary identities. In fact, almost twice as many Tamil respondents said they had a "great deal of trust in the central government" (58%) as did the overall Indian group (30%). Also, 82% of Tamil respondents had a "great deal" of trust in the Indian Army compared to the 64% Indian average. Very importantly, 35% of Tamils stated that they were "very satisfied" with the way democracy works, 12 points above the Indian average. On these results, despite their very strong "only Tamil" self-identification, respondents in Tamil Nadu seem to confirm our hypotheses about their state-nation integration into Indian politics (see table 4.3).

In our initial theoretical presentation of our state-nation ideal type in chapter 1, we made the case that if multinational societies are to approach the state-nation ideal type—as opposed to only being a state with a group of aspirant, or emerging, nation-states within its territory—it should become a "political community" with some shared symbols. Collective memories of some state icons play a crucial role here. If some of the "founding fathers" are remembered and respected in one part of the country and not in the rest, it can be a source of weak polity integration. We decided to try to test this in our surveys for India as a whole, and especially for Tamil Nadu. We designed our question to explore three dimensions: (1) name recognition in India and Tamil Nadu; (2) positive ratings in India and Tamil Nadu; and (3) negative ratings in India and Tamil Nadu.[52]

The responses to our questions indicate that Tamil Nadu is indeed not only strongly Tamil but also strongly a part of the Indian political community. Of the seven political leaders on our list, Mahatma Gandhi, the major mobilizer of the Indian Independence movement and the Congress Party, had the greatest name recognition, 92% in India, and the highest positive rating, 72%. In Tamil Nadu, Gandhi also ranked first in both categories, but with slightly higher scores, 96% and 79%, respectively.

Jawaharlal Nehru, a major independence leader who was prime minister of India from Independence in 1947 until his death in 1964, ranked second in both categories in India, with a name recognition of 86% and a positive ranking of 58%. But in Tamil Nadu, Jawaharlal Nehru had even higher name recognition, 93%, and a greater positive approval rating, 77%, than the rest of India. Thus the two major political leaders of India, even though both are north Indian, are shared icons among Tamils and other Indians alike. The "Father of the Constitution," the north Indian Dalit, Bhimrao Ambedkar, has a quite comparable positive rating in Tamil Nadu (50.4%) and the rest of India (53%).

Of the seven political figures on our list, the closest to being a polarizing figure is Vinayak Savarkar, the founder of the Hindu Mahasabha, an early ideologue of "Hindutva," or Hindu fundamentalist politics. However, even Savarkar is ranked the same—last—in terms of positive, and explicitly negative, rating in India as a whole and in Tamil Nadu. The key difference is in the lowness of the positive ratings, 7% in Tamil Nadu versus 33% in the rest of India, and the greater explicit negative rating, 58% in Tamil Nadu, versus 18% in the rest of India. No one on our list is a major polarizing icon that profoundly divides the Indian political

52. See the note to table 4.4 for how we constructed an index for positive and negative ratings.

TABLE 4.4
Name Recognition and Evaluation of Some Major Political Figures, Tamil Nadu and the Rest of India, 2005

Name of leader (place of origin, social category, and ideological orientation)	Name recognition		Positive rating		Negative rating	
	Tamil Nadu	Rest of India	Tamil Nadu	Rest of India	Tamil Nadu	Rest of India
Mahatma Gandhi (Hindu merchant caste from Gujarat). Congress. Leader of mass mobilization in the freedom movement. Known as "father of the nation." Founder of a new political ideology centered around nonviolence and a critique of modern civilization.	96%	92%	79%	72%	1%	15%
Jawaharlal Nehru (Kashmiri Brahmin settled in Uttar Pradesh). Congress. First prime minister, 1947–64. Modern, secular, and democratic in orientation, strongly influenced by socialist ideology and state building.	93	86	77	58	1	14
Bhimrao Ambedkar (Dalit from Maharashtra). Known as the "father of the Indian constitution." Believed in equality and social justice. Opposed to the Congress.	59	78	50	53	5	16
Bhagat Singh (Sikh from the Punjab). Modern, secular, and socialist. Opposed Congress and Gandhi. Advocated, and was hanged by the British for, the use of revolutionary violence for nationalist purposes.	64	71	20	55	7	15
Sardar Patel (Dominant peasant caste, Patidar, from Gujarat). Congress. The first home minister. "Iron man" responsible for the integration of principalities into the Indian union. Opposed to "appeasement of minorities."	63	67	20	49	10	10
Jayaprakash Narayan (Upper caste, Kayastha from Bihar). Leader of the Socialist Party and the Gandhian movement after Gandhi. Led resistance to "Emergency" in 1975–77.	29	56	28	34	12	13
Vinayak Savarkar (Brahmin from Maharashtra). Founder of Hindu communal organization, the Hindu Mahasabha, an early ideologue of Hindutva politics.	18	45	7	33	58	18

Source: SDSA 2005, India main dataset, weighted by state electorate, CSDS Data Unit, Delhi.

Note: "Name recognition" stands for percentage of respondents who answered in the affirmative to the question about having heard the name. "Positive rating" stands for percentage of respondents who, from among those who recognized the name, placed the leader from 8 to 10 on a ten-point scale. "Negative rating" stands for percentage of respondents who placed the recognized leader from 1 to 3 on a ten-point scale.

Question Q-59: "Now I will read out the names of Indian leaders. You tell me about these leaders one by one, as to what was their contribution to Democracy in India. I will show you a ladder with 1 to 10 marked on it [show card]. If 1 represents such a leader who has contributed very little to democracy and 10 represents such a leader who has made great contribution to democracy, then where will you place [the leader]?"

community.[53] For a more complete presentation and explication of our results concerning political heroes in the Indian political community, see table 4.4.

In terms of positive integration and identification with Indian democracy, we believe the survey data support our argument that opinions in Tamil Nadu vis-à-vis India approach those in a political community we would call a state-nation. However, we would like to close this chapter with an excursus on the concept of identity.

EXCURSUS ON THE MEASUREMENT AND MEANINGS OF IDENTITY

Throughout this book we have spoken of political identities. However, the section we have just finished, concerning the difficulty of interpreting the political signifi-cance of "only Tamil" identities, calls for explicit reflection on the uses and abuses of "identity" in modern social science. Questions on identity can create a false appearance of polarization if only two choices are given, of which the respondent is forced to choose one. For example, a two-point-scale question, of the sort that explicitly asks respondents to give a "primary identity" (when they may not in fact want to choose between their various identities) was used in the World Values Survey for the United States. The question itself would seem to have played an important role in producing the following responses (see table 4.5).

We ask the reader to carry out a simple thought exercise. Assume that, instead of the two-point scale in table 4.5, the respondents were given a five-point-scale question of the sort we have reproduced for Spain, Belgium, and India. Is there some chance that on a five-point scale, (only American, more American than Latino, equally American and Latino, more Latino than American, only Latino), the modal response among second- and third-generation Latinos would in fact be, "equally American and Latino"?[54]

53. This said, we should acknowledge that on later reflection, and unfortunately too late to be included in this round of surveys, we realized that our list had no Muslim or South Indian leaders. In the next round of these surveys, we will certainly include a major nationalist Muslim leader such as Maulana Azad and leaders from South India like C. Rajagopalchari, Kamaraj, and Periyar.

54. Narayani Lasala-Blanco, Ph.D. candidate at Columbia University, conducted a June 2006 survey of the two hundred most prominent Mexican-American leaders in California. From a Hunt-ingtonian perspective, one would expect them to be the most "Mexican" in their self-identity. Lasala-Blanco asked both the two-point and the five-point identity questions to the same people during the same interview. In the two-point question, "Do you identify yourself as primarily Mexi-can or primarily American?" 50% defined themselves as primarily Mexican. In contrast, when given the choice to answer the five-point scale question, only 5% defined themselves as "Mexican only"

TABLE 4.5
Self-identification of Americans within a Binary Ethnic Scale

Self-identification	Largest historic minority (blacks)	Largest current minority (Hispanics)	Majority (whites)
Above all, I am an American first and a member of some ethnic group second.	18%	22%	28%
Above all, I am a Black American.	80		
Above all, I am an Hispanic American.		76	
Above all, I am a White American.			65

Sources: World Values Survey: 1990–93, Ronald Inglehart et al., Inter-University Consortium for Political and Social Research, University of Michigan, questions 208, 233. For the United States, a cross-tabulation between questions 208 and 233 was used.

Note: Question 208 is the following: "Which of the following best describes you?" The columns do not add up to 100 because of "do not know" and some isolated "other" answers.

But our excursus needs to go even further. The data we have produced about #5, "only Tamil" responses, for Tamil Nadu, raise another set of concerns of the sort that need to be more systematically incorporated into studies of identity— especially of identities with some presumed political implications. Is it correct to assume that respondents who express very strong ethnic, regional, or national identity, such as "only Tamil," would have a lower degree of trust in the central government, or a lower degree satisfaction "with the way democracy works" than the polity-wide average? We designed our battery of questions to shed light on such questions. In the case of Tamil Nadu, our results distinctly call into doubt the index value of responses to identity questions, taken in isolation. In fact, those respondents who self-identified as "only Tamil" were more than twice as likely (62.6%) as the all-India average (29.5%) to express a "great deal of trust in the Central Government." The "only Tamil" respondents were also above the all-India average in saying that they were "very satisfied with the way democracy works in our country." For the complete results and breakdown, which show that no matter which of the five self-identities they chose in Tamil Nadu, all five of them are at or substantially above the all-India average, see table 4.6.

and only 15% identified themselves as "more Mexican than American." Thus, 95% of them included American as part of their identity. Indeed, the modal self-identification was "equally Mexican and American." See Lasala-Blanco, "Who Are 'They'? The Real Challenges of Mexican Immigration," paper presented at the 2006 Midwest Association of Public Opinion Research Conference, November 17–18, 2006, Chicago, Illinois.

TABLE 4.6

*Identity by Level of Trust in Central Government and Satisfaction
with Democracy in India and Tamil Nadu, 2005*

Those who say they . . .	All-India average	Those in Tamil Nadu who identify themselves as:				
		Only Tamil	More Tamil than Indian	Equally Indian & Tamil	More Indian than Tamil	Only Indian
Are "very satisfied" with the way democracy works in our country	23%	31%	23%	54%	32%	37%
Have a "great deal" of trust in the central government	30	63	50	61	45	71

Source: SDSA 2005, India main dataset, weighted by state electorate, CSDS Data Unit, Delhi.

Note: Total number of respondents in Tamil Nadu is 391; the rest of India, 4,811. The exact N varies slightly for each question due to some missing cases.

Questions:

C-13a: "How much trust do you have in the Central Government?"

C-12: "On the whole, how satisfied are you with the way democracy works in our country—very satisfied, somewhat satisfied, somewhat dissatisfied, totally dissatisfied?"

C-16: "When we ask people as to who they are, we get different answers. Some people say that they are only Indian while others say that they are more Indian and less Tamil. Some people say that they are as Indian as they are Tamil. And others say that they are more Tamil than they are Indian, while some other people say that they are only Tamil. How do you identify yourself?"

Questions that entail an "either/or" response or elicit answers such as "what is your primary identity *above all*" are methodologically flawed. They are bad social science that *systematically produces* evidence of patterns that may not exist (polarization) and *systematically precludes* documentation of empirical patterns that may exist (multiple but complementary identities). Many analysts commit a different fallacy about identities when they conflate "cultural identities" with "political preferences." In fact, it is both theoretically possible and empirically the case that these two phenomena sometimes, in any period of time, go in opposite directions. For example, in the first five years after devolution in Scotland, people who self-identified on the five-point scale as "only Scottish" increased significantly, while the percentage of people who said they were in favor of independence decreased.

In fact, when we look at the results of our battery of questions on pride and identity for Tamil Nadu, it is clear that multiple but complementary identities exist. By almost thirty percentage points, respondents in Tamil Nadu expressed more pride in their regional identity than did the rest of India; 67.3% versus 49%. At the same time, however, consistent with our state-nation theory concerning multiple but complementary identities, respondents from Tamil Nadu were also

TABLE 4.7
National and Regional Pride in India and Tamil Nadu, 2005

Pride	Tamil Nadu	Rest of India
Very proud of state or regional identity	67%	49%
Very proud of being Indian	73	65

Source: SDSA 2005, India main dataset, weighted by state electorate, CSDS Data Unit, Delhi.

Note: Total number of respondents in Tamil Nadu is 391; the rest of India, 4,811. The exact N varies slightly for each question due to some missing cases.

Questions:

48: "How proud are you to be a [regional identity name, e.g. Tamil]—very proud, proud, not proud, or not at all proud?"

49: "How proud are you to be an Indian—very proud, proud, not proud, or not at all proud?"

"very proud of being Indian." Indeed, they were somewhat more proud of being Indian than the all-India average; 73% versus 65%. Pride, like trust, can be a multiple-sum rather than a zero-sum relationship (see table 4.7).[55]

The whole ideology of self-determination and nationalism that undergirds nation-state theory and the democratic conception of "let the people decide" means that solving the nationality conflict normally entails the holding of a plebiscite wherein people decide between two mutually exclusive alternatives. Such formulations ignore the fact that many people might have dual identities and may not want to make what seems to them a dichotomous decision that precludes living in a political community we would call a state-nation.

55. For the overlap, or non-overlap, between identity and attitude toward independence in the Basque Country in Spain, see the analysis and the table in Juan J. Linz, *Conflicto en Euskadi* (Madrid: Espasa Calpe, 1986), pp. 136–148.

Tamils in Sri Lanka

How Nation-State Policies Helped Construct
Polar and Conflictual Identities

The literature on nationalism is filled with warnings about the "slippery slope of ethno-federalism," which in the case of Yugoslavia (but not in India, Belgium, and Spain) we are in substantial agreement.[1] However, much less studied and equally prevalent is the "slippery slope toward violence and secession" in countries that have employed aggressive nation-state building policies in societies that are multi-national. We hope that this chapter is a contribution to that undertheorized issue.

THE SRI LANKAN PUZZLE

There are three issues concerning Sri Lanka about which there is a domestic and international consensus.[2] First, even though about 70% of the population was Sinhalese (92% of whom were Buddhists and almost all of whom spoke Sinhalese) and 23% were Tamil (about 86% of whom were Hindus and most of whom spoke Tamil) at Independence in 1948, there had been *no* riots or any other form of collective violence between Sinhalese and Tamils for hundreds of years before Independence.[3]

---

1. The most influential book cited to advance this argument is Bunce, *Subversive Institutions: The Design and the Destruction of Socialism and the State* (New York: Cambridge University Press, 1999). The "subversive institutions" of the title are those institutions with some ethno-federal dimensions that deviate from the classic nation-state model.

2. Until 1972 Sri Lanka was called Ceylon. In this chapter we will use the names interchangeably, with the aim of achieving historical and contextual appropriateness.

3. The only major ethnic riot had been between Sinhalese and Muslims in 1915. Muslims, who in 1946 constituted 6% of the population, were predominately Tamil-speakers and thus on many, not

Gananath Obeyesekere, a distinguished anthropologist of Sinhalese origins, asserts that "the antagonism between Tamils and Sinhalese is rooted in the country's
history but has been exacerbated into inter-ethnic violence *only since 1956*."[4] S. J.
Tambiah, an equally distinguished anthropologist of Tamil origins, writing in 1986,
argued that "Sinhalese-Tamil tensions and conflicts in the form known to us today
are of relatively recent manufacture. . . . [They] owe more to the ideas and polemics
of contemporary 'nationalist' ideologues and the politics of nation making and
election winning than to earlier concerns and processes."[5] Donald L. Horowitz,
one of the world's leading legal scholars on patterns of ethnic conflicts, opened an
article about Malaysia and Ceylon with the statement: "If we were to go back to independence and ask which of these two countries was likely to have the more
serious ethnic conflict in the decades ahead, the answer would have been unequivocal. Any knowledgeable observer would have predicted that Malaysia (then Ma-
laya) was in for serious, perhaps devastating, Malay-Chinese conflict, while Sri
Lanka (then Ceylon) was likely to experience only mild difficulty between Sinhalese and Tamils."[6] The classic political development book on Ceylon was written
by Howard Wriggins, who commented that "unique among South Asian countries,
Ceylon's decade of independence was without civil war or protracted public disorder." And, further: "In no other country in the whole of South and Southeast Asia,
from the Persian Gulf to the arc of Indonesia, had there been such public peace."[7]
    The second consensus was found in socioeconomic development publica-
tions. Wriggins, citing the standard statistical and development accounts of the
day, wrote that "of the ten newly independent countries of South and South

---

all, policy issues of language often allied with the Hindu Tamil-speakers. The population estimates
are from the 1946 Census as reported, with more data on territorial concentrations of different
categories of Sinhalese, Tamils, and Muslims in Chandra Richard de Silva, "Sinhala-Tamil Relations and Education in Sri Lanka: The University Admissions Issue—The First Phase, 1971–77," in
From Independence to Statehood: Managing Ethnic Conflict in Five African and Asian States, ed.
Robert B. Goldman and A. Jeyaratnam Wilson (London: Francis Pinter, 1984), table 9.1, p. 136. For a
number of tables on Ceylon's religious, linguistic, and ethnic composition at independence, see
Robert N. Kearney, *Communalism and Language in the Politics of Ceylon* (Durham: Duke Univer-
sity Press, 1967), pp. 1–18.
    4. See Obeyesekere, "Origins and Institutionalization of Political Violence," in *Sri Lanka in
Change and Crisis*, ed. James Manor (New York: St. Martin's Press, 1984), pp. 153–174, quotation
from p. 153, emphasis added.
    5. See Tambiah, *Sri Lanka: Ethnic Fratricide and the Dismantling of Democracy* (Chicago:
University of Chicago Press, 1986), esp. pp. 13–64, quotation from p. 7.
    6. Donald L. Horowitz, "Incentives and Behavior in the Ethnic Politics of Sri Lanka and
Malaysia," *Third World Quarterly* 11 (October 1989), p. 18. His monumental book on about 150
ethnic conflicts is *Ethnic Groups in Conflict* (Berkeley: University of California Press, 1985).
    7. See Howard Wriggins, *Ceylon: Dilemmas of a New Nation* (Princeton: Princeton University
Press, 1960), quotations from pp. 328 and 282, respectively.

East Asia, Ceylon has more of the attributes of a modernized social and political system than any other." These attributes included 60% literacy at the time of Independence—higher than India in 2000. Ceylon also had "the highest per capita income of any country in Asia except for Japan." Using contemporary vocabulary, we would say that Ceylon at Independence had a much more "useable state" than most developing countries. For, as Wriggins argues, the civil service by 1949 was "almost exclusively Ceylonese. The public service has always had a high reputation for integrity and the impersonal application of the law." Ceylonese society was also admirably progressive: "Important social welfare programs accounted on the average for over 35 per cent of the government's expenditure for the first ten years of independence," which was almost twice the amount of the budget India spent on social welfare. Indeed, Ceylon was considered such an outstanding social model of development that it was "used as a training ground for South Asian administrators to study public health administration . . . low cost housing and the development of cooperatives."[8]

The third consensus is that there were major Sinhalese/Tamil riots in 1958, 1977, 1981, and 1983, and that since 1983 Sri Lanka was in the grip of a brutal internal war of secession over the independence of the Tamils. Meanwhile, the quality of democracy, once seen as one of the best in Asia, deteriorated—indeed, at times, broke down.[9] The magnitude of the breakdown may surprise some: according to one of the standard compilations of deaths by political violence, it appears that for the 1946–2007 period, the Sinhalese/Tamil civil war in Sri Lanka contributed to the highest per capita death rate among democracies or near-democracies in the world.[10] The death rate intensified in the (Sinhalese-led) army assault of 2008–2009 against the (Tamil-led) LTTE insurgents, resulting in an estimated twenty thousand deaths.[11]

8. Ibid., pp. 6, 68, 100, 289, 318.

9. In 2007 *The Economist* estimated that seventy thousand people had been killed in this war since 1983. See "A War as Strange as Fiction," *The Economist*, June 7, 2007. On the descent into civil war and the erosion of democratic practices, see Sumatra Bose, *States, Nations, and Sovereignty: Sri Lanka, India, and the Tamil Eelam Movement* (London: Sage, 1994); A. Jeyaratnam Wilson, *The Break-Up of Sri Lanka: The Sinhalese-Tamil Conflict* (Honolulu: University of Hawaii Press, 1988); and the previously cited works by Obeysekere, Tambiah, and Manor.

10. See Monty G. Marshall, "Major Episodes of Political Violence: 1946–2006," Center for Systemic Peace, February 5, 2007, available at http://members.aol.com/cspmgm/warlist.htm. Marshall estimates eighty thousand people killed in Sri Lanka since 1983, even higher than *The Economist*.

11. Between 2007 and 2008, total deaths increased by 170%. According to the South Asia Terrorism Portal, in 2007 there were 4,369 total terrorism-related deaths in Sri Lanka, 11,144 in 2008, and 15,565 in 2009. Of the 13,503 civilian deaths since 2000, 11,111 occurred in 2009; data available at www.satp.org. See also Catherine Philip, "The Hidden Massacre: Sri Lanka's Final Offensive against Tamil Tigers," *The Times*, May 29, 2009.

Given these three patterns, it is clear that we cannot explain Sri Lanka's recent ethnic conflicts by recourse to arguments about "historic hatreds," "statelessness," or "absolute poverty." This, then, presents a puzzle: Why did the non-issue of Tamil separatism become *the* issue? What explains the outbreak of unprecedented violence in Sri Lanka a decade after Independence?

In our chapter on Tamil Nadu, we analyzed how an issue became a non-issue. In this chapter, we will attempt to analyze and explain how a potential issue became a civil war. In terms of the overall framework we developed in the first chapter, Ceylon at Independence was a society with some multinational dimensions. But it was not, as India was at Independence and Spain and Belgium were in the 1970s, a "robustly multinational" polity. We say this because there were no significant political leaders in the territory of the new state who were seeking independence from Ceylon.

One of the many reasons that no important Tamil leaders argued for independence in the 1940s was that the Tamil population was physically divided into three quite separate territories. The populations in each of these three territories had significantly different cultures, language traditions, employment patterns, and, from the orientation of rational choice theory, preferences, concerning their needs as "Tamils" in Ceylon. One group of Tamils have been concentrated in the northern peninsula of Ceylon, where they established the sixteenth-century Tamil Hindu kingdom of Jaffna in which they were a linguistic, religious, and ethnic majority. Many Tamils from this area eventually settled in Colombo, the capital of Ceylon, located in the country's southwest. This group included many Tamil civil servants, lawyers, merchants, and workers. In the historical literature about Ceylon, these two groups of Tamils are referred to as "Ceylon Tamils." The surveys we utilize later in this chapter refer to these two groups as "Tamils." Therefore, for simplicity's sake, we will also refer to these two groups as "Tamils." A third territorially concentrated group of Tamils exists in Ceylon/Sri Lanka. This group began coming from India as laborers in the mid- to late nineteenth century to work on the new tea plantations in the central highlands of Ceylon. In the historical literature, these later-arriving, plantation-based Tamils are called "Indian Tamils." In this book, and in the surveys we use, they are referred to as "Up-Country Tamils." At Independence, the Up-Country Tamils, and the Tamils around Colombo—who constituted approximately half of all the Tamils in Ceylon and lived in Sinhalese-speaking majority districts—were unenthusiastic about purely territorial responses to Tamil needs such as federalism, much less independence.

Just as important, as we shall soon document, Tamils at Independence, because they had a tradition of strong university education in English, were well

represented, indeed numerically overrepresented, in the higher echelons of the
Sri Lankan administrative service (SAS) and in the professions. They also were
prominent in the Independence movement. Indeed, in 1919, the founder of the
first pro-Independence organization, the Ceylon National Congress, was a Tamil,
Sir Ponnambalam Arunachalam. While the Tamils were well integrated, they
offended some Sinhalese nationalists by arguing for a variety of constitutional
formulas to protect and advance their ethnic and linguistic interests.[12]

But Sri Lanka did not become "robustly multinational" until the mid-1970s,
almost thirty years after Independence. For example, as late as 1970, while some
Tamil voices were asking for much greater territorial autonomy within Sri Lanka,
there were no Tamil guerrillas yet in the jungle. The strongest Tamil voice
for greater territorial autonomy was that of the democratically elected members
of parliament of the Federal Party. However, their 1970 general election manifesto still categorically stated: "It is our firm conviction that *the division of
the country* in any form would be beneficial neither to the country nor to the
Tamil-speaking people. Hence we appeal to the Tamil-speaking people not to
lend their support to any political movement that advocates *the bifurcation of
the country.*"[13]

In terms of the categories we developed in table 1.1 and figure 1.1, we will
attempt to show that, given its political context, Ceylon after Independence probably could have remained a peaceful unitary state but only as long as no aggressive
nation-state policies were followed that reduced the quality and participation of
Tamils in the political system and as long as some form of decentralization, not
necessarily full federalization as in India, was established. We will argue that
a combination of some, not too aggressive, nation-state policies and moderate
state-nation policies would probably have maintained social peace and a well-
functioning democracy.

However, what actually happened in Ceylon, particularly from 1956 to 1983,
was that highly aggressive nation-state policies ended up not only *not* fostering
a unified nation-state in Ceylon—and certainly not a state-nation—but also con-
structing two warring aspirant nation-states in one state.[14] Aggressive nation-state-

12. For a review of non-territorial proposals to protect their interests advanced by the Tamils
before Independence, see Wilson, *Break-Up of Sri Lanka*, pp. 1–24.
13. See Wilson, *Break-Up of Sri Lanka*, p. 86, emphasis in original.
14. See figure 1.1. Our position is that after 1983, Sri Lanka's polity increasing was in the upper
right hand circle, the position we argued was most difficult and unlikely for peace and unity in one
democratic state.

building policies in Sri Lanka put the multinational society on the "slippery slope" of state erosion and democratic decay. Let us examine five major steps down this slippery slope.

THE "POLITICAL CONSTRUCTION" OF POLITY FRAGMENTATION

Let us analyze five different but compounding political choices that helped deconstruct Ceylon's multicultural and peaceful polity and construct two warring nations in one territory.

1. *The disenfranchisement of the "Up-Country Tamils" in 1947–48.* The Up-Country Tamils had voted in all of the general elections in Ceylon since the securing of universal suffrage in 1931. The Up-Country Tamils constituted just over half of the entire Tamil population in Ceylon.[15] By 1948, however, they had been disenfranchised by the Sinhalese-dominated government. The justification for this disenfranchisement advanced by the government in the parliamentary debates was that many of the Up-Country Tamils had come from South India to work in the tea plantations in the late nineteenth century and were not really part of the Ceylonese nation. Thus, they should not be voters in Ceylon. In fact, many of the Up-Country Tamils were second- and third-generation residents in Ceylon and had severed most of their ties with India.

The Up-Country Tamils were situated in central Ceylon in the hill country and were physically separated from the more educated Tamils in the north around Jaffna, the Jaffna Zone Tamils. For this reason and others, Up-Country Tamils developed their own political associations. Their party, the Ceylon Indian Congress, won seven seats in the general election of 1947.[16] More important, they were a substantial minority in many other constituencies, forming coalitions with polity-wide non-Tamil parties, especially the Marxists. Sir Ivor Jennings, the eminent British constitutionalist and drafter of the Ceylonese constitution, estimates that the Up-Country Tamils were "decisive" in the election of twelve to fourteen Marxist candidates.[17] Since the All Ceylon Tamil Party won seven seats in the north, Tamils thus had a significant impact on about twenty of the ninety-one

15. See Amita Shastri, "The Tamil Citizenship Act of 1948 and Sri Lanka Partition," *Contemporary South Asia* 8 (March 1999), pp. 25–86.

16. See Kearney, *Communalism and Language*, p. 104.

17. Sir Ivor Jennings, *The Constitution of Ceylon*, 3rd ed. (London: Oxford University Press, 1953), p. 29.

constituency races for the first parliament. In this context, the leader of the All Ceylon Tamil Party, G. G. Ponnambalam, argued for "constructive collaboration" and allied his party with the governing United National Party (UNP). For this support, Ponnambalam was made minister for industries.

We should note that the disenfranchisement had three consequences. First, by disenfranchising the Up-Country Tamils in the name of nation-state ethnic authenticity, the ruling centrist party of course conveniently eliminated the electoral ally that had been "decisive" for the victory of at least twelve ethnically "pure" Sinhala, but politically "impure" Marxist, party seats. Second, after the disenfranchisement, the Tamil parties never again had such a high percentage of seats in parliament and never again formed so many electoral alliances with winning (Marxist or non-Marxist) polity-wide non-Tamil parties. Third, and most important, their disenfranchisement contributed to the number two leader of the All Ceylon Tamil Party, S. J. V. Chelvanayakam, leaving this polity-wide party on the argument that the Tamils needed a territorial electoral base in the north to protect Tamil interests. He founded the Federal Party, which, after more rebuffs of Tamil "recognition" that we shall analyze later, increasingly became the political base for Tamil demands for some form of territorial autonomy.

The disenfranchisement also had an effect on competitive politics within the Sinhalese/Buddhist majority. With the reduced coalitional capacity of the Tamils, the temptation increased for winner-take-all outbidding among Sinhalese parties for the votes of Sinhalese for the control of their nation-state. It was not inevitable, however, that such outbidding would occur, or, if it did occur, that it would be successful.

2. *The 1956 "Sinhalese Only" electoral campaign and the marginalization of polity-wide careers for Tamil- and English-speakers.* The political leader who initiated the appeals to aggressive nation-state policies was S. W. R. D. Bandaranaike. Born into an aristocratic family, Bandaranaike was raised as an English-speaking Christian. A brilliant orator, he first won recognition in Ceylon by being elected secretary of the Oxford Union in 1923. He converted to Buddhism upon his return to Ceylon and, by the mid-1930s, combined the portfolios of the ministries of local government and health and was later a minister in the first post-Independence cabinet. He used this power base to increase his personal following by appealing to problems involving the Sinhalese language and of Buddhists. Language and religion are of course highly interconnected, but let us first begin with an analysis of the ethnic mobilization of language and its divisive effects.

It is crucially important to stress that Bandaranaike initially found scant support from his target audiences. Bandaranaike's distinguished biographer James Manor notes that after Bandaranaike began to give "hard hitting speeches advocating the . . . uplift of the vernacular languages. . . . This provoked fierce attacks in the press."[18] Indeed, by 1951 Bandaranaike had been forced out of the top leadership of the ruling party and had decided to form his own party, the Sri Lankan Freedom Party (SLFP). In the 1952 general elections he intensified his appeals to Sinhalese nationalism. Nonetheless, his party won only 16% of the vote. However, as the head of the second-largest party in parliament after the elections, Bandaranaike won the formal title, Leader of the Opposition, which gave him a valuable platform.

The 1956 general election saw the birth of institutionalized outbidding among the two Sinhalese parties. Originally Bandaranaike's party was not given much chance of winning. Many issues besides ethnicity were initially involved. The popular longstanding moderate Sinhalese leader and first prime minister of independent Ceylon, D. S. Senanayake, died in 1952, and his successors were lackluster. In 1953, the government eliminated subsidies for rice, causing the staple of Ceylonese diets to rise threefold in price. The Marxist parties, which had previously advocated "parity" between Sinhala and Tamil, so wanted to defeat the government that they swallowed their principles and entered into a "no-compete" agreement with Bandaranaike's SLFP party, which greatly helped Bandaranaike in Ceylon's "first past the post" electoral system.[19] In this context, the populist message and style of Bandaranaike gained great momentum. He campaigned to the Sinhalese-speaking voters on the simple idea of "Sinhalese Only." The only official language of Ceylon would be Sinhalese, and it would be adopted immediately. In his campaign he mobilized local Buddhist monks, teachers of Sinhalese, and practitioners of traditional Ayurvedic medicine, virtually all of them outside of organized party structures.

Not to be left behind, the ruling United National Party, which had long supported the gradual upgrade of Sinhalese and Tamil along with the retention, as in India, of some use of English, began to radicalize its approach to language and tried to catch up by virtually advocating "Sinhalese Only" themselves. In the end,

18. For his biography, see James Manor, *The Expedient Utopian: Bandaranaike and Ceylon* (Cambridge: Cambridge University Press, 1989), quotation from p. 201. The government wanted to introduce more Sinhalese and Tamil gradually, but Bandaranaike wanted them adopted as the "official languages immediately." Wriggins, *Ceylon*, p. 121.

19. On the "no compete" agreement and the language issue in the 1956 campaign, see Kearney, *Communalism and Language*, pp. 68–89.

the 1956 campaign revolved around the extreme nationalist competition of the two largest parties for, in effect, nationalist Sinhalese votes. Bandaranaike won with a strong parliamentary majority.

The bill to make Sinhalese the "one official language" of Ceylon was introduced on June 14, 1956, and was passed nine days later. Four sentences in the fine book on Ceylon by Wriggins capture the tone of the aggressive nation-state policy making process that followed.

- "Proponents of changing the language of government rapidly advanced within public service."
- "The Minister of Education argued in public that the English medium for schools should be abolished in 1958."
- "It was announced that one of the leading teacher training colleges would be reserved for Sinhalese teachers only."
- "The government made no moves to allay the Tamil fears."[20]

The polarization in the campaign was such that neither the former ruling party, UNP (which had won 40% of the seats in the northeast in 1952), nor the new ruling party, SLFP, contested a *single* constituency in this Tamil-speaking zone in 1956. For their part, the Tamil parties, especially the Federal Party, limited their campaigning almost entirely to Tamil-speaking areas.[21] In our theoretical framework, this means that Ceylon ceased to have any major polity-wide parties after the aggressive nation-state-building policies were initiated in 1956.

In our conceptual framework, we also argued that given the inherent tensions in a multinational society, polity-wide jobs in the state apparatus for all citizens are normally useful for polity-wide integration. The "Sinhalese Only" nation-state policies eroded this source of Tamil integration and identification with the Ceylonese political community.

After the laws on language of 1956, Tamil-speakers could still take the higher civil service entrance exam in English but, after admission, further tests for promotion would be conducted in Sinhalese only. Existing Tamil-speakers would have to show proficiency in Sinhalese by 1960. English was abolished for the liberal arts at the university level. Tamils had been overrepresented in public employment, but the rapidity in the drop of their numbers in the state sector caused growing alienation in this politically critical group.

20. Wriggins, *Ceylon*, pp. 262–263.
21. Kearney, *Communalism and Language*, p. 77. In the 1952 election, the ruling party, UNP, had won 40% of the seats in these areas.

In 1955, 26% of the members of the elite and politically powerful Sri Lankan administrative service (SAS) were Tamils. By 1979 this figure had been cut in half.[22] But for younger Tamil aspirant professionals, recruitment trends into the SAS were even more ominous. From 1970–77, of the 467 admissions via the Open Competitive Examination route, 34 (only 7.2%) were Tamils. In the 1977–81 period, of the 159 new admissions via this route, *none* were Tamils.

A new set of admissions criteria to universities also reduced Tamil chances of getting professional qualifications for private sector jobs. This was particularly so in engineering and medicine, where Tamils had been traditionally strong. In 1969, 48% of the new admissions in engineering, and 49% in medicine, were Tamils. In 1974, these figures had dropped to 16% and 26%, respectively.[23]

Concerning primary and secondary education, the principal goals of nation-state policies were to eliminate English and to make it compulsory for all children of Sinhalese parents to learn Sinhalese. Children of Tamil parents were taught Tamil but were often not provided with teachers to learn Sinhalese. Thus, ironically, this nation-state policy was for "Sinhalese Only."

3. *The mobilization of religious differences.* A potential problem of harmony in Ceylon's multiethnic but not yet "robustly multinational" polity that needed addressing at Independence was the status of the Buddhist community. Smith's standard account of religion and politics in South Asia in the postcolonial era opens its discussion of Buddhism with the following assessment of the colonial legacy: "The Sinhalese Buddhist majority was in a markedly inferior position vis-à-vis other communities, and its language, religion and culture had been relegated to a secondary place."[24] This is true. At Independence, Buddhist monuments, which had received very little support during the period of colonial rule from the Catholic power Portugal, the Dutch Protestants, or from the successor Anglican/secular power Britain, were in a sad state of disrepair. Also, during the British period, much of the public expenditures for schooling went to "state-assisted" English-language privately run schools. These schools, the best in Ceylon, often had British and American missionary origins. They were attended

22. These data are from the official publication, *Ceylon Civil List*, and were reported in S. W. R. de A. Samarasinghe, "Ethnic Representation in Central Government Employment and Sinhala-Tamil Relations in Sri Lanka: 1948–81," table 11.3, p. 177.

23. See C. R. de Silva, "The Impact of Nationalism on Education: The Schools Takeover (1961) and the University Admissions Crisis, 1970–1975," in *Collective Identities, Nationalisms, and Protest in Modern Sri Lanka*, ed. Michael Roberts (Colombo, Sri Lanka: Marga Institute, 1979), pp. 474–499, data from table 8.

24. Donald E. Smith, "The Sinhalese Buddhist Revolution," in *South Asian Politics and Religion*, ed. Smith (Princeton: Princeton University Press, 1966), p. 454.

disproportionately by the minority "Ceylonese Tamil" community, which, due to its high-quality education in English, won a larger relative share of appointments, via competitive exams, to the highly coveted Ceylonese administrative service than did the Sinhalese. In fact, the Sinhalese were often said to be a "majority with a minority complex." Moreover, starting in the late nineteenth century, a number of changes occurred within Ceylonese Buddhism that made Buddhism potentially an even more "useable resource" for religious nationalism. Major scholars have written extensively about the "Buddhist revivalism" in Ceylon from 1860 to 1915 and its aftermath.[25]

Obeyesekere argues that in the Buddhist *doctrinal* tradition, "there is little evidence of intolerance, no justification for violence, no conception of just wars."[26] But he also notes that the construction of Ceylonese Buddhist *historiographical* tradition included foundational myths about Buddha creating Ceylon for Buddhists. This foundational myth has been selectively read by monks to create a history of "ethnic separation and integration."[27] In this sense, "every single Buddhist history . . . takes it as axiomatic that the country is Buddhist."[28]

This mythic tradition, however, did not have much impact on political life in Ceylon until the 1860s, because monks, especially the senior monks who controlled the Sangha (Buddhist Brotherhood), until then had a normative and political tradition of abstaining from direct political involvement. However, in the 1870s Buddhist nationalism began to focus on foreign control of education and were given a great boost by the arrival in Ceylon in 1880 of Colonel Henry Steel Olcott. Obeyesekere says of Olcott that "as a Westerner and an anti-imperialist American who had fought in the Civil War, Olcott possessed enormous charisma" and goes on to describe his "almost single-handed construction of a fundamentalist Buddhism."[29] In Tambiah's judgment, "the most significant activity of the

25. Among the most important works are Richard Gombrich and Gananath Obeyesekere, *Buddhism Transformed: Religious Change in Sri Lanka* (Princeton: Princeton University Press, 1988); Gananath Obeyesekere, "Buddhism, Nationhood, and Cultural Identity: A Question of Fundamentals," in *Fundamentalisms Comprehended*, ed. Martin E. Marty and R. Scott Appleby (Chicago: University of Chicago Press, 1995), pp. 231–258; Stanley J. Tambiah, "Buddhism, Politics, and Violence in Sri Lanka," in *Fundamentalisms and the State: Remaking Politics, Economies, and Militance*, ed. Martin E. Marty and R. Scott Appleby (Chicago: University of Chicago Press, 1993), pp. 589–619; and Heinz Bechert, "S.W.R.D. Bandaranaike and the Legitimation of Power through Buddhist Ideals," in *Religion and Legitimation of Power in Sri Lanka*, ed. Bardwell L. Smith (Chambersburg, PA: Anima Books, 1978), pp. 199–211. Also useful, especially because it implicitly introduces an Indian perspective, is Urmila Phadnis, *Religion and Politics in Sri Lanka* (New Delhi: Manohar, 1976).
26. Obeyesekere, "Buddhism, Nationhood, and Cultural Identity," p. 233.
27. Ibid., p. 236.
28. Ibid., p. 254.
29. Ibid., p. 247.

Buddhist revivalism stimulated and sponsored by Colonel Olcott and the Buddhist Theosophical Society [he] founded in 1880 was the establishment of Buddhist schools to counter the near monopoly that the Protestant missions (and to a
lesser extent the Catholic Church) had over the educational system."[30] Olcott also
contributed to a tradition of charismatic younger monks such as Dharmapala
taking up Buddhist mobilization directly.

But there is no direct line between this period and the 1956 events we have
described. In point of fact, this brand of Buddhist nationalism went into abeyance.
As Tambiah writes, "A remarkable feature of the Buddhist fundamentalist and
Sinhala movement is [that in 1915 it] seemed to lose prominence and surrendered
the lime light to a different cast of Sinhalese and Tamil politicians, who were to
initiate a phase of collaboration rather than confrontation."[31]

The 1947 election witnessed another period of Buddhist involvement in nationalist politics in which monks (bhikkus), particularly younger Marxist-influenced
monks, created a party, the Ceylon Union of Bhikkus (LEBM), that played a major
mobilizing role in the election. However, this movement also rapidly lost momentum partly because the young bhikkus were too leftist for the mainstream parties
(particularly the ruling, center-right UNP party) and too radical, too young, and
too autonomous for the senior monks traditionally in charge of the Sangha. As
Tambiah writes, "Once the election of 1947 was over and the UNP was elected,
[the LEBM] soon became defunct."[32] The Indian scholar Urmila Phadnis concurs
that "the LEBM virtually became defunct once the 1947 election was over. Its
leadership lost its initiative, and the group broke up." She goes further, establishing that religious issues themselves lost salience in Ceylonese public debates. In
fact, she makes the surprising assertion that "in such a setting, religious issues were
relegated to a peripheral position, if at all in the 1952 election. In fact, several
parties ignored the subject altogether in their manifestos."[33]

The above discussion underscores our central point, that religion only emerged
as the critical dividing point in the Ceylonese polity once a major party leader
found a way to mobilize it in order to ride into state power by polarizing the
majority Sinhala/Buddhists against the Tamil/Hindus. S. W. R. D. Bandaranaike,
as we have already shown, did precisely this to win the 1956 election. As Tambiah
writes, the leadership was not from within the Sangha; political bhikkus had
to wait to "join a more congenial political coalition under the leadership of

30. Tambiah, "Buddhism, Politics, and Violence in Sri Lanka," p. 590.
31. Ibid., pp. 590–591.
32. Ibid., p. 593.
33. Phadnis, Religion and Politics in Sri Lanka, pp. 172–173.

S. W. R. D. Bandaranaike."[34] This time, however, the political mobilization of religion was so intense that more than fifty years later, Buddhist mobilization still plays a major structuring role in Sri Lankan politics.

Before discussing this fatal mobilization of religious difference, let us briefly note how India-style state-nation policies could have addressed many of the admittedly serious problems Buddhism faced in Ceylon at Independence. With the ample economic and political resources Howard Wriggins documents were available to political leaders and the state apparatus at Independence, noninflammatory but effective policies to improve the status of the Buddhist majority could have been possible, but all such opportunities were lost.

When the first prime minister of newly independent Ceylon, D. S. Senanayake, was approached by a delegation of Buddhists with a request for some state support for monuments and schools, he refused. His stated reason was that "the Buddha has pointed out the path of development, and no state aid can take man there."[35] An alternative response to this nineteenth-century British liberal formula could have been that of India's. India's Constituent Assembly created a distinctive form of secularism based on a "respect all and support all" formula for religions.[36] This formula allows the Indian secular state to spend extensive monies to keep religious monuments and pilgrimage sites presentable and safe. As the largest religion in India, Hinduism receives the largest share. Also, while the Indian state continued to give support to religious "state-assisted schools," which also had a bias toward English and many of which had missionary origins, the secular government in India rapidly created a polity-wide network of high-quality universities and technical institutes. Indeed, five very high-quality Indian Institutes of Technology have helped pave the way for India's growing world prominence in areas

34. Tambiah, "Buddhism, Politics, and Violence in Sri Lanka," p. 593.
35. Ibid., p. 457.
36. Something very similar to the Indian formula is also found in Indonesia and Senegal. See Alfred Stepan, "The Multiple Secularisms of Modern Democratic and Non-Democratic Regimes," in Rethinking Secularism, ed. Mark Juergensmeyer, Craig Calhoun, and Jonathan Van Antwerpen (New York and London: Oxford University Press, forthcoming). For the Indian model, see Rajeev Bhargava, "The Distinctiveness of Indian Secularism," in The Future of Secularism, ed. T. N. Srinivasan (Oxford: Oxford University Press, 2006), pp. 20–53. For the moral and political theory behind India's secularism, see Bhargava, "Political Secularism," in The Oxford Handbook of Political Theory, ed. John S. Dryzek, Bonnie Honig, and Anne Phillips (Oxford: Oxford University Press, 2006), pp. 636–655. See also the volume Bhargava edited, Secularism and its Critics (Delhi, Oxford, and New York: Oxford University Press, 2004), especially the articles by Bhargava, Akeel Bilgrami, and Amartya Sen. Under this somewhat state-nation formula, even the Hindu nationalist BJP-led government gave substantial subsidies for Muslims to make pilgrimages to Mecca. Indeed, one of the three terminals at Delhi's international airport, the "Hajj Terminal," is devoted exclusively to facilitating such pilgrimages. For a book-length treatment on the emergence and practice of secularism in India, see Donald E. Smith, India as a Secular State (Princeton: Princeton University Press, 1963).

such as information technology. But when Ceylon began addressing the problems of the Sinhalese-Buddhist majority, political leaders went from relative neglect to aggressive nation-state policies, which contributed to increasingly polarized political identities and eventually to war between the two nations.

Let us look specifically at the role of religion in the years leading up to the 1956 election. Bandaranaike knew he had a powerful conjunctural factor in his favor. The election year coincided with the great celebrations planned to commemorate the 2500th anniversary of the death of Buddha and the first landing of his followers in Ceylon. Bandaranaike initially received quite lukewarm support from important parts of his Buddhist electoral audience. Wriggins writes that Bandaranaike in 1951 "courted Buddhist opinion by protesting against the government's neglect of the Buddhist religion and culture. At the time he publicly proposed making Buddhism a state religion, but both Buddhist priests and laymen objected."[37] Indeed, as late as January 1956, the year of the fatal mobilization, the president of the All Ceylon Buddhist Congress, Dr. G. P. Malalasekera, in a major speech about the forthcoming report on the status of Buddhism, explicitly argued that Buddhists "have no desire to make Buddhism the State religion—in spite of the cry raised by self-seeking politicians—but they do want the State to help them rehabilitate themselves and undo some, at least, of the injustices perpetrated against them during the days of their [colonial] subjection."[38]

After his 1956 electoral victory, Bandaranaike initially concentrated on passing the polity-fragmenting majoritarian language policies we have discussed. However, the political promotion of identification of the state with only one, of what were then two, self-conscious political communities in Sri Lanka (and four significant religions) was deepened in 1978 when the new constitution declared, "The Republic of Sri Lanka shall give Buddhism the foremost place and accordingly it shall be the duty of the State to protect and foster the Buddha Sasana" (Article 9). As the comparativist Donald Horowitz put it, "The Sri Lankan language and state religion provisions symbolically wrote the Sri Lankan Tamils out of the polity."[39]

4. *The privileging of nation-state over state-nation values.* Once these nationalist forces were ushered into existence by political leaders in the 1956 campaign and Sinhalese/Buddhist values and language were accorded primacy, even a major pact by Prime Minister Bandaranaike himself and the Tamil president of the

37. Wriggins, *Ceylon: Dilemmas of a New Nation* (Princeton: Princeton University Press, 1960), p. 121. This particular speech was given at the Young Men's Buddhist Association.

38. Text of speech reproduced in *The Times of Ceylon*, January 15, 1956, cited in Wriggins, *Ceylon*, p. 196.

39. Horowitz, "Incentives and Behavior in the Ethnic Politics of Sri Lanka and Malaysia," p. 28.

Federalist Party, S. J. V. Chelvanayagam, was shattered by many of the same political forces Bandaranaike had mobilized. A similar pact made by the new governing party in 1965 met the same fate.[40]

Major Sinhalese-Tamil riots occurred in 1958, 1977, and, worst of all, 1983, right before the start of the civil war. Wriggins draws a direct link between the nation-state policies and state ambivalence about enforcing public order against Sinhalese nationalist forces: "The alarming riots of 1958, unparalleled in the island's history, were the direct result of these reforms and of government reluctance to insist that public order be maintained."[41] As the riot cycle progressed, the state security apparatus increasingly abandoned serious efforts at representing state neutrality. As Tambiah writes of the police and the armed forces, "In 1958 they saved many Tamil lives and earned their reputation as upholders of law and order; in 1977 they turned indifferent; but from 1981 onwards they have become a party to the riots, frequently figuring as prime villains."[42] Two of the main reasons for this decreasing neutrality of the state security forces were their sense of what political leaders wanted and the near-total shift away from recruiting any Tamils into the security apparatus. By the time of the devastating riots of 1983, probably no more than 5% of police officers in the police, and less than this in the army, were Tamils.[43]

The 1978 constitution, hastily drafted and approved when the ruling party controlled five out of every six seats in parliament, deliberately shifted Sri Lanka to a directly elected semi-presidential system that gave the president more powers than in France. Some of the powers of the president include the right: to "be head of the Cabinet of Ministers" (article 43); to appoint all members of the "Public Service Commission" (article 56); to "submit to the people by Referendum any Bill" so long as it does not change the constitution (article 85); and appoint the chief Justice and, after ascertaining his views, appoint "every other Judge of the

40. We are referring to the Bandaranaike-Chelvanayagam Pact of July 1957 and the Dudley Sennayake–Chelvanayagam Pact of March 1965. Both pacts are reproduced in Ambalavanar Sivarajah, *Politics of Tamil Nationalism in Sri Lanka* (New Delhi: South Asian Publishers, 1996), pp. 202–205. Many analysts and policy makers, Sinhalese and Tamil alike, now argue that if either pact had been implemented, the civil war would not have happened.
41. Wriggins, *Ceylon*, p. 270.
42. Tambiah, *Sri Lanka*, p. 26.
43. See Newton Gunasinnghe, "Community Identity and Militarization in Sri Lanka: Sri Lankan Armed Forces," in *The Challenge in South Asia: Democracy, Development, and Regional Cooperation*, ed. Ponna Wijnaraja and Akmal Hussain (New Delhi: Sage Publications, 1989); and Bose, *States, Nations, and Sovereignty*, p. 75. See also Darina Rajasingham-Senanayake, "Sri Lanka: Transformation of Legitimate Violence and Civil-Military Relations," in *Coercion and Governance: The Declining Political Role of the Military in Asia*, ed. Muthiah Alagappa (Stanford: Stanford University Press, 2001).

Supreme Court and Court of Appeals" (article 151). On top of all this, the president may, with some minor limitations, "from time to time, by Proclamation summon, prorogue, and dissolve Parliament" (article 70).

Over the next decade, the president called a referendum under dubious circumstances, extended the life of the parliament (where he had a massive majority) to six years longer than the prescribed term of office, passed some draconian security laws, and replaced most judges.[44] Such a powerful presidential office makes it virtually impossible for the top political office ever to be a serious, chief-executive-binding coalition. It also makes it extremely difficult for that office to be a "divisible good," with many of the groups, or parties, in a multinational society sharing power, as is possible in a multinational society with a parliamentary system. As we noted in chapter 1, all the democracies in the world that are close to the state-nation ideal type are essentially parliamentary and thus have power-sharing potential.

5. *The elimination of the major Tamil party from parliament and the shift of Tamil power to secessionist guerrillas.* Since 1953, in sharp contrast to the pattern we documented for Tamil Nadu, no politician ever elected to parliament from the Tamil base in the north was ever made a cabinet minister. However, they still contested parliamentary seats and participated in parliament. Even this ended in 1983, mostly due to nation-state policy choices.

In May 1976, twenty years after the crises had begun, most of the Tamil parties united to create the Tamil United Liberation Front. At their founding meeting they resolved: "The restoration and reconstitution of the Free, Sovereign, Secular, Socialist State of Tamil Eelam based on the right of self determination inherent in every nation has become inevitable in order to safeguard the very existence of the Tamil nation in this country."[45]

Many Sinhala observers saw this as a Declaration of Independence. However, despite the provocative language, one of the chief Tamil negotiators, A. Jayaratham Wilson, writing in 1978, said that the resolution "still left room for manoeuvre on the question of autonomy or sovereign statehood."[46] Indeed, in a later

44. For a discussion of the president's extensive use and abuse of these powers, see C. R. de Silva, "Plebiscitary Democracy or Creeping Authoritarianism? The Presidential Election and Referendum of 1982," M. P. Moore, "The 1982 Elections and the New Gaullist-Bonapartist State in Sri Lanka," and Priya Samarakone, "The Conduct of the Referendum," all in *Sri Lanka in Change and Crisis*, ed. Manor, pp. 35–50, 51–75, and 76–83, respectively. For a critical analysis of the 1978 constitution by a leading Tamil scholar who frequently represented the Tamil leader, Chelvanaykam, in major negotiations, see A. Jeyaratnam Wilson, *The Gaullist System in Asia: The Constitution of Sri Lanka (1978)* (London: Macmillan, 1980).
45. Wilson, *Break-Up of Sri Lanka*, p. 89.
46. A. Jeyaratnam Wilson, *Politics in Sri Lanka, 1947–79* (London: Palgrave/Macmillan, 1974),

book, Wilson devotes most of his discussion of the 1976–83 period to negotiations between the government and the Tamils about proposals for devolution, in which the Tamil political leaders were apparently still quite interested.[47]

In 1983, the worst riots against the Tamils occurred. Shortly afterward, the president pushed through the Sixth Amendment to the constitution, which required all members of parliament to swear a public oath against secession—and, implicitly, for the continued unitary status of Sri Lanka—or to lose their seat in parliament. From a comparative perspective, it is important to stress that parties that advocate independence, such as the Scottish Nationalists in the United Kingdom, the Parti Québecois in Canada, and the Vlaams Belang in Belgium are able to remain in their respective legislatures. As it was, not a single Tamil member of parliament from the north took the oath in Sri Lanka in 1983; they all walked out of parliament, and they never returned during the civil war.[48] Numerous observers considered this the end of any possibility of peace and democracy between Sinhalese and Tamils in Sri Lanka.

One of the Tamil members of parliament who refused to take the oath insists that, until the riots and the oath in 1983, "the vast majority of the Tamil parliamentary group would have accepted a serious federal alternative. Even outside the Parliament, we were still the most powerful group. But, by 1985–86, the LTTE [the separatist guerrillas] were the most powerful group."[49] Some of the former top guerrilla leaders agree with this assessment. In the early 1980s there were five small guerrilla groups in the jungle: their acronyms were LTTE, PLOTE, EPRL, EROS, and TELOS. In an interview, a former leader of EPRL estimated that before the 1983 pogrom and oath, they "were recruiting but had no fighters—but by 1985, they had a cadre of seven thousand." In his estimation, before 1983 "most Tamils still probably had more faith in their elected officials in Parliament than in

p. 154. A participant at the meeting, Siva Sitaparam, told Stepan in an April 1998 interview in Colombo that a lot of politicians at the meeting had reservations about the resolution, but he had become convinced, after a conversation with the key Tamil leader at the meeting, C. V. Chelvanayakam, that "C. V. was of the view that if a good alternative inside Sri Lanka emerged he would consider it." Sitapuram at the time of the interview was the secretary general of what remained of TULF.

47. For his detailed discussions of various devolutionary schemes (which we consider quite modest by the standards of Canadian, Spanish, Belgium, or Indian devolution), see Wilson, *Break-Up of Sri Lanka*, pp. 141–174.

48. The oath, in its entirety, was: "I will uphold and defend the Constitution of the Democratic Socialist Republic of Sri Lanka and that I will not, directly or indirectly, in or outside Sri Lanka, support, espouse, promote, finance, encourage or advocate the establishment of a separate state within the territory of Sri Lanka." See the Seventh Schedule, Article 157, of the 1978 Sri Lankan constitution.

49. Previously cited interview by Alfred Stepan with Siva Sitaparam, Colombo, April 1998.

the boys in the jungle." A former top leader of PLOT estimates that before 1983, none of the five guerrilla groups had more than thirty "militants" but that by 1985, they had four thousand under arms.[50]

Traumatic events can constitute a strong feeling of "we-feeling," or even of a hostile "nation," among a previously loyal and quite divided minority community. Multiple but complementary identities can be shattered and then replaced by conflictual polar identities. In the judgment of Tambiah, policies "implemented in the name of nation building [Sinhalese] and equitable democratization of society served to deepen the Sinhalese-Tamil rift and increasingly to politicize and make collective adversaries out of the Sinhalese and the Tamils."[51] Bose strikes a similar note: "Nation building, as attempted by those at the helm of the postcolonial Sri Lankan state, actually facilitated the emergence and development of a Tamil national consciousness and eventually precipitated a crisis of the state."[52] Let us now examine the state of opinion in Sri Lanka in 2005.

PUBLIC OPINION IN SRI LANKA

In 2005, the *State of Democracy in South Asia* (SDSA) project of the CSDS carried out a survey with 4,613 respondents in Sri Lanka. In addition to the set of SDSA questions common to all of the five South Asian countries (India, Pakistan, Bangladesh, Sri Lanka, and Nepal), the survey included a special battery of questions designed for Sri Lanka. In the next few pages, "Tamils" refers only to "Jaffna-area Tamils," not to "Up-Country Tamils." The responses to these questions shed great light on Sinhala/Tamil relations after fifty years of aggressive nation-state building policies in Sri Lanka. The results dramatically reveal the majoritarianism among the Sinhala/Buddhist population and the sense of insecurity and low trust in key state institutions among the Tamils of Sri Lanka.[53]

For example, only 9% of Sinhala respondents "strongly disagreed" with the

50. Both the interviews with former guerrilla leaders were by Stepan in Sri Lanka, February 2003. A former AFP correspondent who did over one hundred interviews with guerrillas from 1987 to 1989 estimates that none of the five major guerrilla groups had more than 50 active members in 1981 but that "the July 1983 riots opened a floodgate of young Tamils to various Tamil militant groups. It was a remarkable change in the Tamil heartland. Until then not many had vowed to plunge into militancy." See M. R. Narayan Swamy, *Tigers of Lanka: From Boys to Guerrillas* (Delhi: Konark Publishers, 1994), p. 96.

51. Tambiah, *Sri Lanka*, p. 75.

52. Somantra Bose, "State Crises and Nationalities Conflict in Sri Lanka and Yugoslavia," *Comparative Political Studies* 28 (April 1995), p. 100.

53. Parts of northern and eastern provinces where civil war prevented a survey were excluded from the sampling frame, which did not cause undersampling of Tamils (11% of our sample) and Up-Country Tamils (4%).

TABLE 5.1
Perceptions of Discrimination by Community in Sri Lanka, 2005

Respondents who:	Sinhalas	Tamils	Up-country Tamils	Muslims
Strongly disagree that "everyone enjoys equal rights."	9%	32%	18%	29%
Strongly disagree that "people are free to speak their mind without fear."	6	25	19	15
Say they feel "less safe" now "compared to the situation in this city/town/ village a few years ago."	20	41	21	34
Do not feel or are unsure that, "if you went to the police, you would be treated in the same way as everyone else."	51	73	71	45

Source: SDSA 2005, CSDS, Delhi, Sri Lanka dataset; questions A-10, C-20b.

Note: The overall N for SDSA in Sri Lanka is 4,613. In tables 5.2 to 5.5, the N varies for each question because the number of "do not know" responses varies by question.

statement that "everyone enjoys equal rights," whereas the percentage of Tamils who feel this way is more than three times as high (32%). Only 6% of Sinhala respondents "strongly disagreed" with the statement that "people are free to speak their mind without fear," whereas more than four times as many Tamils (25%) "strongly disagreed" with this statement. The percentage of Tamils who responded that they feel "less safe" than a few years ago is twice as high as among the Sinhala (41% versus 20%). A surprisingly high percentage of Sinhala (51%) were not sure that they would be "treated in the same way as everyone else," but an even higher percentage of Tamils (73%) were unsure of their equal treatment by the police (see table 5.1).

Some of our readers may believe that all majority religions, in any country, will tend toward majoritarianism in politics and public policy. Our SDSA survey reveals that this is not necessarily so. For whatever complex variety of reasons, the majority Buddhist population in Sri Lanka, a polity that has followed robust nation-state policies for fifty years, is much more majoritarian than the majority Hindu population in India, a polity that has followed state-nation policies for sixty years.

In Sri Lanka, 89% of the Buddhist majority "strongly agree" or "agree" with the statement that "in a democracy the will of the majority must prevail," whereas in India the comparable response to this question by the Hindu majority is only 48%.

TABLE 5.2

Majoritarianism in Sri Lanka and India by Majority Religion, 2005

	Sri Lanka (majority Buddhist)	India (majority Hindu)
Those who "strongly agree" or "agree" that "in a democracy the will of the majority community must prevail."	89%	48%
Those who "strongly disagree" or "disagree" that "giving equal treatment is not enough, the government should give special treatment to minorities."	77	29
"Strong majoritarians" on composite index	27	7

Source: SDSA 2005, CSDS, Delhi, Sri Lanka dataset; Sri Lanka–specific questions.

Note: The composite index on majoritarianism uses two items: 31-b ("Giving equal treatment is not enough, the government should give special treatment to minorities") and 31-g ("Minorities should adopt the ways of life of the majority community"). "Strong majoritarians" in our index are those who disagree or strongly disagree with 31-b *and* agree or strongly agree with 31-g. The overall N for SDSA in Sri Lanka is 4,630. Here the N varies for each question because the number of "do not know" responses varies by question.

Affirmative action for minorities is much more opposed by Buddhists in Sri Lanka than it is by Hindus in India. In Sri Lanka, 77% of Buddhist respondents "strongly disagree" or "disagree" with the statement that "giving equal treatment is not enough, the government should give special treatment to minorities." But in India, only 29% of Hindu respondents "strongly disagreed" or "disagreed" with the same statement.

The SDSA survey constructed an index of "strong majoritarianism." Respondents who "strongly agreed" or "agreed" with the statement that "minorities should adopt the ways of life of the majority" *and* who also "strongly disagreed" or "disagreed" with the affirmative action question we just discussed in the preceding paragraph are labeled "strong majoritarians." In the SDSA survey, only 7% of Hindu respondents in India are strong majoritarians, whereas four times as many Buddhists in Sri Lanka (27%) are strong majoritarians. For a summary of these results, see table 5.2.

As early as the 1970s, Sri Lankan administrations became so aware of the impending crisis with the Tamils that they began to relax some of the language strictures against Tamil, but these efforts were never fully implemented, nor the damage undone. Since the 1990s there have been various peace efforts, but the extreme nation-state policies that they had implemented have massively eroded the Sri Lankan state's internal capacity even to communicate to their Tamil-speaking citizens. For example, as late as 1998, the "National Integration Planning Unit" working with the president on peace plans and quasi-federal proposals sent out virtually all of its mass mailings to Tamils in Sinhalese. They did this because they had no Tamil-script computers or Tamil-literate typists in the National Integration Planning Unit.[54]

In early 2002, in response to a Norwegian-led effort to mediate a peace process in Sri Lanka, the Tamil LTTE separatists and the Sri Lankan government agreed to a ceasefire. The ceasefire was in existence at the time of the 2005 survey but broke down in January 2008.

In the SDSA survey, a strong majority of Sinhalas and an even stronger majority of Tamils supported various measures to seek peace. In answer to the statement "it is very important to have a peaceful settlement of ethnic conflict for the existence of a strong democracy in Sri Lanka," 68% of the Sinhalas "strongly agreed" or "agreed," as did 83% of the Tamils, 94% of the Up-Country Tamils, and 87% of the Muslims. A comparable consensus supported the statement "the best way to achieve peace in Sri Lanka is a solution through negotiation": 63% of Sinhalas, 84% of Tamils, 85% of Up-Country Tamils, and 74% of Muslims. Most surprising of all, almost fifty years after the militant nation-state "Sinhalese Only" monolingual campaign had contributed to growing polarization and conflict in multinational and multilingual Sri Lanka, there was nonetheless a strong consensus among all respondents about the desirability of strong language reforms in a more state-nation direction: 60% of Sinhalas, 68% of Tamils, 72% of Up-Country Tamils, and 88% of Muslims strongly agreed that "the state should make it compulsory to learn all the three languages [Sinhala, Tamil, and English] at school."

However, any advance on negotiations during the ceasefire period would almost certainly have had to entail constitutionally embedded concessions granting a serious degree of regional autonomy. On this key issue (after fifty years of unitary state/nation-state rhetoric from Sinhala-led governments), Sinhala opinion was in

---

54. The above is based on long interviews (and observations of working arrangements) by Stepan with Foreign Minister Laksman Kadhirgamar and Minister of Justice and Constitutional Affairs G. L. Peiris, April 2–6, 1998, Colombo. Kadhirgamar, the only significant Tamil minister in the Sri Lankan government, was assassinated in 2004, most analysts believe by the LTTE. In a follow-up interview with a major Sri Lankan political scientist, Jayadeva Uyangoda, in 2004, Uyangoda confirmed Stepan's impression, saying that while some leaders in the government were exploring ways for Sinhala-Tamil rapprochement, the state apparatus had still not become "decommunalized."

sharp disagreement with Tamil opinion. Federalism, indeed asymmetrical federalism, had been crucial to the "holding together" formulas in India, Spain, Belgium, and Canada that we have already discussed. But 82% of Sinhala respondents rejected a formula with asymmetrical dimensions, whereas only 34% of the Tamils did. Even a symmetrical formula that would increase the small level of devolved power they had through Provincial Councils vis-à-vis the center was rejected by three and a half times as many Sinhala respondents (66%) as Tamil respondents (18%).[55] A quarter of Sinhalas favored a combination of negotiated *and* military solutions, whereas only 3% of Tamils favored a solution with any military component. Finally, in the modern world many conflict termination formulas include some discussion of a general amnesty, but 77% of Sinhala respondents opposed general amnesty, whereas only 31% of Tamils did. Significantly, the Up-Country Tamils, who have been on the receiving end of some LTTE military actions, oppose amnesty even more than the Buddhists (80%), and the Muslims, who have also borne the brunt of some LTTE forced migration measures, oppose amnesty by 45% (see table 5.3).

Since there was a civil war for over a quarter of a century and the Sri Lankan military is now "occupying" much of the former war zone, the development of a postwar political solution inevitably entails the Sri Lankan military and police playing some role. But, as the only Tamil minister in the government acknowledged in an interview with Stepan, due to the Sinhalization of the security apparatus, this would be difficult, because in his judgment "there are few, maybe no, high-ranking Tamil Army officers in the Sri Lankan Army. Indeed, of the top fifty police officers, maybe only one or two are Tamils."[56] This has also contributed to a troublesome legacy in terms of Tamil attitudes. In a 2005 survey of Sri Lankan respondents, Tamils were ten times more likely (40%) than Sinhalas (4%) to respond that they had "no trust at all" in the Sri Lankan Army.[57]

55. In 1987, the thirteenth amendment to the Constitution was passed, introducing a degree of self-government at the provincial level. This came in the form of "Provincial Councils." However, to date, serious power has never devolved to the Councils. The central government appoints a governor to the province, and this governor controls the most important part of the budget in the province and de facto controls education, land, police, and health.

56. Previously cited interview by Stepan with Laksman Kadirgamer. Indeed, the U.S. State Department found that staffing in the Sri Lankan armed forces had increased 650% since 1985—but that not one Tamil had been employed. This situation contrasts sharply with the end of the insurgency in the 1990s in Punjab State in India, where the top police officer during the counterinsurgency was K. P. S. Gill, himself a Sikh. For an account of how and why Gill led the military campaign against Sikh separatists, see K. P. S. Gill, *Punjab, The Knights of Falsehood* (New Delhi: Har-Anand Publications, 1997).

57. State of Democracy in South Asia project, 2005, Sri Lanka dataset, questions C-13e, C-13f.

TABLE 5.3
Opinions on Measures to End the Present Conflict by Ethnicity in Sri Lanka, 2005

Those who:	Sinhalas	Tamils	Up-country Tamils	Muslims
"Strongly disagree" or "disagree" with the proposal that "the powers of some Provincial Councils may need to be increased more than others."	82%	34%	46%	47%
"Strongly disagree" or "disagree" with the proposal that "the powers of Provincial Councils should be increased, even if those of the government at the center have to be decreased."	66	18	17	24
"Strongly disagree" or "disagree" with proposal for general amnesty.	77	31	80	45
Favor "military solution by defeating the LTTE by itself or with negotiations as the best way to achieve peace in Sri Lanka."	25	3	2	16

Source: SDSA 2005, CSDS, Delhi, Sri Lanka dataset.

Note: The overall N for SDSA in Sri Lanka is 4,613. Here the N varies for each question because the number of "do not know" responses varies by question.

Questions:

S-9: "Now I am going to ask you about some proposals with regarding to the ethnic conflict that have been discussed recently. For a peace agreement, please state whether you very much agree, agree, somewhat agree, do not agree with the following proposals:"

S-9b: "The powers of some Provincial Councils may need to be increased more than others."

S-9a: "The powers of Provincial Councils should be increased, even if those of the government at the center have to be decreased."

S-9d: "There should be a general amnesty (that is, freedom from criminal prosecution) for people who may have committed illegal political violence against civilians during the war."

REFLECTIONS ON SRI LANKA AND INDIA

In the last two chapters we have addressed a puzzle: after Independence, why did the issue of Tamil separatism become a non-issue in India while the non-issue of Tamil violence and separatism become a war for Tamil independence in Ceylon?

Let us look at comparative levels of trust and distrust in the two countries. In the state-nation of India, there are surprisingly small differences between majority Hindu and minority Muslim opinions on such key matters as trust in the army and perceptions of inequality in the polity. In strong contrast, in Sri Lanka, which has tried to impose aggressive nation-state policies for fifty years, there are extremely

TABLE 5.4
Opinions on Trust in the Army and Unequal Treatment in Sri Lanka and India, 2005

	Sri Lanka		India	
	Majority Buddhist	Minority Hindu	Majority Hindu	Minority Muslim
Those who have "no trust at all" in the army	4%	34%	5%	7%
Those who strongly disagree that "everyone enjoys equal rights"	9	28	9	8

Source: SDSA 2005, CSDS, Delhi, Sri Lanka dataset.
Note: The overall N for SDSA in Sri Lanka is 4,613. Here the N varies for each question because the number of "do not know" responses varies by question.

sharp differences between majority Buddhist and minority Hindu opinions on these same questions (see table 5.4).

In table 5.2 we documented that in India, only 7% of the respondents from the majority religion, Hinduism, gave answers to a battery of questions that led us to classify them as "majoritarian." In sharp contrast, in Sri Lanka, 27% of respondents from the majority religion, Buddhism, were majoritarian. For the 2005 SDSA survey, we created an index for "religiosity" and an index for "support for democracy." For India, we documented the surprising finding that, the higher the degree of religiosity among the majority religion, the greater the support for democracy. In Sri Lanka, the exact opposite relationship exists: the higher the degree of religiosity, the lower the support for democracy (see figure 5.1).

There are of course many historically specific reasons in each country that contributed to these outcomes. We have discussed some of these for India already. A historically specific complicating factor in Ceylon was what is commonly referred to as their "majority with a minority complex" because Sri Lanka's Tamil minority is historically related to the community in India of over 40 million Tamils that control their own state, Tamil Nadu, twenty miles across the straits. Another complicating factor was that Ceylon lacked a powerful polity-wide independence movement, which would have been crucial in developing a constituent assembly to argue out, craft, and legitimate their constitution. Indeed, the British played such a powerful constitutional development role that from 1948 to 1972 the constitution of Ceylon was called the "Soulbury Constitution" after Lord Soulbury, Herwald Ramsbotham, the head of the British commission that began the constitutional drafting process.

However, we feel that a considerable part of the difference is the dramatically different "policy grammar" that was used in India and Sri Lanka to manage

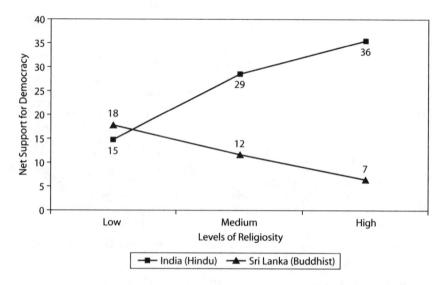

Figure 5.1. Opposite Relationship between Intensity of Religious Practice and Support for Democracy by Majority Religion in India and Sri Lanka

Notes: Table entries are for "net support for democracy," which is measured here by subtracting the percentage of "non-democrats" from the percentage of "strong democrats." We classify respondents as "strong democrats" if they (1) "prefer democracy" in C23 *and* (2) "strongly approve" or "approve" of rule by "elected leaders" in C18d *and* (3) "strongly disagree" or "disagree" with rule by army *and* (4) "strongly disagree" or "disagree" with rule by the king. We classify respondents as "non-democrats" if they (1) say they prefer dictatorship or say it doesn't matter in C23 and (2) either "strongly disagree" or "disagree" with rule by elected leaders *or* "strongly agree" or "agree" with rule by army or king.

Source: SDSA 2005, CSDS, Delhi, India and Sri Lanka main dataset.

their respective multinational societies peacefully and democratically. Using the framework we presented in chapter 1, India and Sri Lanka employed diametrically opposite strategies toward our eight categories (see table 5.5).

Looking at the 1996–2008 period, it is clear that any peace process could only have advanced if the "outbidding" in Sri Lanka between the two largest traditional Sinhalese parties had stopped and if they had formed a grand coalition to produce the constitutional amendments required for any form of serious devolution that might be acceptable to the Tamils. By the late 1990s, there was in Sri Lanka certainly a degree of mutual exhaustion of the sort that Dankwart Rustow has argued is useful to end a stalemate.[58] However, a grand coalition was made more

58. Dankwart Rustow, "Transitions to Democracy: Toward a Dynamic Model," *Comparative Politics* 2, no. 3 (1970), pp. 337–363.

TAMILS IN SRI LANKA   169

difficult in Sri Lanka's version of a "semi-presidential" system, which, as we have argued, is a less potentially "sharable office" than the office of the prime minister in a parliamentary system. Certainly, given the frequent tensions between the president and the prime minister to date, such power-sharing has not occurred.

In any case, the refrain often heard in the 1990s in Sri Lanka was that despite the acknowledgment of the failure of aggressive nation-state-building policies, "the most the government can give is still less than the insurgents can accept." This was especially so by 2007 when a hardline Buddhist monk party (JHU) temporally joined the governing coalition led by the populist, Sinhalese-nationalist president, Mahinda Rajapaksa, and the Tamils were still led by the pro-independence LTTE. The often-violated (by both sides) ceasefire agreement brokered by Norway that began on February 23, 2002, was terminated by the Sri Lankan government on January 16, 2008.[59]

Once again, this reminds us of the importance of *timing* in politics.[60] One often also hears in Sri Lanka that if the government had been willing in 1956, or even in 1975, to offer half of what they have occasionally offered in the last few years, the elected Tamil politicians probably could have convinced their fellow Tamils to accept such terms as the price of peace and democracy.

POST–CIVIL WAR AFTERMATH

Sri Lanka's civil war ended in May 2009 with the death of the LTTE leader Velupillai Prabhakaran and the military victory of the Sinhalese nationalist leader, President Rajapaksa. The consequences of Sri Lanka's long conflict over nation-state grammar in a robustly multinational context had taken a secular toll on democracy. On Freedom House's seven-point scale on "political rights," where the best score is 1, Sri Lanka never scored worse than 2 from 1973 to 1981; however, Sri Lanka has not scored as high as 2 since 1983. Indeed, in every full year of Rajapaksa's government from 2006 to 2009, Sri Lanka never received a "political

59. See "Sri Lanka Notifies Broker Norway of End to Rebel Peace Deal, Nordic Monitors to Leave," *Associated Press*, January 4, 2008. There is a rich literature on previously failed devolution and peace discussions. See, for example, M. Somasundram, ed., *Reimagining Sri Lanka: Northern Ireland Insights* (Colombo, Sri Lanka: International Centre for Ethnic Studies, 1999). See also Regi Siriwardena, ed., *Sri Lanka: The Devolution Debate* (Colombo, Sri Lanka: International Centre for Ethnic Studies, 1996).

60. On the vital role of timing in politics, see Juan J. Linz, "Democracy's Time Constraints," *International Political Science Review* 19, no. 1 (1998), pp. 19–37; and the chapter by Linz, "Time and Regime Change," in his *Robert Michels, Political Sociology, and the Future of Democracy* (New Brunswick, NJ: Transaction Books, 2006). Houchang Chehabi edited this book and added a valuable bibliography.

TABLE 5.5

Contrasting Policies of India and Sri Lanka toward Their Tamil Minority Populations

Policy grammar	Tamils in India	Tamils in Sri Lanka
1. An asymmetrically federal *but not* a unitary state or symmetrically federal state	The constituent assembly created an asymmetrical federal system that enabled state boundaries to be redrawn and eventually regional cultural majorities to rule these states in their own languages. Non-Tamil speaking areas were carved out of the then Madras state.	No constituent assembly was held, but the parliament approved a constitution that declared Sri Lanka a unitary state. After 1956, the Sinhalese-Buddhist majority increasingly advanced majoritarian state policies. No significant devolutionary policies were ever implemented.
2. Individual rights *and* collective recognition	*Language:* In 1965, after intense mobilizations and political negotiations, plans for implementing Hindi as the official language of the Indian union were abandoned. The "three-language formula" for education was adopted. Tamil is the official language of Tamil Nadu, and the state is not obliged to use Hindi in its communication with the Union. *Religion:* All major religions were constitutionally recognized. Minority institutions are eligible for financial support from the state.	*Language:* In 1956, Sinhalese was made the only official language. *Religion:* Article 9 of the 1978 constitution assigned Buddhism "the foremost place" among religions. State subsidies favor Buddhists.
3. A parliamentary *instead of* a presidential or semi-presidential system	Parliamentarianism created a "sharable good" in the executive, which allowed regional, even potentially secessionist, parties to help form ruling coalitions at the center. Since 1996, the ruling coalition at the center has always included one of the Dravidian parties from Tamil Nadu.	In 1978, Sri Lanka created a semi-presidential system executive system in which the president has more powers than in France. No northern-based Tamil party has been in any ruling coalition at the center in the last 35 years.

rights" score higher than 4. Civil liberties, such as freedom of the press, fared even worse. Reporters Sans Frontières, in the *Press Freedom Index: 2008*, noted that for the first time ever they included Sri Lanka, "which has an elected government and where the press faces violence that is all too often organized by the state" as one of the ten worst offenders of the more than 150 countries included in their rankings.[61] We stated previously that between 1983 and 2006, Sri Lanka had more estimated

61. See the Asia section of their annual report, available at www.rsf.org/en-classement794-2008.html. For articles discussing assassinations and imprisonment of journalists, including some of the most important Tamils, see "Chronicle of a Death Foretold," *The Economist*, December 1, 2009, and the UNHCR, *Refworld*, September 4, 2009. One of the most prestigious Tamil journalists, three months after the military triumph, was sentenced to twenty years of hard labor for his reports considered too sympathetic to the LTTE.

TABLE 5.5 *(continued)*

Policy grammar	Tamils in India	Tamils in Sri Lanka
4. Polity-wide *and* "centric-regional" parties and careers	Tamil-centric regional parties, due to their great coalitional ability with polity-wide parties, have enjoyed substantial presence in the Indian parliament and a disproportionate share of powerful ministries. After the mid-1970s, no significant "regional separatist" parties existed, and all Tamil parties turned "centric regional."	Tamils, especially after 1956, lost virtually all their coalitional ability in polity-wide politics and government formation. No elected Tamil from the North ever became a federal minister after 1957. After the mid-1970s, no major "centric-regional" Tamil parties existed, and all subsequent major Tamil parties were "regional separatist."
5. Politically integrated *but not* culturally assimilated populations	Tamils became politically integrated into the Indian polity but maintained very strong pride in Tamil culture. Different governments in Tamil Nadu have aggressively taken up the promotion of Tamil language and culture, including in state schools and educational curricula.	"Indian Tamils" were disenfranchised in 1948; all members of pro-autonomist Tamil parties had to leave parliament in 1983. By the mid-1980s Sri Lanka was "robustly politically multinational" with politically unintegratable Tamil LTTE guerrilla leaders.
6. Cultural nationalists vs. territorial nationalists	Cultural nationalists achieved many of their goals. Territorial nationalists, advocating separatist goals, virtually disappeared.	Violent guerrilla territorial nationalists with explicit separatist goals led the Tamil community in the northeast by the late 1970s.
7. A pattern of multiple but complementary identities	Strong Tamil identities remained, but polity-wide Indian identity grew. Trust in the central government is higher in the state of Tamil Nadu than in the rest of the country.	Due to marginalization in electoral politics and growing state discrimination and repression, polarized and conflicting identities became dominant among the Tamils in the northeast. In the end, over 100,000 Sri Lankans (disproportionately Tamil) had been killed in the long civil war that ended with the bloody defeat of the Tamil-led LTTE in 2009.

internal conflict–related deaths, eighty thousand, than any other democracy in the world in this period.[62] But the three bloodiest years were yet to come. An estimated thirty-one thousand people died in the brutal "endgame" of the civil war (2007–2009).[63] Three months after the end of the conflict, almost three

62. See Marshall, "Major Episodes of Political Violence: 2004–2006."
63. This estimate comes from the South Asia Terrorist Portal, "Total fatalities from terrorist violence, 2007–2010." The portal has tracked terrorist violence in Sri Lanka since 2000. Available at www.satp.org.

hundred thousand internally displaced civilian Tamils were still confined to heavily guarded camps.[64]

Hard nation-state policies contributed to the outbreak of this internal war and to its bloody conclusion. The war, if anything, increased the distance between Sri Lanka's Sinhalese Buddhists and Tamil Hindus and virtually eliminated the multiple but complementary identities so crucial to state-nation "we-feeling." What can be done? Most analysts, even those who are not familiar with our arguments for state-nation policies, would now suggest that some form of what Charles Taylor would call "recognition" of the Tamil minority might be socially and politically useful, coupled with devolution, even if full asymmetrical federalism is not on the table.

However, in a long three-part interview with the editor-in-chief of India's authoritative and widely circulated English daily newspaper, *The Hindu*, the Sinhalese leader Rajapaksa, still basking in a victor's justice glow, did not seem to feel that he needed to consider any of these policies: "My theory is: there are no minorities in Sri Lanka, there are only those who love the country and those that don't. . . . The people have given me the mandate, so I am going to use it. . . . No way for federalism to happen in this country."[65]

64. For estimates of deaths and casualities in the end-game of 2007–2009, see Michael Renner, "The Casualties of Sri Lanka's Intensifying War," *World Watch Institute*, July 18, 2007; "War on the Displaced: Sri Lankan Army and LTTE Abuses against Civilians in the Vanni," *Human Rights Watch*, February 2009; and U.S. Department of State, "Report to Congress on Incidents during the Recent Conflict in Sri Lanka," available at www.state.gov/documents/organizations/.

65. See the three-part interview with N. Ram, editor-in-chief of *The Hindu*, July 6, 7, and 8, 2009. These quotations are from the July 6 interview.

CHAPTER SIX

Ukraine

State-Nation Policies in a Unitary State

Thus far in this book, we have presented nation-states and state-nations as sharply contrasting ideal types for how to nurture democratic political communities. We have also noted that a characteristic political institution of the state-nation ideal type is federalism, indeed asymmetrical federalism. However, theoretically and empirically, we can imagine geopolitical and domestic contexts where *neither* full state-nation *nor* full nation-state policies are plausible as a way of managing the multinational dimensions of a polity. Why?

Geopolitically, states are members of a world of states, and it is possible that in some international contexts, especially if a country has borders with a more militarily powerful state that has some irredentist tendencies toward it, asymmetrical federalism, indeed any type of federalism, may present dangers for the nurturing of a new democratic political community via this classic state-nation policy. The safest solution might be a unitary state.

Domestically, meanwhile, if politically significant elites are divided deeply over cultural policies, it would also be democratically dangerous and politically unfeasible to try to impose classic strong nation-state policies. If we take as given in some countries such geopolitical and domestic constraints, some key questions automatically arise. Are mixed state-nation and nation-state policies possible? Specifically, is it possible to follow many state-nation policies in a unitary state? Also, is it possible to utilize some "soft" nation-state policies within an overall state-nation strategy, for example by using some consociational practices without institutionalizing a full consociational regime?

The goal of our book has not been to extol state-nations over nation-states but rather to expand our collective political imaginations about what is feasible, and unfeasible, in different contexts. One possible context is that which we have just discussed in which the utilization of the full set of either state-nation or nation-state policies would seem inadvisable. It is thus incumbent on us in the remainder of this book to identify and empirically examine some examples of what might be plausible in such contexts. In this chapter we will explore what political formulas are possible where aggressive nation-state policies are unlikely to lead toward societal peace and inclusive democracy but a full state-nation strategy, especially the use of the key state-nation policy—federalism—would also be dangerous. The analysis of independent Ukraine will allow us to study such a situation.

We examine Ukraine here from the perspective of three issues. First, we examine some conditions and identities that make the implementation of aggressive nation-state policies in Ukraine difficult and dangerous, if the goal is social peace and democracy.[1] Ukraine at independence in 1991 was a multinational society but not a "politically robust multinational" polity, as we have been using that term in this book. The data contained in this chapter suggest that if aggressive nation-state policies had been pursued in Ukraine at independence, self-identifying Russians in Crimea, and especially some of their political leaders, would most likely (as in Sri Lanka) have become "robustly multinational." Some Russians in Crimea, especially if they felt the only language permissible in the state would be Ukrainian, could have become secessionist and, as in Transnistria in Moldova, could have appealed for and received Russian military support. Second, we will examine compromises, conditions, and identities that facilitated the use of some state-nation policies for both the ethnic Russian and the ethnic Ukrainian communities. Third, we suggest some potential reforms, ones not yet tried in Ukraine, that might do what many theorists of nationalism think an impossibility: simultaneously deepen nation-state as well as state-nation democratic loyalties and iden-

---

1. Concerning the status of democracy in Ukraine before the Orange Revolution, Lucan A. Way nicely analyses the formal, and especially informal, "limitations on democracy [but also] the reasons why authoritarianism never became consolidated in Ukraine." He asserts that "Ukraine under Kuchma's presidency was a model case of 'competitive authoritarianism'—a civilian nondemocratic regime with regularly held elections that are competitive but extremely unfair." See his "Ukraine's Orange Revolution: Kuchma's Failed Authoritarianism," *Journal of Democracy* 16 (April 2005), p. 131. It is probably also useful to note that on Freedom House's seven-point scale of political rights (1 being the best score), Ukraine is the only one of the twelve non-Baltic former members of the Soviet Union never to have had a political rights score in 1992–2005 worse than 4. To be sure, it also never had a score better than 3. Also, the constitution was deeply debated and was not designed by the president only, as Russia's was in 1992, and some features of this constitution were useful to the Orange Revolution activists. On constitution building in Ukraine, see Kataryna Wolczuk, *The Moulding of Ukraine: The Constitutional Politics of State Formation* (Budapest: Central European University Press, 2001).

tities without becoming a federal state. In a brief conclusion, we will offer some comparative reflections concerning whether the unusual amalgam of policies implied in the title of this chapter is making an inclusive and peaceful democracy possible in independent Ukraine.

WHAT MAKES AGGRESSIVE NATION-STATE POLICIES DIFFICULT AND DANGEROUS?

For a newly independent country to opt for aggressive but socially peaceful and democratic nation-state strategies, it is very useful if three conditions are present: (1) a strong overlap of the cultural *demos* and the political *polis*; (2) a relatively unified, electorally based political elite that is in agreement about pursuing such policies; and (3) a geopolitical situation that supports, or at least is not outright hostile to, the pursuit of such strategies. At independence, Ukraine met none of these criteria.

1. *Cultural* demoi, *not* demos. In a 2005 public opinion survey in Ukraine, 81% of the respondents self-identified as being of "Ukrainian nationality" and only 17% self-identified as being of "Russian nationality."[2] But identities and everyday language use in Ukraine create many more obstacles for aggressive nation-state-building strategies than these figures indicate. In 1995, for example, in the five eastern provinces close to Russia, 59% of the population defined themselves as "ethnic Ukrainian" but only 15% spoke Ukrainian as their "language of preference."[3]

Ukraine's history has created an especially complex multinational society.[4] The territory that is now independent Ukraine only attained its present borders in 1954, when Soviet leader Nikita Khrushchev assigned Crimea, the home of the Soviet Black Sea Fleet, to Ukraine. The majority of the population in Crimea is made up of ethnic Russians, and there is a sizeable Islamic Tatar population. As late as 1994, only 6% of the total Crimean population completely supported Ukrainian independence because they wanted their own sovereignty if not necessarily full independence.[5] Important cities in western Ukraine, such as Lviv, until

2. Richard Rose, "Divisions within Ukraine: A Post-Election Opinion Survey," *Studies in Public Policy*, no. 403 (2005), question C-2a, p. 23.

3. See Dominique Arel, "Ukraine: The Temptation of the Nationalizing State," in *Political Culture and Civil Society in Russia and the New States of Eurasia*, ed. Vladimir Tismaneanu (Armonk, NY: M. E. Sharpe, 1995), p. 170, table 6.5. In all of his work, Arel draws the important distinction between "native language" and "language of preference."

4. Numerous footnotes and analysis to follow on all these points.

5. See Roman Solchanyk, "The Post-Soviet Transition in Ukraine: Prospects for Stability," in *Contemporary Ukraine: Dynamics of Post-Soviet Transformation*, ed. Taras Kuzio (Armonk, NY: M. E. Sharpe, 1998), pp. 30–33.

their annexation by the U.S.S.R. at the end of the Second World War, had for hundreds of years been a part of the Polish-Lithuanian Commonwealth, the Austro-Hungarian Empire, and later Poland, while eastern Ukraine was under Imperial Russia or the U.S.S.R.

Strong nation-state strategy advocates would have had to put great emphasis on making the Ukrainian language the de facto, as well as de jure, dominant language throughout the territory. This would have been difficult because, even if we exclude Crimea, only 44% of Ukraine's population shortly after independence used Ukrainian as their "language of preference." This percentage varied from a high of 92% in the west, to only 24% in the capital of the country, Kiev, to less than 15% in the east and south.[6]

Religion is not a homogenizing factor or even a cross-cutting cleavage in creating a common cultural *demos*. Indeed, in many parts of Ukraine, religion contributes to compounding cleavages. Since the Union of Brest in 1596, many Orthodox bishops in the West, virtually alone among the Orthodoxy in the world, broke away from Orthodoxy and pledged allegiance to the Pope in Rome as Uniates, in return for which they were allowed to retain their Eastern Rites. The Orthodoxy who are not allegiant to Rome are probably more fragmented (or pluralistic) in Ukraine than in any country in the world, with three intensely competing Orthodox organizations. Some bishops accept the Moscow Patriarchate, while others accept the Kyivan (Kiev) Patriarchate. There is also the Ukrainian Autocephalous Orthodox Church. Finally, and very importantly, a third of the population self-identify as "not religious."[7]

From August 10 to September 29, 1991, Richard Rose, in collaboration with the All-Russian Public Opinion Research Center (VCIOM), conducted a survey among the Russian minorities in eleven of the fifteen republics of the U.S.S.R.[8] The responses from *self-identifying* ethnic Russians in Ukraine graphically document how, on some critical attitudes, only a few months before independence, they were very far from feeling like members of the Ukrainian nation-state, or

6. Arel, "Ukraine: The Temptation of the Nationalizing State," in *Political Culture and Civil Society in Russia and the New States of Eurasia,* ed. Tismaneanu, p. 170.

7. See José Casanova, "Ethno-Linguistic and Religious Pluralism and Democratic Construction in Ukraine," in *Post-Soviet Political Order: Conflict and State Building,* ed. Barnett R. Rubin and Jack Snyder (London: Routledge, 1998), pp. 81–103, esp. table 5.2. In the 2004 presidential election, followers of the Kyivan and Autocephaelous Orthodox churches tended to support the Orange Revolution, whereas priests and monks from the Moscow Patriarch often paraded in support of Moscow-supported Yanukovych. "Ukrainians Threaten Orthodox Split" in *The Ukraine List,* no. 355, pp. 17–20.

8. For the Gorbachev and early post-Gorbachev period, VCIOM was by far the best Moscow-based survey institute for Russia and key post-Soviet states like Ukraine.

"demos." In answer to the question, "With what nationality do you define your-self?" 89% answered "Russian" and only 7% answered "Ukrainian." In answer to the question, "When you say 'in our country' what do you most often mean?" 79% answered "Soviet Union," 11% answered "this republic." Concerning the inquiry as to the language spoken by their children and grandchildren, 67% said it was Russian, 2% said it was Ukrainian, and 29% said it was both. Significantly, 52% of the ethnic Russians felt that knowledge of the Russian language should be compulsory for ethnic Ukrainians. In an important political sense, the ethnic Russians were happy if the U.S.S.R. or the new state of Russia retained some political responsibility for protecting the Russian diaspora in Ukraine. In answer to the question, "Who should be responsible for protecting Russians' interest in the republic?" (with multiple answers allowed), Russians in eastern Ukraine indicated Republican leadership (74%), U.S.S.R. leadership (44%), Russian leadership (40%), and the Soviet Army (7%).[9]

2. *Existing sharp divisions among the major politically relevant elites.* National-ism and the demand for independence had an early champion in the People's Movement of Ukraine, also called Rukh, which later became a political party. Among these early nationalists, there were certainly many who would have liked to press for strong nation-state policies. However, unlike Poland's Solidarity, Rukh had trouble building a strong and active constituency outside of its original base, which was in the predominantly Ukrainian-speaking, pro-European, anticommu-nist, western part of Ukraine centered around Lviv (with some strong followers in the capital Kiev in the center of the country). Rukh was close to the zenith of its powers in 1989, but at its First Congress 85% of its members were from the west and the center and only 6% from eastern Ukraine.[10] In the 1991 presidential elections, the Rukh candidate came in second, with 23% of the vote. In the first two competitive elections for the parliament, in 1990 and 1994, Rukh and its allies managed to win only slightly more than a quarter of the seats.[11]

The other major political elite group came from the Ukrainian Communist Party (CPU). The former ideological secretary of the Communist Party, Leonid Kravchuk, won the first presidential elections in 1991 with 62% of the vote. In the

9. See VCIOM (with Richard Rose), "Russians outside Russia: A 1991 Survey" and "Russians in the Baltic: A 1991 Survey," *Studies in Public Policy*, nos. 283 and 287 (1991), respectively, Center for the Study of Public Policy, University of Strathclyde, Glasgow, 1997.

10. Wolczuk, *Moulding of Ukraine*, p. 96.

11. On the 1990 elections, see Arel, "Parliamentary Blocs in the Ukrainian Supreme Soviet," *Journal of Soviet Nationalities* 1, no. 4 (Winter 1991), pp. 108–154. On the limits these elections presented to any ethnic-based nationalism, see Roman Szporluk, "Reflections on Ukraine after 1994," *Harriman Review* 7 (March–May 1994), p. 2.

first parliamentary elections of 1990, the CPU emerged as the largest party.[12] In fact, while many of the 450 members of the Ukrainian parliament in 1990 were formally listed as independents, Wolczuk asserts that "only 68 deputies were not CPU members," although real partisan membership was certainly less strong than these data indicate because, among other things, an individual could be a member of CPU and Rukh.[13] With a strong base among Russian-speakers, especially in the eastern parts of Ukraine, the Communist Party and its allies had very few incentives to champion aggressive nation-state policies that would lead to a marginalization of the Russian language.

There were in fact some disincentives. A rapid movement toward Ukrainian as the only usable language in parliament may well have hurt the careers of the members of the largest party in the parliament, the CPU. A content analysis of speeches in the parliament reveals that only 30% of CPU deputies spoke Ukrainian in parliamentary debates in the early 1990s.[14]

3. *Geopolitical constraints on aggressive nation-state policies.* At the time of Ukranian independence, it was by no means clear how strong irredentism might, or might not, become in the rump state of Russia. However, what was clear is that by far the largest number of ethnic Russians who were "lost to Russia"—11.3 million—were in Ukraine.[15] Also, Ukraine still had a much greater density of Russian soldiers on its territory than did Russia itself. At independence, Ukraine had a soldier-to-inhabitant ratio of one soldier for every 98 inhabitants, whereas Russia only had one soldier for every 634 inhabitants—and many of these Russian soldiers in Ukraine were still under Russian commanders supported by a still world-class military system.[16] Moreover, prominent Russian citizens from elite institutions repeatedly referred to Ukrainian independence as "temporary." Numerous public opinion polls by the Moscow-based Public Opinion Foundation found that "Russians could not accept Ukrainian independence."[17]

In comparative terms, it is important to stress that geopolitically, none of

---

12. Szporluk, "Reflections on Ukraine after 1994."

13. Wolczuk, *Moulding of Ukraine*, p. 96.

14. See Arel, "Ukraine," p. 186n45. Indeed, Arel states that these deputies denounced Ukrainian-language nationalists as "linguistic fundamentalists."

15. Alexander Motyl and Bohdan Krawchenko, "Ukraine: From Empire to Statehood," in *New States, New Politics: Building the Post-Soviet Nations*, ed. Ian Bremmer and Ray Taras (Cambridge: Cambridge University Press, 1997), p. 244.

16. Motyl and Krawchenko, "Ukraine," p. 294.

17. On the Ukrainian security situation, Taras Kuzio, "National Identity and Foreign Policy: The East Slavic Conundrum," and James Sherr, "Ukrainian Security Policy: The Relationship between Domestic and External Factors," both in *Contemporary Ukraine*, ed. Kuzio, pp. 221–244 and 245–266, respectively.

the multinational societies that we consider close to the state-nation pole, such as India, Belgium, Spain, and Canada, had at independence a potentially hostile *irredentist* relationship with a militarily more powerful neighboring country. Ukraine, at independence, potentially had such a politically significant irredentist relationship with Russia.

To some extent Ukraine has a mutually dependent energy situation, because most of Russia' exports to Europe pass through Ukraine; however, in a short-term crisis, Ukraine is extremely vulnerable to Russian retaliation. Estimates are that as much as 90% of Ukrainian oil and 60% of Ukrainian gas comes from Russia, at highly subsidized prices.[18] On a few occasions, Russia has literally turned the lights out in parts of Ukraine.[19] Geopolitical as well as domestic power balances therefore made aggressive nation-state policies in the aftermath of independence both difficult and dangerous.

Enabling Factors for Some State-Nation Policies

Two months after the Orange Revolution, Stepan asked one of the world's leading political science specialists on Ukraine, Dominique Arel, the following question: "If, at independence, a full nineteenth-century French-style nation-state strategy had been attempted, what are the chances that Ukraine would have remained united and peaceful?" Arel's answer: "Nil."[20]

There was certainly no conceptually conscious effort to follow strategies close to what we have called the state-nation ideal type, but there were conscious efforts to avoid the nation-state dangers.[21] Stepan first became aware of this in the

18. See the discussion by Sherr, "Ukrainian Security Policy," p. 263. This situation led some wags to say that "in the spring Ukraine leans toward the West, but in the fall toward the East."

19. Communication with an IDB official based on his personal observations in Eastern Ukraine, London, June 2005. See Jonathan Stern, "The Russian-Ukrainian Gas Crisis of January 2006," Oxford Institute for Energy Studies, available at www.oxfordenergy.org/pdfs/comment_0106.pdf. See also "Russia, Ukraine Gas Dispute Turns Ugly," *Associated Press*, December 14, 2005.

20. Dominique Arel, chair of Ukrainian Studies at the University of Ottawa and coordinator of the *Ukraine List* newsletter, is the author of numerous works on Ukraine and comparative nationalism. He coordinated the Ukraine section of the comprehensive project on "Identity Formation" led by David D. Laitin. Stepan's interview with Arel was in February 2005 at the University of Ottawa. We should note that a standard assertion in the literature on Ukraine is that there was virtually no ethnic or political violence during or after the drive for independence. In 1994, there were a rash of articles about the possible breakup of Ukraine. Thus the formulation of Stepan's question.

21. However, José Casanova cites an early discussion by Juan Linz of our state-nation concept and argues that it was the most appropriate strategy for Ukraine to follow and that many of the policies actually negotiated, and implemented, were close to state-nation policies. Casanova, "Ethno-Linguistic and Religious Pluralism," esp. pp. 87–88. Similarly, Roman Szporluk does not use the state-nation terminology, but the implications are consistent with our argument. Szporluk, "Reflections on Ukraine after 1994."

mid-1990s in conversations with Ukrainian politicians. He had been invited to Kiev by Ukrainian parliamentarians when they were discussing the draft constitution. They wanted him to explain to them how to avoid loopholes in decree legislation that might facilitate presidential authoritarianism. They were also interested in Stepan's (and Linz's) thoughts on how Spain handled its multinationalism democratically and relatively peacefully. In informal discussions, a frequent cautionary theme, among Russian and Ukrainian participants alike, was that they could build a state, if they were careful, but if they allowed themselves to get into irresolvable fights over their ethnic identities or divisive symbols, they could easily lose their historic opportunity.[22] State building, not nation building, was their essential effort. How did they do this? Let us briefly discuss seven important conditions and compromises, with state-nation overtones, that helped state building.

1. *Positive Russian attitudes toward living in an independent state-nation of Ukraine.* As we have just seen, many self-identifying ethnic Russians (and even some self-identifying Ukrainians) had attitudes and language preferences that would have made them resistant to nation-state-building policies at independence. The utility of our state-nation ideal type is that it directs attention to the possibility that within the set of attitudes that might be hostile to nation-state-building policies, there may be a politically useable set of attitudes that support many state-nation-building policies.

We claim that the state-nation ideal type of "multiple and complementary identities" is useful in multinational societies; we also claim it is possible.[23] The Richard Rose/VCIOM study supports this thesis. Since our purpose is to expand our understanding of different ways to build commitment and loyalty to a democratic state, let us examine the attitudes of self-identifying Russians carefully. In those areas outside the Ukrainian nationalist stronghold in western Ukraine, the following sets of self-identifying ethnic *Russian responses* to questions reveal attitudes, three months before independence, quite supportive of state-nation policies.[24]

---

22. For a well-documented article that argues that Ukranian nationalists appreciated this multinational power diffusion reality and looked for ways to accommodate it inside newly independent Ukraine, see Paul D'Anieri, "Ethnic Tensions and State Strategies: Understanding the Survival of the Ukrainian State," *Journal of Communist Studies and Transition Politics* 23 (March 2007), pp. 4–29. This article contains bibliographic references to a CIA report discussing the very real threat of the breakup of Ukraine by the CIA. Journals such as *The Economist, Foreign Policy,* and *Forbes* magazine also contained similar reports.

23. Much documentation supportive of the reality of multiple but complementary identities in Ukraine is found in Henry E. Hale, *Foundations of Ethnic Politics* (Cambridge: Cambridge University Press, 2008).

24. A separate sample was made for Russians in western Ukraine.

- "All people in the republic, both Russians and titular residents, share the same hardships now." (Agree: 96%)
- "Russians in this republic are being discriminated against." (Agree: 3%)
- "I don't feel alien in this republic." (Agree: 86%)
- "How would you evaluate relations between different nationalities in the republic?" (Cordial: 28%; Normal: 58%; Tense: 9%; Hostile: 0%)
- "Do you intend to emigrate from this republic or do you intend to stay for the rest of your life?" (Firmly decided to emigrate: 2%)
- "Pogroms of Russians are possible in the foreseeable future." (Agree: 3%)[25]

Attitudes, of course, are highly malleable. What is impressive in Ukraine is that, by and large, both the Ukrainian ethnic majority and the Russian ethnic minority made a series of compromises and decisions that built upon, rather than eroded, attitudes that were supportive of state-nation policies.

2. *The wording of the Declaration of Independence.* As the eminent Harvard-based historian of Ukraine, Roman Szporluk argues, "It is essential to remember that the independent Ukraine proclaimed in August 1991 did not define itself as an ethnic state. It was a jurisdiction, a territorial and legal entity. . . . The new state declared that all power in it derives from 'the people of Ukraine.' "[26]

3. *The inclusive law on citizenship.* Unlike Estonia and Latvia, which at independence passed exclusionary citizenship laws that disenfranchised many Russians, Ukraine, in October 1991, passed a very inclusive citizenship law. In her important account of the negotiations on the constitution, Wolczuk argues that this law "adopted a territorial definition of citizenship and membership in the new state was granted automatically to almost everyone who was living in Ukraine at the time the law was passed (the "zero option"). As no category of the population was formally excluded from the political community, citizenship based on *ius soli* became one of the fundamental attributes of the new political community."[27]

Timing helped secure this compromise. The referendum on independence was scheduled to take place two months later, in December 1991. Ukrainian nationalists accepted this inclusive wording in the citizenship law as a way to encourage a positive vote for independence in Crimea and in the Russophone

25. VCIOM (with Rose), "Russians outside Russia," questions 43, 44, 41, 81, 31, and 48, respectively. In Latvia and Estonia, the titular populations were attempting nation-state policies, and Russian-minority answers on these six questions were much more wary. The only area where Ukrainian nation-state advocates were in the majority at the time of the survey was in western Ukraine, and Russian-minority attitudes in western Ukraine were substantially more skeptical of the neutrality and fairness of a potential Ukrainian state.
26. "Reflections On Ukraine in 1994," p. 1.
27. Wolczuk, *Moulding of Ukraine*, p. 89.

eastern part of the country. The compromise was also deliberately crafted as a way of blunting the warnings by Communist Party hardliners on the dangers of ethnic exclusion modeled on the Baltics.[28]

4. *Growing strategic cooperation between Rukh and the communist leadership over statehood.* As the Rukh-based nationalists began to realize that their electoral upper base was probably only between 20% to 30% of the vote and that they needed the cooperation of Communists to win and sustain an independent Ukrainian state, they increasingly shifted from an exclusive, "nation-based" discourse to a more inclusive, "state-based" one. As Alex Motyl and Bohdan Krawchenko note, "Rukh's language was palatable to the Communists such as Kravchuk because it was nationalist, but neither chauvinist, nor racist; it had at its core the attainment of statehood for the Ukrainian people, whom Rukh carefully defined in non-ethnic terms that permitted Russians, Jews, and Poles, and others to take part in and support its cause. Such a nationalism was at least as potentially appealing to Communists, as it promised them the opportunity of continuing to serve as an elite, if not the only elite, within a future Ukrainian state."[29]

With the two major political elite groupings cooperating strategically in their advocacy of independence and an inclusive citizenship law already passed, on December 1, 1991, a republic-wide referendum approved the independence of Ukraine by 90%, including 80% support in the heavily Russophone eastern oblasts (regions) and 54% in Crimea.[30] On the same day, the once anti-nationalist but now pro-independence Kravchuk was elected president of Ukraine with 62% of the vote.

5. *Partial compromises over the constitutional preamble.* As in many countries with a multinational society, there was a heated constitutional debate over the preamble. Who are the people? The preamble to the constitution adopted in 1996 was indeed a partial victory for the nationalists, but in the same long and tortuous sentence, there is a partial compromise for all nationalities. The parliament voted for the constitution "on behalf of the Ukrainian people—citizens of all nationalities, expressing the sovereign will of the people, based on the centuries-old history

---

28. Ibid.

29. Motyl and Krawchenko, "Ukraine," pp. 250–251. Casanova is in agreement. He writes that "Rukh had incorporated explicitly such an inclusive policy in its platform." Casanova, "Ethno-Linguistic and Religious Pluralism," p. 86. The fact remains, however, that the core membership and electorate of Rukh retained a Ukrainian ethnic base.

30. The incentives for strategic cooperation by the communist elites were enhanced because some of them supported the failed coup of August 1991 in Moscow and wanted to be protected from reprisals by Yeltsin.

of Ukrainian state building and on the right to self-determination realized by the Ukrainian nation, all the Ukrainian people . . . adopts this Constitution."

As a tradeoff for this partial compromise with the nationalists, the constitution went on in its next fifteen chapters to embed one of the most rights-protecting (but often not enforced) constitutions of any postcommunist European state. As previously mentioned, Ukraine has one of the most inclusive citizenship laws in postcommunist Europe. Article 55 also gives citizens the right to seek redress for the violation of their rights from any international judicial organization of which Ukraine is a member. Article 15 also created a Human Rights Representative located in the parliament, not the executive. Dominique Arel implicitly affirms the state-nation, as opposed to nation-state, policies that Ukraine pursued after independence. Arel argues that "Ukraine strove to convince the world that, unlike many of the successor states of the former Soviet bloc, its state was being built on territorial and civic principles, eschewing any privilege for the titular Ukrainian group. . . . In terms of civic rights, one can hardly disagree with the assertion that Ukrainian state policy has been all-inclusive. . . . It is difficult to disagree with the contention that the Ukrainian state-building project is resting on territorial, as opposed to ethnic, foundations."[31]

6. *The de facto, if not de jure, compromise over language.* As late as 1968, only 17% of the post-secondary textbooks in Ukraine were in Ukrainian.[32] However, in 1989 the Ukrainian parliament, still under Gorbachev's U.S.S.R., passed the "Law on Language" establishing Ukrainian as the state language of Ukraine, and stipulated that Ukrainian be introduced in higher education and state bodies within ten years. At independence, some Ukrainian nationalists wanted to push for "Ukrainian Only," but a strong group of Russophones in Crimea and eastern Ukraine wanted then, and want now, Russian to be established as the second official state language.

Article 10 of the constitution adopted in 1996 covers the creation of a de jure nation-state language. The first two clauses read:

- The state language of Ukraine is the Ukrainian language.
- The state ensures the comprehensive development and functioning of the Ukrainian language in all spheres of social life throughout the entire territory of Ukraine.

31. Arel, "Ukraine," pp. 167–168.

32. Motyl and Krawchenko, "Ukraine," p. 243. Historically, the key issue was enrollment in Ukrainian courses. In a private communication to Stepan, Dominique Arel wrote that such enrollment "was almost nil in Imperial Russia, very high in the 1920s-30s, decreasing after World War II, and near extinction in urban areas of East and South Ukraine, as well as in Kiev, from the 1960s on."

However, the third clause of Article 10 (especially if one substitutes "nationalities" for "national minorities") has some state-nation overtones:

- In Ukraine, the free development, use and protection of Russian, and other languages of national minorities of Ukraine, is guaranteed.

Article 53 further entrenches Russian and makes illegal any aggressive nation-state, homogenizing, "Ukrainian Only" state policies:

- Citizens who belong to native minorities are guaranteed in accordance with the law the right to receive instruction in their native language, or to study their native language in state and communal educational establishments and through national cultural societies.

An ideal-type state-nation strategy would probably call for Russian to be one of the two official languages of Ukraine. The countries closest to the state-nation ideal type, such as Switzerland, Belgium, Spain, India, and Luxembourg, all of course have more than one official language in the state.

The key question for us to analyze is how much the de jure language of Article 15 actually impeded some core state-nation values such as multiple but complementary identities and polity-wide access to public and private careers.

As we saw in chapter 5, Sri Lanka's decision to make Sinhalese the only official state language and to eliminate English as a vital link language virtually precluded important polity-wide public sector careers or state-nation identities for Tamil-speakers, very few of whom spoke or wrote Sinhalese fluently.[33] Within a decade, almost no important state bureaucrats were Tamil-speakers. Sri Lanka, at independence, had many conditions that would have facilitated state-nation policies and the prolongation of its unified and democratic polity. Moreover, as we argued in chapter 5, Sri Lanka could have pursued some non-zero-sum "soft" nation-state policies like improving the educational quality of Sinhalese-language schools or refurbishing the many run-down Buddhist shrines. However, as we documented, the aggressive, zero-sum pursuit of "hard" nation-state policies in Sri Lanka's multinational society helped bring about a civil war that eroded the country's democracy and threatened its physical integrity.[34]

Independent Ukraine developed quite different language policies than those

33. Many prominent Tamils did have a second language, but it was English.
34. See chapter 5. Since 1997 Stepan has made three research trips to Sri Lanka. Virtually all the key participants he interviewed, from the prime minister on down, now think that their aggressive nation-state policies, especially toward the privileged place of Sinhalese and Buddhism, and their complete hostility to decentralization contributed directly to the crisis.

adopted in Sri Lanka, policies that make state-nation identities possible, notwithstanding the fact that Ukrainian is the only official language of the country. The pattern of the everyday use of language in Ukraine helps defuse the issue. In a 1995 poll, 32% of respondents said that they used Ukrainian as their predominant language at home, 33% used Russian as their predominant language, and 35% used *both* Ukrainian and Russian.[35] In any case, in Ukraine, the language of preference is not necessarily a marker of self-identity. Although only 32% of the population said that Ukrainian was the predominant language they spoke at home, 70% of them nonetheless self-identified as ethnic Ukrainians.[36] Finally, the Russian and Ukrainian languages are sufficiently close that in parliament, on television, and elsewhere, it is common for conversations to proceed with one person that speaks exclusively Russian while the other person speaks exclusively Ukrainian, and often speakers switch languages in the same sentence.[37] Thus, whatever language is spoken, there is normally not a problem of complete mutual incomprehension, at least in the linguistic sense.

Those self-identified ethnic Ukrainians who are in fact Russophone understandably might not want to jeopardize their careers by having to speak Ukrainian at the workplace or to use it in exams for entry into the public service. However, while only 40% of self-identified Ukrainians in Kiev spoke Russian at home, 98% of them said that they wanted their children to be "fluent" in Ukrainian.

A promising sign for the long-term possibility of multiple but complementary identities in a possible state-nation polity in Ukraine is that over 90% of self-identified ethnic Russians in Lviv expressed a desire that their children be fluent in Ukrainian.[38]

7. *The use of some key common symbols.* If a multinational society is to have a political community close to the state-nation ideal type, its citizens and political leaders need to have recourse to some common symbols.[39]

In Ukraine, there are more facilitating conditions concerning nonpolar identities than the huge literature on the "two Ukraines" indicates. Fortunately, an important longitudinal study of the supposedly polar opposite cities, Lviv in the

---

35. In 2005, the figures were 42%, 36%, and 22% respectively. See Oleh Protsyk, "Majority-Minority Relations in the Ukraine," *JEMIE* 7 (2008), p. 24. *JEMIE* is a publication of the European Centre for Minority Issues.

36. Ibid. This is a standard finding in surveys on Ukraine.

37. This is called "Surzhyk," or "code switching."

38. See Ian Bremmer, "The Politics of Ethnicity: Russians in a New Ukraine," *Europe-Asian Studies* 46, no. 2 (1994), table 12.

39. For example, the king in Spain and Belgium and, as we showed in chapter 4, Nehru and Gandhi for citizens in Tamil Nadu and India are shared positive symbols throughout the polities.

so-called nationalist west and Donetsk in the so-called pro-Russian east, has been carried out by the Ukrainian scholar Yaroslav Hrytsak. In this study, the overwhelming percentage of people polled agreed that the medieval Kyivan Rus period was the starting point of Ukraine. There are thus not competing but rather complementary founding myths about Ukraine. Also, throughout all of Ukraine, the most popular historical figure is the Cossack leader Bohdan Khmelnytskyi, whom both ethnic Ukrainians and ethnic Russians in Ukraine (unlike Russians in Russia) see as a major state-builder. Indeed, even President Leonid Kuchma, often accused of pro-Russian tendencies, made a major speech on the four hundredth anniversary of Khmelnytskyi's birth suggesting his "we-feeling" with him: "Today, carrying on Bohdan's work, we are realizing the third attempt at the revival of our state."[40] In fact, Kuchma's most important book, which is half-memoir and half-history, has a title that translates as "Ukraine Is Not Russia."

The theoretical literature on nationalism often points to the utility of an "other" in forging common identities. In Ukraine, ethnic Ukrainians, ethnic Russians, and Crimean Tatars have a shared historical "other"—Stalin. The famine in Ukraine, which led to millions of deaths, and the expulsion of the Tatars from Ukraine in 1944, are seen as direct results of the policies of Stalin. Thus, ethnic Russians and ethnic Ukrainians alike "both in the West and East, are unanimous in their negative evaluation of Stalin and his acts of repression; they see him as the main villain in Ukrainian history, the number one anti-hero. And this is exactly what makes them different from Russians [in Russia]: a majority of the Russian population [in Russia] considers Stalin in rather positive terms, as a great state builder, who turned the Soviet Union into a world superpower."[41] A more recent pre-independence appearance of an external "other" that forged some commonalities among virtually all citizens of Ukraine, vis-à-vis Russia, was the Chernobyl disaster and its callous handling by Moscow.[42]

40. Wolczuk, Moulding of Ukraine, p. 177.

41. Yaroslav Hrytsak, "On the Relevance and Irrelevance of Nationalism in Ukraine," Second Annual Cambridge-Stasiuk Lecture on Ukraine, February 20, 2004, quotation from p. 8. For example, in the year 2000, when asked in Russia to name the "most outstanding" politician to have headed the state in the twentieth century, Stalin emerged as number one. Archie Brown, "Cultural Change and Continuity in the Transition from Communism: The Russian Case," "Culture Matters" Project Final Conference, Tufts University, Medford, Massachusetts, March 26–28, 2004. Survey conducted by VTsIOM.

42. Another "othering" factor from the time of independence in Ukraine is that many mothers, whether they were ethnically Russian and ethnically Ukrainian, worried that a reunification with Russia would incur the danger of having their sons drafted in the Russian army and killed in the war against Chechnya.

Does Voter Polarization Preclude State-Nation Building?

Too many observers conflate voter, identity, and issue polarization. To understand the possibilities of some state-nation policies in Ukraine, it is imperative that we disaggregate polarization. "Voter polarization" in Urkraine is of course by comparative standards very high. But "identity polarization" is less so, and there is far less "issue polarization" that most of the literature indicates.

To be sure, as the literature on the "two Ukraines" suggests, there are strong voting differences between Lviv and Donetsk and what would appear to be dangerous voter polarization between East and West.[43] For example, in the third and final round of voting for the president during the Orange Revolution, the pro-Orange Viktor Yushchenko won 93.7% in Lviv but only 4.2% in Donetsk.[44]

But, a few years earlier, when a hard question was asked of the population of the two cities if they should become divided into several different countries, only 1% of Lviv residents and 5% of Donetsk residents chose the option of radically dividing the political community.[45] Conclusion: voter polarization does not necessarily reflect polarization about desired future political identities.

Fortunately for the political community of Ukraine, voter polarization is only one type of polarization. Conceptually and empirically, we can also speak (and measure) identity polarization and issue polarization as well as voter polarization. Identity polarization is substantially lower in Donestsk than voter polarization. For example, on a three-point scale of identity, only 20% of respondents said they were "only Russian," but 28% said they were "only Ukranian," and the modal response was bi-ethnic, at 48%. Thus, 76% of respondents in Donetsk have some degree of Ukrainian in their self-definition of identity.

43. For an excellent review of the extensive literature on the polarization debate in Ukraine and a very informative quantitative analysis that leads the authors to the conclusion that it makes sense to speak of eight, as opposed to two, regions, see Lowell W. Barrington and Erik S. Herron, "One Ukraine or Many? Regionalism in Ukraine and its Political Consequences," *Nationalities Papers* 32, no. 1 (March 2004), pp. 53–86.

44. See Rose, "Divisions within Ukraine," pp. 49–50. In the 2004 U.S. presidential elections, the most polarized state was Utah (Bush 71%, Kerry 26%), but the District of Columbia resembled Donetsk in that the losing presidential candidate won overwhelmingly (Kerry 90%, Bush 9%). One of the leading Ukraine analysts, Andrew Wilson, after a July 2005 visit to Donetsk, wrote that polarization was declining somewhat and that "most east Ukrainian elites are regrouping under party labels that accept the agenda set by the new regime." See *The Ukraine List*, no. 354, July 15, 2005, p. 11.

45. See the fascinating studies by Yaroslav Hrytsak, "National Identities in Post-Soviet Ukraine: The Case of Lviv and Donetsk," in *Cultures and Nations of Central and Eastern Europe*, ed. Zvi Gitelman, Lubomyr Hajda, John-Paul Himka, and Roman Solchanyk, *Harvard Ukrainian Studies*, vol. 22 (1998), pp. 263–282, and "Ukrainian Nationalism, 1991–2001: Myths and Perceptions," Austrian Institute for Eastern and South-Eastern Europe, Vienna, Austria, October 15, 2001.

Issue polarization is also strikingly lower than voter polarization. The north-west, where Lviv is located and which voted overwhelmingly for Yushchenko in 2004, was presented in the Russophone media during the 2004 elections as sup-porting extreme "Ukrainian Only" language plans and opposing good trade rela-tions with Russia. In fact, 68% of those surveyed in the northwest, far from being in favor of *more restrictive* policies toward the status of Russian were actually in favor of *more permissive* policies toward the Russian language than the constitu-tion prescribed: 45% were in favor of Russian being made an official language at the local level if people want it, and 23% were in favor of Russian being made the second official language. In terms of Ukrainian government relations with West-ern Europe and Russia, there was surprisingly little issue polarization in north-western Ukraine. On a five-point scale, 56% of respondents in the northwest chose the middle position, "equal orientation toward the West and toward Russia." This was also—barely—the modal position (36%) chosen in the southeast.[46]

These data offer some hope that, provided that future electoral campaigns are waged in a context of a freer press and that less government-controlled "admin-istrative resources" are used to generate polarization than there was in the 2004 elections and that the pro- and anti-Orange polarization of the 2004, 2006, and 2008 struggles dies out, new politicians might find it increasingly productive to devise policies that appeal to citizens on issues where there is in fact not over-whelming polarization.[47] If so, voter polarization could diminish, and multiple but complementary identities of the state-nation sort could increase. However, it should be noted that in the 2010 presidential election, geographical polarization was still powerful.[48]

Nation-State and State-Nation Identities: Not Mutually Exclusive?

The above heading may strike some readers as a contradiction in terms, because they may assume that the two ideal types are always in an either/or relationship. Let us see why this is not necessarily so, either theoretically or empirically.

---

46. All these data are drawn from Dominique Arel and Valeri Khmelko, "Regional Divisions in the 2004 Presidential Elections in Ukraine," paper written for the First Annual Danyliw Seminar on Contemporary Ukrainian Studies, University of Ottowa, Canada, September 29–October 1, 2005.

47. In a private note, Henry E. Hale commented to Stepan that this may be beginning to happen in that in the 2010 presidential election, a "new generation" type of candidate, Sergei Tyhypko who tried to bridge the east/west divide came in a surprisingly strong third.

48. For example, the map of electoral results, which depicted Yanukovych in blue, shows the east and southeast as a solid blue. See *Kyiv Post*, January 18, 2010, available at www.kyivpost.com/news/politics/detail/57376/.

The goals of both ideal types include the creation of a useable state, without which a democracy is impossible. Both ideal types can also have policies that may help develop commitment and loyalty to the democratic institutions of the state. We have argued that Ukraine has a better chance of creating a democratic political community if it does not pursue aggressive nation-state policies. However, in theory, there can be policies that may look like nation-state policies but that, if implemented softly and widely, also facilitate the multiple but complementary identities that are crucial both for state-nations and for democracies in multinational societies. Let us explore this proposition in the case of Ukraine.

Adult Russophones do not want to be forced to speak Ukrainian in the workplace or in the exercise of their full rights of citizenship. Nonetheless, the overwhelming percentage of them want their children to have the opportunity to speak Ukrainian fluently. However, in many schools in the east and the south, there are not enough Ukrainian-speaking teachers, and many of the textbooks are not only in Russian but were also written in the Soviet era in what is now Russia.[49] If Russophone parents see that state policies are improving their children's capacity to function successfully in Ukraine, these same Russophone parents might well increase their trust in the state-nation policies of the Ukrainian state. If in two generations, virtually every adult in Ukraine speaks Ukrainian (even though many of them will continue to speak Russian), the policy would also have been also been a good nation-state policy.

A somewhat more complex matter is the role of Russian-language news on television. Because of financial constraints and sensitivity to nation-state sensibilities, the Ukrainian government television channels, such as UT-1, are in Ukrainian. This meant that most Russophones, especially in eastern Ukraine, watched Moscow-originated programs during the 2004 presidential elections and during the Orange Revolution. The production of high-quality television news programs in Russian by the time of the Orange Revolution may have been seen as a linguistic compromise on nation-state goals, but it would probably would have been a plus for building a political community in Ukraine that is at ease with Ukraine as a viable democratic nation-state for some of its citizens and a viable democratic state-nation for other of its citizens. Certainly the goal of having Russophones with multiple but complementary identities would have been served.

What about federalism? Every country close to the state-nation pole (with the exception of tiny Luxembourg) is federal. Must Ukraine become federal to main-

---

49. See Nancy Popson, "The Ukrainian History Textbooks: Introducing Children to the 'Ukrainian Nation,'" *Nationalities Papers* 29, no. 2 (2001), pp. 325–50.

tain itself as a country with many state-nation qualities? Most of the scholars we have asked are somewhat worried about territorially concentrated power under the existing conditions of polarization and policy conflicts with its large neighbor Russia. As we discussed earlier, Ukraine—unlike the near-state-nations of Spain, India, Belgium, or Canada—had a potentially threatening irredentist situation on its borders. Under such circumstances, federalism might not have been prudent. However, is federalism nonetheless the only solution? Not necessarily. But serious decentralization and center-regional development projects should be considered. Many of the east-west conflicts find their roots in economic as much as cultural factors. For example, part of the reason that Viktor Yanukovych received 93.5% of the vote in Donetsk in the third round of the 2004 presidential election was that industrial production in Donetsk had declined by nearly 60% in the 1990–98 period. However, Yanukovych was appointed governor of Donetsk in 1997. He worked with the central government on a series of industrial promotion poli-cies and created two new "special economic zones." By 2003, Donetsk's indus-trial production had improved substantially, the unemployment rate had declined, and Yanukovych received much of the credit. Correctly or not, Yushchenko was presented in the 2004 elections as an opponent of these regional development zones.[50]

Much of eastern Ukraine is dominated by state-owned Soviet-era mines and factories. At the moment, every governor is appointed directly by the president, and municipal budgets are small. A model for Ukraine to consider is the Scan-dinavian countries, which combine unitary states with much greater budgets for cities than the federal states of Europe.[51]

---

50. These figures on Donetsk come from Svitlana Kalinina, Alexander Lyakh, Galina Sav-chenko, and Adam Swain, "Regional 'Lock-In' or Local Hegemonic Bloc? Industrial Restructuring in the Ukrainian Donbas," paper prepared for the Danyliw Research Seminar in Contemporary Ukrainian Studies at the Chair of Ukrainian Studies, University of Ottawa, September 29–October 1, 2005. See also Barrington and Herron, "One Ukraine or Many," pp. 70–71. From a comparative viewpoint of political symbols, it should be noted that in Donetsk, the Ukrainian flag is flown (unlike Kurdistan, where the Iraqi flag is not flown), and no one has reported a Russian flag flying in Donetsk, as some were briefly flown in Crimea.

51. For example, from 1992 to 1996 municipalities in the four democratic federal systems of Western Europe spent 14.3% of total public expenditures, whereas municipalities in the eleven unitary states spent 24.6% of total public expenditures. In Denmark, Finland, and Sweden, munici-pal expenditures in this same period accounted for 44%, 37%, and 35% of total public expenditures, respectively. See *Government Finance Statistics* (Washington, DC: International Monetary Fund), various issues. For an analysis of these robust municipal expenditures in unitary states, see Juan J. Linz and Alfred Stepan, "Inequality Inducing and Inequality Reducing Federalism: With Special Reference to the 'Classic Outlier'—The USA," paper given at the 18th Congress of the International Political Science Association, Quebec City, Canada, August 1–5, 2000, esp. table 2.

SUCCESSES AND FAILURES IN UKRAINE'S USE
OF STATE-NATION POLICIES

What can we say after nearly twenty years of Ukraine's independence and its use of many more state-nation policies than nation-state policies? Specifically, what can we say about violence, stateness, democracy, and the possibility of moving toward power-sharing arrangements normally associated with parliamentarism?

Internal Peace and Stateness

We have argued that one of the goals of state-nation policies is to help facilitate domestic peace and a high degree of stateness in multinational polities. There had been, of course, much speculation in many major journals that Ukraine might fragment. *The Economist*, for example, ran an article called, "Ukraine: The Birth and Possible Death of a Country," a *Foreign Policy* article was entitled, "Letter from Eurasia: Will Ukraine Return to Russia?" and the Central Intelligence Agency leaked a report about the likely fragmentation of Ukraine.[52]

However, in a recent review of ethnic tension and state survival in Ukraine, Paul D'Anieri wrote that "secessionist movements have made few inroads, and violence has been non-existent."[53] Dominique Arel asserted that "regionalism in Ukraine does not constitute a threat to the territorial integrity of Ukraine. . . . Russian-speaking elites and the general population in the East seek inclusion, not separation."[54]

This peaceful situation in Ukraine contrasts sharply with Sri Lanka, where, as we documented earlier, aggressive nation-state policies led to civil war and nearly to state disintegration. Ukraine's peace is also in sharp contrast to two of its Black Sea post-Soviet neighbors, Moldova and Georgia, both of which lost sovereignty over part of their states largely due to conflicts over their hardline nation-state policies in multinational settings.

In Moldova, the nation-state-building Moldovian Popular Front at independence pushed hard for Romanian as the national language, for union with Romania, and for a radical downgrading of the Russian and Ukrainian languages

---

52. Full references to all these reports and others are contained in Paul D'Anieri, "Ethnic Tensions and State Strategies."

53. Ibid., p. 4.

54. Dominique Arel, "The Hidden Face of the Orange Revolution: Ukraine in Denial Towards Its Regional Problem," a translation of "La face cachée de la Révolution Orange: l'Ukraine en négation face á son problèm régional," *Revue d'études comparatives Est-Ouest* 37 (December 2006), p. 38.

widely spoken in the Transnistria district of Moldova: "In August and September 1989, the Moldovan parliament adopted a number of interrelated language laws. Moldovan/Romanian was declared the sole state language; in the future it was to be written with Latin characters. While the legal texts in themselves were rather liberal, allowing for substantial use of the minority languages in a transitional period, nationalist enthusiasts among Moldovan bureaucrats, locally and in the capital, often gave them a most wanton interpretation and used them as a weapon of linguistic discrimination."[55] Lucan Way, a close follower of Moldovan politics, writes that most analysts "agree that the ethnic tension and brief civil war/separation of Transnistria [which endures to this day] was facilitated by pro-Romanian rhetoric of the front."[56] From March 2 to July 21, 1992, there was what was called the "War of Transnistria." In the final stage of the civil war, the former Soviet 14th Guards Army entered the conflict, opening fire and deploying combat tanks. Since then, Moldova has exercised no effective control over Transnistria.[57] In 1995, the former Soviet 14th Army Unit in Transnistria was redesignated the "Operational Group of Russian Forces in Transnistria."[58] The former Soviet combat unit still consisted of "one motorized infantry division and a number of specialized subunits, 6,000 men in all. . . . In the army depots enormous quantities of military hardware, ammunition, and weaponry remained."[59]

In Georgia, from August to September 2008, the interaction between growing autonomous efforts in the ethnically and linguistically distinct regions of South Ossetia and Abkhazia, and Georgia's aggressive nation-state effort towards them, led to militarized violence in both areas and to an eventual war between Russia and Georgia. Russia not only defeated Georgia but also rapidly recognized South Ossetia and Abkhazia as independent countries.[60] In February and April 2010, Russia signed agreements with Abkhazia and South Ossetia to place military bases in both territories.[61]

55. Pål Kolstø and Andrei Malgin, "The Transnistrian Republic: A Case of Politicized Regionalism," *Nationalities Papers* 26, no.1 (1998), p. 107.

56. Personal correspondence between Alfred Stepan and Lucan Way, April 22, 2010. See also William Crowther, "The Politics of Ethno-National Mobilization: Nationalism and Reform in Soviet Moldavia," *The Russian Review* 50 (April 1991), pp. 183–202.

57. On how strong nation-state demands for the use of Romanian in Moldova contributed to the involvement of the Russian military, see William Crowther, "Politics of Ethno-National Mobilization."

58. Andreas Johannson, "The Transnistrian Conflict after the 2005 Moldovan Parliamentary Elections," *Journal of Communist Studies and Transition Politics* 22 (December 2006), p. 509.

59. Kolstø and Malgin, "Transnistrian Republic," p. 111.

60. On the war in Georgia and its impact in Ukraine, see Dominique Arel, "Ukraine since the War in Georgia," *Survival* 50, no. 6 (December 2008–January 2009), pp. 15–25.

61. See "Russia Recognizes South Ossetia and Abkhazia to Save People's Lives," *Pravda*, Au-

As we have already documented in this chapter, the first two decades of Ukraine's independence have shown a generally inclusionary and accommodative approach to the use of the Russian language in Ukraine that is dramatically different to the nation-state language policies followed in Sri Lanka, Moldova, and, to a lesser extent, Georgia. Indeed, even though Yushchenko, who emerged as president after the Orange Revolution, would have personally preferred to have advanced a very strong nation-state agenda concerning language, he accommodated the multinational realities of Ukraine. In order to alleviate ethnic Russian fears about his possible Ukrainian nationalist policies about language, Yushchenko made explicit pledges "that his government would not shut down a single Russian school."[62]

Democracy

We also argued that in a robust multinational polity, state-nation policies, if well implemented, would not hurt the building of democracy, and might even facilitate it. To evaluate this argument, let us analyze the state of democracy in the twelve countries that were members of the U.S.S.R. since the 1920s to see where Ukraine stands comparatively within this set.[63] One of the most cited annual reviews of the state of democracy in the world is the Freedom House Survey. This survey ranks countries on a seven-point scale (with 1 being the best score and 7 being the worst) for "political freedoms" and an identical seven-point scale for "civil liberties." Of the twelve countries in the set, Ukraine in 2010 has the best total of the two scores: 3 on political freedoms and 2 on civil liberties, for a total of 5. The average total of the other twelve countries in the set is 9.7. Russia receives a 6 on political rights and a 5 on civil liberties, for a total score of 11.[64] For the five years since the Orange Revolution in 2004, the only country in the twelve-country set ever to have been listed as "free" has been Ukraine, and Ukraine has been listed as "free" every year since 2005.

---

gust 28, 2008; and "Russia to Sign Deal on Military Base in South Ossetia on Wednesday," *Ria Novosti*, April 6, 2010.

62. Oleh Protysk, "Majority-Minority Relations in the Ukraine," p. 30. Protsyk went on in the same quotation to say that this pledge has been kept by successive post-Orange cabinets.

63. From the fifteen countries that were once part of the Soviet Union, we therefore omit the three Baltic countries and what is now called Moldova (then called Bessarabia), as they only became part of the U.S.S.R. via the Molotov-Ribbentrop Pact of 1939. Unlike any of the eleven countries in our set, all three of the Baltic countries had substantial experience with democracy in the interwar period, and all have been members of the European Union since 2006.

64. For the raw data for 194 countries, see "The Freedom House Survey for 2009," *Journal of Democracy* 19, no. 2 (April 2010), pp. 142–143.

Another sign of Ukraine's democratic credentials, particularly if we focus on elections, is that it is the only country of our set of twelve where an incumbent (or a candidate enjoying the full support of an incumbent) has been defeated in a contested election and thus produced alternation in power. This has happened three times. In 1994, Leonid Kuchma challenged the incumbent, Leonid Kravchuk; in a run-off election, the challenger, Kuchma, received 52% of the vote while the incumbent, Kravchuk, received only 45%. In 2004, Kuchma could not run for a third term, but his administration used what are called "administrative resources" to support his nominee, Yanukovych. The Orange Revolution's effective resistance to what appeared to be election fraud led to a third round of voting in which the challenger, Viktor Yuschenko, won with almost 52% of the vote, to beat the incumbent's nominee, Yanukovych. In the 2010 presidential election, Yushchenko, the presidential incumbent, contested the election but only won 6% of the vote for a fifth-place finish, and Yanukovych won in the second round against Yulia Tymoshenko, who was the sitting prime minister.

This series of closely contested elections that have led to alternations in power does not mean that democracy in Ukraine is consolidated. However, many people in Ukraine are beginning to think that elections are becoming "the only game in town." Indeed, there is evidence that this assumption began to develop as early as the second alternation in 2004. Richard Rose has created an innovative battery of questions to determine the percentage of respondents in the country who are what he calls "confident democrats." Rose calls a respondent a "confident democrat" if he or she "disapproves of the suspension of parliament and considers suspension unlikely." In 1996, only 30% of Ukrainians were "confident democrats," which was the lowest of the ten postcommunist countries surveyed, the average result of which was 59%. However, in 2005, "confident democrats" in Ukraine had more than doubled, to 63%. Of critical and positive significance for our concern with multiple but complementary identities in possible state-nations in multinational societies is that ethnic Russians and ethnic Ukrainians both scored an identical 63% on the "confident democrat" score in Ukraine in 2005, which, among other things, implies that ethnic-Russians were reasonably confident that they had weight in the political system (see table 6.1).

Unfortunately, to our knowledge, there is no survey data since 2005 that utilizes the classic three-part support for democracy or dictatorship question that we have used in many countries.[65] However, a Rose survey in 2005 did use this question. Notwithstanding the low quality of democracy in Ukraine, Ukrainians

65. See, for example, table 2.5.

TABLE 6.1

Percentage of "Confident Democrats" in Ukraine, Russia, and Eight Central European Post-Communist Countries, 1996 and 2005

	% of "confident democrats"	
	1996	2005
Eight Central European post-Communist countries	59%	
Russia	36	
(Self-defined Russian nationality)		(63)
Ukraine	30	63%
(Self-defined Ukrainian nationality)		(63)

Sources: For the ten countries (eight—Bulgaria, Czech Republic, Slovakia, Hungary, Poland, Romania, Slovenia, Croatia—compared to Ukraine and Belarus), see Richard Rose and Christian Haerpfer, "New Democracies Barometer IV: A Ten Nation Survey," *Studies in Public Policy*, no. 262 (1996), p. 86. For Russia, see Richard Rose, "Getting Things Done with Social Capital: New Russian Barometer VII," *Studies in Public Policy*, no. 303 (1998), p. 44. For Ukraine in 2005, see Richard Rose, "Divisions within Ukraine: A Post-election Opinion Survey," *Studies in Public Policy*, no. 403 (2005), p. 32.

Note: The definition Richard Rose uses for "confident democrats" is the same as he used in the ten-country survey—that is, a respondent "disapproves suspension of parliament" (Q.29) *and* "considers suspension unlikely" (Q.28). The definition used for nationality is not essentialist but self-definition. The question was, "What do you consider your nationality now?"

had a higher percentage of respondents who answered that "democracy is preferable to any other form of government" (57%) than did Chileans (52%) or Brazilians (41%). The survey results also remind us that situationally specific political context is often more important than ethnicity itself. For example, while only 24% of Russians in Russia answered that "democracy is preferable to any other form of government," 43% of self-defined ethnic Russians in Ukraine did so (see table 6.2).

However, it must be acknowledged that Ukraine's democracy (partly due to ongoing and entrenched conflicts over the prerogatives of the President) is of a low quality. For example, on Transparency International's corruption perception index for 2009, Ukraine ranks 154th of 180 countries.[66] While in 2005 support for democracy was high, in the same year Richard Rose identified that Ukraine still had one of the lowest levels of trust in the police and courts of any of the twelve postcommunist countries. For example, 30% of respondents in the twelve postcommunist countries said they trusted the police but only 10% of respondents in Ukraine trusted the police. And while 29% of respondents in the twelve postcommunist countries said they trusted the courts, only 16% said they did in Ukraine.[67]

66. "Global Corruption Barometer 2000," Transparency International, available at www.transparency.org/policy_research/surveys_indices/gcb/2009, accessed May 26, 2010.

67. See Richard Rose and Christian Haerpfer, "New Democracies Barometer V: A Twelve Nation Survey," *Studies in Public Policy*, no. 306 (1998), questions 27a, b, c, and p.

TABLE 6.2
Opinions on Democracy and Authoritarianism in Ukraine, Russia, and Selected Latin American Democracies

	Consolidated democratic state-nations					Citizens of Ukraine (2005)		Two key Latin American democracies (1996)	
	Spain	Belgium	India	Russia	Ukraine	Self-defined Ukrainian nationality	Self-defined Russian nationality	Chile	Brazil
"Democracy is preferable to any other form of government." (Valid responses excluding "do not know/no answer")	78% (83%)	70% (78%)	60% (83%)	24% (25%)	57% (66%)	60% (70%)	43% (51%)	52% (54%)	41% (48%)
"In some circumstances an authoritarian government can be preferable to a democratic government."	9	10	6	41	18	17	25	18	21
"For someone like me, a democratic or a nondemocratic regime makes no difference."	7	10	6	33	11	9	17	25	23
Do not know/no answer	6	10	27	2	14	14	15	4	15
(N)	(1,000)	(1,036)	(8,133)	(2,107)	(2,000)			(1,200)	(1,240)

Sources: The data for India are from National Election Study, 1998, coordinated by Yogendra Yadav of the Center for the Study of Developing Societies, Delhi. The data for Ukraine come from Richard Rose, "Divisions within Ukraine: A Post-Election Opinion Survey," Studies in Public Policy, no. 403 (2005), Question D-7, p. 29. The data for Russia are from Richard Rose, "New Russia Barometer: 2005," Studies in Public Policy, no. 402 (2005), Question D-7, p. 33. Data for Brazil and Chile are from Latino Barometer 1996, directed by Marta Lagos. The Spanish and Belgian data are from Eurobarometer 37 (1992).

Note: Percentages may not add up to 100 due to rounding. The definition used for nationality is not essentialist but self-definition. The question was, "What do you consider your nationality now?"

In a November 2009 poll, in a context when Ukraine was experiencing a 14% decline in its rate of growth, in answer to the question "How satisfied or dissatisfied are you with the political situation in Ukraine today?" 51% or respondents were "very dissatisfied" and 40% were "somewhat dissatisfied." In contrast, only .2% were "very satisfied," and only 5% were "somewhat satisfied." Very disturbingly, in answer to the question "Is Ukraine a democracy?" twice as many respondents said "No" (49%) as said "Yes" (24%).[68]

Is a Power-Sharing "Parliamentarized Semi-Presidentialism" Possible?

On theoretical and political grounds, we have already argued in our discussion of the "nested grammar" in chapter 1 that for democracy in multinational societies, parliamentarism has a number of advantages that presidentialism, and most types of semi-presidentialism, do not have. In postcommunist Europe, the most frequently chosen model to produce an executive was semi-presidentialism. However, in many cases, this semi-presidentialism in fact turned into something like "super-presidential semi-presidentialism." Fortunately, while it has been imperfectly recognized and not yet theorized, a new model that we will call "parliamentarized semi-presidentialism" has emerged. This variant of semi-presidentialism allows for a sharable executive.[69]

The Ukrainian constitution of 1996 adopted a model of governance close to the French-style, dual-executive, semi-presidentialism created by Charles de Gaulle for the Fifth Republic, with a directly elected president with significant executive powers and a prime minister responsible to parliament. This system works best when the president and the prime minister come from the same political party or coalition and support each other and have a majority in parliament; the constitutional court's legitimacy and authority concerning the prerogatives of the president, the prime minster, and the parliament are respected; and the president is what Cindy Skach calls a "party man." None of these conditions have emerged as a routine in Ukraine.

In the classic theory of semi-presidentialism, if the president does not have a parliamentary majority, political power should pass to the prime minister if he or

68. "Change on the Horizon? Public Opinion in Ukraine Before the 2010 Presidential Election," International Foundation for Electoral Systems, November 2009.

69. For a more extensive discussion of the new concept, and the new practice, of "parliamentarized semi-presidentialism," see Alfred Stepan, "Introduction: Undertheorized Political Problems in the Founding Democratization Literature" in *Democracies in Danger*, ed. Alfred Stepan (Baltimore: Johns Hopkins University Press, 2009), esp. pp. 9–14.

198 CRAFTING STATE-NATIONS

she controls a majority in parliament.[70] However, classical theory and the modern French experience are virtually silent on how the system should work if (as in Yeltsin's Russia) neither the president nor the prime minister has a majority.[71] In the case of Russia under Yeltsin—and in many of the post-Soviet cases—the president, in the absence of a party majority, often rules on the margin of constitutionality by decree or moves out of the democratic box entirely by closing the parliament, tightly controlling the rewriting of a constitution in which presidential powers are greatly enhanced, and then holding a plebiscitary ratification of a model that is most aptly called "super-presidential semi-presidentialism."[72]

Something like the above, except for the very important facts that no president ever dissolved the parliament or was able to rewrite the constitution completely, occurred in post-independence Ukraine.[73] There are two key points about "super-presidential semi-presidentialism" that are central to our inquiry as to whether Ukraine can become a consolidated democratic state-nation. First, no stable democracy in the world, certainly no European Union member country, has a constitution that comes remotely close to being "super-presidential semi-presidentialism." Second, state-nations are facilitated if there is some degree of a

70. For an important new work on the theory of semi-presidentialism, see Cindy Skach, *Borrowing Constitutional Designs: Constitutional Law in Weimar Germany and the French Fifth Republic* (Princeton: Princeton University Press, 2006).

71. On these silences and the very exceptional conditions that allowed this model to function reasonably well in France, see Alfred Stepan and Ezra Suleiman, "The French Fifth Republic: A Model for Import? Reflections on Poland and Brazil," in Stepan, *Arguing Comparative Politics*, pp. 257–275.

72. See Timothy J. Colton and Cindy Skach, "The Predicament of Semi-Presidentialism," in *Democracies in Danger*. A shorter version of their argument appeared as "The Russian Predicament," *Journal of Democracy* 16 (July 2005), pp. 113–126.

73. For Kuchma's augmentation of his powers, see Wolczuk, *Moulding of Ukraine*, pp. 205–209. Oleh Protsyk, who wrote his 2000 Ph.D. dissertation at Rutgers on semi-presidentialism in Ukraine, argues that both Russia and Ukraine are what Shugart and Carey would call "president-parliamentary" and that Russia's version gave the president more powers than in Ukraine. Nonetheless, he wrote that for most of his time as president, Kuchma, tried to "increase the formal powers of the presidency" and that he "consistently played the role of a challenger to the existing constitutional status quo." See Oleh Protsyk, "Troubled Semi-Presidentialism: Stability of the Constitutional System and Cabinet in Ukraine," *Europe-Asian Studies* 55, no. 7 (2003), p. 1087. See also Andrew Wilson, "Ukraine: Two Presidents and their Powers," in *Post-Communist Presidents*, ed. Ray Taras (Cambridge: Cambridge University Press, 1997). In the same volume, see the essay by Juan Linz, "Introduction: Some Thoughts on Presidentialism in Post-Communist Europe," pp. 1–14. On attempts to measure presidential powers in postcommunist Europe, see Timothy Frye, "A Politics of Institutional Choice: Post Communist Presidencies," *Comparative Political Studies* 30, no. 5 (1997), pp. 523–552. Whereas Frye scored presidential powers in Slovenia, Slovakia, Latvia, the Czech Republic, and Estonia as all in the 4.5 to 5.5 range, he gave Kuchma's Ukraine a score of 15 and Yeltsin's superpresidential Russia a score of 16. Due to politics, however, unlike Putin's Russia, there was often gridlock under the first two directly elected presidents in Ukraine.

"shared executive," but by definition "super-presidential semi-presidentialism" is an indivisible good. Let us elaborate.

A look at the eight postcommunist countries admitted to the European Union in 2004 is instructive. Five—Hungary, the Czech Republic, Estonia, Latvia, and Slovakia—are parliamentary. The other three—Slovenia, Poland, and Lithuania— have directly elected presidents. None comes constitutionally or politically close to Kuchma's Ukraine. Like Portugal in the 1980s, Slovenia, Poland, and Lithuania (and likely EU member Croatia) adopted semi-presidential systems that so reduce presidential authority and so increase the parliament's and the court's powers that they are most accurately described as "parliamentarized semi-presidential" systems.[74]

Where is Ukraine in terms of semi-presidential type? A major issue raised and not yet resolved by the Orange Revolution concerns presidential powers. Many Yushchenko loyalists, who would have been happy with much stronger nation-state policies, would have liked a presidency with strong executive powers. They were thus extremely upset that, in exchange for the outgoing pro-Russian Kuchma government agreeing to fairer election rules and a rerun of the presidential election, Victor Yushchenko agreed to a transfer of some presidential powers to the parliament and to the prime minister by January 1, 2006.

These powers are still the subject of vitriolic political and constitutional debates, but the prime minister, since these agreements went into effect in January 2006, has had the power to appoint most ministers. As long as this situation obtains, Ukraine does not function as a "super-presidential semi-presidential" system. Many analysts, in fact, argue that Ukraine's dual executive system has contributed to a balance of power that has made the construction of a Russian-type of "vertical power" system unlikely. Henry E. Hale has argued that it was precisely the division of executive power that sustained Ukrainian democracy. "Democracy can endure in the space created by president-versus-premier infighting, which gives the two, fairly evenly matched sides ample incentive to check and confound

74. Steven D. Roper, in his combined score of presidential powers—in each of the ten regimes in Europe he classifies as "premier-presidential"—gives Slovenia and Lithuania the lowest scores, that is, he considers that they have the weakest presidents. See Roper, "Are All Semipresidential Regimes the Same? A Comparison of Premier-Presidential Regimes," *Comparative Politics* 34 (April 2002), table 3, p. 260. Roper does not give a score for Ukraine because he classified its regime as "presidential-parliamentary." For the reduction of presidential powers in Poland and Portugal, see Colton and Skach, "Predicament of Semi-Presidentialism." For a more extensive analysis of "parliamentarized semi-presidentialism" and details on the political conditions in Lithuania and Croatia that made its adoption much more constitutionally rooted and consensual than in Ukraine, see Stepan's introduction in *Democracies in Danger*.

each other. The rivalry even helps to keep elections honest, since each side can expose any attempt to falsify the ballot count.[75]

If somehow Ukraine were to evolve more toward the Portuguese, Polish, Slovenian, or Croatian version of parliamentarized semi-presidentialism, the Ukrainian presidency would potentially be a "sharable" or "coalition-friendly" institution and could become less a political source of ethnic polarization. Such a coalition-friendly institution might help overcome the dual-government policy paralysis and provide incentives for some state-nation style policy coalitions supported by parties with different multinational configurations.

Such parliamentarized semi-presidentialism seems unlikely for Ukraine in the foreseeable future. Viktor Yanukovych, who won the presidency in a close election in February 2010, disliked the constraints on him in the semi-presidential 2004 Constitution. In July 2010 Yanukovych tried to get the two-thirds parliamentary approval needed to hold a referendum on abolishing semi-presidentialism. The opposition, and even two parties in his ruling coalition (the Communist Party and the Lytvyn Bloc), refused to endorse a referendum.[76] However, after four Supreme Court judges resigned under what some of them complained was undue pressure from the Yanukovych administration, the Supreme Court unanimously declared the 2004 Constitution unconstitutional and reestablished the 1996 Constitution, with its much stronger presidential powers. Now the president can select the prime minister and name cabinet ministers.

More than thirty years ago, in *The Breakdown of Democratic Regimes*, Linz and Stepan argued that, even in once consolidated democracies, acts by democratic incumbents can erode or even break down democracy. Ukraine has avoided fragmentation by following some creative state-nation, as oposed to hard nation state, policies. But the presidency of Yanukovych has weakened democracy. Most observers said the October 31, 2010, municipal and regional elections were less free and fair than the earlier 2010 presidential election. Reporters Without Borders dropped Ukraine 42 places in its most recent world rankings of press freedom, and there are increasing analogies between Putin and Yankovych. Yet Ukraine still has more areas of political autonomy than Putin's Russia. Democratic breakdown in Ukraine is not over-determined. But democracy, as always, will have to be produced by struggle.

75. Henry E. Hale, "Ukraine: The Uses of Divided Power," *Journal of Democracy* 21 (July 2010), p. 86.
76. "Ukraine's Yanukovych Fails in Move to Strengthen Powers," *Reuters*, 10 July 2010.

CHAPTER SEVEN

Federacy

A Formula for Democratically Managing
Multinational Societies in Unitary States

The major subject of this book has been how states can democratically manage multinational societies. We developed an ideal-type model, which we called a state-nation, as a possible way to respond to this challenge, and then demonstrated how some countries such as India and Spain have approximated empirically this ideal type with relatively good results. A major component of our state-nation model involved asymmetrical federalism.

However, we want to raise here a hard problem we have not yet discussed. Can a unitary polity respond effectively to the nationalism of a territorially concentrated cultural minority within the state with its own "politically robust multinational leaders" while nonetheless remaining a unitary and democratic state?

We will address this theoretical and political challenge in four steps.

First, we will identify the special nature of this problem and demonstrate why and how unitary states do not normally have adequate political formulas available to address this challenge.

Second, we will propose a political formula for how unitary states could democratically address this problem; we will call our newly conceptualized ideal-type arrangements a "federacy." We will advance a new ideal-type definition of federacy and its seven ideal-type institutional arrangements.

Third, we will shift from ideal-type analysis to comparative empirical analysis. Have any actual unitary states resolved their problems with territorially concentrated cultural minorities by using policies that actually conform relatively closely to our ideal type of federacy? Empirically, we will document why, and how, small

Scandinavian unitary states have constructed, and managed democratically, their multinational challenges via three federacies that conform very closely to our ideal type. These three federacies are: Finland–Åland Islands, Denmark–Faroe Islands, and Denmark-Greenland.

Fourth, we will address the all important "scope value" question. Can the concept and some of the practices of federacy travel beyond the longstanding peaceful, small democratic welfare states of Scandinavia? Might federacy be useful in some transitions to democracy after authoritarianism or defeat in war? Could the practice of the shared sovereignty that is intrinsic to federacy arrangements be acceptable—indeed, under some circumstances, attractive—even to major political leaders in a polity with extremely strong nation-state values and practices? Might federacy arrangements help end a longstanding civil war even in a populous and predominantly Muslim polity that many argue is particularly resistant to dual sovereignty governance arrangements essential to federacies? Might federacy arrangements be of use in mitigating ethnic and religious conflicts even in a polity, such as China, shaped by revolutionary communism and Han nationalism? If the answer to even some of these questions is yes, our version of the federacy concept travels well, and its scope value warrants inclusion in the theoretical and practical repertoire of modern democratic governance.

As we document in the rest of this chapter, federacies played a crucial facilitating role in the transition to democracy in Italy after the fall of Fascism and defeat in war. Federacy arrangements were created in the midst of the most volatile period of Portugal's revolution and eventual transition to democracy. In France—the world's doctrinal and organizational template of a unitary nation-state—the National Assembly in 2001 voted in favor of some partial federacy arrangements to mitigate tensions over Corsica's role in the French polity. The long separatist armed conflict in Aceh Indonesia that threatened the democratic transition in the world's most populous Muslim-majority polity made the greatest progress toward peace ever when—facilitated by the mediation of a former president of Finland who pointed out the possible utility of the Finnish-Åland Islands formula—the polity consensually agreed to federacy arrangements in 2005. On a number of recent occasions, the Dalai Lama indicated that he would accept federacy-type arrangements with China for Tibet, and China extended, but did not honor fully, federacy arrangements for Hong Kong. If China were ever a democracy, might federacy arrangements be useful? We will explore all these cases, except for the hypothetical case of a democratic China, which would require another chapter, for the light they shed on the concept and practice of federacies in the modern world.

CONCEPTUALIZING THE UNITARY STATE–TERRITORIALLY
CONCENTRATED MINORITY PROBLEM

In keeping with our goal of expanding our imaginations beyond nation-states and state-nations, let us first briefly hypothesize the character of the political problem of territorially concentrated minorities in a unitary state.

Let us imagine an existing small or medium-sized independent state with a unitary constitution, a relatively culturally homogeneous population, and a proud nation-state sense of identity. Let us further assume that this otherwise well-functioning unitary state has a territorially concentrated population that does not identify with the history and culture of the unitary state. Its different identity will most likely stem from one or more of the following six factors:

1. Physical separation or great distance from the unitary state;
2. Linguistic or religious difference;
3. A previous, self-governing tradition it wants to restore or expand;
4. A geopolitical or cultural sense that it was, and should be, part of a neighboring state with which it identifies;
5. A radically different economy that the population believes needs special laws to help preserve its own livelihood and way of life; and
6. A history of warfare with, or coercive repression by, the unitary state within which it is located.

Let us make a further, not unreasonable assumption that this territorially concentrated minority population is unhappy with the status quo. At the very least, they want more autonomy and self-governing arrangements that recognize their culture and facilitate its development; some of the population may identify with leaders and organizations who demand independence or seccession. This combination of factors gives a multinational dimension to the unitary state.

Let us make some further constraining assumptions about two possible solutions to this political problem: federalism or independence. Concerning federalism, if the population and dominant political actors of the unitary state agree to become an asymmetrical federal system, many of the problems of territorially concentrated minority population, short of independence, could be addressed reasonably well. However, if we assume that the vast majority of the state's population and its major political actors do *not* want to depart from what they perceive as a well-functioning unitary state, we should assume that a federal state, much less an option for an asymmetrical federal state, is highly unlikely.

Let us also assume that a full exit from the unitary state of the territorially concentrated minority, either by independence or joining an irredentist neighbor, is extremely unlikely for the foreseeable future, due to one or more of the following factors: (1) strong sentiments in the unitary state opposing such an exit and the military capacity to back up such policy preferences; (2) geopolitical opposition by many neighboring states to the emergence of a new, small, and possibly weak independent state in the region or to unification with the irredentist neighbor; (3) divided sentiments in the minority population about the political and financial costs of independence.

If we rule out federalism and complete exit, are there any other political arrangements that could possibly increase the "voice" and "loyalty" of the territorially concentrated minority community or nation?[1] Can their desires for greatly enhanced autonomy and self-government be addressed from *within* the unitary state? Specifically, can we imagine a possible formula for managing this potential threat to a peaceful, inclusionary democracy in the existing state that could be acceptable to both the majority and the minority "nations"? We believe there is. At the theoretical, ideal type conceptual level, we can imagine what we call a "federacy" formula.

FEDERACY AS AN IDEAL TYPE

Our short ideal-type definition of a federacy is the following.

> *A federacy is a political-administrative unit in an independent unitary state with exclusive power in certain areas, including some legislative power, constitutionally or quasi-constitutionally embedded, that cannot be changed unilaterally and whose inhabitants have full citizenship rights in the otherwise unitary state.*

The minimal agreed set of arrangements for such a federacy, as an ideal type, would have to satisfy the five institutional requirements.

Defining Characteristic 1: Federal-like division of state and federacy functions. In order that the federacy, unlike other parts of the unitary state, can pass special self-governing laws and administer their polity in such a way that it can address many of the areas of greatest tension with the unitary state, there must be a classic

---

1. The reference, of course, builds on the reflections of Albert Hirschman's *Exit, Voice, and Loyalty: Responses to Declines in Firms, Organizations, and States* (Cambridge: Harvard University Press, 1972).

federal-like agreement concerning the division of powers in the polity. These federal-type arrangements are: (1) explicit powers that fall in the exclusive domain of the federacy; (2) powers that remain in the domain of the center; and (3) powers that might be shared or even remain with the center but that can be progressively transferred permanently to the federacy.

Powers in the exclusive domain of the federacy are the vital culture-making and culture-preserving powers, such as the right to establish the indigenous language as an official language of the federacy, control over the content and administration of education, the hiring and promotion of federacy civil servants, and possibly the granting of citizenship in the federacy to supplement their full citizenship in the unitary state. The federacy may have a range of prerogatives not found in any other part of the unitary state, such as the legal right to create extremely restrictive immigration policies in the federacy and to prohibit those citizens of the polity who are not also citizens of the federacy from buying land or establishing commercial enterprises. The federacy might also have the right to create its own rules governing the federacy's legislature and executive and have extensive control over local development plans. Some powers, such as foreign affairs, defense, currency, and a final court of appeals, would generally remain the exclusive prerogatives of the center.

Finally, unlike most federations, there can be a presumption that some powers, especially the provision of costly services such as pensions, welfare, and hospitals that may have been originally created by the center, may eventually be transferred, by mutual agreement, to the federacy, as it develops the financial and administrative capability to be fully self-governing in these areas. The center would have cost-sharing formulas with the federacy and would normally contribute a significant amount to the federacy's budget.

Defining Characteristic 2: Quasi-constitutionally embedded political autonomy of the federacy. The territorially concentrated minority population would have a constitutionally, or quasi-constitutionally, embedded degree of political autonomy well beyond that found in any other part of the unitary state. Ideally, the legislatures of the unitary state and the newly created federacy would both agree to the new autonomy arrangements, but at an absolute minimum it would be stipulated that the act of autonomy, or federacy agreement, would not be able to be unilaterally altered without substantial supermajorities on both sides. The federacy situation might begin by negotiations and agreements between states as a way of settling their disputes over the demands of two of the most important competing principles of modern politics, the right of state sovereignty and the right of the self-determination of populations. Eventually however, representative bodies of the territorially concentrated population and the unitary state would have to debate about, and vote for, the federacy arrangements. Legally, politically, and often internationally, federacy arrangements would be much more binding on the central government of the unitary state than devolution or decentralization. The latter two might be unilaterally reversed by parliamentary majorities, whereas a constitutionally embedded federacy would only be changed by mutual supermajorities.[2]

Defining Characteristic 3: Existence of dispute resolution procedures. The federacy and the state, as part of the eventual autonomy agreement, would have dispute resolution procedures about their respective powers and prerogatives. Only in exceptional circumstances would a dispute go to the state's highest court, and this court would be able to make binding decisions for the entire polity only as long as it does not in any way violate the constitutionally embedded autonomy agreement. If the legislature of the center were considering a bill within its powers that might have a special impact on the federacy, the federacy would often have the right to present its views; on many matters, not only would *consultation* with the federacy be required, but its *consent* as well.

Defining Characteristic 4: Reciprocal representation between the unitary state and the federacy. The goal of the federacy arrangement is to create a high level of trust, voice, and loyalty between the federacy and the center, so there is joint citizenship in the federacy and the center. The citizens of the autonomous unit would therefore be full citizens of the state, vote in state wide elections, and have representatives in the parliament of the state as well as in their own parliament. The center would have an official representative in the federacy who would also help coordinate those activities in the federacy that fall under central state powers.

Defining Characteristic 5: The federacy is part of an internationally recognized independent state. The autonomy agreement would be an internal law of the unitary state and not part of international law. The autonomy agreement might be derived from international agreements, but it is not part of international law

---

2. Some important constitutional theorists such as Geoffrey Marshall argue that political traditions and a sense of what is politically appropriate can give regular law de facto constitutionally constraining qualities, even without written constitutional status. See Marshall, *Constitutional Conventions: The Rules and Forms of Political Accountability* (Oxford: Oxford University Press, 1984). We will see such constitutional accretion in some of the cases we analyze, especially the Denmark parliament's acceptance of the de facto constitutional convention that its federacies had a right to negotiate an exit from the state of Denmark. However, such conventions are normally only produced over time, so our focus will be on written constitutionally embedded agreements.

(unless the state makes a specific exception) and would not create a "subject" of international law.

If these five *requirements* are functioning, federacy arrangements *may* additionally contain and legitimate two peace-facilitating features that are not normally found in unitary or federal states.

Facilitating Characteristic 1: Role of international guarantors in the founding of the federacy. A federacy arrangement, especially if it emerges in the context of geopolitical conflict, may well combine elements of two of the greatest principles in conflict since the late nineteenth century, the right of state sovereignty and the right of self-determination of populations. In such cases, federacy arrangements, more than in unitary or federal states, may involve some participation of concerned neighboring states and international organizations in their emergence and even in the establishment of some arrangements, particularly the distinctive cultural rights of the federacy's population.

Facilitating Characteristic 2: Role of the federacy in international treaties signed by the center. More than in a federation, and totally unlike a unitary state, it is possible that the very existence of a federacy may facilitate the federacy's advocacy and creation of some "opt-out" arrangements of treaties into which the unitary state enters. This will be most likely if the leaders of the federacy, with the support of the unitary state, believe that certain provisions of the treaty would be hurtful to the preservation of the distinctive economy and way of life of the population that the federacy had been created to protect. No other part of the unitary state would have the status to construct such opt-out arrangements with the participation and help of the center that normally negotiates them.

FEDERACY'S CONCEPTUAL DISTINCTIVENESS FROM "UNITARY STATES," "ASYMMETRICAL FEDERATIONS," "CONFEDERATIONS," AND "ASSOCIATED STATES"

Given the defining characteristics of our ideal type of federacy, it should be clear that it is quite different from the ideal type of a unitary state. This is so because of the high degree of a federacy's constitutionally embedded autonomy and prerogatives that are not enjoyed by other jurisdictions of the unitary state. However, as we have seen, a unitary state can enter a federacy agreement; indeed, such an agreement may be a particularly useful formula for managing a small or medium-sized unitary nation-state's problems with a territorially concentrated minority population or nation.

As an ideal type, a polity that contains a federacy is also analytically quite different from a federal polity, even an asymmetrical federal system. True, the unit that we call a federacy, especially in the first and second defining requirements of our ideal type, has a federal quality in its relations to the state. However, in the ideal type of federalism, the *entire* polity is federal. Some readers might think that the powers of what we call a federacy are close to the autonomy and special prerogatives that are found in what we have called asymmetrical federalism. This is true, but some differences are nonetheless fundamental. In asymmetrical federalism, *every* unit in the polity is part of a federation, and *no* part of the polity is part of a unitary state. Further, in our judgment, an asymmetrical federal system does not need a federacy, because the specific prerogatives obtainable for minority populations can be established in an asymmetrical federal system. Witness the vast amount of special prerogatives India has negotiated and delivered for Mizoram, where a once war-torn secessionist society now has high degrees of voice and loyalty inside India.

Contrary to what some readers may assume, federacies are also fundamentally different from confederations. A confederation is an agreement *between* states. A federacy is an agreement *within* a state. In a confederation, a member state may make a *unilateral* decision not to participate in a collective foreign policy endeavor, unless such a decision violates the specific treaty creating the confederation. However, in a federacy, opting out of a decision unilaterally is not constitutional. "Opt outs" by a federacy can only be undertaken with the *prior agreement and help* of the center.

Finally, some observers might feel that federacies and "associated states" that do not qualify for membership in the United Nations (or even some colonies) are analytically the same. However, our ideal-type federacy has the requirement that citizens resident in the autonomous unit participate fully in elections for the central government of the polity, have their own representatives in the parliament, and thus in a parliamentary system can play a play a role in government formation. In a presidential system citizens who reside in the autonomous unit have the right to participate in the election of the president. In any case, if the autonomous unit were actually still a colony, this would violate our ideal-type stipulation that the federacy is an integral part of an independent state.

We do not claim to have invented the word *federacy*, which has a long history going back to the Greeks and which has been briefly and variously used by social scientists and lawyers interested in discussing new forms political autonomy for many decades. However, in our judgment, the term is used in so many ways that nothing like a cumulative literature in comparative politics has, or can, emerge unless an attempt at closure is made. We hope this chapter contributes to that task because the concept, as well as the practice, could be of conceptual and political use, especially for managing multinational societies democratically.

The scholar who did most to introduce the concept was probably Daniel J. Elazar. However, when Elazar advanced his definition in the introduction to his extremely useful compendium, *Federal Systems of the World: A Handbook of Federal, Confederal and Autonomy Arrangements*, he gave only two specific examples of federacies—Puerto Rico and the United States, and Bhutan and India.[3] Neither meets our definition of a federacy.

Puerto Rico's commonwealth status with the United States is a very interesting arrangement, but Puerto Rican residents do not have their own representatives with a vote in the U.S. Congress, and they cannot vote in federal elections for the president of the United States even though Puerto Rican delegates participate in national party conventions to select nominees. (Puerto Ricans who are residing in the United States are permitted to vote in political elections.)

In the case of Bhutan and India, both have been, since independence in 1949 and 1947, respectively, independent states. Bhutan has been a member of the United Nations since 1971. Bhutan's elected bodies and judicial systems are fully separate from India's. Bhutan, which borders China, has, if you will, "outsourced" much, but not all, of its defense tasks to India.[4] Bhutan is possibly thus an interesting case of an "associated state," but it is not a case of federacy. Elsewhere, Elazar classifies Jammu and Kashmir as a federacy of India, but it is actually a disputed component of an asymmetrical federation.

David Rezvani's dissertation on federacy contains much useful documentation and analysis, especially of what we call the requirement in a federacy for constitutionally embedded political autonomy and the requirement for conflict adjudication procedures.[5] However, like Elazar, he does not stipulate that citizens of a federacy must have representatives in the legislature of the state or the right to vote for the president; this leads him to classify such entities as Puerto Rico, Northern Marianas Islands, and the Palau Islands as federacies. Like Elazar, he often classi-

---

3. Daniel J. Elazar, *Federal Systems of the World: A Handbook of Federal, Confederal and Autonomy Arrangements* (Essex, UK: Longman Group, 1991), pp. xvi–xvii.

4. We say "much, but not all" because Bhutan has the right to reject Indian security advice. For example, in 1961–62, during a time of great Sino-Indian tension, Bhutan unilaterally denied India permission to guard the Bhutan-Tibetan border.

5. David A. Rezvani, "Federacy: The Dynamics of Semi-Sovereign Territories," unpublished D. Phil in Politics, University of Oxford, 2004.

fies cases of asymmetrical federalism as federacies. Thus, two of the four "federacies" he selects for special attention in an eleven-page appendix, along with the Åland Islands and Greenland, are Catalonia and the Basque Country, neither of which fits our definition of a federacy.[6]

FROM IDEAL TYPE TO EMPIRICAL REALITY?
THREE FEDERACIES IN SMALL SCANDINAVIAN DEMOCRACIES

We can insist on our five defining characteristics (and two facilitating conditions) for a federacy in an ideal type; however, when we turn to the empirical analysis of the contemporary world, is our ideal type an elegant but insignificant category in world affairs, because there are few, if any, actual examples which approximate the type? If there are examples, can we make cogent arguments about the conditions in which they will tend, or tend not, to emerge? Can we make theory-based predictions about the conditions in which federacies will function well or function poorly? Here we begin with an examination of three cases; The Åland Islands–Finland, the Faroe Islands–Denmark, and the Greenland-Denmark arrangements. We will ask the following questions for each case; did a crisis concerning exit or loyalty ever exist between a territorially concentrated minority population and the relatively homogeneous unitary nation-state? Were policies relatively close to some or all of our seven ideal-type federacy arrangements created in response to the crisis? If they were created, what effect would we predict they would have, and what effect did they have?

The Åland Islands: Finland, Sweden, and Czarist or Soviet Russia
Origins and Nature of the Crisis

The Åland Islands illustrates very well some of the conditions and processes leading to the creation of a federacy that is embedded in laws, treaties, international agreements, and, increasingly, the constitution of a unitary state.[7] Ruth Lapidoth, in her valuable book on varieties of autonomy, sets out very nicely the geopolitical importance of the 6,500 islands and skerries that make up the Åland Islands: "The islands are located in a strategically important area in the Baltic Sea between Sweden and Finland, at the entrance to the Gulf of Bothnia. This

---

6. See Rezvani, "Federacy," Appendix C.

7. There are four different combinations of spellings and accents used in the English-language literature to refer to the Åland Islands. In this chapter we will follow the spelling and accent used by the Åland legislature in their English-language publications. Our only exception to this practice will be for book titles.

location also dominates the access to St. Petersburg, and is thus of great importance for the defense of three states: Sweden, Finland and Russia."[8]

The history of the islands reflects the contributing role of geography and geopolitics as well as the tension between two powerful forces in international politics—nationalism and the self-determination of peoples versus state building and state maintenance. The institutional arrangements, their processes of enactment, and the role of international actors, particularly the League of Nations, exemplify how federacies can emerge.

From the Middle Ages until 1809, the Åland Islands were under Swedish rule and were Swedish in language and culture. Finland was also under Swedish rule, and the Åland Islands were administered by a governor from Abo, a city on the Finnish coast. In 1809 Sweden was forced to yield Finland and the Åland Islands to Russia. Within Imperial Russia, the Åland Islands were part of the Grand Duchy of Finland, an entity that had a high degree of democratic self-government, with its own parliament.[9] Tore Modeen, a Scandinavian legal historian, describes how, in the turmoil surrounding the Russian March Revolution of 1917, "just as the Finns aimed at the independence of their country (including Åland), so the Ålanders in turn wanted their islands to be detached from Finland and put under Swedish sovereignty."[10] In this standard work Modeen shows how, on the Åland Islands, there had "arisen a strong separatist movement. . . . The Ålanders feared that Finnish dominance when Finland gained its independence would be very strong. They therefore looked upon union with Sweden as the surest guarantee for the preservation of the national identity of the Åland Islands."[11] Sweden encouraged this prospect. Indeed, they sent a naval expedition in 1918, and Åland delegations were well received in Sweden. Few authorities or contemporary observers who have speculated on the subject doubt that if the principle of self-determination had resulted in a plebiscite, Ålanders would have voted to join Sweden.[12]

8. Ruth Lapidoth, *Autonomy. Flexible Solutions to Ethnic Conflicts* (Washington, DC: U.S. Institute of Peace Press, 1997), p. 70.

9. For example, in Finland in 1907 universal and equal suffrage was extended to all women and men over 24 years of age. Thus Finland in 1910 had the highest percentage of voters in the 20-and-over population of any of the fourteen West European countries documented in Peter Flora et al., *State, Economy, and Society in Western Europe, 1815–1975: A Data Handbook in Two Volumes* (Frankfurt: Campus Verlag, 1983), pp. 93 and 108. The party in the 1910 elections with the highest percentage of votes was the Social Democratic Party, p. 111. See also Osmo Jussila, *From Grand Duchy to Modern State: A Political History of Finland since 1809* (London: Hurst, 1999).

10. Tore Modeen, "Åland Islands," in Rudolf Berhardt, ed., *Encylopedia of Public International Law*, vol. 12 (Amsterdam: North Holland, 1990), p. 1.

11. Tore Modeen, "The International Protection of the National Identity of the Åland Islands," *Scandinavian Studies in Law* (1973), pp. 178–179.

12. See in particular the sections "Swedish Occupation of the Aland Islands" and "Swedish

212 CRAFTING STATE-NATIONS

When we look at the six factors that we suggest might make a territorially concentrated minority population feel quite distinct from the ethos of a unitary nation-state, the Åland Islands in 1920 scored reasonably high on five of the six, namely: (1) moderate but not great physical separation; (2) a different language; (3) a moderate self-governing tradition they wanted to expand; (4) a belief that, geopolitically speaking, their self-government could best be pursued by joining Sweden; and (5) an economy and way of life sufficiently different that its residents wanted to restrict ownership of property and most businesses to themselves. Fortunately, there was no major history of warfare or coercive repression by Finland. The absence of this feature, and the fact that both Åland and Finland were parliamentary democracies, made the construction of a federacy feasible.

On the other side of the conflict however, the principle of state sovereignty and state interests was also very strong. Finland objected to what it saw as an attack on its sovereignty and territorial integrity, and insisted on maintaining the Åland Islands as part of Finland. The French Prime Minister, Georges Clemenceau, was particularly interested in strengthening the anti-Bolshevik *cordon sanitaire* and thus wanted to back Finland which, unlike Sweden, had indicated its potential support for the *cordon sanitaire*.[13] The U.S.S.R., for its own reasons, also implicitly supported Finland because it wanted to maintain the demilitarization of the Åland Islands and knew it had much more geopolitical-military leverage over Finland than it had over Sweden, which was still a major regional power.

The international diplomacy involved in resolving the Åland controversy has been well documented.[14] However, in our judgment, a fundamental part of the solution devised by the League of Nations involved federacy arrangements. Following the state sovereignty principle (and the pressure of the major victor powers of World War I, mainly France, Britain, and the United States, all of whom wanted to avoid more conflict and instability in the region), the Åland Islands were awarded to Finland. But the price of the award of the Åland Islands to Finland was limitations of a federacy nature on the Finnish unitary nation-state. Numerous "self-determination of peoples" principles were built into the Åland Agreement of 1921 and increasingly codified and consensually expanded in 1951 and 1991.[15]

Desires for a Plebiscite" in the extremely well-documented book by James Barros, *The Aland Islands Question: Its Settlement by the League of Nations* (New Haven: Yale University Press, 1968), pp. 75–84, 99–101.

13. Ibid., pp. 203–204.
14. Ibid.
15. See "Finland: Aaland Islands," in *Federal Systems of the World*, ed. Elazar, pp. 98–100.

Earlier we mentioned five defining characteristics and two facilitating features, all seven of which are unusual or impossible in a unitary state but common in a federacy. To a strong degree, at least six (with some elements of the seventh) are found in the Åland Islands.

Defining Characteristic 1: Federal-like division of state and federacy functions. Our first ideal-typical defining characteristic is a federal-like agreement on the division of powers and responsibilities. The federacy-type arrangement for Åland is called the "Act on the Autonomy of Åland." The act was originally passed in 1921, with new acts increasing the federacy's autonomy in 1951, and 1991. We will use the current 1991 Autonomy Act in our analysis to see how it conforms or deviates from our ideal type. Unlike the 1921 agreement, the 1991 Autonomy Act has no international guarantors and was approved by both the Finnish parliament and the freely elected Legislative Assembly of Åland before it went into effect. We should note, however, that even the 1921 agreement was judged by Tore Modeen to be the "most radical form of international guarantee for a national minority ever to have been drawn up. In no other treaty have such far-reaching guarantees been given for the preservation of a national minority's language and culture and the protection of the national character of the area inhabited by the minority."[16]

Building on the 1922 and 1951 Autonomy Acts, the 1991 Autonomy Act devotes Chapter 4 to the "Authority of Åland" and Chapter 5 to "Authority of the State." As we shall document later, even Chapter 5 legislates some constraints on the otherwise exclusive powers given to the Finnish state.

Some of the key, embedded, culture-making, and identity-sustaining prerogatives explicitly given in Chapter 5 to the self-governing legislature of Åland are the following:

1. The Official language of Åland shall be Swedish. The language used in State administration, Åland administration and municipal administration shall be Swedish. (Section 36)

16. Modeen, "International Protection," pp. 183–184. What is called the 1921 Agreement was actually a decision that the Council of the League of Nations passed on June 24, 1921, with representatives of Finland and Sweden present. The government of Finland presented a bill to the Finnish parliament containing the League of Nations provisions three days later. The first election of the Åland parliament under their new prerogatives was not held until 1922. The 1951 Autonomy Act was largely a response by the Finnish government and parliament to Åland Island demands since the 1930s for greater clarity about the various understandings and agreements that collectively were called the 1921 agreement. After the end of World War II, the 1920s documents about Åland were mutually negotiated between the federacy and Finland and were signed separately by the Finnish parliament, the legislature of the Åland Islands, and finally by the president of Finland, see ibid., pp. 190–191.

2. The language of education in schools maintained by public funds or subsidized by public funds shall be Swedish, unless otherwise provided by an Act of Åland. (Section 40)

3. The power to grant the right of domicile is vested in the Government of Åland. (Section 7)

4. Only a person with the right of domicile may participate in elections of the Åland Parliament, the municipal councils and the other positions of trust in the Åland and municipal administration. (Section 9)

5. The right of a person without the right of domicile to exercise a trade or profession in Aland for personal gain may be limited by an Act of Åland. (Section 11)

6. The limitations of a person without the right of domicile to acquire real property or property of a similar nature in Åland with full legal title or with the right to enjoy are as provided in the [quite restrictive] Act on the Acquisition of Real Property in Åland." (Section 10)

In addition, Section 18 stipulates that "Åland shall have legislative powers in respect of: public order and security, (Article 6), health care and medical treatment, (Article 12), the design and use of the Åland flag and coat of arms (Article 3), farming, forestry, hunting and fishing (Articles 15–16), the creation of an offense and the extent of the penalty for such an offense in respect of a matter falling within the legislative competence of Åland (Article 25), an administrative court may be established in Åland by a State Act, such a court may by an Act of Åland be granted jurisdiction over administrative matters within the competence of Åland."

Chapter 5 spells out the areas where the state of Finland has authority to pass legislation, such as: the armed forces and border guards (Article 34), the issuing of paper money and foreign currencies (Article 37), foreign relations (Article 4), foreign trade (Article 12), nuclear energy (Article 18), civil defense (Article 28), and telecommunications (Article 40).

However, embedded in the 1991 Act of Autonomy of Åland are quite a number of explicit restrictions that relate to Åland but to no other part of Finland. For example, with respect to the armed forces, given that Åland is demilitarized and neutral, "residents of Åland . . . shall be exempt from conscription for military service" (Section 12); the Articles on labor law, mineral development, criminal law, and taxes all state that there may be some explicit exceptions concerning Åland. In three key areas—telecommunications, nuclear development, and civil defense—there are explicit requirements for the *consent* of Åland for the exercise of these state functions in Åland. Concerning civil defense, the evacuation of residents of Åland "may only be made with the consent of the Government of Åland" (Article 28). Nuclear energy is an exclusive function of the state of Finland— "however, the consent of the Government of Åland is required for the construction, possession and operation of a nuclear power plant and the handling and stockpiling of materials therefore in Åland" (Article 18). Telecommunications is a state function—"however, a state official may only grant permission to engage in general telecommunications in Åland with the consent of the Government of Åland" (Article 40).

Defining Characteristic 2: Quasi-constitutionally embedded political autonomy of the federacy. No prerogative is worth much if the central state can unilaterally reverse it. All constitutions have provisions for amendment, but the norm for amendment is to require exceptional majorities. The Autonomy Act of Åland does precisely this. The act stipulates that it can only be amended by a two-thirds majority of both the Finnish parliament and the Åland parliament (Section 69). Modeen is emphatic on the constitutional embeddedness of the Autonomy Act and the restriction that neither Åland nor Finland can unilaterally alter the Autonomy Act: "The Autonomy Act cannot be repealed or amended without the approval of the Landsting [the Åland parliament]. Any such decision by the Finnish parliament (Riksdag) shall follow the specific rules regulating constitutional amendments."[17] Lapidoth concurs, stressing that amending the Act requires the joint action of Åland and Finland: "Collaboration or agreement between the central authority and the province is indispensable."[18]

Defining Characteristic 3: Existence of dispute resolution procedures. This defining characteristic of an ideal-type federacy is not met explicitly in the case of the Åland Islands. The Act of Autonomy states that "if a conflict of authority arises between Åland officials and State officials on a given administrative function, a decision on the matter shall be rendered by the Supreme Court [of Finland]" (Section 60). However, the spirit and practice of the Act of Autonomy builds in a type of dispute regulation. New state laws affecting only Åland cannot be made, nor policies of the central state executed, *in* Åland—even in areas of state responsibility such as civil defense and the development of nuclear energy and telecommunications—without the express *consent* of the Åland legislature or government. As we shall see when we discuss treaties, although foreign policy is an

17. Modeen, "Åland Islands," p. 4.
18. Lapidoth, *Autonomy*, p. 71.

exclusive state function, consent of the Åland Islands is frequently required if a treaty has a special impact on them. Also, in numerous areas within the state's prerogatives, the act stipulates that no measures can go forward that will have a special effect on Åland without *consultation* with Åland authorities. For example, "A decision of the Bank of Finland that may be presumed to be especially important for the economic life or employment in Åland shall, if possible, only be made after negotiations with the government of Åland" (Section 29, clause 18). Procedures encouraging co-participation are seen even in the prescribed way by which the state of Finland appoints its governor, who, the Autonomy Act states, "shall represent the Government of Finland in Åland" (Section 4). Further, "The President of the Republic shall appoint the Governor after having agreed on the matter with the Speaker of the Åland Parliament. If a consensus is not reached, the President shall appoint the Governor from among five candidates nominated by the Åland Parliament" (Section 52).

Defining Characteristic 4: Reciprocal representation between the unitary state and the federacy. Both of these characteristics are fulfilled in the Åland Islands: "In Parliamentary and Presidential elections Åland shall constitute an electoral district" [of Finland]. (Section 68). As we have just discussed, Finland has a governor to "represent Finland in Åland" (Section 4).

Defining Characteristic 5: The federacy is part of an internationally recognized independent state. Finland is a member of the United Nations, and Åland is represented there by the Government of Finland. Due to its representation in the Finnish parliament, and its well-developed, constitutionally embedded self-governing prerogatives, Åland is part of the state of Finland.

Facilitating Characteristic 1: Role of international guarantors in the founding of the federacy. As we documented, a variety of international guarantors, particularly the League of Nations, were involved in setting up Åland Islands as a federacy. However, the question of the disarmament and neutrality of the Åland Islands preceded federacy arrangements, because they had been a key subject of the international negotiations among France, Britain, and Russia in the 1856 Treaty of Paris that ended the Crimean War. Continuation of Åland disarmament and neutrality was a crucial precondition of the U.S.S.R. and Sweden accepting Finland's award of the Åland Islands by the League of Nations. In fact, as Modeen shows, "a convention on the non-fortification and neutralization of the Åland Islands was concluded between Denmark, Estonia, Finland, France, Germany, Italy, Latvia, Poland, Sweden, and the United Kingdom on October 20, 1921."[19]

19. Modeen, "Åland Islands," p. 2.

Facilitating Characteristic 2: Role of the federacy in international treaties signed by the center. When Finland applied for membership in the European Community, "the Åland islanders vehemently opposed the move. There [was] concern that their demilitarized status might be affected by the Maastricht Treaty's provisions for a common foreign and defense policy. They also were concerned about what would happen to tax-free sales on board the Åland-owned ferries running between the islands and Sweden and Finland. The ferries and the tourists they bring contribute about 70 per cent of the island's income."[20] That the Åland Islands and Finland had an internationally accepted federacy arrangement allowed Finland, with the strong support of Åland, to negotiate some opt-out provisions from Finland's commitments when it joined the European Community in 1994. It is important to stress that federacy arrangements are flexible and can expand in what they cover. Such opt-out provisions were not in the 1921 or 1951 Autonomy Acts. However, after Finland negotiated opt-out arrangements with the EC for the Åland Islands, the 1991 Autonomy Act added in 2004 an amendment stating that "in the decision-making on the measures in Finland relating to decisions made in the European Union, the legislative power and the administrative power shall be divided between Åland and the State as provided in this Act" (Section 59b).[21]

How Successful Has the Åland Islands Federacy Been?

Partly because the federacy arrangements have been honored by Finland's one-time irredentist neighbor, Sweden, and honored also by the democratic polities of Finland and the Åland Islands, and partly because the federacy involves a flexible, living, growing set of mutually beneficial arrangements that has the capacity to respond to new problems such as the EU case, no significant political movement has emerged in Åland since the federacy was created in 1922 that might have led Åland to break its federacy commitments, join Sweden, or become independent. Writing in 1973, Modeen judged that "the people of Åland will continue to live in surroundings which are Swedish in both language and culture: this lies not only in their own interest but in that of both Sweden and Finland. . . . The people of Åland have the advantage of enjoying a marked degree of autonomy, which gives them as independent a status as a small community of some 20,000 inhabitants can hope to achieve."[22] Writing almost a quarter of a century later, Lapidoth

20. "Finland: Aaland Islands," *Federal Systems of the World*, ed. Elazar, p. 87.
21. For a discussion of the exact opt-out provisions approved by the EC, see Lapidoth, *Autonomy*, pp. 237–238n38.
22. Modeen, "International Protection," pp. 204–205.

asserted, "Because the Åland Islands have had autonomy for more than seventy years and all those involved seem satisfied, it may be considered a successful case of Autonomy."[23]

The Faroe Islands; Crisis between a Unitary Nation-State and a Distant Minority Population

The Faroe Islands, if they had been an independent state in 2008, with its population of about 50,000, would have constituted the eleventh least populous state in the United Nations. The Islands, which have been linked to the Danish Crown since the fourteenth century, are located between the Shetland Islands northwest of Scotland and Iceland and are situated 1,300 kilometers from Copenhagen.[24] As Debes writes, "During the Middle Ages, Faroese developed into a separate Nordic language. . . . No section of the Faroese people became Danish-speaking, while Danish became the language of the authorities, in church, court, trade and the administration at large."[25]

In the first constituent assembly in Denmark, three-quarters of the members were elected by popular suffrage, but the Faroes were represented by a Crown nominee. The new constitution, still without Faroese elected representation, was applied to the Faroes in 1850, and the island was considered a province in the unitary state of Denmark. The Faroes were given one seat in the Danish lower house and one in the upper house and the right to an elected provincial assembly, the Løgting, in its capital, Torshavn.

Competitive party divisions only really began early in the twentieth century. "The issue on which the first Faroese political parties were formed was whether to maintain or loosen the constitutional link with metropolitan Denmark," writes West.[26] The Unionist Party favored the former and the Home Rule Party the latter. Due to the Unionist Party's successful electoral appeals to the islanders' worries about losing valuable financial and cultural links to Denmark, the Unionist Party was the dominant force in Faroese politics from 1906–36. The Social Democratic Party was in the middle. It favored more home rule and greater language auton-

23. Lapidoth, *Autonomy*, p. 70.

24. John F. West argues that "the crown of Norway was united with that of Denmark in 1380, and from that time, Iceland and the Faroe Islands came to be governed more and more not as Norwegian, but as Danish provinces." See his useful volume on the historical development of the Faroe Islands, *Faroe: The Development of a Nation* (London: Hurst, 1972), p. 8.

25. Hans Jacob Debes, "The Formation of a Nation: The Faroe Islands," in Sven Tägil, ed., *Ethnicity and Nation Building in the Nordic World* (London: Hurst, 1995), p. 67.

26. West, *Faroe*, p. 154.

omy, but it never sought a complete break with Denmark because its social policies were helped by the high welfare subsidies Denmark gave the Faroes.

However, electoral sentiments in favor of the equality of the Faroese language with Danish and stronger home rule were growing by the late 1930s. At this point, a context-changing geopolitical event happened. Germany occupied Denmark in April 1940. The Danish king and government almost immediately capitulated to Germany. All communications between Denmark and the Faroes were severed. But the Faroes did not surrender. The day after the Danish surrender, the leader of a new, more militant home-rule People's Party in the Faroes, which had just won six of the twenty-four seats in the Faroese legislature, "declared in the Lögting that Faroe had passed from Danish sovereignty, and that the Lögting should now be fully responsible for legislative and executive acts in the islands. This declaration was coupled with the threat that if secession from Denmark had not been accomplished by 6 o'clock that evening, its proposers would themselves take whatever steps were necessary."[27]

The People's Party did not carry the day in the Løgting, but the legislature passed a new provisional constitution that augmented Faroe's capacity to govern itself in virtually all domestic matters, while the friendly power, Britain, whose protective presence was accepted, occupied the island and attended to the war. After the 1943 elections, the nationalistic People's Party was only one seat short of an absolute majority. There was an economic boom owing to the Faroes' key role in providing fish to the hard-pressed British food market. In this context of isolation from Denmark and growing self confidence in its self-governing capacities, "there was a remarkable intensification of nationalist agitation and the growing support for the self-rule movement."[28]

At the end of the war, both the Danish and the Faroese authorities knew that they could not go back to the prewar political arrangements, so negotiations began. While the discussions were still going on, with the Danish government's proposal containing only modest new autonomy provisions, the People's Party argued for a plebiscite, as a way of informing their negotiators about the opinion of the islanders. The moment of constitutional crisis in Faroe islands occurred on September 1946. An inconclusive, Faroe-drafted plebiscite on independence posed three alternatives: (1) "Do you want the Faroe Islands to secede from Denmark?" (2) "Do you want the Danish government's proposal to be put into effect?" or (3) spoil your ballot if you want neither of the above but prefer a dominion

27. Ibid., p. 175.
28. See Debes, "Formation of a Nation," p. 79.

status short of complete independence. The second choice was favored not only by the Unionists but also by the large Social Democratic Party, which wanted autonomy but wanted maintenance of the traditionally large Danish welfare subsidies to Faroe even more. The results in the September 14, 1946, vote were: 48.7% for secession, 47.2% for the Danish government's position, and 4.1% spoiled ballots.[29] Danish Prime Minister Knud Kristensen, who did not have a parliamentary majority, took the view that the vote, though narrow for secession, should be respected, and the Faroes were granted independence. However, the Danish parliament, taking the view that the vote for independence was inconclusive, did not support Kristensen. In the Faroes, the People's Party now had a majority of one and was able to pass a resolution to proceed with setting up a government to negotiate independence.[30] In Denmark "this resolution was widely seen as a coup d'etat . . . the King, on the advice of the Danish government dissolved the Løgting. . . . The Danish corvette, *Thetis*, was sent to Tórshaven . . . as a deterrent to any popular disorder."[31]

For the Danish government to be seen as threatening force in the North Atlantic against its own citizens was a national and international embarrassment. For many in the Faroes also, a complete and costly break with Denmark was to be avoided. New elections in the Faroes produced a coalition government: "In March 1947 the Løgting voted unanimously in favor of a request to the Danish government to grant legislative power to the Løgting, but on a basis of Faroe continuing to be part of the Danish Kingdom. The result was the negotiation, over the next twelve months, of the Faroese Home Rule Act. This was approved by both the Danish Parliament and the Faroese Løgting."[32]

The Faroes, with their great physical separation from Denmark, separate language, World War II legacy of de facto self-government, and fragile reliance on low-technology fishing within their own shores and extremely vulnerable to outside fishing fleets, had four of the six features we have argued would make a territorially concentrated minority population difficult to manage peacefully and democratically within a unitary state. The negotiation of home rule was helped by the complete absence of an irredentist power or any historical memory of actual

29. West, *Faroe*, p. 188.
30. To this day, there is some scholarly disagreement over exactly what the Faroese government intended. Lapidoth called the actions a "unilateral declaration of independence," but others see it as the putting together of a government to negotiate much greater autonomy from Denmark. Lapidoth, *Autonomy*, p. 113.
31. West, *Faroe*, pp. 189–190.
32. Ibid., p. 190.

warfare or the use of armed coercive repression. But how close to our ideal type of federacy was this Faroese Home Rule Act?

The Faroese Home Rule Act of 1948

Defining Characteristic 1: Federal-like division of state and federacy functions. The Home Rule Act of 1948, in a very federal way, explicitly divides powers into List A, List B, and residual powers. List A are called "special Faroese affairs." If the Faroese home government wanted to assume them and would pay all the expenses, all list A powers were the exclusive responsibility of the Faroes. These functions, among many others, included; Faroese administration, including appointment, dismissal, conditions of service and salaries of Faroese civil servants, schooling, public welfare services, territorial fishing and protection of fish, rural and agricultural matters, harbors, coastal protection, trade licensing, and direct and indirect taxes (Section 16). List B included administrative fields that "shall be the subject of further negotiation in order to determine whether and to what extent they can be recognized as Special Faroese Affairs." These included the established church, the police, the land fund, the radio, natural resources, and import and export controls. By the 1970s radio and import and exports had passed to the federacy. In 1994 the federacy and the state agreed on a natural resources formula in which most of the powers went to the federacy. For all the new powers the federacy assumed, they also agreed to pay the expenses. The major residual powers are covered by Section 6, which states that "matters which do not, according to this Act, come under the Faroese Home Government shall be handled as joint concerns by the national [state] authorities." This means that in the domain of the state are foreign affairs, defense, currency, and the final court of appeals.[33]

Defining Characteristic 2: Quasi-constitutionally embedded political autonomy of the federacy and *Defining Characteristic 3: Existence of dispute resolution procedures.* We have combined these two defining functions for analysis because the situation is not as clear-cut as in the Åland federacy, and much of the embeddedness comes from British-style dispute resolution procedures and practices. Nowhere does the Home Rule Act state how the act shall be amended or that unilateral change is forbidden. However, Lapidoth, writing almost fifty years after its adoption, writes, "The Home Rule Act establishes an elaborate system for settling disputes: Four persons, two of them nominated by the central government and two by the home rule authorities, are to try to resolve the dispute. If they fail to

---

33. For a discussion of the division of powers see Lapidoth, *Autonomy*, pp. 113–114.

reach agreement, the matter is to be decided by three judges of Denmark's Supreme Court. The system has never been used."[34] The system may never have been used, because if the Danish state were to violate the spirit of the Home Rule Act in some egregious way, the Faroes would probably exercise what is understood as their right to secede.

Notwithstanding the absence of explicit wording against a unilateral decision to alter the Home Rule Act on the part of the unitary state, the Home Rule Act does contain frequent references to the obligation of the state to discuss and negotiate with the federacy if it passes laws, even in the area of state residual powers, that affect the Faroes. For example, Section 7 of the Home Act states: "In order to ensure for the Løgting the widest possible influence on the formulation of special provisions relating exclusively to the Faroes in Acts passed by the national authorities, National Government Bills containing provisions relating exclusively to the Faroes shall be put before the Home Government for consideration before they are tabled in the national parliament. Other national legislation affecting local Faroese matters shall be put before the Faroese Home Government for consideration before they are put in force in the islands. . . . The same procedure shall be followed with regard to treaties and other international agreements which require the sanction of the national parliament and which affect special Faroese interests."[35]

Defining Characteristic 4: Reciprocal representation between the unitary state and the federacy. Here we find full congruence with the ideal-type federacy: "The Faroese shall be represented in the Danish parliament by at least two members" (Section 14). The Danish state sends to the Faroes a "High Commissioner, who is the highest representative of the State in the Faroes and the head of the national administration on the Islands" (Section 15).

Defining Characteristic 5: The federacy is part of an internationally recognized independent state. As the first sentence of the Home Rule Act states, "Within the framework of this Act the Faroe Islands shall constitute a self-governing community within the State of Denmark." As the expert on Faroe matters in the Danish Ministry of Foreign Affairs stresses, the Home Rule Act "does not create a new subject of international law."[36] At the United Nations there is one ambassador who represents both Denmark and the Faroes, namely the Ambassador of Denmark.

34. Ibid., p. 115.
35. All of the above patterns of action by Denmark and the Faroes approximate what constitutional theorists such as Geoffrey Marshall would call "conventions" that are de facto, even though unwritten, parts of the working constitution. For a useful discussion of such "conventions," see Rezvani, *Federacy*, esp. ch. 4.
36. Árni Olafsson, "International Status of the Faroe Islands," *Nordisk Tidsskrift*, no. 29 (1982), p. 30.

Facilitating Characteristic 1: Role of international guarantors in the founding of the federacy. Neither Denmark nor the Faroes wanted, or needed, international guarantors to set up or monitor the federacy arrangements in 1948.

Facilitating Characteristic 2: Role of the federacy in international treaties signed by the center. Both Denmark and the Faroes were especially prescient about how to craft the Home Rule Act so that it could, if needed, allow the federacy to help structure and approve international agreements that might have a crucial impact on fishing "geopolitics" in the Faroes and be of mutual interest to the state of Denmark. The Home Rule Act explicitly states that "after consultation with the Faroese Home Government provision should be made for the latter to assert in each case the special interests of the Faroes in negotiations with foreign countries for agreement concerning trade and fishery. . . . Where special Faroese matters are concerned, the Ministry of Foreign Affairs may, where it is not deemed incompatible with national interests, authorize representatives of the Home Government, if a wish to that effect has been expressed, to carry on direct negotiations with the assistance of the Foreign Service" (Section 8).

These prescient provisions have become standard international practice for Denmark. As the Faroe expert of the Danish Foreign Ministry wrote more than thirty years after the Home Rule Act was passed: "It is considered general practice by the Danish Ministry of Foreign Affairs that during the process of concluding an international agreement endeavors are made to identify whether the treaty is relevant to the Faroe Islands, and if it is the case contacts are made with the Prime Minister's Office and the Faroese Home Government as to the acceptability of the treaty to the Faroe Islands. If the treaty is not considered acceptable, Denmark may either make use of a territorial clause in the treaty or make a declaration, at the latest at the time of signature or ratification, that the treaty does not apply to the Faroe Islands."[37]

When Denmark joined the European Community in 1973, the Faroe Islands argued that the treaty's provisions on fishing would have a dangerous impact on their fish mono-culture economy and society. Lapidoth describes the subsequent opt-out agreement as follows "The Faroe Islands have remained outside [the EC and later the EU], they have instead concluded a trade agreement with the EC (1974), as well as with certain member states of the European Free Trade Association. These agreements were formally concluded by Denmark for the Faroes. . . . If the Faroese government is opposed to the conclusion of a treaty, Denmark will usually make a statement excluding the islands from the application instru-

37. Ibid., p. 33.

ment. Not being a state, the Faroes cannot join international intergovernmental organizations."[38]

Challenges to the Continuation of the Faroe Federacy

In many ways the federacy has been a success. The Federacy has endured for sixty years. There has never been any political violence. Both Denmark and the Faroes are solid parliamentary democracies. The standard of living in the Faroes has been helped greatly by Danish subsidies that aim at maintaining near-parity of the Danish welfare state provisions between the Faroes and the inhabitants of the unitary state.

Nonetheless, Faroe governments announced in 1999, 2001, and 2007 that they wanted to hold a referendum on independence. The Danish parliament and government stated on various occasions that the Faroese people could decide whether they wanted independence or not and that the result of their vote would be honored. But, in three rounds of negotiations about the procedures to be followed, a sticking point emerged. The Faroe government wanted subsidies to be maintained at current levels for twelve years after independence. The Danish parliament and prime minister insisted that the subsidies would terminate after four years of independence. Faroese citizens watched this debate carefully and revealed in numerous public opinion polls that they were extremely sensitive to the post-independence duration of subsidies. For example, in April 2000, about half of those polled favored independence if the Danish subsidies were maintained for twenty years, but only a quarter did if the subsidies were terminated in four years. To date all three proposed referendums have been postponed by Faroese governments.

It is possible that a referendum might be held some day, and the vote for independence could well carry the day. This depends on economics much more than on issues of identity or politics. In 1992 the Faroes reached an agreement with Denmark giving them full ownership of any hydrocarbons discovered in their offshore waters. These waters are quite close to some British-controlled oil fields. In 2001 twelve major oil companies signed contracts giving them exploration rights if they drilled eight wells in eight years.[39] Independence plans were based on future oil largesse. But, as of 2007, no successful wells had been developed. The 2008 referendum on independence was cancelled, and for the first time

38. Lapidoth, *Autonomy*, p. 114.
39. See Matthew Jones, "Faroese Explore Prospects for New Economic Base," *Financial Times*, July 10, 2001.

in almost twenty years an election was fought virtually without debate about independence.[40]

If oil were ever discovered in the Faroes, and the islanders voted for independence, the outcome would be completely unlike the 1946 crisis. There would be no Danish corvette, no unilateral dissolution of the Faroe government by Denmark. Following the spirit of the Home Rule Act, a mutual "velvet divorce" would be negotiated by two consenting democracies.

Greenland

We will be much shorter in our discussion of the Greenland-Denmark federacy, because it is very similar to the Faroes-Denmark arrangements.[41] However, the origins of the federacy arrangements were somewhat different and illustrate how a unitary state may find federacy arrangements useful.

Unlike in Åland, in Greenland there was no strong desire to join another country, and unlike the Faroes, there was no contested vote for independence. But even more than either Åland or the Faroes, Greenland was radically different from the unitary state to which it was attached as a colony, Denmark.[42] On three of the six factors that can make a territorial unit difficult to absorb democratically into a unitary state—distance, different language and culture, and a precarious and unique economy that its inhabitants felt needed special protective legal measures to preserve their livelihood and way of life, Greenland was radically distinct from Denmark.

Distance from the unitary state. Greenland is the world's largest island that is not a continent; it is located more than 2,000 miles from Copenhagen, but less than 70 miles off Canada's northeastern coast. In fact, according to Harhoff, "Geographically, Greenland belongs to the North American continent, and Greenland has been traditionally been encompassed by the Monroe Doctrine."[43]

Linguistic and cultural difference from the unitary state. A Danish legal adviser to the Greenland Home Authorities says that "there is no resemblance or linguistic community between Greenland and the Danish language: Danish is as different from Greenlandic, as English is from Chinese. . . . Greenland is inhabited

40. See "Faroe Islanders Head to the Polls Saturday," Agence France-Presse, January 17, 2008.
41. See Lapidoth, *Autonomy*, p. 144; and Frederick Harhoff, "Greenland's Withdrawal from the European Communities," *Common Market Law Review*, no. 20 (1983), p. 18.
42. Harhoff writes that "Greenland has belonged to the Danish Crown since the fourteenth century, but was first properly colonized by Denmark in the beginning of the eighteenth century and administered by the Royal Greenland Trade Department in Copenhagen," Ibid., p. 14.
43. Ibid.

by 52,000 persons, 42,000 of which are Eskimos of the same origin and culture as the Eskimos of arctic Canada and Alaska."[44]

Economic differences from the unitary state and the desire for special protective legislation. Greenland's culture and way of living is exceptionally vulnerable: "Greenland is totally dependent upon its fishery. . . . Greenland's fisherman fish exclusively within Greenland's own fishing territory, thus having no interest in fishing in foreign waters."[45] Because Greenlanders are so dependent on fishing off their own shores, they feel very threatened by the prospect of allowing other countries to fish in their waters. A common market agreement by the unitary state that would allow other states to fish off Greenland's shores, while also permitting Greenlanders to fish thousands of miles away off member states' shores, is thus quite threatening.

Three things happened to put pressure on Denmark's colonial arrangements concerning Greenland. First, like the Faroes, Greenland was completely cut off from Denmark by the German occupation in World War II. Being so close, the United States, and not Britain, became the occupying country during the war. Second, in 1946, in the postwar atmosphere of de-colonization, Denmark in 1946 felt obliged to acknowledge to the United Nations that Greenland was a "non-self-governing territory."[46] Third, in November 1947 a new Social Democratic government came to power in Denmark. The Social Democrats were not comfortable with Denmark's classification by the UN as a colonial power subject to routine reports and inspections, so in 1953 the government decided to alter Denmark's colonial power status by making Greenland a full voting member of the unitary state of Denmark.[47]

Before colonization, Greenland had a robust tradition, which Elazar calls "tribal republicanism."[48] However, at the time of incorporation into Denmark as a normal voting province in 1953, Greenland had a very low level of political mobilization and no political party life. The trigger to mobilization and the development of a party system involved the European Community. As Axel Sørensen, a historian of Greenland nationalism, explains, "The Danish entry into the Common Market in 1972 was the clearest single impetus which got the political development in Greenland moving. A referendum was taken all over the realm.

44. Ibid.
45. Ibid., p. 22.
46. Ibid., p. 14.
47. See Axel Sørensen, "Greenland: From Colony to Home Rule," in *Ethnicity and Nation Building in the Nordic World,* ed. Sven Tägil (London: Hurst, 1995), pp. 98–102.
48. "Finland: Aaland Islands," *Federal Systems of the World,* ed. Elazar, p. 80.

Denmark (continental) was in favor, while Greenland voted against. . . . Green-land [as part of the unitary state] had to follow Denmark in joining the EC. The [newly mobilized Greenlandic politicians] . . . took the initiative to change the constitutional relations to Denmark to get out again."[49] They wanted to get out of the EC precisely because joining the EC would allow all EC members to fish in their waters. To avoid this without leaving Denmark and its important subsidies, the only formula was to campaign for a federacy similar to that of the Faroe Islands. The first step was that the Greenland Provincial Council pressured suc-cessfully for a committee consisting exclusively of Greenlanders to study a home rule proposal. The Danish parliament received the proposal in 1975 and agreed to set up a commission to negotiate and draft a home rule bill for consideration. The commission consisted of seven Greenlandic elected legislators, seven members of the Danish parliament, and a Danish chair, Isi Foighel. Foighel later wrote that Greenlanders were "fighting not for national independence but for an identity of their own, or rather for better possibilities of strengthening and developing their identity through increased self-responsibility . . . [while remaining] a constituent part of Denmark."[50]

The commission's report was approved by the Danish parliament, which passed the Greenland Home Rule Act in 1978. Greenland, by a three-to-one referendum margin, voted for the act in 1979.[51] By 1985, Denmark and Greenland, using the provisions made possible by the federacy arrangements, had negotiated Green-land's withdrawal from the EC.[52]

As in the Faroe Islands, there have been periodic expressions in Greenland of the desire for independence. But independence movements have always been, until recently, constrained by the exceptionally important role of Danish assis-tance, which represents, according to some assessments, approximately 40% of the gross national product of the island.[53] A hostile independence with no further Danish assistance is not desired by authoritative Greenlandic political leaders. However, global warming is causing some of Greenland's glaciers to retreat, mak-ing on-shore mineral excavation and off-shore oil exploration possible and, with it, the possibility of economic independence and thus, the possibility of political independence. On November 25, 2008, Greenland held a referendum on greater

49. Sørensen, "Greenland," p. 103.
50. Foighel, "Home Rule in Greenland 1979," *Nordic Journal of International Law* 48 (1979), p. 6.
51. Ibid., pp. 4–9.
52. Harhoff, "Greenland's Withdrawal," pp. 13–33.
53. See Stephan Faris, "Ice Free: Will Global Warming Give Greenland its Independence?" *New York Times Magazine*, July 27, 2008, p. 20.

autonomy from Denmark. The referendum passed with approximately 75% of the vote.[54] Negotiations ensued between Greenland and Denmark about what were the autonomies for which Greenland would like to assume full financial and political responsibility. The new "Act on Greenland's Self Government," an agreement between the Greenland government and the Danish government as "equal partners," dated June 2009 and signed by Denmark's Queen Margrethe II, explicitly recognized in the first sentence of the preamble that "Greenland is a people pursuant to international law with the right of self-determination."[55] Article 8 of the act goes on to say, "Decision regarding Greenland's independence shall be taken by the people of Greenland." Article 3 of the act stipulates that, until such time as there is independence, Denmark will continue to give Greenland an annual subsidy of 3,439.6 million kronor per year (approximately 633 million USD, or approximately $11,000 per capita). This sum will decline as revenues from Greenland's mineral resources increase. Greenland's competencies in arranging international agreements with the consent of Denmark were also increased in the 2009 agreement.

BEYOND SCANDINAVIA?

Can the concept and some of the practices of federacy travel beyond the small, relatively peaceful democracies we have explored so far? What is the scope value of our concept? Can it travel into much more conflictual situations? Can it travel to non-Western, especially Islamic, cultures? In the second half of this chapter, we examine four different cases. Might federacy be useful in some transitions to democracy after authoritarianism or defeat in war? For this we examine Italy in the immediate aftermath of World War II, when the unitary state had a "politically robust multinational" situation in which five peripheral regions either had leaders and movements who wanted to exit or were demanding greater autonomy. In less than a decade, Italy was a consolidated democracy with no secessionist movements. Why? How? Our second case is Portugal in 1974, when the Carnation Revolution broke out in one of Europe's oldest unitary states. Why and how did the constituent assembly defuse a secessionist movement on the Azores? Third is the case of Corsica. The basis for our ideal type of a normatively grounded, unitary nation-state model is, of course, France. Why did the National Assembly

54. Alan Cowell, "Greenland Vote Favors Independence," *New York Times*, November 26, 2008, available at www.nytimes.com/2008/11/27/world/europe/27greenland.html, accessed November 30, 2008.

55. Denmark. Act no. 473 of June 12, 2009, *Act on Greenland Self-Government*.

try to alter this model in the case of Corsica in 2001? Fourth, and last, concerns Indonesia. Can a federacy be constructed between two opponents in an ongoing civil war? Can federacy travel well even to a Muslim context, which is often alleged to be particularly hostile to shared sovereignty? We will look at Indonesia and Aceh to explore these last two questions. Let us begin our exploration of the scope value with Italy after World War II.

The Role of Federacies in the Italian Postwar Democratic Transition

Italy's economy, politics, and unitary state at the end of World War II were all facing crises. Due to Mussolini's alliance with Hitler, Italy's international and domestic legitimacy was dangerously low. In the country's peripheries, territorially concentrated minority populations, in five different areas, partly in response to Mussolini's authoritarian centralizing policies, had leaders and movements seeking exit or self-government from the Italian state. These areas were: German-speaking South Tyrol, where the vast majority of the population wanted to rejoin their irredentist neighbor, Austria; the French-speaking province of Valle D'Aosta on the alpine border with France, which had recently sent troops and agents to the province, making annexation a live issue; Friuli-Venezia Giulia on the border with Yugoslavia, with many Slovene speakers, much of the territory of which the Allies' war partner Tito was occupying and claiming as part of Yugoslavia; and the islands of Sicily and Sardinia, with their very distinctive social structures and problems.[56] In terms of the categories we have developed in this book, Italy in 1944–45 was a "politically robust multinational polity" governed by a unitary state.

South Tyrol, in what is now the province of Bolzano, is adjacent to the strategically valuable Brenner Pass connecting the Alps with northeastern Italy. Before World War I this territory was part of Austria, with a population that was approximately 86% German-speaking, 8% Italian-speaking, and 4% Ladino-speaking.[57] In 1919, in the Treaty of St. Germain, the territory was given to Italy as part of a secret agreement (later published) for joining the allies in World War I. Mussolini's fascist regime imposed a particularly harsh and authoritarian set of unitary-state and Italian nation-building policies on South Tyrol. The German schools were closed, Italian was made the only official language, there was extensive state-

---

56. For an invaluable map showing these five peripheral regions and the fifteen other regions of Italy, see "Italy," *Federal Systems of the World*, ed. Elazar, p. 121.

57. For rapidly changing language estimates for the province of Bolzano in 1910, 1921, 1939, 1943, 1946, 1951, 1953, and 1961, see Anthony Evelyn Alcock, *The History of the South Tyrol Question* (Geneva: Graduate Institute of International Studies, 1970), p. 497, table D.

sponsored Italian immigration into the area, and the name of the territory was changed to Alto Adige. In 1926 Mussolini proudly announced: "The Germans of the Alto Adige are not a national minority but an ethnic remnant."[58]

Not so. German speakers were still the largest and most politically organized part of the population in South Tyrol (Alto Adige) in 1945. Almost immediately after the war, a German-speaking party, the South Tyrolean People's Party (Süd-tiroler Volkspartei, SVP), was formed and rapidly became the dominant social movement and political party in South Tyrol. In the name of self-determination, the SVP demanded a plebiscite over their status. With the strong domestic political and international diplomatic irredentist support of Austria, the SVP's goal was to exit Italy and accede to Austria.[59] The Italian-speaking minority in South Tyrol and the Italian-speaking majority in Italy were in turn deeply suspicious of the German-speakers of South Tyrol. Hitler and Mussolini had arranged for a plebiscite of sorts in South Tyrol in which German-speakers could opt to retain Italian nationality or migrate to Hitler's Reich and receive German citizenship. Out of a total number of the 229,500 inhabitants of Bolzano entitled to opt out of Italy and to migrate to the Reich, 166,488 did so.[60]

A second troubling area for the unitary state was the Alpine province of Valle d'Aosta, situated in northwestern Italy, bordering France, Switzerland, and Piedmont, the powerhouse of Italian unification in the nineteenth century.[61] Historically, Valle d'Aosta had had a French-speaking population, which in return for pledging loyalty to the Savoias in 1191, received special "rights and privileges and some self government" and gradually developed substantial identity with Italy.[62] Up until unification in 1860, if the question "Can you be Italian while continuing

58. Rolf Steininger, "Back to Austria? The Problem of South Tyrol in 1945/46," *European Studies Journal* 7, no. 2 (Fall 1990), p. 52.

59. For an excellent analysis of the SVP from 1945 to the present, see Günther Pallaver, "The Südtiroler Volkspartei: From Irrendentism to Autonomy," in *Autonomist Parties in Europe: Identity Politics and the Revival of Territorial Cleavage*, vol. 2, ed. Lieven De Winter, Margarita Gómez-Reino, and Peter Lynch (Barcelona: Institut de Ciències Polítiques i Socials, 2006), pp. 161–188.

60. For an thorough treatment of this episode, see Alcock, "Hitler, Mussolini, and the Options Agreement of 1939," in *History of the South Tyrol Question*, pp. 45–59. On the immensely complicated and fraught national and international negotiations on the rights of the 70,000 "optants" who migrated to the Reich to return to Italy as citizens, and thus as voters in the South Tyrol, see "Autonomy and Options: October 1946–February 1948" in the same volume, pp. 148–194. See also Steininger, "Back to Austria?" p. 54.

61. For an important account of the Italian unification process, and particularly the central role of Piedmont, see Daniel Ziblatt, *Structuring the State: The Formation of Italy and Germany and the Puzzle of Federalism* (Princeton: Princeton University Press, 2006).

62. See Marco Cuaz, "La Valle d'Aosta. Un'identità di frontiera fra Italia, Europa ed etno-nazionalismi," in *Altre Italie: Identità nazionale e Regioni a statuto speciale*, ed. Gaspare Nevola (Rome: Carocci editore, 2003), pp. 1–18, esp. pp. 1–3.

to speak French?" was asked, the most likely voluntary answer in Valle d'Aosta probably would have been, "I am an Italian who speaks French."[63] Such an answer would have been a clear illustration of what we have called multiple but complementary identities. Unification of Italy, with its increased taxes and greater centralization, eroded these pro-Italian sentiments somewhat, but it was Mussolini's Tyrolean-type, authoritarian Italianization policies that turned these multiple identities into polar identities. Within Valle d'Aosta, sentiments in favor of joining France emerged and were encouraged by irredentists in France. As Kogan's exemplary political history of early postwar Italy states: "In April 1945, French troops crossed the Alps to occupy adjacent territory in Piedmont and the Val d'Aosta. French agents tried to win the French-speaking *Valdostani* over to the idea of annexation."[64] At a meeting of the Council of Foreign Ministers of the victorious allies, France gave up some, but not all, of its demands. A lot was at stake for potentially fragmenting Italy: "The French demands, if realized, would bring France down onto the Italian side of the Mountains and eliminate the natural barriers to invasion routes into the Po Valley. Also on French soil would be some major hydroelectric power installations that provided substantial portions of electric current to such cities as Genoa and Turin."[65]

In the atmosphere of a weakened Italian state, facing since 1943 a resurgent communist movement aiming at control of the Italian polity, separatist movements emerged in Sicily and Sardinia. Sicily had the third-largest population of any Italian province and a history of pre-unification autonomy and post-unification conflict with the unitary state of Italy. Sardinia was once the proud Kingdom of Sardinia. Kogan writes: "Separatist organizations had begun to operate in . . . Sicily after the liberation of these two major islands of Italy. Conservative and reactionary forces feared that radicals would take over the central government on the mainland. The more substantial landowners believed they could better protect their holdings by separation. Although in 1944 the Americans and British repudiated the separatists' claims of Allied support, the agitation nevertheless continued. Its peak was reached in the immediate postwar period."[66]

The fifth peripheral area in the postwar conflicts was on the border with Yugoslavia. Yugoslavia was a victor country in World War II on the side of the Allies. Tito used Mussolini's repression of minorities to fan Slovene and Slav

63. Ibid., pp. 4–5.
64. Norman Kogan, *A Political History of Italy: The Post-War Years* (New York: Praeger, 1983), p. 6.
65. Ibid., p. 7.
66. Ibid., p. 21.

desires to join Yugoslavia. Tito gave the fragile Italian government a major blow by occupying many areas with Italian populations. Italy was particularly worried about losing much of the Friuli-Venezia Giulia area, especially the great port city of Trieste, which had an important Slovene minority.[67]

How was Italy to respond to these five simultaneous challenges to its unitary-state authority? The political history of unified Italy did not offer much in the way of a useable past. In theory, federalism, especially asymmetrical federalism, would have seemed to have offered the most possibilities. However, Italy, which, despite its pre-unification character, was divided into five various kingdoms and a papal state, a situation that might naturally have led to German-style confederation morphing eventually into a federation, in fact became a unitary state in 1860. None of Italy's major unification leaders, Cavour, Garibaldi, or Mazzini, were sympathetic to federalist ideas. In any case, the largest political force in 1945 in Italy were the Christian Democrats. Their major challenger was the Communist Party of Italy. While in theory, the Christian Democrats were in favor of decentralization, in reality they feared passing power to the regions. The regions of the famous "Red Belt" of central Italy—such as Umbria, Emilia-Romagna, Tuscany, and to some extent Marche—were the strongholds of the Communist Party. In fact, while the constitution of 1948 called for regionalization and decentralization, formal bills to transfer more power to the regions were not passed until 1970. Actual power transfers were only implemented in the late 1970s, thirty years after the crisis in the five peripheral regions described above.[68]

So, if the government of the unitary state had neither the will nor the time to decentralize, and if full federalization, much less asymmetrical federalism, was not on the agenda, what could the Italian government do in a hurry? The answer, in essence, was to create de facto federacies (called "regions of special statute") with enhanced cultural and political prerogatives as rapidly as they could. In the case of Valle d'Aosta, this was done by a decree law on September 7, 1945, to blunt French territorial claims and, in Sicily, on May 15, 1946, to defuse the separatist movement. These decrees were later made Constitutional Laws on February 20, 1948, the same day that Trentino Alto Adige and Sardinia were also made federacies by Constitutional Laws.[69] The Italian constitution of January 1, 1948, in

67. Ibid., pp. 3–6.
68. See "Italy," *Federal Systems of the World*, ed. Elazar, pp. 116–121, esp. p. 116.
69. The special statute for Friuli-Venezia Giulia, due to political problems, was not spelled out in a Constitutional Law until 1963. For details on these five different special statutes, see Robert C. Friend, *The Italian Prefects: A Study in Administrative Politics* (New Haven: Yale University Press, 1963), pp. 236–246.

Article 116, divided Italy into twenty regions and created the category of "regions of special statute" for five regions. The five peripheral regions were made "regions of special statute" with separate powers and prerogatives spelled out in their special statutes.[70] The fifteen other regions were "normal" regions with identical powers and no special prerogatives. The goal of the special statutes—which we call federacies—in the words of one of its intellectual authors, Federico Chabod, was to establish territorial autonomy without encouraging an ethnic minority that was "critical and distinct from the Italian people."[71] All five crises were substantially defused, and a degree of multiple but complementary identities was gradually restored. Italy, though still a unitary state, had completed its transition to democracy by the late 1940s.[72]

The most complicated case was that of South Tyrol, and this case tells us a lot about some of the special international and national arrangements that can be negotiated once a context of a federacy is on the table. The origin of the special statute for South Tyrol was not in a constituent assembly but in the De Gasperi–Gruber Accord signed by the foreign ministers of Italy and Austria on September 5, 1946, and linked to the Paris Peace Treaty (which involved the United Nations).[73] Some of the specific commitments were expanded and constitutionalized in 1948 and 1972 in further special statutes. The De Gasperi–Gruber Accord was helpful in defusing the crisis, especially in the area of equal cultural, political, and employment rights for German-speaking citizens. Some of the key agreements that allowed Karl Gruber, the Austrian foreign minister, to stress that the accord would significantly improve the rights of the German-speaking former Austrian citizens in South Tyrol, were the following:

70. The indispensible book on these special statute regions, and how each special statute, in different ways, helped defuse the crises we have discussed, is Nevola, ed., *Altre Italie.*

71. Cuaz, "La Valle d'Aosta," p. 7.

72. For a classic study of the Italian democratic transition, see Gianfranco Pasquino, "The Demise of the First Fascist Regime and Italy's Transition to Democracy, 1943–1948," in *Transitions from Authoritarian Rule: Southern Europe,* ed. Guillermo O'Donnell, Philippe C. Schmitter, and Laurence Whitehead (Baltimore: Johns Hopkins University Press, 1986). For excellent analyses of democratic consolidation in postwar Italy, see Maurizio Cotta, "Elite Unification and Democratic Consolidation in Italy: An Historical Overview" in *Elites and Democratic Consolidation in Latin America and Southern Europe,* ed. John Higley and Richard Gunther (Cambridge: Cambridge University Press, 1992), pp. 146–177; and Leornado Morlino, *Democracy between Consolidation and Crisis: Parties, Groups, and Citizens in Southern Europe* (Oxford: Oxford University Press, 1998).

73. The full Italian version of the accord, and a full English language translation, is found in Andrea Di Michele, Francisco Palermo, and Günther Pallaver, eds., *1992: Fine di Un Conflitto: Dieci anni dalla chiusura della questione sudtirolese* (Bologna: il Milano, 2003), pp. 77–79. This accord was an appendix to the Treaty of Paris.

1. German-speaking inhabitants of the Bolzano Province . . . will be assured a complete equality of rights with the Italian-speaking inhabitants within the framework of special provisions to safe guard the ethnical character and the cultural and economic development of the German-speaking element.

In accordance with legislation already enacted or awaiting enactment the said German-speaking citizens will be granted in particular:

(a) elementary and secondary teaching in the mother-tongue;

(b) parification of the German and Italian languages in public offices and official documents;

(c) The right to re-establish German family names which were Italianized in recent years;

(d) Equality of rights as regards the entering upon public offices with a view to reaching a more appropriate proportion of employment between the two ethnical groups.

2. The populations of the above mentioned zones will be granted the exercise of autonomous legislative and executive regional power. The frame within which the said provisions will apply, will be drafted in consultation also with local representative German-speaking elements.

The accord enabled Austrian political leaders not to be too adamant in their irredentist drive. It also enabled Alcide De Gasperi, the Italian foreign minister, to stress that the major concessions to German-speakers would strengthen Italy's frontiers and protect its electrical resources while ensuring the language rights of the Italian minority in South Tyrol. These and many other issues were included in The Special Statute for the Trentino–Alto Adige as Constitutional Law of February 2, 1948.

This Constitutional Law meets our embeddedness requirement for a federacy. Article 88 of this statute stresses its constitutional embeddedness by stating: "For the amendment of the present law the procedure established by the Constitution shall be applied." Articles 4 through 17 spell out the federal-like constitutionally embedded powers of the region. Citizens of Bolzano are full citizens of Italy, and since 1948 have received six seats in the Italian parliament, four in the lower house and two in the upper house. As in the Scandinavian federacies, the unitary state is represented in the federacy by a commissioner.[74]

Notwithstanding these gains, there was still a major point of contention in the new federacy. It was solved in a novel form of dispute settlement involving sub-

74. See Pallaver, "Südtiroler Volkspartei," p. 175, table 16.9.

stantial international participation. The population of Bolzano were in a German-majority province. However, not really in the spirit of the De Gasperi–Gruber Accord, Bolzano was joined with a more populous Italian-speaking province, Trentino, to make the Trentino–Alto Adige Region. Austria in 1960 appealed to the United Nations, stating that some of the Paris Peace Treaty provisions implied in the De Gasperi–Gruber Accord, which was attached to the Paris Peace Treaty, had not been fully honored. In response to Austria's complaints, the UN General Assembly adopted a resolution urging Italy and Austria to reopen negotiations. Italy then created a mixed commission, with substantial South Tyrolean, German-speaking representation, which produced a 137-point agreement approved by both the Austrian and Italian parliaments. This agreement was incorporated in the new 1972 autonomy statute. The last of its 137 measures went into force in 1988, and in a 1992 exchange of notes to the United Nations, Austria and Italy confirmed that all outstanding issues had been settled.

Some of the key outcomes were: a treaty recognizing the jurisdiction of the International Court of Justice for some disputes; public posts to be filled on a proportional basis according to self-identified language groups (as of the 1981 census, this meant that 65% of the posts went to German-speakers); and the explicit right granted to Bolzano to challenge state legislation in case of infringement of the region's constitutionally embedded autonomy.[75]

Political party institutions played a key role in this conflict resolution by negotiation. The central party in South Tyrol since 1945 has been the SVP. It was initially strongly secessionist and wanted to rejoin irredentist Austria. However, the SVP, in the context of the De Gasperi–Gruber Accord and sensing that the victorious Allied powers, for their own geopolitical interests, were gradually aligning themselves with Italian state-building and state-maintenance principles instead of German speaking self-determination and nation-building principles, shifted its stance from a politics of secession to a politics of autonomy.

The SVP can justly claim many of the achievements gained by the autonomy statutes of 1948 and 1972 and the robust economic growth of Bolzano. The SVP has been one of Europe's most successful autonomist parties for the last sixty years. They have won an absolute majority at the provincial level in all elections since 1948, they are the major winners of South Tyrol's "outward representation" to the

75. See Dietrich Schindler, "South Tyrol," in *Encylopedia of Public International Law*, vol. 12, ed. Rudolf Berhardt (New York: North-Holland, 1990), pp. 348–350; and R. Steininger, "75 Years After: The South Tyrol Conflict Resolved; A Contribution to European Stability and a Model for Settling Conflicts?" in *Austria in the 1950s*, ed. Gunter Bischof, Anton Pelinka, and Rolf Steininger (New Brunswick, NJ: Transaction Publishers, 1995), pp. 116–137.

Italian parliament and to the European Parliament, and they staff much of the public administration in South Tyrol. But, very importantly, the SVP has high prestige with *all* three language groups. Günther Pallaver, in his review of late 1990s public opinion surveys, reports that 78% of the German-speaking voters responded that they were happy with the work of the regional government, but significantly, an impressively high 62% of Italian speakers and 60% of Ladin speakers, also expressed satisfaction with the regional government, which of course was run by the SVP. All three language groups also answered that they saw advantages in autonomy (German 83%, Ladin 68%, and Italian 60%).[76]

Nationally and internationally, the SVP was an active, and fairly positive, political presence. The SVP maintained good relations with most parties in the Italian parliament, especially the Christian Democrats, who were the dominant party in the first three decades of the Italian democratic transition. The SVP also maintained close contacts with the Austrian governments of the day. In Austria, public posts are distributed proportionally to party members of the two major parties, the Christian Democrats and the Social Democrats, in a system known as *proporz*, so they understood South Tyrol's politics of "language proporz" for all public posts.

The conflict in Valle D'Aosta was settled much more rapidly but along similar lines. The Allied Powers wanted a strong postwar Italy but could not come out against French demands until Italy publically reversed all of Mussolini's anti-French policies. Italy rapidly did this with the September 7, 1945, Decree Law setting up the federacy we discussed earlier. The federacy's new language policies, combined with the well-supported and self-administrating French-language schools, a robust economy helped by subsidies built into the special statute, and large tourist and hydro-electric investments, turned Valle D'Aosta into a multiethnic frontier province with one of the highest standards of living in Italy.[77]

The peak of separatist demands in Sardinia and Sicily was right before the granting of their special statutes.[78] In the judgment of Daniel J. Elazar, "Sicily and Sardinia had . . . active secessionist movements which the general government successfully defused through the granting of special regional status."[79] In Sicily, one observer asserts that Sicilian regionalism "concentrated itself in the separatist

---

76. Pallaver, "Südtiroler Volkspartei," pp. 184–185.
77. See Cuaz, "La Valle D'Aosta," pp. 1–18. For the Valle D'Aosta special statute, see p. 16; for information on the recent political economy, see pp. 10–14.
78. See Kogan, *Political History of Italy*, p. 21.
79. "Italy," *Federal Systems of the World*, ed. Elazar, p. 117.

phase in the first half of the 1940s."[80] In the case of Sardinia, this would also seem to be the case, because military observers estimated that in 1944–45, the autonomist party was the largest party in Sardinia, with forty thousand members, but experienced rapid decline in the 1950s.[81]

The peripheral crisis with Slovenians and Yugoslavia took longer to solve. Italy did lose substantial Italian-speaking areas to Yugoslavia but was eventually awarded Trieste after it agreed to protect Slovene language rights and put credible guarantees to this effect in the 1963 special statute.[82]

Portugal

Portugal is one of the relatively few nation-states in the world with no national, ethnic, linguistic, or "native" minorities. Its borders date back centuries, and it has no irredenta (except for a claim to the border city of Olivenza it lost to Spain in the eighteenth century). It has always been a unitary state. Even recently, the citizens overwhelmingly rejected in a referendum a reform that would have represented a possible move toward federalism precisely because they have historically conceived their state as a unitary nation-state.

However, in the archipelago of the Azores, 800 miles west of Lisbon, during the turmoil of the 1974 Portuguese Revolution, also called the Carnation Revolution, secessionist sentiments emerged. While the constitution-makers were working, many people in Portugal feared that the radical junior officers who had started the revolution in April 1974 might end up having the power to install a communist regime. The secessionist sentiments in Azores were driven by these fears but also had a special contributing geopolitical dimension. The United States had a major strategic air base in the Azores, Lajes Field, which was co-administered by Azoreans and gave them substantial employment. This, and the close ties to Azorean immigrants in the United States, strengthened anticommunist sentiments, which in turn led to secessionist activities. Opello's standard history of the Carnation Revolution analyzes its separatist impact in the Azores: "Powerful separatist tendencies . . . appeared on the islands in 1974 and 1975 when it seemed that Portugal would likely have a communist government. In those years, the desire to separate was given voice by the . . . Azorean Liberation Front

---

80. See Christophe Roux, "The Partito Sardo D'Azione: Regionalist Mobilization in Southern Italy," in *Autonomist Parties in Europe*, ed. De Winter, Gómez-Reino, and Lynch, p. 191.

81. Ibid., p. 211.

82. See Kogan, *Political History of Italy*, pp. 3–6.

which sabotaged government facilities and . . . actively sought to detach the Azores from Portugal and seek to become a protectorate of the United States."[83]

The framers of the constitution in Lisbon responded to this particular secessionist threat, and to the distinctive needs of the islands far from the mainland, by creating for them a special status in the constitution.[84] The constitutional text is particularly emphatic about the general unitary character of the Portuguese state, when it declares in Article 227, paragraph 3, "The political and administrative autonomy of the regions in no way affects the State's full sovereignty and is exercised within the limits of the constitution." But at the same time, and in the same Article, the constitution institutionalizes the autonomous regions (as distinct from normal regions) and defends why it is making this great exception to the unitary nature of the Portuguese state:

> The special political and administrative arrangements for the archipelagos of the Azores and Madeira are based on their geographic, economic, and social and cultural characteristics and on the historic aspirations of the peoples of the islands to autonomy.
>
> The autonomy of the regions serves the interests of democratic participation by their citizens, their economic and social development, the promotion of national unity and of the bonds of solidarity among all Portuguese.

Article 6 of the constitution states that 1) "the state is a unitary one organized to respect the principles of autonomy of local authorities and democratic decentralization of the administration; and 2) the archipelagos of Azores and Madeira constitute autonomous regions with their own political and administrative status and self-governing organs." This formula fits well within our concept of federacy.

What for our purposes is particularly important is that in Article 288, paragraph O, the constitution lists which matters can only be changed by amendment and therefore require exceptional majorities. The new federal arrangements were given such constitutionally embedded status: "The laws revising the constitution safeguard . . . the political and administrative autonomy of the archipelagos of the Azores and Madeira."

Our reading of the constitutional norms leads us to consider Azores as a clear

83. Walter C. Opello Jr., *Portugal: From Monarchy to Pluralist Republic* (Boulder, CO: Westview Press, 1991), p. 16, quotation from p. 153. For U.S. policies in this period, see Kenneth Maxwell, "The Thorns of the Portuguese Revolution," *Foreign Affairs* 54 (January 1976), pp. 250–270.

84. The same provisions were extended to the archipelago of Madeira, but more for reasons of political symmetry than political threat. Because the constitutional writers' fundamental concern was the Azores, we will restrict our analysis to the Azores.

case of a federacy. However, we also think that, given the unitary conception of the state in Portugal, and their otherwise strong nation-state character, it is doubtful, with no secessionist dangers or foreign threat, that a federacy in Portugal is as necessary now as in the other cases we have considered.[85]

Why France, the Paradigm of a Unitary Nation State, Considered a Federacy with Corsica

Corsica is an island in the western Mediterranean that had a brief period of virtual independence (1755–69) but was eventually sold by Genoa to France. To this day the vast majority of the total population of 260,000 inhabitants of Corsica speak Corsican, a language which is closer to Italian than to French. In a 1982 survey of those inhabitants who defined themselves as of Corsican origin, 96% said they understood Corsican, and 86% said they regularly spoke it.[86] The "administrative and legal role [of Corsican] is minimal for it has no official status."[87] This linguistic marginalization of the majority was a longstanding source of tension on the island. However, sustained violence with autonomist dimensions began in the early 1970s. Between 1971 and 1998 there were 45 political murders in Corsica, 21 of which were explicitly claimed by nationalists.[88] In 1995 and 1996 there were 1,172 bomb attacks. On February 6, 1998, Claude Erignac, the prefect of Corsica, the senior French official in the governing structure of France on the island, was assassinated.

The origins of the political violence have a temporal relationship to two major policy initiatives, taken near-unilaterally by the French state, that directly allocated scarce resources in Corsica to non-Corsicans. Daftary describes these French state policies thus: "A major reorganization of the agricultural sector introduced in 1957 . . . failed to bring any benefits to the local population for it was used to relocate 17,000 *pied-noir* colonists from Algeria who were given preference

---

85. For an overall view of the turmoil of the Portuguese political process in 1974–1976, see the classic work by Kenneth Maxwell, "Regime Overthrow and the Prospects for Democratic Transition," in *Transitions from Authoritarian Rule: Southern Europe*, ed. O'Donnell, Schmitter, and Whitehead, pp. 109–137. For the placement of the Portuguese democratic transition in comparative perspective, see Juan J. Linz and Alfred Stepan, "From Interim Government to Simultaneous Transition and Consolidation," in *Problems of Democratic Transition and Consolidation*, ed. Linz and Stepan (Baltimore and London: Johns Hopkins University Press, 1996), pp. 116–129.

86. Farimah Daftary, "Insular Autonomy: A Framework for Conflict Resolution? A Comparative Study of Corsica and the Alland Islands," *Global Review of Ethnopolitics* 1, no. 1 (September 2001), pp. 19–40, data on p. 24.

87. Ibid.

88. J. L. Briquet, "Le problème corse," *Regards sur l'actualité*, no. 240 (April 1998), pp. 25–37.

in obtaining land. The state policy of development of tourism starting in the late 1960s was also perceived as colonial expansion."[89] In the judgment of Marc Smyrl, "The rise of militant modern separatist movements since the 1960s in Corsica is linked directly to" such policies. "The first violent manifestations of separatist sentiment in Corsica came with bomb attacks against *pied noir* property."[90]

In 1997 a Socialist prime minister, Lionel Jospin, came to power in France and indicated his government's interest in opening a dialogue about ways to reduce conflict in Corsica. Before Jospin's arrival in Corsica in September 1999, a process of internal political unification had begun in Corsica, and the center-right president of the Corsican Assembly publically called for political autonomy.[91] A seven-month process of negotiation between the French government and representatives of all parties to the Corsican Assembly began, including the deputies from Corsica Nazione, the only separatist organization in the Assembly. The result, in the summer of 2000, was the crafting of a concord, to be implemented gradually over four years, that Smyrl argues was "accepted by all but the most intransigent forces on each side."[92] By May 2001, the French Assembly had passed a bill which contained, strikingly for the French unitary nation-state, certain asymmetrical, federacy-like features. In the judgment of Smyrl, "in a significant departure from past French practice" the Assembly of Corsica was given the "power to pass secondary legislation—that is to adapt national laws to the special conditions of the island." In addition, there were "provisions encouraging the teaching of the Corsican language in public schools and generally reinforcing Corsica's cultural autonomy."[93]

The key point we would like to make is that the most important democratically elected body of French representatives, the French National Assembly, after a number of years of reflection and negotiation, decided that political practices and principles restricted to a nation-state repertoire were not appropriate for the peaceful and successful management of French-Corsican relations. A federal alternative, especially of the full state-nation sort, was not on anyone's political agenda. In

89. Daftary, "Insular Autonomy," p. 24.

90. See Marc Smyrl, "France: Challenging the Unitary State," in *Federalism and Territorial Cleavages*, ed. Ugo M. Amoretti and Nancy Bermeo (Baltimore: Johns Hopkins University Press, 2004), p. 214.

91. Daftary, "Insular Autonomy," p. 31.

92. Smyrl, "France," p. 218; *Le Monde*, July 12, 19, 21, and August 5, 2000, and "French MPs Back Corsica Devolution," available at news.bbc.co.uk/2/hi/europe/1344285.stm.

93. Smyrl, "France," p. 218. See also Élisabeth A. Vallet, "L'Autonomie Corse Face à L'Indivisibilite de la République," *French Politics and Culture* 22, no. 3 (Fall 2004), pp. 51–75.

the specific context of the perceived unsuitability of strict nation-state policies by key French and Corsican political actors and the normative undesirability of federal state-nation policies for the overwhelming majority of French citizens, the response to the "Corsican problem" that was collectively crafted by the French government, the National Assembly, and the Assembly of Corsica, turned out to have substantial federacy features.

Many of the factors that make a territory difficult to govern in the context of a democratic unitary state—a distinct language, distance from the mainland of the unitary state, a previous history of self-government, an economy and landscape whose valued characteristics some nationalists believe can only be preserved by greater local control—were clearly present. However, we should note that Corsican politics has never produced a unified, much less a hegemonic, movement, such as the SVP in South Tyrol. Most important, the fractious and clientelistic Corsican political groupings have never generated a solid, sustained majority for increased democratic autonomy of a federacy nature.

But, in any case, a full federacy was never created. The process was stopped by the Constitutional Court. On January 17, 2002, the court decided that the key aspect of the reform, the power of the Assembly of Corsica to modify some laws to suit local conditions, was an "impermissible delegation of the National Assembly's constitutional monopoly on legislative authority."[94] However, the Constitutional Council compromised somewhat by judging that as long as the teaching of Corsican during normal school hours was not compulsory, it is "not contrary to the principle of equality" and was thus allowable. With respect to the controversial French state-structured tourist facilities and programs in Corsica, the council also compromised by judging that the Corsican Assembly could pass its proposed regulations managing the cultural policy of tourism without "violating the indivisibility of the Republic, the integrity of the territory or national sovereignty."[95]

It could be that the decentralizing measures short of full federacy measures that the French National Assembly approved, and the Constitutional Court allowed, may be sufficient in the Corsican case. Since the decision, political violence has not increased; indeed, it may have decreased.[96]

94. Smyrl, "France," p. 218. For the exact wording of the council, see France; Constitutional Council, Decision 2001-454 DC of January 17, 2002, paragraphs 18–21.

95. France; Constitutional Council, Decision 2001-454 DC of January 17, 2002, paragraph 29.

96. For two well-documented articles on the still fragmented nature of party politics in Corsica, see Isidre Molas, "Partis nationalistes, autonomie et clans en Corse," and Thierry Dominici, "Le système partisan nationalitaire corse contemporain: étude d'un phénomène politique," both in the Barcelona journal, BCN Political Science Debates 4 (2005), pp. 5–42 and 43–88, respectively.

Did the Idea of Federacy Play a Crucial Role in the
Peace and Democratization Process in Indonesia and Aceh?

In 1998, when the thirty-two-year-long military regime of General Suharto fell in Indonesia, the world's most populous Muslim majority country, democratization was one possible outcome. But by 2003, a fourth Indonesian president since Suharto was already on the horizon; the new political managers of the state's two-thousand-mile archipelago were trying to manage secessionism in its eastern periphery of Papua and in its northwestern periphery of Aceh, while East Timor had already won its struggle for independence; Muslim-Christian riots (with some military and police complicity) had occurred on islands such as Ambon and Sulawesi; and massive al-Qaeda–linked explosions had killed 202 in Bali and wounded approximately 170 in the Marriott Hotel in Jakarta. Thus, while democratization was still a possibility, crises of "stateness," intensified religious conflicts, and growing military autonomy, were other possibilities.

To many in the country's capital, Jakarta, the crisis in Aceh presented particularly dangerous problems for the unitary state of Indonesia. Except for the absence of irredentism, Aceh scores relatively high on all the variables we argued make it difficult to manage politics democratically and peacefully in a unitary state. Many of Aceh's people pride themselves on practicing a stricter form of Islam than in the Indonesian heartland of Java; many think of themselves as members of the Acehnese, not Indonesian, nation; many want more control over their oil resources; and Aceh as a territory has had a long history of resistance to, and armed repression by, the unitary state. Many Acehnese gave active or at least passive support to the armed resistance to colonial rule in the late nineteenth century and to armed rebellions and separatist or independence movements in the 1950s and for much of the last thirty years. The most recent insurgent group, the Gerakan Aceh Merdeka (GAM), started an insurrection in 1976 and intensified their struggle for independence in 1999 in the political and coercive spaces created by the fall of Suharto.[97] There were failed peace processes in

97. The best documentation and analysis of Aceh's conflicts with Indonesia is found in Edward Aspinall, *Islam and Nation: Separatist Rebellion in Aceh Indonesia* (Stanford: Stanford University Press, 2009). Also see his "Modernity, History, and Ethnicity: Indonesian and Acehnese Nationalism in Conflict," *Review of Indonesian and Malaysian Affairs* 36, no. 1 (2002), pp. 3–33. For a convincing argument that for GAM, nationalism eventually became more important than Islamism, see Aspinall, "From Islamism to Nationalism in Aceh, Indonesia," *Nations and Nationalism* 13, no. 2 (2007), pp. 245–263. Also useful on GAM is Anthony Reid, ed., *Veranda of Violence: The Background to the Aceh Problem* (Singapore: Singapore University Press, 2006). For a detailed analysis of the military and ideological dimensions of GAM as a separatist movement, see Kirsten E. Schulze, *The*

2000 and a "Cessation of Hostilities Agreement" (COHA), which began in December 2002. However, the government of Indonesia, backed or pushed by the military and many parliamentarians, who were convinced that GAM was only using the ceasefire to strengthen its guerrilla forces for a further independence drive, declared martial law in May 2003. The chief of the armed forces, General Endriartono Sutarto, told troops their mission was "destroying GAM forces down to their roots" and "finishing off, killing those who still engage in armed resistance."[98]

Yet, as of this writing, Aceh and the central government were in their fifth year of peace; the World Bank office in Aceh stressed that "political commitment to the peace process remains strong on both sides"; Indonesia was ranked as one of the two most politically democratic of the world's forty-seven Muslim majority polities; and scholarly debates were less about the challenges of "stateness," or political Islam, than about what still needs to be done before Indonesia is democratically consolidated.[99]

Did federacy or, better, the *idea* of federacy, contribute to this startling change, especially peace in Aceh? We believe that we can make a strong case that it did.

One of the major reasons why the cessation of hostilities broke down in 2003 was the continuing clash of fundamental goals. The central government and the military were worried about the territorial fragmentation of Indonesia and were deeply suspicious of any formula other than a unitary state. GAM, for their part, could not see how they could advance their social and developmental goals outside of independence.

Under these circumstances, four facilitating events happened, all of which

Free Aceh Movement (GAM): Anatomy of a Separatist Organization (Washington, DC: East-West Center, 2004).

98. Edward Aspinall and Harold Crouch, "The Aceh Peace Process: Why It Failed," *Policy Studies* 1 (Washington, DC: East-West Center, 2003), p. 1.

99. On Freedom House's seven-point scale for political rights—where 1 is the best possible score and 7 the worst—Indonesia receives a 2. See *Freedom in the World: Political Rights and Civil Liberties: 2010* (New York: Freedom House, 2010), available at www.freedomhouse.org. For the argument by two leading political scientists who specialize on Indonesia that Indonesia is close to democratic consolidation, see R. William Liddle and Saiful Mujani, "Indonesian Democracy: From Transition to Consolidation," paper prepared for an International Conference on "Islam and Democracy in Indonesia: Comparative Perspectives," Center for Democracy, Toleration, and Religion, Columbia University, New York, April 2–3, 2009. The World Bank quotation is from Samuel Clark and Blair Palmer, "Peaceful Pilhada, Dubious Democracy: Ache's Post Conflict Elections and Their Implications," *Indonesian Social Development Papers*, no. 11 (Jakarta: World Bank, November 2008), p. vi. The word "dubious" comes from Clark and Palmer's focus on the need to improve the quality of election procedures and practices in order to deepen democracy. Indeed, in the runup to the 2009 elections, while there were no signs of the resurgence of the civil war, there was some use of intimidation and violence by participants in the electoral struggle.

helped the peace outcome. Three of the events have been well written about, but in our judgment none were sufficient.

First, a tsunami killed upwards of 150,000 people in Aceh on December 26, 2004. Within a week, GAM and Susilo Bambang Yudhoyono, the newly elected president, expressed interest not only in a ceasefire but also in negotiations. However, as a single causal exogenous explanation, the tsunami disaster is not satisfactory. The same tsunami smashed neighboring Sri Lanka, with the opposite political effect. The struggle over relief resources worsened. Eventually the Norwegian peacekeeping mission was asked to leave so that the government could make one more attempt to eliminate the Tamil Tigers (see chapter 5). Furthermore, it has also now been documented that significant preparations for secret peace discussions about Aceh had already begun at least a month before the tsunami.[100]

The second explanation draws on Dankwart Rustow's classic "Transitions to Democracy: Toward a Dynamic Model," where he advances the argument that if two opponents are engaged in an exhausting major political struggle, and one side can defeat the other, victory by one side, rather than democratic concession or democratic peace accords, may well be the outcome. For Rustow it is precisely "prolonged and inconclusive political struggle" that can be conducive to the construction of new master frameworks of peace or democracy.[101] Modern conflict settlement theory employs the analogous concept of "hurting stalemates."[102] Specialists on the military dimension of the conflict in Aceh have made a strong case that a stalemate had occurred by late 2003. The May 2002 military offensive against GAM had indeed taken a great toll. GAM had been forced to retreat to the mountains and had virtually ceased offensive actions. Nonetheless, even though the commander of the Indonesian armed forces had vowed to root out GAM completely, he later reluctantly acknowledged that they could not be defeated: "We cannot do what we hoped. . . . Two die but four take their place."[103] However,

---

100. See the memoirs of a key Australian adviser to the GAM, Damien Kingsbury, *Peace in Aceh: A Personal Account of the Helsinki Peace Process* (Jakarta: Equinox Publishing, 2006), pp. 15–22; and Edward Aspinall, "The Helsinki Agreement: A More Promising Basis for Peace in Aceh?" *Policy Studies* 20 (Washington, DC: East-West Center, 2005), pp. 14–19.

101. See Dankwart Rustow, "Transitions to Democracy: Toward a Dynamic Model," *Comparative Politics* 2 (April 1970), p. 352.

102. See, for example, William Zartman, "The Timing of Peace Initiatives: Hurting Stalemates and Ripe Moments," *Global Review of Ethnopolitics*, no. 1 (2001), pp. 8–18. In fact, one of the sections of Aspinall's "Helsinki Agreement" monograph is called "Toward a Hurting Stalemate?"

103. Statement of Armed Forces Chief Endriartono Sutarto, cited in Aspinall, "Helsinki Agreement," p. 21. True, Sutarto did not make this statement until 2005, but evidence suggests that this was the situation by late 2003.

even if there were a complete stalemate, the theory is not necessarily a sufficient explanation in itself. Stalemate does not necessarily produce peace if the long-term goals of the two adversaries are still locked in a zero-sum relationship. GAM could and did withdraw to the mountains with virtually all their leaders and command structure intact. The military could and did continue to occupy all the urban space of Aceh. The new equilibrium was simply a less hurting stalemate, a possibly fragile ceasefire but certainly not yet peace.

The third explanation of the origins of the surprising peace was the election in November 2003 of retired military general Susilo Bambang Yudhoyono (normally referred to as "SBY") as president and Jusuf Kalla as vice president; both were creative, hands-on advocates of a serious new peace process in Aceh.[104] This was certainly extremely helpful, and a new peace process began in Helsinki in January 2003. However, the emergence of these new leaders was not necessarily sufficient for the achievement of peace. A strong case could be made that unless GAM had radically and credibly renounced its goal of independence, even these new leaders would not have been able to build and sustain a winning peace coalition among the nationalist majority in the military and the parliament, whose collaboration was necessary for the crafting of a sustainable peace. Indeed, the first round of the Helsinki Peace talks, on January 27–30, 2005, yielded nothing but pessimism. In fact, in Aspinall's judgment, "On the eve of the second round of talks on February 21–23, 2005, the gulf between the two sides seemed as wide as ever. Collapse seemed a real possibility."[105]

However, soon after the second round began, a spokesperson of GAM announced at a press conference on February 23, 2005: "The demand for Independence is no longer on the table. They are demanding self-government now and the Indonesians [government representatives] understand this very clearly."[106] As Aspinall put it, "This was a shift of historic proportions. It was the first time that GAM had ever indicated that it was prepared to accept anything less than independence or a referendum [on independence]. As such, it was widely viewed as major breakthrough, and it made all subsequent progress in the talks possible."[107]

104. On the contributions of this exceptional new SBY-Kalla team, the most detailed report of the government side of the Helsinki negotiations, based on extensive interviews with SBY and Kalla and all the key government negotiators, is Michael Morfit, "The Road To Helsinki: The Aceh Agreement and Indonesia's Democratic Development," *International Negotiation* 12, no. 1 (2007), pp. 111–143.

105. Aspinall, "Helsinki Agreement," p. 27.

106. Associated Press, February 23, 2005, cited in Aspinall, "Helsinki Agreement," p. 26.

107. Ibid.

What contributed to this major compromise on the part of GAM? It would seem that the *idea* of federacy-type arrangements broke the bargaining deadlock. Why, how, and with what consequence?

More has to be written by key participants, but it seems that on the eve of the second round, the head of the Helsinki mediation team, the former president of Finland, Martti Ahtisaari, in a television address on February 20, 2005, alluded to "self-government" for Aceh as a possible goal of the negotiations. On February 22, the GAM spokesperson said—rightly or wrongly—that self-government "is the main thing on the table." The next day GAM renounced independence and accepted a goal of self-government.[108]

It may be that Ahtisaari's informal conversations with the GAM were even more important than his television address. One of the GAM negotiators in Helsinki, Nur Djuli, told Stepan the following account about why he personally came to believe that an Åland Island type of arrangement could lead to self-government.[109] One evening he and some other GAM negotiators were sitting with Ahtisaari looking out at the sea. They respected Ahtisaari, who among many other accomplishments had been nominated for a Nobel Prize for Peace for his peace-keeping achievements in the Balkans as a high official of the United Nations.[110] Ahtisaari noticed a ship going by and asked Nur Djuli if he recognized the flag the ship was flying. Djuli said he did not. Ahtisaari said the flag was that of the Åland Islands. Ahtisaari went on to say that the Åland Islands were a part of the unitary state of Finland with special self-governing arrangements. He said that he, as president, could not send a Finnish ship to the Åland Islands without the permission of the legislature of the Åland Islands. He said further that no major domestic law or treaty affecting the Åland Islands could go into effect without the *consultation* and *consent* of the government and legislature of the Åland Islands. Djuli later insisted that he and some of the other GAM negotiators virtually did

108. Ibid., p. 27.

109. Djuli was a significant figure in many stages of the peace process, and his opinion is important in itself. Djuli was member of the GAM team that led to the aborted 2002 Cessation of Hostilities Agreement and was later critical of its failure to address basic political differences. After being a member of the much more successful MoU negotiating team, Djuli was the architect of a GAM draft of the future Law on Governing Aceh. At the time of his interview with Stepan, Djuli was the Head of BRA, the World Bank–supported Aceh Reintegration Board. See the section "Nur Djuli to the Rescue" in International Crisis Group, "Aceh: Post Conflict Complications," *Asia Report* no. 139, October 4, 2007, pp. 11–12.

110. In 2008, Ahtisaari was awarded the Nobel Peace Prize, in part because his work was "central to the solution of the complicated Aceh question in Indonesia." See "The Nobel Peace Prize for 2008," available at www.nobelprize.org/nobel_prizes/peace/laureates/2008/press.html.

not sleep that night. They spent the night looking up the Åland Islands, and then Greenland, on the Internet. They may or may not have heard of the word *federacy*, but they increasingly began to feel that the Finnish–Åland Islands federacy arrangement might produce a serious form of "self-government" for Aceh.[111]

Whatever the exact reasons for GAM's withdrawal of their demand for independence, the bargaining situation in Helsinki was no longer zero-sum. A non-zero-sum game was now on the table. If GAM were able to negotiate for a federacy of the Åland Islands type, they believed many of their goals concerning self-government could be met. If the central government's negotiators were able to get such a federacy, their central goal of peacefully keeping Aceh inside of the unitary state of Indonesia would be met. Such a mutually acceptable treaty, called the "Memorandum of Understanding between the Government of the Republic of Indonesia and the Free Aceh Movement" (MoU), was signed on August 15, 2005, and witnessed by Martti Ahtisaari.[112]

The major goal of the central government was achieved in the second paragraph of the MoU Preamble: "The parties commit themselves to creating conditions within which the government of the Acehnese people can be manifested through a fair and democratic process *within the unitary state and constitution of the Republic of Indonesia*" (emphasis added).

In addition to forgoing their independence claims, GAM agreed to demobilize "all of its 3000 military troops" and to undertake "the decommissioning of all arms, ammunition and explosives held by the participants in GAM activities" under the supervision of the newly created EU-ASEAN–led "Aceh Monitoring Mission," no later than December 31, 2005.

The quid pro quo for GAM were new federacy prerogatives, many quite similar to those agreed to in the Åland Islands–Finland federacy, that were to be the principles of a new Law on the Governing of Aceh. Four of our five defining characteristics of a federacy, and both of our facilitating features, are clearly involved in the MoU.

Defining Characteristic 1: Federal-like division of state and federacy functions.

For GAM negotiators, some of the most important self-governing prerogatives were spelled out in Article 1 of the MoU, which set out federal-type arrangements: "Aceh will exercise authority within all sectors of public affairs . . . except in the

---

111. Interviews of Alfred Stepan with Nur Djuli in Banda Aceh, Aceh, Indonesia, November 2, 2007, and Bireuen, Aceh, November 4, 2007.

112. A complete English copy of the MoU is available in Aspinall, "Helsinki Agreement," pp. 75–84.

fields of foreign affairs, external defense, national security, monetary and fiscal affairs, and justice and freedom of religion."[113]

Defining Characteristic 3: Existence of dispute resolution procedures. In most policy areas where Aceh would not be self-governing because they involved state powers, the MoU stipulated that policies would be crafted "in consultation with and with the consent of" the relevant authorities of Aceh. Specifically, Article 1.1.2(c) stipulates that "Decisions with regard to Aceh by the legislature of the Republic of Indonesia will be undertaken in consultation with and with the consent of the legislature of Aceh," and 1.1.2(d) that "Administrative measures undertaken by the Government of Indonesia with regard to Aceh will be implemented in consultation with and with the consent of the head of the Aceh administration."

In police and military affairs, an important distinction was made in the MoU between "organic" and "non-organic" personnel. The Government of Indonesia, subject to binding verification by the Aceh Monitoring Mission, agreed to "withdraw all elements of non-organic military and non-organic police forces from Aceh" (Article 4.5).[114] Very importantly, "The appointment of the Chief of the organic police forces and the prosecutors shall be approved by the head of the Aceh administration" (Article 1.4.4).

Defining Characteristic 4: Reciprocal representation between the unitary state and the federacy. Under the section called "Political Participation" (Article 1.2), it is explicitly stated that "Full participation of all Acehnese people in local and national elections will be guaranteed in accordance with the Constitution of the Republic of Indonesia." The MoU is silent on the question of the unitary state having a representative in the federacy; however, it does speak of central state functions being carried out by a variety of state representatives.

Defining Characteristic 5: The federacy is part of an internationally recognized independent state. Indonesia is a member of the United Nations, but Aceh is not.

Facilitating Characteristic 1: Role of international guarantors in the founding of the federacy. The chair of the Helsinki peace process that created the federacy was not an Indonesian but rather Martti Ahtisaari, the former president of Finland, who was also a major UN negotiator in Bosnia. Furthermore, the MoU explicitly states in Article 5.1 that "An Aceh Monitoring Mission (AMM) will be established

---

113. Indonesia's general decentralization law of 1999 had given extensive new rights to provinces, but GAM negotiators evidently saw Article 1 of the MoU as more significant and more binding on Jarkarta.

114. "Non-organic" personnel meant any extra central government troops that had been sent in to bolster the numbers and capacity of the regular "organic forces." This distinction implied a significant reduction of the number of Indonesian government security forces in Ache.

by the European Union and ASEAN contributing countries with the mandate to monitor the implementation of the commitments taken by the parties in this Memorandum of Understanding." In cases of a dispute between the government of Indonesia and GAM, Article 6.1 stipulates that "The Head of the Monitoring Mission will make a ruling which will be binding on the parties." Some of the key issues that the AMM monitored were the disarmament of GAM, the exit of the "non-organic" Indonesian military forces from Aceh, and the supervision of free elections in Aceh—all three of these issues were crucial to the successful setting up of the federacy in Aceh.

Facilitating Characteristic 2: Role of the federacy in international treaties signed by the center. The MoU may be more explicit about this than any other federacy. Article 1.1.2(b) asserts that "International agreements entered into by the government of Indonesia which relate to matters of special interest to Aceh will be entered into consultation with and with the consent of the legislature of Aceh."

While they are not defining conditions, some other aspects of the MoU helped end the civil war and facilitate the construction of the federacy and the deepening of democracy. In one of the most contested and important prerogatives, the MoU stated that, "understanding the aspirations of Acehnese people for local political parties, the Government of Indonesia will create . . . the political and legal conditions for the establishment of local political parties" (Article 1.2.1). This was crucial for GAM, because Indonesia's parliament, fearing regional fragmentation, had passed an exceptionally restrictive law mandating that *all* political parties must have a recognized party committee in at least 60% of Indonesia's provinces and in 50% of the districts in those provinces. If a party does not meet these requirements, it is not recognized as a legal body.[115] Such a law would, of course, have banned the most important ethno-regional parties in Canada, Spain, Belgium, and India, all of which we have discussed in this book. Without this special prerogative, GAM, being exclusively Aceh-based, would not have been able to run for the upcoming elections as a political party. With this special prerogative, however, GAM, running as independents but clearly representing GAM, was able to enter democratic political competition for the governorship and for all district heads and mayors in Aceh in the December 2006 elections. To ensure fair elections, there was an EU Election Monitoring team present. To the surprise of many people, the formerly Aceh-based head of intelligence for GAM, Irwandi Yusuf, won the governorship. Also to the surprise of many, the president of Indonesia immediately sent his warmest congratulations. After the MoU (and the tsunami),

115. Private correspondence with Edward Aspinall.

the governor's office was worth controlling. According to the World Bank, the budget of Aceh in 2008 would be around 1.5 billion dollars, seven times that of the 1999 figure. GAM also won about a third of the mayorships in Aceh.[116] In addition to these federacy-like prerogatives, a number of provisions ending the civil war were offered to GAM, such as amnesty, release of all political prisoners, and reintegration funds to be administered by GAM.[117]

Four months after the Helsinki Agreement was signed and the deadline for disarmament arrived, one of Aceh's longest and most respected observers, Sidney Jones, released a report declaring that "the Aceh peace process is working beyond all expectations. Guerrillas of the Free Aceh Movement, GAM, have turned in the required number of weapons. The Indonesian military, TNI, has withdrawn troops on schedule. The threat of militia violence has not materialized. Amnestied prisoners have returned home without incident. The International Aceh Monitoring Mission, AMM, led by the European Union's Peter Firth, has quickly and professionally resolved the few violent incidents between GAM and the TNI. . . . The peace process has active support of the Indonesian government."[118]

Recently, two events have happened that some interpret as implying GAM support for harsh shari'a and violence. Neither event does. In October 2009, four years after the Helsinki agreement, the legislature of Aceh passed a law supporting death by stoning in cases of adultery. Two things should be noted. One, this law was passed in the last days of an outgoing legislature that contained no GAM members. The legislature had been based on elections that occurred before GAM could compete as a party in elections. After the law was passed, the governor of Aceh, Irwandi Yusuf, who was the former head of GAM intelligence for Aceh,

116. See the article by Edward Aspinall, "Guerrillas in Power," in the special issue edited by Edward Aspinall, "Aceh: Two Years of Peace," in *Inside Indonesia*, no. 90 (October–December 2007). Stepan visited a former GAM exile, Dr. Nurdin, who was elected district head of Bireuen, one of the most militarily contested war zones of Aceh. Nurdin said that the process was working reasonably well despite the local history of great conflict. He had the flags of Aceh and Indonesia and the standard photograph of the president of Indonesia that one sees in every public office in Indonesia above his desk. The data on Aceh's 2008 budget were given to Stepan by the World Bank office in Aceh.

117. MoU, Section 3, "Amnesty and Reintegration into Society."

118. See International Crisis Group, "Aceh: So Far, So Good," *Asia Briefing*, no. 44, December 13, 2005, p. 1. GAM was both proactive and active in the peace process; for example, one of the most senior former GAM commanders, Darwis Jeunieb, turned over to the police a former GAM soldier who was still trying to enforce GAM's now renounced "intelligence tax," and GAM leaders were in charge of the compensation program for the demobilized GAM troops, pp. 4, 6.

Stepan interviewed Sidney Jones in Jakarta on November 4, 2007. For additional corroborative accounts of the peace dimensions two years after Helsinki, see the special issue edited by Edward Aspinall, "Aceh: Two Years of Peace." Stepan interviewed Aspinall in Aceh on November 6, 2007.

criticized the law and said that he would never implement it.[119] The second major event was the discovery that a terrorist base camp was being constructed in Aceh in April 2010. In their assessment on the event, the International Crisis Group asserted, "Former rebels from [GAM] were not involved in any significant way."[120] They also note that the information about the base was given to the police by an Acehnese.

In a survey conducted in 2006 among 1,075 former GAM militants by Columbia University professor Macartan Humphreys, the former GAM militants were asked to indicate their degree of satisfaction or dissatisfaction "with MoU implementation." "Satisfied" former GAM militants outnumbered "dissatisfied" former GAM militants nine to one: 46% were "very satisfied," 44% "satisfied," 7% "not satisfied," 2% "very dissatisfied," with only 1% refusing to answer.[121] The prospect of a federacy—and of peace—was an acceptable alternative to the former fighters for independence.

This section would not be balanced, however, if we did not point out how Aceh falls short of the ideal-type federacy we discussed at the beginning of this chapter. Aceh is the only case of federacy-type arrangements being constructed by two forces actively engaged in civil war. In the case of Aceh, this contributed to one major limitation. The MoU was a peace agreement signed by the government of Indonesia and GAM. But in the new democracy of Indonesia, MoU could not become a law, much less be constitutionally embedded, until the parliament ratified it. The sitting parliament, without GAM representatives—because GAM, as a revolutionary force turned provincial political party, would participate in parliamentary elections for the first time in 2009 as Partai Aceh—passed a Law on the Governing of Aceh (LOGA) that incorporated many but by no means all parts of the MoU.[122] The most important watered-down provision was that instead of LOGA stipulating that laws, treaties, or administrative measures affecting Aceh must be with the "consultation and consent" of the relevant Aceh authorities, only the word *consultation* was included, not *consent*. Also, in our ideal type of federacy the arrangements should be constitutionally embedded. However, to GAM's great disappointment, LOGA is a law that can be amended by an ordinary

119. In a conversation with Alfred Stepan on May 19, 2010, Sidney Jones, the widely respected project director for the International Crisis Group in Jakarta, told Stepan that she doubted whether the law would ever be implemented in Aceh. We hope the law will be formally abrogated.

120. International Crisis Group, "Indonesia: Jihadi Surprise in Aceh," *Asia Report*, no. 189, April 20, 2010.

121. Unpublished results provided to Alfred Stepan by Macartan Humphreys on March 6, 2009.

122. See, President, Republic of Indonesia, Law of the Republic of Indonesia, Number 11 of the year 2006 Regarding Governing of Aceh.

majority in the lower house of parliament.[123] At the very least, we have to acknowledge that our second defining condition of a federacy, constitutional embeddedness, is not fully met.[124]

Nonetheless, we think that we have produced strong evidence indicating that the surprising emergence of social peace and political incorporation in Aceh would not have been possible without the *idea* of federacy and without the utilization of many important federacy-type arrangements in Indonesia. In an October 2009 interview with Stepan, Vice President Kalla stressed the helpfulness of federacy for the peace process.

In future studies of federacy, more consideration of the particular asymmetrical bargaining powers of armed separatists versus the government in Time 1 (during negotiations) and in Time 2 (after the separatists' disarmament and participation in elections) should be analyzed. During Time 1, both the government and the separatists may have strong *incentives* and *capacities* to make federacy arrangements. However, during Time 2, if the former separatists want to return to armed violence, their disarmament, demobilization, and the public disclosure of members in hiding will have greatly *decreased* their capacity to launch another rebellion. Also, because many of their most effective fighters may now be in important public positions of power, they will have less incentive to resist. Asymmetrically, the government's capacity and incentive to resist a new rebellion would in no way be diminished; in fact, the government's relative capacity to resist would be *increased*.

REFLECTIONS ON FEDERACIES, IRREDENTAS, AND IDENTITIES

Building on (but at times going beyond) the cases discussed in this chapter, let us offer some reflections as to why federacies might emerge, and the conditions that

123. Nur Djuli, the GAM negotiator at Helsinki who told Stepan about his conversation with the former President of Finland, Martti Ahtisaari, about the "self-governing" qualities of federacy in the Åland Islands, felt particularly betrayed by the changes by parliament and constructed and circulated a "matrix" illustrating how some key guarantees of autonomy were less strong in the LOGA than in the MoU. Indeed, the danger of the parliament attempting to erode MoU further was evident in January 2008, when, led by former President Megawati Sukarnoputri's coalition building efforts among the opponents of MoU, the parliament passed a law recommending that in a future reorganization of Indonesia's administrative units, some units that are now a part of Aceh should be transferred elsewhere. This would not only be a violation of MoU but also of LOGA. The bill never went into effect because President Yudhoyono did not sign it. See "Indonesia: Pre-Election Anxieties in Aceh," International Crisis Group, *Asia Briefing*, no. 81, September 9, 2008, pp. 6–8.

124. LOGA, by what constitutional theorists call embedded political "convention," might have become de facto constitutionally embedded, and therefore requiring exceptional majorities to amend, but the Megawati initiative would indicate that such a convention was lacking for her. For the classic treatment of political constraints and conventions producing unwritten forms of constitutional embeddness, see Marshall, *Constitutional Conventions*.

might support or hinder their relative success, from the perspective of irredentas and identities.

The crafting of a federacy is less complicated if there are no irredentist neighbors. Denmark had no neighbors with irredentist ambitions toward the Faroe Islands or Greenland. Some secessionists in the Azores were interested in being an "associated state" of the United States, but as soon as the Social Democrats and their allies had clearly secured control, the secessionists no longer aspired to this exit option; in any case, the United States never explicitly articulated any version of irredentism comparable to that articulated by Austria toward South Tyrol or Yugoslavia toward much of Friuli-Venezia Giulia and Trieste. In the case of Aceh, no neighbor articulated irredentist claims, and all of Indonesia's neighbors participated as monitors of the Helsinki Peace Agreement.

However, this does not necessarily mean that the existence of an irredentist power reduces the likelihood of a federacy being attempted. Quite the opposite. If a unitary state is faced with a secessionist territory but does not want to use coercion, grant independence, or allow its annexation, the existence of an irredentist neighbor could well be an *incentive* to adopt a federacy as a "holding together" strategy, because a de facto federacy may be the best available option.

Furthermore, federacy arrangements, particularly if an irredentist neighbor is part of a network of democratic powers, much more than a unitary state arrangement or even asymmetrical federal arrangements, can allow space for foreign states or international organizations to be involved in negotiating, and eventually endorsing or even guaranteeing, arrangements to protect the rights of members of a minority linguistic community. Witness the De Gasperi–Gruber Accord between the foreign ministers of Austria and Italy and the later appeal, building on this accord, by Austria to the United Nations that led to the 1972 and 1992 extensions of linguistic, cultural, and political rights in the South Tyrol statute of autonomy. Recently, the North Tyrol province of Austria, and the South Tyrol province of Italy, wanted to engage in bilateral negotiations to create a Euroregion. The governments of Italy and Austria discouraged this, because both felt that it might endanger the carefully crafted and negotiated cultural autonomy statutes and violate the preeminent role of the sovereign states in foreign policy affairs.[125]

The settlement of the Åland controversy, with the award by the League of Nations of the islands to Finland and not to Sweden, was facilitated by the

125. See Bruno Luverà, "L'Euregio tirolese. Tra regionalismo transfrontaliero e micronazionalismo di confine," in *Altre Italie*, ed. Nevola, pp. 19–33.

understanding that Finland would in essence create a federacy that constitutionally embedded Swedish-speakers' cultural and political rights in the Åland Islands.

The unitary state of Indonesia was adamant that no foreign powers should be involved in mediating or monitoring any peace process, but in the end, EU and ASEAN states played a crucial role in monitoring the surprisingly successful process of military disengagement and peaceful elections.

What is the political impact of *identities* in federacies, as opposed to identities in a unitary state or an asymmetrical federal system? Even though federacies have some federal-like features, their emergence is not due to a federalist tradition or identity or to the strength of federalism in the country. On the contrary, the states that created federacies all had a unitary tradition and did not want to change it (Finland, Denmark, Italy, Portugal, and even Indonesia). The elites in the center opted for "federacies" for pragmatic reasons, forced by circumstances, sometimes reaffirming their unitary and even nation-state character in the very act of crafting a federacy.

Some observers might suppose that this lack of a strong affirmation of a polity-wide federacy ideology and identity is a weakness. After all, both nation-states and state-nations are strengthened by supportive identities. These same observers may also believe that the special prerogatives of federacies will inevitably be resented or envied by the citizens who live in the unitary state. This misses the special character of identities in a unitary state with a federacy. The institutional arrangements of a federacy work precisely because the federacy does not have a broader base of support in the rest of the country based on identity and because the prerogatives, especially cultural prerogatives, do not respond to a felt need in other parts of the country. For instance, none of the provinces in the mainland of Denmark wanted the right to "opt out" of the European Union following the federacy arrangements involving Faroes or Greenland; likewise, no other part of Finland demanded the specific prerogatives the Ålands received. This means that federacies do not normally (except sometimes over their generous subsidies) generate demands for the extension of their special federacy principle. This contrasts sharply with asymmetrical federalism, where member units are all federal units and tend to want any special prerogative given to one unit to be extended to them as well. Witness Spain, where member units are increasingly demanding that what is a right of Catalonia or the Basque Country should be a right for them too. This syndrome in Spain is called "café para todos" (coffee for everyone).

There is another political reason why federacies do not tend to generate the institutional hostility of the members of the unitary state. Federacies have representation in the national legislature, sometimes disproportionate to their number of votes, and sometimes their representatives constitute an ethno-federal party of the federacy. However, only in a highly fragmented, multi-party, parliamentary system with a minority government would their small vote give them the major coalitional or blackmail potential that an ethno-federal party from a populous unit often has in a federal system.

There is one aspect of identity that is especially useful in a federacy that is quite different from the types of identity that are supportive of a unitary nation-state or an asymmetrical federal state-nation. In a unitary nation-state, a single, relatively homogeneous identity is often the goal of state leaders. In a state-nation, multiple and complementary identities are the most polity-conducive pattern. However, in a unitary state with a federacy, there is no particular need for citizens in the unitary state to have a multiple but complementary identity with the federacy. What is important is that they should think of the inhabitants of the federacy as full and equal members of the state. A federacy will work best, however, if the citizens resident in the federacy identify positively to some extent with the state as well as with their federacy. If such mutual feelings are completely absent, the tendency will be for a breakup of the federacy or a somewhat coercively imposed unity that lowers the democratic quality of the state.

Are there other territories where the idea of federacy might conceivably some-day be of use? If China ever becomes a democracy, it is likely that one of its most intractable problems will be Tibet. On a number of occasions the Dalai Lama has indicated that he would accept federacy-type arrangements. Of course, if China continues "Cromwellian" policies of encouraging Han immigration into Tibet and Chinese nationalism grows more intense, there might not be sufficient politi-cal space for such initiatives even in a democratic China. But as the conversation facing the sea off the coast of Finland between the Aceh independence leaders and the former president of Finland shows, possibilistic political theories with success-ful examples might someday be emulated with surprising speed and success.

CONCLUSION

We live in a world of both states and nations. Federacies are a response to the problems of "holding together" a unitary state while also responding to the claims of the minority nation principle within that state. Federacies can work, but only if there is minimum loyalty to the state and if the principle of national self-determination is not exploited by other states. In the case of an area that has been considered an "irredenta" by a neighboring state, this means support of the federacy by that potentially irredentist power. The legitimacy of the "voice" and the "exit" of the federacy population, in addition to the ability of the unitary state to control its own elites, is often a result of the world—especially the regional— system of states within which the possible federacy would exist. What is often called the international dimension of politics is of course more often an interstate dimension. As we write this, we think of the interstate system that would have affected a potential federacy in South Ossetia in 1991 in contrast to that facing South Tyrol in 1945. Ultimately, we are living in a world of states, united or dis- united, and not of nations—but also of nations disturbing the status quo of states.

CHAPTER EIGHT

The U.S. Federal Model and Multinational Societies

Some Problems for Democratic Theory and Practice

The purpose of this chapter is to explore the question: How appropriate or inappropriate is U.S.-style federalism in robust multinational societies if our goals are democracy, reasonably inclusive social welfare policies, and relative political tranquility? We ask this question because, even though we argued in chapter 1 that the United States was multicultural but not multinational, many readers may have reservations with both the ideal types we have examined so far, nation-state and state-nation. Why then, they may ask, not just follow the U.S. model, especially since we have stressed the critically helpful role of federalism?

For many theorists and political leaders, the U.S. model of federalism is held up as not only the first, but also the most authentic—indeed, the best—model of federalism. Thus, one of the most prestigious political scientists of federalism in the English-speaking world, William H. Riker argues in many of his works that U.S. federalism is "the model to which all others aspire."[1] In a very influential early analysis of Indian federalism Kenneth C. Wheare termed India's model "quasi-federalism," mainly because of its deviations from the U.S. model.[2] Even in modern Spain, some influential critics do not consider Spain's current model "federal," because it was not, as in the United States, created by autonomous political units that came together and decided to pool some of their sovereignty

1. William H. Riker, *Federalism: Origin, Operation, Significance* (Boston: Little Brown, 1964). See also his influential *The Development of American Federalism* (Boston: Kluwer Academic Publishers, 1987) and "Federalism," in *Handbook of Political Science*, ed. Fred Greenstein and Nelson W. Polsby (Reading, MA: Addison-Wesley, 1975), vol. 5, pp. 93–172.

2. Kenneth C. Wheare, *Federal Government* (Oxford: Oxford University Press, 1963), pp. 26–28.

to create a federal system. Indeed, on more than one occasion during our research, it was clear to us in conversations with important politicians in unitary countries such as Sri Lanka, Indonesia, and the Philippines, that one of the reasons they had difficulty considering a federal option is that, considering the U.S. model to be the most authentic, they thought that they would have to dissolve the unitary state and then let those units who wanted to join have a constituent assembly in order to construct, as in Philadelphia in 1787, a federal constitution. Many of the leaders of nationalist armies in Burma who have been struggling for independence, when they got together to draft a constitution in which they would possibly agree to remain within Burma, looked to the U.S. model as the one that would be the be the most appropriate, that would most protect their rights.

Given all the above arguments, we think it is imperative for us to try to answer a fundamental question. Is the U.S. federal model particularly useful for democratic governance in robustly multinational societies, is it neutral in its impact, or could it be particularly harmful?

We believe that we can get some leverage on these issues by carrying out a simple but potentially powerful exercise revolving around two interrelated subquestions we will ask. First, what are the key features of the specific type of federalism in the United States? How do they relate to the rest of the U.S. Constitution? How do they compare with the features found in the other seven long-standing OECD advanced-economy federal systems? These countries are Germany, Austria, Belgium, Spain, Switzerland, Canada, and Australia. Note that four of these countries, Belgium, Canada, Switzerland, and Spain, are close to the state-nation ideal type. Second, what are some of the implications for governance in a robust multinational society, if the *entire* U.S. package of distinctive federal features were adopted?

We realize that this is a thought exercise. No country would probably adopt the entire package. However, carrying out such an exercise will generate great analytic (and political) opportunities. It will enable us to analyze many aspects of U.S. federalism comparatively, both in its component parts and as an interrelated system. In the preface of this book, we argued that one of our purposes was to expand our imaginations concerning possible new and constructive ways of managing multinational polities. We hope our concept of the state-nation has expanded political imaginations. Another way of doing this is to carry out a thought exercise like the one we will do now, one that asks us to systematically "re-imagine" what a well-known, classic model, such as U.S. federalism, may or may not actually imply.

THE SEVEN KEY FEATURES OF U.S. FEDERALISM
IN COMPARATIVE PERSPECTIVE

1. *The upper chamber is extremely malapportioned.* Each state in the U.S. federation, no matter how large or small its population, receives the same number of seats in the Senate. This is, of course, a massive violation of the democratic principle of "one person, one vote." Article 5 of the U.S. Constitution stipulates that "the Senate of the United States shall be composed of two Senators from each State." This means that, in terms of producing a U.S. senator, a vote in Wyoming, with its population in 2009 of only 544,270 people, had the approximate value of sixty-eight votes in California, with its population of 36,961,664.[3] Furthermore, Article 5, one of the least democratic articles in the Constitution, is the only part of the constitution that was framed to be impossible to amend without complete unanimity in the Senate. The Constitution expressly mandates that "no state, without its consent, shall be deprived of its equal suffrage in the Senate."[4] In Robert A. Dahl's judgment, "The likelihood of reducing the extreme inequality of representation in the Senate is virtually zero."[5]

In comparison with the other members in our set of the eight longstanding federal democracies in advanced economies, as shown in table 8.1, the United States has the most extreme Gini index of malapportionment.

2. *The upper chamber has major and unique constitutional powers.* This extremely malapportioned chamber, the U.S. Senate, has an absolute veto on all legislation (Article 1, section 7). The Senate also has many exclusive and critical prerogatives *denied* to the very well apportioned House of Representatives, such as the veto power over all presidential nominations for major judicial positions, cabinet members, and heads of major government agencies as well as the ratification of treaties (Article 2, section 2). Also, the "Senate shall have the sole power to try all impeachments" (Article 1, section 3).

In comparative terms of our set of eight countries, the upper chambers in Austria and Belgium do not have an absolute veto. Canada's upper chamber de jure has an absolute veto but, as an appointed body, de facto would not dare use it.

---

3. Population estimates come from the U.S. Census Bureau. See http://quickfacts.census.gov/qfd/states/56000.html for Wyoming and http://eadiv.state.wy.us/pop/st-09est.htm for a fifty-state comparison.

4. U.S. Constitution, Article 5.

5. See the excellent and sobering book, Robert A. Dahl, *How Democratic Is the American Constitution?* (New Haven: Yale University Press, 2001), p. 154. For some of the negative effects of this malapportionment in the Senate on social policies aimed at reducing inequality in the United States, see pp. 13–15, 46–54, and 144–145.

TABLE 8.1

Overrepresentation in the Upper Houses of Eight Longstanding OECD Federal Democracies and India

Gini index of malapportionment		Ratio of best-represented to worst-represented federal unit (by population)		Percentage of seats of best-represented decile	
Nation	Index	Nation	Ratio	Nation	%
United States	.49	United States	66/1	United States	39.7
Switzerland	.45	Switzerland	40/1	Switzerland	38.4
Australia	.36	Canada	21/1	Canada	33.4
Canada	.34	Australia	13/1	Australia	28.7
Germany	.32	Germany	13/1	Germany	24.0
Spain	.31	India	11/1	Spain	23.7
India	.10	Spain	10/1	India	15.4
Austria	.05	Belgium	2/1	Austria	11.9
Belgium	.02	Austria	1.5/1	Belgium	10.8

Sources: Data come from *Whitaker's Almanack* (London: I. Whitaker, 1997); *The Europa World Year Book 1995* (London: Europa Publications, 1995); and Daniel Elazar et al., *Federal Systems of the World* (Harlow, U.K.: Longman, 1994). For the constitutional provisions on second chambers, see S. E. Finer, Vernon Bogdanor, and Bernard Rudden, *Comparing Constitutions* (Oxford: Oxford University Press, 1995), and A. P. Blaustein and G. H. Flanz, eds., *Constitutions of the Countries of the World* (Dobbs Ferry, NY: Oceana Publications, 1991–).

Note: The inequality (malapportionment) index is computed as $(1/2) \Sigma |s_i - v_i|$ where s_i = % of seats and v_i = % of population. This calculation follows the formula proposed by David Samuels and Richard Snyder in "The Value of a Vote: Malapportionment in Comparative Perspective," *British Journal of Political Science* (October 2001), p. 655.

In Germany, the upper chamber has an absolute veto for only about 60% of legislation. In Spain, the upper chamber has a veto only on issues that directly relate to the constitutionally embedded prerogatives of the member units of the federation. Only the three classic "coming together federations," the United States, Australia, and Switzerland, have an absolute veto on all legislation.

The upper chamber, by itself, seldom blocks legislation in Switzerland, occasionally does so in Australia, and frequently does so in the United States. None of the other upper chambers in the set has as many unique prerogatives as does the U.S. Senate.[6]

3. *U.S. federalism is symmetrical, not asymmetrical.* The framers negotiated a Constitution in which every state has the same rights and obligations, that is to say, U.S. federalism is symmetrical, not asymmetrical. In an asymmetrical federation, some federal members could constitutionally be given special prerogatives concerning some cultural features. This symmetrical feature of U.S. federal arrange-

---

6. For details and documentation on the veto powers of the second chambers in all advanced economy OECD countries, see Stepan, "Electorally Generated Veto Players."

ments is not unusual in aggregate comparative terms, because more than half of our set (Germany, Austria, Australia, and Switzerland, as well as the United States) are symmetrical. But, if we disaggregate our set so as to identify those polities that have a territorially based robust multinational dimension, we notice that *all* of them (India, Spain, Belgium, and even Canada) are asymmetrical. As we saw in our discussion of "policy grammars" and have seen in the rest of this book, whether a constitution is symmetrical or asymmetrical has important consequences for what can be done, or especially for what *cannot* be done, to manage politics in a polity with multinational dimensions. To return to India and Mizoram, a key part of the agreement to end the civil war was to constitutionally grant two special prerogatives to the state of Mizoram. Non-Mizos are prohibited from buying property in Mizoram, and non-Mizos cannot run in a local election.

4. *"Residual powers"—not to the union but to the individual states.* In the demarcation of union and state tasks in the U.S. Constitution, the states of the federation were assigned many key tasks. On top of this, any tasks that were not explicitly assigned to the federal center were assumed not to be federal, or joint, but under the authority of the states; that is, "residual powers" were granted to the states.[7] In Spain, residual powers belong to the center; in Germany most powers are de facto concurrent.

5. *Senate and states must both vote approvals of any amendment by super-majority.* The above four features, taken together, are not only (as we shall see) highly unusual in the world of developed country democratic federal systems but are also embedded in a constitution that is one of the hardest, if not the hardest, in the world to change. As John Elster has argued, the most difficult rules to change are those that most favor actors who are charged with amending them. In the case of the U.S. Constitution, exceptional majorities by the two political actors most favored by the Constitution, the Senate and the states, are required for any amendment. An amendment must be approved by two-thirds of the state legislatures or of both houses and then ratified by three-fourths of the states, either by special conventions or by their legislatures (Article 5). On Lutz's index for assessing the relative difficulty of the amendment process, the United States is rated as having the most difficult amendment process, not only of all of the countries in our eight country set but also of the thirty-two countries calculated by Lutz.[8]

---

7. This was inserted into the U.S. Constitution under the 10th Amendment, which states, "The powers not delegated to the United States by the Constitution, nor prohibited by it to the States, are reserved to the states respectively, or to the people."

8. See Donald S. Lutz, "Toward a Theory of Constitutional Amendment," *American Political Science Review* 88, no. 2 (June 1994), pp. 355–370. In Lutz's rankings, the higher the index number,

Two other features of the U.S. political system are not about federalism per se but about the separation of powers, within which U.S. federalism is embedded.

6. *A supreme court with strong and extensive judicial review capacity.* Even if both houses and the president approve a bill to extend the powers of the federal government via new legislation that they consider does not require an amendment, this legislation can be declared unconstitutional by the Supreme Court, as the Supreme Court has done in many cases.[9]

7. *The U.S. presidential system entails a directly elected, "unsharable" executive with a fixed term and strong veto powers.* In a parliamentary system, executive power is often "shared" by a coalition of parties. In the U.S. presidential system however, the incumbent is necessarily one person, so the office is normally referred to as an "indivisible good" that is unsharable. The incumbent does not have an absolute veto but is considered by Tsbellis to be a "veto player" because a presidential veto can only be overridden by exceptional majorities in two houses (Article 1, section 7 of the U.S. Constitution).[10]

THE IMPLICATIONS OF THESE SEVEN FEATURES FOR A DEMOCRACY IN A ROBUST MULTINATIONAL POLITY

1. *The inability to utilize "asymmetrical" federal formulas.* Every democratic and relatively peaceful polity that is what we have called "robustly multinational"—that is, composed of more than one territorially based cultural group with leaders who consider themselves a nation and advanced claims for independence—has elected to hold the polity together by creating a "asymmetrical" federal system.[11] By this definition, as we have argued before, Spain, Belgium, Canada, and India are robustly multinational. Switzerland is deeply multicultural but is not robustly multinational, because none of the cantons, or parties in parliament, seeks independence.

---

the greater the degree of difficulty in amending the constitution. The United States scores highest with a score of 5.1, whereas Australia, Portugal, Canada, and New Zealand all score less than 1.0. India is 1.8.

9. In an analysis of all cases decided up to June 28, 2002, by the U.S. Supreme Court, the Government Printing Office found that 158 acts of Congress had been declared unconstitutional. See www.gpoaccess.gov/constitution/pdf2002/046.pdf.

10. See G. Tsbellis, *Veto Players: How Political Institutions Work* (Princeton: Princeton University Press, 2002); and G. Tsbellis, "Decision Making in Political Systems: Veto Players in Presidentialism, Parliamentarism, Multicameralism, and Multipartyism," *British Journal of Political Science* 25 (1995), pp. 289–325.

11. Even the unitary state of the United Kingdom has responded to the diversity of cultural identities by a devolutionary process creating national legislatures: the Scottish Parliament (1999–), the Welsh National Assembly (1998–), and the Northern Ireland Assembly (1998–). England itself has no legislature.

The reason why polities that have a multinational dimension to their society find the asymmetrical formula politically useful is that it allows them, without violating individual rights or the constitution, to give some special recognition to some important cultural feature such as the language of a territorially concentrated minority nationality that also forms a majority in at least one of the units of the federation. This is often seen by most designers of the federation as a legitimate part of the strategy for maintaining unity amidst diversity, for nurturing multiple but complementary identities.

Most analysts of the Spanish transition to democracy in the mid-1970s believe that the successful transition was facilitated not only by federalism but also by the ability, within an asymmetrical constitution, to recognize some historic prerogatives of the role of the Catalan language in Catalonia and tax privileges in the Basque Country as well as recognition of the Basque language. In Canada, in 1867, the asymmetrical formula allowed a special place in Quebec for the Napoleonic Code as well as for the French language. Asymmetrical federalism in Belgium granted special status to Wallonia and Flanders, while also according an innovative "personal federalism" to Brussels. Personal federalism, which is not found in Wallonia or Flanders, allows those citizens who self-identify as individuals as members of different linguistic or religious communities to vote in separate cultural constituencies for boards that supervise social services, such as hospitals or schools.[12] Similarly, India's asymmetrical federal constitution would allow a special status for Kashmir should peace ever be achieved. It also allowed the central government to negotiate successfully an end to the decades-long war of independence with the tribal Mizos by granting them a state with special rights that would have been impossible in a symmetrical constitution. These special Mizo rights included the right of their state assemblies to preclude non-Mizos from buying property without their permission and the prohibition of non-Mizos from voting in local, basically tribal elections. These special arrangements have contributed, as we have seen, not only to the end of the civil war but also to high degree of pride among Mizos in being Indian, even though less than 5% of the Mizos speak Hindi or are Hindus.[13]

If we examine the entire universe of the eleven countries that have been continuous federal democracies since 1988, we note that *all* of the polities that have a territorially based multinational dimension to their societies are asymmetrical,

12. William Swenden, "Federalism and Second Chambers: Regional Representation in Parliamentary Federalism," D. Phil in the Department of Politics, University of Oxford, 2000.

13. See *Jammu and Kashmir; Assembly Election 2002: Findings of a Post-Poll Survey* by Lokniti, Delhi, February 2003.

	Constitution	
	Symmetrical	Asymmetrical
Not Robustly Multinational	Austria Germany Australia United States Argentina Brazil Switzerland (state-nation)	
Robustly Multinational		India Belgium Canada Spain

Figure 8.1. Constitutional-Legal Arrangements of Entire Universe of the Eleven Federal Systems That Have Been Democracies since 1988

whereas all of the others—many of which, like Switzerland, are deeply multi-cultural but not multinational—have been able to function with symmetrical federal systems.

The fundamental thing we want to stress is that a U.S.-style symmetrical constitutional model would have made almost all of the special arrangements that we have discussed for managing democracy in the territorially based multinational contexts such as those found in Spain, Canada, India, and Belgium *unconstitutional* and therefore politically impossible, in a democracy (see figure 8.1).

2. *The weakness of coalitional incentives in the U.S. presidential system.* Let us now discuss the *presidential,* as opposed to the parliamentary, component of the U.S. federal model and its theoretical and practical implications for democracy in a robust multinational society.

For our purposes, the fundamental feature of presidentialism is that a directly elected president, with a fixed term, is an "indivisible good," that is, it cannot be shared. One consequence of this is that if there is more than one nation in the state, the president can only come from one of the nations. Also, such a president can only be democratically removed by an impeachment, no matter what new intra-nationalist conflicts or other problems might emerge in the short term.

This contrasts sharply with parliamentarism, which can be a "divisible good." As we saw in chapters 2 to 4 when we discussed India, numerous parties, with different constituencies in communities comprised of different nationalities, can negotiate a programmatic pact and then agree to form a coalition government. The parties in the coalition may even decide to support as prime minister a political leader from a small party—or a small nation—and they have the capacity to bring down the government if the prime minister violates the pact that they negotiated when they agreed to form a ruling coalition. Because a prime minister can only rule with a parliamentary majority, or at least with minority support from the outside, the possibility of the government falling often creates "coalition requiring" and even "coalition sustaining" incentives among the national groups forming the government or at least supporting it from the outside.

In terms of the "grammar" of managing multinational polities we discussed in chapters 1 through 4, a parliamentary system can allow a territorially based minority nationalist party to be part of the ruling majority at the center. Parliamentarianism also allows the ruling party at the center to form a coalition in a state with a minority-based party so that the minority party can become the ruling party in its own state. This coalitional calculus may help the democratic management of multinationalism, because it creates incentives for potentially "regional-secessionist" parties to become what we call "centric-regional" parties. Also, if the largest party in the coalition at the center happens to have as its base the largest nationality group in the country but that nationality group by itself does not form a majority in the parliament, the ruling party may well only be able to continue in power if it has the support of some "centric-regional" parties. The potential loss of its necessary parliamentary majority may act as a disincentive to the ruling party at the center, inhibiting it from imposing extreme nationalist policies. Thus, a multinational, multiparty parliamentary coalition at the center may create useful moderating incentives on both majority and minority nationalities, precisely because the government in a parliamentary democracy has the potential to be a divisible good.

None of these potentially useful incentives for democratically managing societies with multinational dimensions are available if the chief executive is a directly elected president with a fixed term, as in the United States.

With this logic in mind, it is illustrative that all four continuous democracies with strong multinational dimensions to their societies, Canada, India, Belgium, and Spain, are parliamentary. Not only are they parliamentary, but all four have had recent governing coalitions at the center that have combined polity-wide parties with some nationalist regional parties. To be sure, such coalitions do not guarantee continued stability, and it does give the minority nationalities veto— one might even say blackmail—potential. However, it does give the polity extra "degrees of freedom" to manage multinationalism via coalitions, degrees of freedom that would not be as broad if a polity selects, as part its constitutional formula, a U.S.-style presidency.

3. *The potentially severe political problem of every full federal unit having the same number of seats (regardless of population) in the upper chamber.* Is the malapportion and inordinate power of the upper house in the U.S. federal model less or more problematic in a robust multinational federal polity than it is in a more homogeneous polity?

We think there could be demographic contexts where the U.S. formula for the upper chamber would be potentially quite problematic. Let us take the hypothetical case of a potentially democratizing polity in a multinational society. Let us assume that our hypothetical polity is territorially divided among segmented nationality groups. Let us assume ten such groups, each of which has a state named after the dominant nationality in that state.[14]

If state "A" contained the largest nationality in the polity and constituted 50% of the total population in the polity but was only a majority in one state, state "A" would receive only 10% of the seats in the extremely powerful, U.S.-style upper chamber we will call the Senate. To further complicate the scenario, let us make the not impossible assumption that there is in state "B" a territorially concentrated, quite distinctive linguistic and religious nationality constituting only 1% of the total population of the polity. Using the U.S. senatorial formula, state "A" and state "B" would each receive the same number of seats in the Senate. This would give nationality group "B" fifty times greater per capita representation in the most powerful house in our hypothetical democracy than nationality group "A." Clearly, this is not an auspicious recipe for a successful democratic transition.

Let us shift to a real country, where the situation is actually worse than the very bad scenario just explored. In June 2001, Stepan participated in a meeting with members of the Burmese democratic opposition, drawn heavily from political and military leaders of nationality groups and armies.[15] Most of the leaders had fought long, but still unsuccessful, wars of independence. However, at the meeting the guerrilla nationalist leaders wanted to discuss a draft constitution they had drawn

14. India is not a perfect example, but it is useful to remember that many of the current states in India, such as Tamil Nadu, Kerala, Mizoram, Kashmir, and Bengal, are composed of a dominant linguistic and ethnic group, some of whom have sometimes seen themselves as a nation.

15. This is reported in more detail in Andrew Reynolds, Alfred Stepan, Zaw Oo, and Stephen Levine, "How Burma Could Democratize," *Journal of Democracy* 12, no. 4 (October 2001), pp. 94–108.

TABLE 8.2
Malapportionment in Burma's Proposed Upper Chamber

State	Population	% of total population	% seats	Malapportionment index
"Ministerial Burma"	40,647,593	75.93	12.5	63.43
Kayah	246,000	0.46	12.5	12.04
Chin	458,000	0.86	12.5	11.64
Kachin	1,202,000	2.25	12.5	10.25
Kayin	1,403,000	2.62	12.5	9.88
Mon	2,337,000	4.37	12.5	8.13
Rakhine	2,610,000	4.88	12.5	7.62
Shan	4,629,000	8.65	12.5	3.85
Total	53,532,593	100	100	63.42

Source: Population data for Burma, see www.myanmar.com.

up under which they would agree to stay within Burma. They were very attracted by the U.S. federal model because it seemed to them to protect the interests of their various states. Their draft constitution enshrined three key principles of U.S. federalism. First, every state would receive an equal number of seats in the upper house. Second, the upper house was made a bit stronger than the lower house, in that all important executive positions were subject to the approval of the upper chamber but not the lower chamber. Third, the draft constitution was symmetrically federal.

In the guerrillas nationalist's proposal, there would be eight states, each composed of the territory of a major nationality. The U.S.-type decision rule meant that two states, Kayah and Chin, each with less than 1% of Burma's total population, would receive the identical number of seats in the upper chamber as the state known as Ministerial Burma, which has 76% of Burma's population (see table 8.2).

In terms of malapportionment, this proposal would have made Burma by far the most malapportioned federal polity of the entire universe of the eleven federal democracies in the world even if we add the non-OECD countries of India, Brazil, and Argentina to our original eight-country advanced democracy comparison set (see table 8.3).

Over 90% of the Burmese officer corps is ethnic Burmese and from the state called Ministerial Burma, which would be massively underrepresented by the application of the U.S. formula. With 76% of the total population of Burma, the state of Ministerial Burma would only receive 12% of the seats in the potentially powerful upper chamber. This is the same percentage of seats as Kayah which has

TABLE 8.3
A Continuum of the Degree of Overrepresentation in the Proposed USA Territorial-style Seat Allocation of the Upper House in Burma in Comparison with the Upper Houses of the Entire Universe of the Eleven Longstanding Federal Democracies

Malapportionment in upper houses[a]		Ratio of best-represented to worst-represented federal unit (by population)[b]		% of seats of best-represented decile[c]	
Nation	Index	Nation	Ratio	Nation	%
Burma	.634	Burma	165/1	Burma	62.5
Argentina	.485	Brazil	144/1	Argentina	44.8
Brazil	.403	Argentina	85/1	Brazil	41.3
United States	.364	United States	68/1	United States	39.7
Switzerland	.344	Switzerland	40/1	Switzerland	38.4
Canada	.340	Canada	21/1	Canada	33.4
Australia	.296	Australia	13/1	Australia	28.7
Spain	.285	Germany	13/1	Germany	24.0
Germany	.244	India	11/1	Spain	23.7
India	.074	Spain	10/1	India	15.4
Austria	.030	Belgium	2/1	Austria	11.9
Belgium	.015	Austria	1.5/1	Belgium	10.8

Sources: The data for Burma comes from the county's official web page: www.myanmar.com. The data for all other countries, including the malapportionment indexes for Canada and Belgium, comes from Alfred Stepan, "Toward a New Comparative Politics of Federalism, (Multi)Nationalism, and Democracy: Beyond Rikerian Federalism," in *Arguing Comparative Politics* (Oxford University Press, 2001), p. 334.

Note: The malapportionment index is computed as $(1/2) \Sigma |s_i - v_i|$, where s_i = % of seats and v_i = % of population. This calculation follows the formula proposed by David Samuels and Richard Snyder in "The Value of a Vote: Malapportionment in Comparative Perspective," *British Journal of Political Science,* 2001.

[a]If there were perfect one-person, one-vote representation in the upper house, the index of malapportionment would be zero. In the worst possible case, where the least populated state has all the seats in the upper chamber, the index would be 1. In the case of Austria, each state is represented in the upper chamber, but the total number of representatives is allocated almost according to population. In Germany, the 1949 Basic Law stipulates that all of the sub-units (or *Länder*) of the federation shall have at least three votes, but that *Länder* with more than 2 million inhabitants shall have four, *Länder* with more than 6 million inhabitants five, and *Länder* with more than 7 million inhabitants six. On the opposite end is Burma, where equal representation is given to all states, some of which have very small populations and one of which has an extremely large population, thus resulting in the most malapportioned upper house in the whole country set.

[b]This ratio compares the value of a vote in the least populous sub-unit of the federation with the value of a vote in the most populous sub-unit. In Germany, the least populous *Land* in 1993 was Bremen, with a population of 686,000, which was allocated three votes in the upper house. The most populous *Land*, North Rhine–Westphalia, had a population of 17,679,000 and was allocated six votes. Thus, one vote in Bremen was worth 13 votes in North Rhine–Westphalia. In the case of Burma, one vote in the Kayah State, with 246,000 inhabitants, would be worth 165 votes in "Ministerial Burma," with a population of 40,647,593. In this scenario, Burma's potential best- to worst-represented state ratio is thus 165/1, which is *fifteen* times greater than the average of the world's longstanding asymmetric federation, which is 11/1.

[c]In this scenario, in Burma, five states—Kachin, Kayah, Kayin, Chin, and Mon—constitute only 10.52% of Burma's total population. However, under one NCUB constitutional proposal—in which "Ministerial Burma" is one of the total of eight ethno-federal states in the federation, each of which would receive 12.5% of the upper house seats—these five states would receive 62.5% of the seats in the upper chamber and thus would constitute an overwhelming "blocking win-set" for any constitutional change and also a majority in simple majority votes.

a population of only 246,000, making a vote in Kayah worth 165 votes in Ministerial Burma. Thus, insistence on the application of the U.S. formula would
enhance incentives (already high) for the military to stay in power and to resist any
free elections.

After some discussion, the negotiators came to appreciate the obstacles to any
potential democratization the U.S.-style upper chamber formula would present in
Burma. There was also a growing interest in asymmetrical federalism. This formula was seen as a potential way of constitutionally embedding some of the
specific desires of different minority nationalities for protection, such as the rights
of non-Buddhists in the state of Karen (where there are sizeable numbers of
Christians, who feared persecution) or the minority-language rights for the Shan-
speaking majority in the state of Shan.

4. *A high number of electorally based veto players and their constraining impact on inequality-reducing legislation.* Let us now analyze the question of "veto
players" in the U.S. model of federalism. George Tsbellis defines a veto player
as "an individual or collective actor whose agreement is required for a policy
decision."[16] Using spatial modeling and empirical arguments, Tsbellis makes a
convincing case that the more institutional veto players there are in a political
system—unitary or federal, parliamentary or presidential—the more difficult it is
to construct a win-set to alter the political status quo, say, by passing a bill to
extend welfare coverage to previously excluded minority groups.[17]

All federal democracies with a multinational dimension, as we have seen, have
created a series of special arrangements to accommodate the social diversity in
their polities. However, federal democracies in multinational societies have as
much, indeed possibly more, need to produce reasonable material standards of
welfare for all its citizens as other types of democracies. But do the special arrangements, accommodations, and constitutional asymmetries of Canada, Belgium,
Spain, and India make ordinary legislation exceptionally difficult, because they
produce a higher number of "veto players" compared to the U.S. model? Also,
how do they compare with the U.S. model of federalism on some of the standard
indicators of poverty and inequality? Is the cost of multinational accommodation
and asymmetry weak polity-wide welfare policies?

Let us first focus on veto players that are electorally based. As we have seen, in
the U.S. federal model, the approval, in separate votes, of both the lower chamber
and the upper chamber are required for legislation. Two veto players.

---

16. See Tsbellis, "Decision Making in Political Systems," p. 293.
17. For the full argument with empirical demonstrations, see Tsbellis, *Veto Players.*

Tsbellis considers the U.S. president a veto player because two separate significant supermajorities (one in each chamber) are needed to override a presidential veto. Three veto players.

Also, unless three-fourths of the states vote to accept a new amendment to the Constitution, that amendment cannot pass. Thus, there are four electorally based veto players in the U.S. system for something as basic as a constitutional change: the states, the Senate, the House of Representatives, and the president.

How many veto players are necessary, in the admittedly complex political arrangements crafted to accommodate the social diversity of multinational societies in Spain, Belgium, Canada, and India?

Spain, Canada, Belgium, and India are all parliamentary democracies in which the lower house has an absolute veto on legislation. One veto player.

In all four countries, the constituent units on some issues relating to their constitutionally embedded "asymmetrically federal" prerogatives, have veto powers. Two veto players.

In the judgment of most analysts, the upper house in these four countries cannot exercise an absolute veto.[18] Still only two veto players.

Should we count the prime minister as a veto player? In the technical literature on counting veto players, the prime minister's blocking capacity is counted as being "absorbed" within the parliament's veto power, so it does not count as a separate veto. The (correct) reasoning behind this counting convention is that the prime minister's mandate can be revoked by a hostile vote of a simple majority of the parliament. In that sense, unlike a directly elected president of the U.S. sort, a prime minister does not have a fixed and independent mandate and cannot sustain a long conflict with the majority in the parliament or even within his or her party. Grand total: two veto players.

Thus, none of the admittedly complex, multinational, parliamentary, asymmetrically federal democratic polities of Spain, Canada, India, or Belgium have more than two "electorally based" veto players. In fact, when we look at the entire universe of the world's twenty-three longstanding democracies from the set of advanced OECD member economies, the United States is the only country in the set to have more than three "electorally based" veto players (see table 8.4).

How does having a high number of veto players correlate with poverty and

18. See Stepan, "Electorally Generated Veto Players in Unitary and Federal Systems," in *Federalism and Democracy in Latin America*, ed. Edward L. Gibson (Baltimore: Johns Hopkins University Press, 2004).

TABLE 8.4

Classification of the Number of Electorally Based Institutional Veto Players in the Universe of the Twenty-three Longstanding Advanced Economy OECD Democracies

	State structure			
Democracies with four institutional veto players	Federal; presidential, bicameral with both houses having extensive veto powers; member states have absolute veto over proposals to amend the Constitution unless three-fourths of them ratify the amendment (United States)			
Democracies with three institutional veto players	Federal; parliamentary, or collective executive generated by parliament, upper chamber has veto; frequent referendums in which a law passed by both houses can be vetoed unless a majority of the cantons or member states approve the law (Switzerland and Australia)			
Democracies with two institutional veto players	Federal; parliamentary, bicameral, with upper chamber veto; member states exercise veto power only through upper chamber (Germany)	Asymmetrical federal; parliamentary, bicameral with weak upper chamber veto power, but regions have some constitutionally embedded veto powers (Belgium, Spain, Canada)	Unitary state; bicameral but upper chamber has weak veto; semi-presidential system when the president does not command a legislative majority (France during "cohabitation")	Unitary state; parliamentary, bicameral where upper chamber has some veto capacity (Italy, Japan, Netherlands)
Democracies with one institutional veto player	Federal; parliamentary, bicameral, where upper chamber and member states have no veto (Austria)	Unitary state; parliamentary, bicameral, but upper chamber has weak veto, or semi-presidential system when the president controls a majority in both houses (France during "non-cohabitation")	Unitary state; parliamentary, bicameral but upper chamber lacks veto (Ireland, Sweden, Norway, U.K.)	Unitary state; parliamentary, unicameral (Finland, Greece, Luxembourg, Portugal, New Zealand, Denmark, Iceland)

Sources: Alfred Stepan, "Electorally Generated Veto Players in Unitary and Federal Systems," in *Federalism and Democracy in Latin America*, ed. Edward L. Gibson (Baltimore: Johns Hopkins University Press, 2004), pp. 323–364, esp. 325–333; George Tsebelis and Jeannette Money, *Bicameralism* (New York: Cambridge University Press, 1997).

inequality levels in this universe? Let us look at four comparative measures of politically produced poverty and inequality.

The first measure is the World Bank's Gini index of inequality where a score of 1 would be perfect equality (because every person in the polity has identical wealth) and a score of ten would be absolute inequality (because one person has all the wealth in the polity). A country's Gini index is to a significant extent politically produced because it reflects a country's post-tax, post-government transfer and post-government income, support, and equalization schemes.[19]

Another widely cited source used to analyze comparative inequality is the Luxembourg Income Study (LIS), coordinated for many years by three distinguished social scientists, Anthony B. Atkinson, Lee Rainwater, and Timothy M. Smeeding. In most advanced industrial democracies, two groups of citizens are particularly dependent on the income-maintenance formulas produced by the political system. The largest group of such dependent citizens is children in "solo mother" households. Our indicator of inequality will be the country's percentage of such children below the poverty threshold after all government transfers. The other group is the population of those over the age of sixty. Part of the elderly's net income, of course, comes from savings from their previous market-related earnings. However, to a significant extent, government-structured social security schemes and a variety of social services for the elderly will determine the percentage of the over-sixty population who live in poverty. These will be our second and third indicators.

Our fourth indicator concerns health. All citizens are directly affected by a country's national health delivery and health insurance plans. Our fourth indicator was developed by the World Health Organization. The WHO has recently constructed a measure of "fairness of financial contribution" to the country's health system in terms of how much citizens in the poorest and wealthiest deciles gave to, and received from, the country's public health system. Such a result is a function not of the market but of the government.

We are now in a position to compare the number of veto players and comparative levels of inequality and poverty. As table 8.5 shows, on *each* of our four measures of inequality, three- and four-veto-player countries have *worse* scores—indicating greater inequality—than one- and two-veto-player countries.

Finally, where does the United States stand, by these inequality measures, with respect to the other seven longstanding federal democracies in advanced-economy OECD member countries? On each of the four measures, the United States has the worst possible comparative ranking. When we expand our analysis to include the entire universe of the twenty-two longstanding, advanced-economy OECD democracies, whether they are unitary or federal states, the United States scores the worst on three indicators and the second-worst on the other one (see table 8.6).

Our thought exercise concluded, we find that the exercise stands much of the argumentation supporting U.S. federalism on its head. For robust multinational

19. *World Development Indicators: 2007* (Washington, DC: World Bank, 2007), pp. 66–67.

TABLE 8.5
Veto Players and Inequality in OECD Advanced Democracies

	Average Gini index (the higher the number, the greater the inequality)	Average poverty rate of children of "single mothers" after all government transfers	Average percentage of population over 60 years old living in poverty	Fairness of financial contribution to health system (the higher the number, the greater the unfairness)
Countries with three or four veto players	0.366	47.1	18.4	40.3
Countries with one or two veto players	0.313	19.1	9.8	18.3

Sources: For Gini index figures, see *World Development Indicators: 2010* (Washington, D.C.: World Bank, 2010), pp. 94–96. For poverty rate in children of "single mother" families, see *Luxembourg Income Study*, as discussed in Lee Rainwater, "Legality and Poverty in Comparative Perspective," p. 16. For population over 60 living in poverty, see Anthony Atkinson, Lee Rainwater, and Timothy Smeeding, *Income Distribution in OECD Countries* (Paris: OECD, 1995), p. 104. For fairness rankings, see World Health Organization, *The World Health Report: 2000*, Annex Table 7, p. 188. For the sources on the number of veto players, see table 8.4.

TABLE 8.6
USA Inequality Indicators in Comparison to Other OECD Federal States and Entire OECD Set

	USA rank against other federal countries in the set	USA rank against entire unitary and federal set
Gini index of inequality	Worst 8/8	Worst 22/22
Average poverty rate of children of "single mothers" after all government transfers	Worst 6/6	Worst 16/16
Percentage of population over 60 living with low income	Worst 7/7	Worst 14/14
Fairness of financial contribution to health system	Worst 8/8	2nd Worst 22/23
Worst possible score on the four indicators	29/29	92/93
Actual U.S. aggregate score	29/29	92/93

Sources: See *Luxembourg Income Study*, as discussed in Lee Rainwater, "Legality and Poverty in Comparative Perspective," p. 16, and the sources indicated in tables 8.4 and 8.5. Robert A. Dahl has a welfare state index and a social expenditures index for eighteen democracies. The United States is the worst or second-worst on each index. Dahl, *How Democratic Is the American Constitution?* p. 169; United Nations Development Programme, "Human Development Report, 2009," http://hdr.undp.org/eng/reports/global/hdr2009/.

societies, U.S.-style federalism, far from being the best possible formula, is likely to be a highly constraining—and possibly the worst—federal governance formula for old, new, and possible future democracies.

CONCLUSION

We have not aspired to write a "cookbook" for policy-makers or constitution-makers. Although some countries have roughly similar characteristics and similar problems, the policies adopted to solve these problems must inevitably deal with a range of historical, social, cultural, and geopolitical specificities that will have a great impact on the policies' appropriateness or inappropriateness, their relative success or failure. We can perhaps be more certain of what might be "possible," "improbable," or "very difficult" to achieve. Unfortunately, social scientists may have to diagnose some problems as intractable—at least under certain conditions and respecting certain values—the same as a physician with the available knowledge at the time has to conclude that a patient is incurably ill. Knowledge in these cases can perhaps contribute to reduce the impact of a hopeless situation, of reducing the pain. Social scientists and policy makers should not deceive themselves that all problems are solvable. However, we should also be aware that more appropriate, more timely actions might prevent some solvable problems from *becoming* insolvable. The timely imagining of alternatives is thus crucial.

Democracy entails the democratic management of a specific territory and its citizens. For too long, the normatively privileged model for a modern state has been the nation-state. But the complexities, conflicts, and identities of citizens require the theoretical, normative, and political imagining of other alternatives. We are convinced that in some circumstances a politics of nation-state-building is in conflict with a politics of peace and a politics of democracy. So we have constructed our state-nation alternative. But we are also convinced that there are conditions where federalism, which is a key contributing component of state-nation policies, is an unlikely outcome in many, if not most, unitary states. So we have constructed our new version of federacy, to expand normatively coherent and politically possible alternative democratic futures.

Bibliography

Alcock, Anthony Evelyn. *The History of the South Tyrol Question*. Geneva: Graduate Institute of International Studies, 1970.

Alemchiba, M. *A Brief Historical Account of Nagaland*. Kohima, India: Naga Institute of Culture, 1970.

Almond, Gabriel A. "Myron Weiner on India and the Theory of Democratization." In *India and the Politics of Developing Countries: Essays in Memory of Myron Weiner*. Edited by Ashutosh Varshney. New Delhi: Sage, 2004, pp. 29–42.

Anderson, Benedict. *Imagined Communities: Reflections on the Origin and Spread of Nationalism*. London: Verso, 1983.

Arel, Dominique. "The Hidden Face of the Orange Revolution: Ukraine in Denial towards Its Regional Problem." Translation of "La face cachée de la Révolution Orange: l'Ukraine en négation face á son problèm régional." *Revue d'études comparatives Est-Ouest* 37 (December 2006).

———. "Parliamentary Blocs in the Ukrainian Supreme Soviet." *Journal of Soviet Nationalities* 1, no. 4 (Winter 1991), pp. 108–154.

———. "Ukraine Since the War in Georgia." *Survival* 50, no. 6 (December 2008–January 2009), pp. 15–25.

———. "Ukraine: The Temptation of the Nationalizing State." In *Political Culture and Civil Society in Russia and the New States of Eurasia*. Edited by Vladimir Tismaneanu. Armonk, NY: M. E. Sharpe, 1995, pp. 157–188.

Arel, Dominique, and Valeri Khmelko. "Regional Divisions in the 2004 Presidential Elections in Ukraine." Paper prepared for the Danyliw Research Seminar in Contemporary Ukrainian Studies at the Chair of Ukrainian Studies. University of Ottawa, September 29–October 1, 2005

Arora, Balveer. "Negotiating Differences: Federal Coalitions and National Cohesion." In *Transforming India: Social and Political Dynamics of Democracy*. Edited by Francine R. Frankel, Zoya Hasan, Rajeev Bhargava, and Balveer Arora. Oxford and Delhi: Oxford University Press, 2000, pp. 176–206.

———. "Spécificité Ethnique, Conscience Régionale et Développement National: Langues et Fédéralisme en Inde." Unpublished Ph.D. dissertation, Fondation Nationale des Sciences, Politiques, Paris, 1972.

Aspinall, Edward. "Aceh: Two Years of Peace." *Inside Indonesia*, no. 90 (October–December 2007).

———. "From Islamism to Nationalism in Aceh, Indonesia." *Nations and Nationalism* 13, no. 2 (October 2007), pp. 245–263.

———. "The Helsinki Agreement: A More Promising Basis for Peace in Aceh?" *Policy Studies* 20 (Washington, DC: East-West Center, 2005).

———. *Islam and Nation: Separatist Rebellion in Aceh Indonesia*. Stanford: Stanford University Press, 2009.

———. "Modernity, History, and Ethnicity: Indonesian and Acehnese Nationalism in Conflict." *Review of Indonesian and Malaysian Affairs* 36 (2002), pp. 3–33.

Aspinall, Edward, and Harold Crouch. "The Aceh Peace Process: Why It Failed." *Policy Studies* 1 (Washington, DC: East-West Center, 2003).

Bardhan, Pranab. *The Political Economy of Development in India*. New Delhi: Oxford University Press, expanded edition 1998.

Barnett, Marguerite Ross. *The Politics of Cultural Nationalism in South India*. Princeton: Princeton University Press, 1976.

Barrington, Lowell W., and Erik S. Herron. "One Ukraine or Many? Regionalism in Ukraine and its Political Consequences." *Nationalities Papers* 32 (March 2004), pp. 53–86.

Barros, James. *The Aland Islands Question: Its Settlement by the League of Nations*. New Haven: Yale University Press, 1968.

Barry, Brian. *Culture and Equality: An Egalitarian Critique of Multiculturalism*. Cambridge, MA: Polity Press, 2001.

Baruah, Sanjib. "Confronting Constructionism: Ending India's Naga War." *Journal of Peace Research* 40 (2003), pp. 321–338.

Basta, Lidija. "Minority and Legitimacy of a Federal State." In *Federalism and Multiethnic States: The Case of Switzerland*. Edited by Lidija Basta and Thomas Fleiner. Fribourg, Switzerland: Institute of Federalism, 1996, pp. 41–69.

Bauböck, Rainer. "United in Misunderstanding: Asymmetry in Multinational Federations." *ICE Working Paper Series*. Austrian Academy of Sciences 26 (May 2002).

BBC News. "French MPs Back Corsica Devolution." May 22, 2001. Available at http://news.bbc.co.uk/2/hi/europe/1344285.stm.

Bechert, Heinz. "S.W.R.D. Bandaranike and the Legitimation of Power through Buddhist Ideals." In *Religion and Legitimation of Power in Sri Lanka*. Edited by Bardwell L. Smith. Chambersburg, PA: Anima Books, 1978, pp. 199–211.

Benhabib, Seyla. *The Claims of Culture: Equality and Diversity in the Global Era*. Princeton: Princeton University Press, 2002.

Beyme, Klaus von. "Die Asymmetrisierung des postmodernen Föderalismus." In *Die Reformierbarkeit der Demokratie und Blockaden*. Edited by Renate Mayntz and Wolfgang Streek. Frankfurt/Main: Campus, 2003, pp. 239–258.

Bhargava, Rajeev. "The Distinctiveness of Indian Secularism." In *The Future of Secularism*. Edited by T. N. Srinivasan. Oxford: Oxford University Press, 2006, pp. 20–53.

——. "Political Secularism." In *The Oxford Handbook of Political Theory.* Edited by John S. Dryzek, Bonnie Honig, and Anne Phillips. Oxford: Oxford University Press, 2006, pp. 636–655.

——, ed. *Secularism and Its Critics.* Oxford: Oxford University Press, 2004.

Bhattacharya, Mohit. "The Mind of the Founding Fathers." In *Federalism in India: Origins and Development.* Edited by Nirmal Mukarji and Balveer Arora. New Delhi: Vikas, 1992.

Billiet, Jaak, Bart Maddens, and André-Paul Frognier. "Does Belgium (Still) Exist? Differences in Political Culture between Flemings and Walloons." *West European Politics* 29, no. 5 (November 2006), pp. 912–932.

Bluhm, William T. *Building an Austrian Nation: The Political Integration of a Western State.* New Haven: Yale University Press, 1973.

Bose, Sumatra. *The Challenge in Kashmir.* London: Sage, 1997.

——. "State Crises and Nationalities Conflict in Sri Lanka and Yugoslavia." *Comparative Political Studies* 28 (April 1995), pp. 87–116.

——. *States, Nations, and Sovereignty: Sri Lanka, India, and the Tamil Eelam Movement.* London: Sage, 1994.

Bowen, John R. *Why the French Don't Like Headscarves: Islam, the State, and Public Space.* Princeton: Princeton University Press, 2006.

Brass, Paul. *Ethnicity and Nationalism: Theory and Comparison.* London: Sage, 1991.

Bremmer, Ian. "The Politics of Ethnicity: Russians in a New Ukraine." *Europe-Asian Studies* 46, no. 2 (1994), pp. 261–283.

Briquet, J. L. "Le problème corse." *Regards sur l'actualité,* no. 240 (April 1998), pp. 25–37.

Brown, Archie. "Cultural Change and Continuity in the Transition from Communism: The Russian Case." "Culture Matters" Project Final Conference. Tufts University, Medford, Massachusetts, March 26–28, 2004.

Bunce, Valerie. *Subversive Institutions: The Design and Destruction of Socialism and the State.* New York: Cambridge University Press, 1999.

Caminal, Miquel. *El federalismo pluralista: Del federalismo nacional al federalismo plurinacional.* Barcelona: Paidós, 2002.

Casanova, José. "Ethno-Linguistic and Religious Pluralism and Democratic Construction in Ukraine." In *Post-Soviet Political Order: Conflict and State Building.* Edited by Barnett R. Rubin and Jack Snyder. London: Routledge, 1998, pp. 81–103.

Census of India 1991, 2001. Registrar General of India, New Delhi.

Chandra, Kanchan. *Why Ethnic Parties Succeed: Patronage and Ethnic Head Counts in India.* Cambridge: Cambridge University Press, 2004.

"Change on the Horizon? Public Opinion in Ukraine before the 2010 Presidential Election." International Foundation for Electoral Systems, November 2009.

Chatterjee, Partha. *Nationalist Thought and the Colonial World: A Derivative Discourse?* Delhi: Oxford University Press, 1986.

——. *The Politics of the Governed: Reflections on Popular Politics in Most of the World.* New York: Columbia University Press, 2004.

——, ed. *State and Politics in India.* Delhi: Oxford University Press, 1997.

Chhibber, Pradeep, and Ken Kollman. *The Formation of National Party Systems: Federalism and Party Competition in Britain, Canada, India, and the U.S.* Princeton: Princeton University Press, 2004.

Colley, Linda. *Britons: Forging the Nation, 1707–1837.* New Haven: Yale University Press, 1992.

Colton, Timothy J., and Cindy Skach. "The Predicament of Semi-Presidentialism." In *Democracies in Danger.* Edited by Alfred Stepan. Baltimore: Johns Hopkins University Press, 2009, pp. 121–136.

———. "The Russian Predicament." *Journal of Democracy* 16 (July 2005), pp. 113–126.

Constituent Assembly Debates. Volume 2. New Delhi, India, 1951.

Cotta, Maurizio. "Elite Unification and Democratic Consolidation in Italy: An Historical Overview." In *Elites and Democratic Consolidation in Latin America and Southern Europe.* Edited by John Higley and Richard Gunther. Cambridge: Cambridge University Press, 1992, pp. 146–177.

Cowell, Alan. "Greenland Vote Favors Independence." *The New York Times,* November 26, 2008. Available at www.nytimes.com/2008/11/27/world/europe/27greenland.html, accessed November 30, 2008.

Crowther, William. "The Politics of Ethno-National Mobilization: Nationalism and Reform in Soviet Moldavia." *The Russian Review* 50 (April 1991), pp. 183–202

Cuaz, Marco. "La Valle d'Aosta. Un'identità di frontiera fra Italia, Europa ed etnonazionalismi." In *Altre Italie: Identità nazionali e Regioni a statuto speciale.* Edited by Gaspare Nevola. Rome: Carocci editore, 2003, pp. 1–18.

Cunningham, David. "Veto Players and Civil War Duration." *American Journal of Political Science* 50, no. 4 (October 2006), pp. 875–892.

D'Anieri, Paul. "Ethnic Tensions and State Strategies: Understanding the Survival of the Ukrainian State." *Journal of Communist Studies and Transition Politics* 23 (March 2007), pp. 4–29.

Daftary, Farimah. "Insular Autonomy: A Framework for Conflict Resolution? A Comparative Study of Corsica and the Alland Islands." *Global Review of Ethnopolitics* 1, no. 1 (September 2001), pp. 19–40.

Dahl, Robert. *Democracy, Liberty, and Equality.* Oslo: Norwegian University Press, 1986.

———. *How Democratic Is the American Constitution?* New Haven: Yale University Press, 2001.

Dang, Satyapal. *Genesis of Terrorism: Analytical Study of Punjab Terrorists.* New Delhi: Patriot Publishers, 1988.

Das Gupta, Jyotirindra. *Language Conflict and National Development: Group Politics and National Language Policy in India.* Berkeley: University of California Press, 1970.

Debes, Hans Jacob. "The Formation of a Nation: The Faroe Islands." In *Ethnicity and Nation Building in the Nordic World.* Edited by Sven Tägil. London: Hurst, 1995, pp. 63–84.

Denmark. Act no. 473 of 12 June 2009, *Act on Greenland Self-Government.*

Desai, A. R., ed. *Violation of Democratic Rights in India*. Bombay: Popular Prakashan, 1986.

Diamond, Larry. "Economic Development and Democracy Reconsidered." In *Re-Examining Democracy*. Edited by Gary Marks and Larry Diamond. Newbury Park, CA: Sage, 1992, pp. 93–139.

Diamond, Larry, Juan J. Linz, and Seymour Martin Lipset, ed. *Democracy in Developing Countries*. Boulder, CO: Lynne Rienner, 1989.

Di Michele, Andrea, Francisco Palermo, and Günther Pallaver, eds. *1992: Fine di Un Conflitto: Dieci anni dalla chiusura della questione sudtirolese*. Bologna: il Mulino, 2003.

Dirks, Nicholas B. *Castes of Mind: Colonialism and the Making of Modern India*. Princeton: Princeton University Press, 2001.

Dominici, Thierry. "Le système partisan nationalitaire corse contemporain: étude d'un phénomène politique." *BCN Political Science Debates* 4 (2005), pp. 43–88.

The Economist. "Chronicle of a Death Foretold." December 1, 2009.

———. "A War as Strange as Fiction." June 7, 2007.

Elazar, Daniel. *Federal Systems of the World: A Handbook of Federal, Confederal, and Autonomy Arrangements*. Essex, UK: Longman, 1991.

Eldersveld, Samuel, and Bashiruddin Ahmed. *Citizens and Politics: Mass Political Behavior in India*. Chicago: University of Chicago Press, 1978.

Embree, Ainslie. *India's Search for National Identity*. Delhi: Chanakya Publications, 1980.

Euskalherria en la encuesta Europea de valores. Bilbao: Universidad de Deusto, 1992

Faris, Stephan. "Ice Free: Will Global Warming Give Greenland Its Independence?" *New York Times Magazine*, July 27, 2008.

"Faroe Islanders Head to the Polls Saturday." Agence France-Presse, January 17, 2008.

Fenet, Alain. "Difference Rights and Language in France." In *Language, Nation, and State: Identity Politics in a Multilingual Age*. Edited by Tony Judt and Dennis Lacorne. New York: Palgrave/Macmillan, 2004, pp. 19–62.

"Finland: Aaland Islands." In *Federal Systems of the World*. Edited by Daniel J. Elazar. Essex: Longman, 1991.

Flora, Peter, ed. *State, Economy, and Society in Western Europe, 1815–1975: A Data Handbook in Two Volumes*. Frankfurt: Campus Verlag, 1983.

Foighel, Isi. "Home Rule in Greenland 1979." *Nordic Journal of International Law* 48 (1979).

Forrester, Duncan B. "Kamaraj: A Study in Percolation of Style." *Modern Asian Studies* 4, no. 1 (1970), pp. 43–61.

———. "The Madras Anti-Hindi Agitation, 1965: Political Protest and its Effect on Language Policy in India." *Pacific Affairs* 39 (Spring–Summer 1966), pp. 19–36.

France. Constitutional Council. Decision 2001–454 DC of 17 January 2002.

"The Freedom House Survey for 2009." *Journal of Democracy* 19, no. 2 (April 2010).

Freedom House. *Freedom in the World: Political Rights and Civil Liberties*. New York: Freedom House, multiple years.

Friend, Robert C. *The Italian Prefects: A Study in Administrative Politics*. New Haven: Yale University Press, 1963.

Frye, Timothy. "A Politics of Institutional Choice: Post Communist Presidencies." *Comparative Political Studies* 30, no. 4 (1997), pp. 523–552.

Furet, François, and Mora Ozouf, eds. *A Critical Dictionary of the French Revolution*. Cambridge: Belknap Press, 1989.

Gandhi, M. K. *Collected Works*. New Delhi: Publications Division, Government of India, 1969.

General Election Study, Belgium 1995. Interuniversitair Steunpunt Politieke-Opinie-onderzoek, K. U. Leuven and Point d'Appui Interuniversitaire sur l'Opinion Publique et la Politique, U. C. Louvain, 1998.

Gellner, Ernest. *Nations and Nationalism*. Oxford: Oxford University Press, 1983.

Gill, K. P. S. *Punjab, The Knights of Falsehood*. New Delhi: Har-Anand Publications, 1997.

Gombrich, Richard, and Gananath Obeyesekere. *Buddhism Transformed: Religious Change in Sri Lanka*. Princeton: Princeton University Press, 1988.

Goswami, B. B. *The Mizo Unrest: A Study of Politicization of Culture*. Jaipur: Aalekh Publishers, 1979.

Gunasinnghe, Newton. "Community Identity and Militarization in Sri Lanka: Sri Lankan Armed Forces." In *The Challenge in South Asia: Democracy, Development, and Regional Cooperation*. Edited by Ponna Wijnaraja and Akmal Hussain. New Delhi: Sage, 1989. 243–249.

Habermas, Jürgen. *Between Facts and Norms*. Cambridge, MA: MIT Press, 1998.

———. *Die Einbeziehung des Anderen: Studien zur politschen Theorie*. Frankfurt am Main: Suhrkamp, 1996.

Habib, Irfan. "Emergence of Nationalities." *Social Scientist*, no. 37 (August 1975), pp. 14–20.

Hale, Henry E. *Foundations of Ethnic Politics*. Cambridge: Cambridge University Press, 2008.

Hardgrave, Richard L. Jr. "Religion, Politics, and the DMK." In *South Asian Politics and Religion*. Edited by Donald Eugene Smith. Princeton: Princeton University Press, 1966.

———. "The Riots in Tamilnad: Problems and Prospects of India's Language Crisis." *Asia Survey* 5 (August 1965), pp. 399–407.

Harhoff, Frederick. "Greenland's Withdrawal from the European Communities." *Common Market Law Review* 20 (1983), pp. 13–33.

Hasan, Mushirul. *Legacy of a Divided Nation: India's Muslims since Independence*. Delhi: Oxford University Press, 1997.

Hazarika, Sanjoy. *Strangers of the Mist: Tales of War and Peace from India's Northeast*. London: Penguin, 1994.

The Hindu. "How India Voted: Verdict 2009." March 26, 2009.

Hirschman, Albert. *Exit, Voice, and Loyalty: Responses to Declines in Firms, Organizations, and States*. Cambridge: Harvard University Press, 1972.

Hooghe, Liesbet. "Belgium: Hollowing the Center." In *Federalism and Territorial*

Cleavages. Edited by Ugo M. Amoretti and Nancy Bermeo. Baltimore: Johns Hopkins University Press, 2004, pp. 55–92.

Horowitz, Donald L. "Incentives and Behavior in the Ethnic Politics of Sri Lanka and Malaysia." *Third World Quarterly* 11 (October 1989), pp. 18–35.

Hrytsak, Yaroslav. "National Identities in Post-Soviet Ukraine: The Case of Lviv and Donetsk." In *Cultures and Nations of Central and Eastern Europe*. Edited by Zvi Gitelman, Lubomyr Hajda, John-Paul Himka, and Roman Solchanyk. *Harvard Ukrainian Studies* 22 (1998), pp. 263–282.

———. "On the Relevance and Irrelevance of Nationalism in Ukraine." Second Annual Cambridge-Stasiuk Lecture on Ukraine, February 20, 2004.

———. "Ukrainian Nationalism, 1991–2001: Myths and Perceptions." Austrian Institute for Eastern and South-Eastern Europe. Vienna, Austria, October 15, 2001.

Human Rights Watch. "War on the Displaced: Sri Lankan Army and LTTE Abuses against Civilians in the Vanni." February 2009.

"Interactive Ukraine Election Maps." *Kyiv Post*. January 18, 2010. Available at www .kyivpost.com/news/politics/detail/57376/.

International Crisis Group. "Aceh: Post Conflict Complications." *Asia Report*, no. 139, October 4, 2007.

———. "Aceh: So Far, So Good." *Asia Briefing*, no. 44, December 13, 2005.

———. "Indonesia: Pre-Election Anxieties in Aceh." *Asia Briefing*, no. 81, September 9, 2008.

International Monetary Fund. *Government Finance Statistics*. Washington, DC: International Monetary Fund, various issues.

Irschick, Eugene F. *Politics and Social Conflict in South India: The Non-Brahmin Movement and Tamil Separatism, 1916–1929*. Berkeley: University of California Press, 1969.

Jaffrelot, Christophe. ed. *Hindu Nationalism: A Reader*. Princeton: Princeton University Press, 2007.

———. *The Hindu Nationalist Movement in India*. London: Hurst, 1996.

Jennings, Ivor. *The Constitution of Ceylon*. 3rd ed. London: Oxford University Press, 1953.

Jodhka, Surinder S. "Looking Back at the Khalistan Movement: Some Recent Researches on its Rise and Decline." *Economic and Political Weekly*, vol. 36, no. 16, April 21–27, 2001, pp. 1311–1318.

Johannson, Andreas. "The Transnistrian Conflict after the 2005 Moldovan Parliamentary Elections." *Journal of Communist Studies and Transition Politics* 22 (December 2006).

Jones, Matthew. "Faroese Explore Prospects for New Economic Base." *Financial Times*, July 10, 2001.

Jussila, Osmo. *From Grand Duchy to Modern State: A Political History of Finland since 1809*. London: Hurst, 1999.

Kailash, K. K. "Coalitions in a Parliamentary Federal System: Parties and Governments in India." Unpublished Ph.D. dissertation, Jawaharlal Nehru University, 2003.

Kalinina, Svitlana, Alexander Lyakh, Galina Savchenko, and Adam Swain. "Regional 'Lock-in' or Local Hegemonic Bloc? Industrial Restructuring in the Ukrainian Donbas." Paper prepared for the Danyliw Research Seminar in Contemporary Ukrainian Studies at the Chair of Ukrainian Studies. University of Ottawa, September 29–October 1, 2005.

Karat, Prakash. "Theoretical Aspects of the National Question." *Social Scientist* 37 (August 1975), pp. 5–13.

Kashmir: An Enquiry into the Healing Touch. Report by the Association for Democratic Rights (ADR), Punjab, Human Rights Forum (HRF), Andhra Pradesh and Organisation for Protection of Democratic Rights (OPDR), Hyderabad, India, 2003.

Kaviraj, Sudipta. "The Imaginary Institution of India." *Subaltern Studies* 7. Edited by Partha Chatterjee and Gyananendra Pandey. Delhi: Oxford University Press, 1993, pp. 1–39.

———., ed. *Politics in India.* Oxford and Delhi: Oxford University Press, 1997.

———. *The Unhappy Consciousness: Bankimchandra Chattopadhyay and the Formation of Nationalist Discourse in India.* Delhi: Oxford University Press, 1995.

Keane, John. *The Life and Death of Democracy.* London: Simon and Schuster, 2009.

Kearney, Robert N. *Communalism and Language in the Politics of Ceylon.* Durham, NC: Duke University Press, 1967.

Khan, Rasheeduddin, ed. *Rethinking Indian Federalism.* Shimla: Indian Institute of Advanced Study, 1997.

Khilnani, Sunil. *The Idea of India.* London: Hamish Hamilton, 1997.

Kingsbury, Damien. *Peace in Aceh: A Personal Account of the Helsinki Peace Process.* Jakarta: Equinox Publishing, 2006.

Kogan, Norman. *A Political History of Italy: The Post-War Years.* New York: Praeger, 1983.

Kohli, Atul, ed. *The Success of India's Democracy.* Cambridge: Cambridge University Press, 2001.

Kolstø, Pål, and Andrei Malgin. "The Transnistrian Republic: A Case of Politicized Regionalism." *Nationalities Papers* 26, no.1 (1998).

Kothari, Rajni. *Politics in India.* Boston: Little Brown, 1970.

———, ed. *State and Nation Building : A Third World Perspective.* Bombay: Allied, 1976

Kumar, Ram Narayan, Amrik Singh, Ashok Agrwaal, and Jaskaran Kaur. *Reduced to Ashes: The Insurgency and Human Rights in Punjab.* New Delhi: South Asia Forum for Human Rights, 2003.

Kumar, Ravinder. "India: A 'Nation-State' or 'Civilisation-state'?" *Journal of South Asian Studies* 25, no. 2, pp. 13–32.

Kumar, Sanjay. "Religious Practices among Hindus: Does This Influence Their Political Choices?" CSDS Working Paper, Delhi, June 2008

Kuru, Ahmet. *Secularism and State Policies toward Religions: The United States, France, and Turkey.* Cambridge: Cambridge University Press, 2009.

———. "Secularism, State Policies, and Muslims in Europe: Analyzing French Exceptionalism." *Comparative Politics* 4 (2008), pp. 1–19.

Kuzio, Taras, ed. *Contemporary Ukraine: Dynamics of Post-Soviet Transformation.* Armonk, NY: M. E. Sharpe, 1998.

Kymlicka, Will. *Multicultural Citizenship: A Liberal Theory of Minority Rights.* New York: Clarendon Press, 1995.

———. *Liberalism, Community, and Culture.* New York: Oxford University Press, 1989.

Lane, J., D. McKay, and K. Newton. *Political Data Handbook: OECD Countries.* Second edition. Oxford: Oxford University Press, 1997.

Lapidoth, Ruth. *Autonomy: Flexible Solutions to Ethnic Conflicts.* Washington, DC: United States Institute of Peace Press, 1997.

Lasala-Blanco, Narayani. "Who Are 'They'? The Real Challenges of Mexican Immigration." Paper presented at the 2006 Midwest Association of Public Opinion Research Conference, Chicago, Illinois, November 17–18, 2006.

Liddle, R. William, and Saiful Mujani. "Indonesian Democracy: From Transition to Consolidation." Paper prepared for an International Conference on "Islam and Democracy in Indonesia: Comparative Perspectives." Center for Democracy, Toleration, and Religion, Columbia University, New York. April 2–3, 2009.

Lijphart, Arend. *Democracies: Patterns of Majoritarian and Consensus Government in Twenty-One Countries.* New Haven: Yale University Press, 1984.

———. "Democratic Institutions and Ethnic/Religious Pluralism: Can India and the United States Learn from Each Other—and from the Smaller Democracies?" In *Democracy and Diversity: India and the American Experience.* Edited by K. Shankar Bajpai. Oxford: Oxford University Press, 2007, pp. 14–49.

———. *Patterns of Democracy: Government Forms and Performance in Thirty-Six Countries.* New Haven: Yale University Press, 1999.

Linz, Juan J. *Conflicto en Euskadi.* Madrid: Espasa Calpe, 1986.

———. "De la crisis de un estado unitario al Estado de las Autonomías." In *La España de las Autonomías.* Edited by Fernando Fernández Rodríguez. Madrid: Instituto de Estudios de Administración Local, 1985, pp. 527–672.

———. "Democracia, multinacionalismo y federalismo." *Revista Española de Ciencia Política* 1 (October 1999), pp. 7–40.

———. "Democracy's Time Constraints." *International Political Science Review* 19 (1998), pp. 19–37.

———. "Democratic States, Nation States, State Nations, and Multinational States." Unpublished manuscript.

———. "Early State-Building and Late Peripheral Nationalisms against the State: The Case of Spain." In *Building States and Nations: Analyses by Region,* Volume II. Edited by S. N. Eisenstadt and Stein Rokkan. Beverly Hills: Sage, 1973, pp. 32–116.

———. "From Primordialism to Nationalism." In *New Nationalisms of the Developed West.* Edited by Edward A. Tiryakian and Ronald Rogowski. Boston: Allen and Unwin, 1985, pp. 203–253.

———. "Introduction: Some Thoughts on Presidentialism in Post-Communist Europe." In *Post-Communist Presidents.* Edited by Ray Taras. Cambridge: Cambridge University Press, 1997, pp. 1–14.

———. "Nationalstaaten, Staatsnationen und multinationale Staaten." In *Staat, Na-*

tion, Demokratie. Traditionen und Perspektiven moderner Gesellschaften. Festschrift für Hans-Jürgen Puhle. Edited by Marcus Gräser, Christian Lammert, and Söhnke Schreyer. Göttingen, Germany: Vandenhoeck und Ruprecht, 2001, pp. 27–38.

——. "Para un mapa conceptual de las democracias." *Politeia,* no. 26 (2001), pp. 25–46.

——. "Parties in Contemporary Democracies: Problems and Paradoxes." In *Political Parties: Old Concepts and New Challenges.* Edited by Richard Gunther, José Ramón Montero, and Juan J. Linz. New York: Oxford University Press, 2002, pp. 291–317.

——. "Spanish Democracy and the Estado de las Autonomías." In *Forging Unity Out of Diversity.* Edited by Robert A. Goldwin, Art Kaufman, and William A. Schambra. Washington, DC: American Enterprise Institute for Public Policy Research, 1989, pp. 260–303.

——. "State Building and Nation Building." *European Review* 1 (1993), pp. 355–69.

——. "Time and Regime Change." In *Robert Michels, Political Sociology and the Future of Democracy.* With editing and bibliography by Houchang Chehabi. New Brunswick, NJ: Transaction Books, 2006, pp. 81–114.

Linz, Juan J., and Alfred Stepan, eds. *The Breakdown of Democratic Regimes.* Baltimore: Johns Hopkins University Press, 1978.

——. "Inequality Inducing and Inequality Reducing Federalism: With Special Reference to the 'Classic Outlier'—the USA." Paper given at the 18th Congress of the International Political Science Association. Quebec City, Canada, August 1–5, 2000.

——. *Problems of Democratic Transition and Consolidation: Southern Europe, South America, and Post-Communist Europe.* Baltimore: Johns Hopkins University Press, 1996.

Linz, Juan J., Alfred Stepan, and Yogendra Yadav. "'Nation State' or 'State Nation'? India in Comparative Perspective." In *Democracy and Diversity: India and the American Experience.* Edited by K. Shankar Bajpai. Oxford: Oxford University Press, 2007, pp. 50–106.

Lipset, Seymour Martin. "Some Social Requisites of Democracy: Economic Development and Political Legitimacy." *American Political Science Review* 53 (March 1959), pp. 69–105.

Llera, Francisco J. *Euskobarometro.* Bilbao: Servicio Editorial Universidad del País Vasco.

——. *Los Vascos y la Política. El proceso político vasco: elecciones, partidos, opinión pública y legitimación en el País Vasco, 1977–1992.* Bilbao: Servicio Editorial Universidad del País Vasco, 1994.

Lokniti. *Jammu and Kashmir; Assembly Election 2002: Findings of a Post-Poll Survey.* Delhi: Center for the Study of Developing Societies, February 2003.

——. *Mizoram Assembly Election Study 2003.* Delhi: Center for the Study of Developing Societies, 2003.

——. *State of the Nation Survey.* Delhi: Center for the Study of Developing Societies, January 2007.

Luithi, Luingam, and Nandita Haksar. *Nagaland File: A Question of Human Rights.* New Delhi: Lancer, 1986.

Lutz, Donald S. "Toward a Theory of Constitutional Amendment." *American Political Science Review* 88, no. 2 (June 1994), pp. 355–370.

Luverà, Bruno. "L'Euregio tirolese. Tra regionalismo transfrontaliero e micronazionalismo di confine." In *Altre Italie*. Edited by G. Nevola. Rome: Carocci, 2003, pp. 19–33.

Lyngdoh, James. *The Chronicle of an Impossible Election: The Election Commission and the 2002 Jammu and Kashmir Assembly Elections.* Delhi: Viking India, 2004.

Madeley, John T. S. "A Framework for the Comparative Analysis of Church-State Relations in Europe." *West European Politics* 26, no. 1 (January 2003), pp. 23–50.

Manor, James. *The Expedient Utopian: Bandaranike and Ceylon.* Cambridge: Cambridge University Press, 1989.

Marshall, Geoffery. *Constitutional Conventions: The Rules and Forms of Political Accountability.* Oxford: Oxford University Press, 1984.

Marshall, Monty G. "Major Episodes of Political Violence: 1946–2006." Center for Systemic Peace, 2009.

Marwah, Ved. *Uncivil Wars: Pathology of Terrorism in India.* New Delhi: Harper Collins, 1995.

Masani, R. P. *Dadabhai Naoroji: The Grand Old Man of India.* London: Unwin Brothers, 1939.

Maxwell, Kenneth. "Regime Overthrow and the Prospects for Democratic Transition." In *Transitions from Authoritarian Rule: Southern Europe*. Edited by Guillermo O' Donnell, Philippe C. Schmitter, and Laurence Whitehead. Baltimore: Johns Hopkins University Press, 1986, pp. 109–137.

———. "The Thorns of the Portuguese Revolution." *Foreign Affairs* 54 (January 1976), pp. 250–270.

McCall, A. G. *Lushei Chrysalis.* London: Luzac, 1949.

McRae, Kenneth D. *Conflict and Compromise in Multilingual Societies*, vol. 1. Ontario, Canada: Wilfred Laurier University Press, 1986.

Meyer, David John. "Ethnic Territorial Autonomy and Post-Soviet Ethnic Political Mobilization." Unpublished Ph.D. dissertation, Department of Political Science, Columbia University, 2007.

Miley, Thomas Jeffrey. Nacionalismo y política lingüística: el caso de Cataluña. Madrid: CEPC, 2006.

Mill, John Stuart. *Considerations on Representative Government* (1861). In *Utilitarianism, On Liberty, Considerations on Representative Government*. Edited by Geraint Williams. London: Everyman, 1993.

Mitta, Manoj, and H. S. Phoolka, *When a Tree Shook Delhi: The 1984 Carnage and Its Aftermath.* New Delhi: Roli Books, 2007.

Modeen, Tore. "Åland Islands." In *Encyclopedia of Public International Law*, vol. 12. Edited by Rudolf Berhardt. Amsterdam: North Holland, 1990.

———. "The International Protection of the National Identity of the Åland Islands." *Scandinavian Studies in Law* (1973), pp. 177–210.

Molas, Isidre. "Partis nationalistes, autonomie et clans en Corse." *Institut de Ciencies Politiques I Socials.* Working paper no. 181 (2000), Barcelona.

Mookerji, Radha Kumud. *The Fundamental Unity of India.* Reprint edition. New Delhi: Bharatiya Vidya Bhavan/Chronicle Books, 2003

Moral, Felix. *Identidad regional y nacionalismo en el Estado de las Autonomías.* Madrid: Centro de Investigaciones Sociológicas, 1998.

Morfit, Michael. "The Road To Helsinki: The Aceh Agreement and Indonesia's Democratic Development." *International Negotiation* 12, no. 1 (2007), pp. 111–143.

Morlino, Leonardo. *Democracy between Consolidation and Crisis: Parties, Groups, and Citizens in Southern Europe.* Oxford: Oxford University Press, 1998.

Motyl, Alexander, and Bohdan Krawchenko. "Ukraine: From Empire to Statehood." In *New States, New Politics: Building the Post-Soviet Nations.* Edited by Ian Bremmer and Ray Taras. Cambridge: Cambridge University Press, 1997, pp. 235–275.

Nandy, Ashis. *Illegitimacy of Nationalism: Rabindranath Tagore and the Politics of Self.* Delhi: Oxford University Press, 1994.

Nehru, Jawaharlal. *Discovery of India.* Delhi: Oxford University Press, 1981.

Nettl, J. P. "The State as a Conceptual Variable." *World Politics* 20 (July 1968), pp. 559–592.

Nevola, Gaspare, ed. *Altre Italie: Identità nazionali e Regioni a statuto speciale.* Rome: Carocci editore, 2003.

Noelle-Neumann, Elisabeth, and Renate Köcher. *Die verletzte Nation: Über den Versuch der Deutschen, Ihren Charakter zu ändern.* Stuttgart: Deutsche Verlags-Anstalt, 1988.

Norris, Pippa. *Critical Citizens: Global Support for Democratic Governance.* Oxford: Oxford University Press, 1999.

Norris, Pippa, and Ronald Inglehart. *Sacred and Secular: Religion and Politics Worldwide.* Cambridge: Cambridge University Press, 2004.

Núñez, Xosé-M. "Historical Research on Regionalism and Peripheral Nationalism in Spain: a Reappraisal." Working paper published by the European University Institute in Florence as ECS no. 92/6 (1992).

Obeyeskere, Gananath. "Buddhism, Nationhood, and Cultural Identity: A Question of Fundamentals." In *Fundamentalisms Comprehended.* Edited by Martin E. Marty and R. Scott Appleby. Chicago: University of Chicago Press, 1995, pp. 231–256.

———. "Origins and Institutionalization of Political Violence." In *Sri Lanka in Change and Crisis.* Edited by James Manor. New York: St. Martin's Press, 1984, pp. 153–174.

O'Donnell, Guillermo, Philippe Schmitter, and Laurence Whitehead. *Transitions from Authoritarian Rule.* Baltimore: Johns Hopkins University Press, 1986.

Olafsson, Árni. "International Status of the Faroe Islands." *Nordisk Tidsskrift,* no. 29 (1982), pp. 29–38.

Opello Jr., Walter C. *Portugal: From Monarchy to Pluralist Republic.* Boulder, CO: Westview Press, 1991.

Orizo, Francisco Andrés, and Maria-Àngels Roque. *Cataluña 2001: Los catalanes en la encuesta Europea de valores.* Madrid: La Fundación Santa María, 2001.

Pallaver, Günther. "The Südtiroler Volkspartei: From Irrendentism to Autonomy." In *Autonomist Parties in Europe: Identity Politics and the Revival of Territorial Cleavage*, vol. 2. Edited by Lieven De Winter, Margarita Gómez-Reino, and Peter Lynch. Barcelona: Institut de Ciències Polítiques i Socials, 2006, pp. 161–188.

Pandian, M. S. S. "Beyond Colonial Crumbs: Cambridge School, Identity Politics and Dravidian Movement(s)." *Economic and Political Weekly*, February 18–25, 1995, pp. 385–391.

Parekh, Bikhu. *Rethinking Multiculturalism: Cultural Diversity and Political Theory*. Basingstoke, UK: Macmillan, 2000.

Pasquino, Gianfranco. "The Demise of the First Fascist Regime and Italy's Transition to Democracy." In *Transitions from Authoritarian Rule: Southern Europe*. Edited by Guillermo O'Donnell, Philippe C. Schmitter, and Laurence Whitehead. Baltimore: Johns Hopkins University Press, 1986, pp. 45–70.

Pew Forum on Religion in Public Life. "Mapping the Global Muslim Population. A Report on the Size and Distribution of the World's Muslim Population." Pew Forum, October 2009.

Phadnis, Urmila. *Religion and Politics in Sri Lanka*. New Delhi: Manohar, 1976.

Philip, Catherine. "The Hidden Massacre: Sri Lanka's Final Offensive against Tamil Tigers." *The Times*, May 29, 2009.

Pinard, Maurice. "Les quatre phases du mouvement indépedantiste québécois." In *Un Combat Inachevé*. Edited by Robert Bernier, Vincent Lemieux, and Maurice Pinard. Sainte-Foy, Quebec: Presses de l'Université du Quebec, 1997.

Plasser, Fritz, and Peter A Ulram. "Politisch-Kulturell Wandel in Österreich." In *Staatsbürger oder Untertanen? Politische Kultur Deutschlands, Österreichs und Schweiz im Vergleich*. Edited by Plasser and Ulram. New York: P. Lang, 1991, pp. 157–245.

Popson, Nancy. "The Ukrainian History Textbooks: Introducing Children to the 'Ukrainian Nation.'" *Nationalities Papers* 29, no.2, pp. 325–350.

Pravda. "Russia Recognizes South Ossetia and Abkhazia to Save People's Lives." August 28, 2008.

President, Republic of Indonesia 2006. Law of the Republic of Indonesia, Number 11, Regarding Governing of Aceh.

Protsyk, Oleh. "Majority-Minority Relations in the Ukraine." *JEMIE* 7 (2008).

———. "Troubled Semi-Presidentialism: Stability of the Constitutional System and Cabinet in Ukraine." *Europe-Asian Studies* 55, no. 7 (2003), pp. 1077–1095.

Przeworkski, Adam. *Sustainable Democracy*. Cambridge: Cambridge University Press, 1995

Puri, Harish K., Paramjit Singh Judge, and Jagrup Singh Sekhon. *Terrorism in Punjab: Understanding Grassroots Reality*. Delhi: Har-Anand, 1999.

Rajasingham-Senanayake, Darina. "Sri Lanka: Transformation of Legitimate Violence and Civil-Military Relations." In *Coercion and Governance: The Declining Political Role of the Military in Asia*. Edited by Muthiah Alagappa. Stanford: Stanford University Press, 2001, pp. 294–316.

Ram, N. "Dravidian Movement in its Pre-Independence Phases." *Economic and Political Weekly*, vol. 14 (February 1979), pp. 377–397.

——. "Visiting the Vavuniya IDP Camps: An Uplifting Experience." Interview with N. Ram. *The Hindu,* July 4, 2009.

Rangasami, Amritha. "Mizoram: Tragedy of Our Own Making." *Economic and Political Weekly,* vol. 13, no. 15, April 15, 1978, pp. 653–662.

Rao, R. V. Ramachandrasekhara, ed. *Indian Unity: A Symposium.* New Delhi: Publication Division, Government of India, 1969.

Raz, Joseph. *Ethics in the Public Domain: Essays in the Morality of Law and Politics.* Oxford: Clarendon Press, 1994.

——. *The Morality of Freedom.* Oxford: Oxford University Press, 1986.

Reid, Anthony, ed. *Veranda of Violence: The Background to the Aceh Problem.* Singapore: Singapore University Press, 2006.

Renner, Michael. "The Casualities of Sri Lanka's Intensifying War." *World Watch Institute.* July 18, 2007.

Requejo Coll, Ferran. *Federalisme, per a què?* Valencia: Tres i Quatre, 1998.

Reynolds, Andrew, Alfred Stepan, Zaw Oo, and Stephen Levine. "How Burma Could Democratize." *Journal of Democracy* 12, no. 4 (October 2001), pp. 94–108.

Rezvani, David A. "Federacy: The Dynamics of Semi-Sovereign Territories." Unpublished D. Phil in Politics, University of Oxford, 2004.

Riker, William. *The Development of American Federalism.* Boston: Kluwer Academic Publishers, 1987.

——. "Federalism." In *Handbook of Political Science,* vol 5. Edited by Fred Greenstein and Nelson W. Polsby. Reading, MA: Addison-Wesley, 1975, pp. 93–72.

——. *Federalism: Origin, Operation, Significance.* Boston: Little Brown, 1964.

Roper, Steven. "Are All Semipresidential Regimes the Same? A Comparison of Premier-Presidential Regimes." *Comparative Politics* 34 (April 2002), pp. 253–272.

Rose, Richard. "Divisions within Ukraine: A Post-Election Opinion Survey." *Studies in Public Policy* 403 (2005).

——. "Russians in the Baltic: A 1991 Survey." *Studies in Public Policy* 287 (1991).

——. "Russians outside Russia." *Studies in Public Policy* 283 (1991).

Rose, Richard, and Christian Haerpfer. "New Democracies Barometer V: A Twelve Nation Survey." *Studies in Public Policy,* no. 306 (1998).

Roux, Christophe. "The Partito Sardo D'Azione: Regionalist Mobilization in Southern Italy." In *Autonomist Parties in Europe: Identity Politics and the Revival of Territorial Cleavage,* vol. 2. Edited by Lieven De Winter, Margarita Gómez-Reino, and Peter Lynch. Barcelona: Institut de Ciències Polítiques i Socials, 2006.

Rubin, Barnett R., and Jack Snyder, eds. *Post-Soviet Political Order: Conflict and State Building.* New York: Routledge, 1998.

Rudolph, Lloyd I. "Urban Life and Populist Radicalism: Dravidian Politics in Madras." *Journal of Asian Studies* 20 (May 1961).

"Russia to Sign Deal on Military Base in South Ossetia on Wednesday." *Ria Novosti,* April 6, 2010.

Rustow, Dankwart. "Transitions to Democracy: Toward a Dynamic Model." *Comparative Politics* 2 (April 1970), pp. 337–363.

Samarasinghe, S. W. R. de A. "Ethnic Representation in Central Government Employment and Sinhala-Tamil Relations in Sri Lanka: 1948–81." In *From Indepen-dence to Statehood*. Edited by Robert Goldmann and A Jeyaratnam Wilson. London: Frances Pinter, 1982, pp. 173–84.

Sapiro, Virginia, and Rosenstone, Steven J. *The American National Election Studies Cumulative Data File, 1948–2004*. National Election Studies, Center for Political Studies, University of Michigan, 2009.

Schindler, Dietrich. "South Tyrol." In *Encylopedia of Public International Law*, vol. 12. Edited by Rudolf Berhardt. New York: North-Holland, 1990, pp. 348–350.

Schulze, Kirsten E. *The Free Aceh Movement (GAM): Anatomy of a Separatist Organization*. Washington: East-West Center, 2004.

SDSA Team. *State of Democracy in South Asia*. Delhi: Oxford University Press, 2008.

Shastri, Amita. "The Tamil Citizenship Act of 1948 and Sri Lanka Partition." *Contemporary South Asia* 8 (March 1999), 25–86.

Silva, Chandra Richard de. "The Impact of Nationalism on Education: The Schools Takeover (1961) and the University Admissions Crisis, 1970–1975." In *Collective Identities, Nationalisms, and Protest in Modern Sri Lanka*. Edited by Michael Roberts. Colombo, Sri Lanka: Marga Institute, 1979, pp. 474–499.

———. "Sinhala-Tamil Relations and Education in Sri Lanka: The University Admissions Issue—The First Phase, 1971–77." In *From Independence to Statehood: Managing Ethnic Conflict in Five African and Asian States*. Edited by Robert B. Goldman and A. Jeyaratnam Wilson. London: Francis Pinter, 1984, pp. 125–146.

Simeon, Richard. "Canada: Federalism, Language, and Regional Conflict." In *Federalism and Territorial Cleavages*. Edited by Ugo M. Amoretti and Nancy Bermeo. Baltimore: Johns Hopkins University Press, 2004, pp. 93–122.

Singh, Devinder. *Akali Politics in Punjab: 1964–1985*. Delhi: National Book Organization, 1993.

Siriwardena, Regi, ed. *Sri Lanka: The Devolution Debate*. Colombo: International Centre for Ethnic Studies, 1996.

Sivarajah, Ambalavanar. *Politics of Tamil Nationalism in Sri Lanka*. New Delhi, South Asian Publishers, 1996.

Skach, Cindy. *Borrowing Constitutional Designs: Constitutional Law in Weimar Germany and the French Fifth Republic*. Princeton: Princeton University Press, 2006.

Smith, Donald E. *India as a Secular State*. Princeton: Princeton University Press, 1963.

———, ed. *South Asian Politics and Religion*. Princeton: Princeton University Press, 1966.

Smyrl, Marc. "France: Challenging the Unitary State." *Le Monde*, July 12, 19, 21, and August 5, 2000.

———. "France: Challenging the Unitary State." In *Federalism and Territorial Cleavages*. Edited by Ugo M. Amoretti and Nancy Bermeo. Baltimore: Johns Hopkins University Press, 2004, pp. 202–225.

Snyder, Jack. *From Voting to Violence: Democratization and Nationalist Conflict*. New York: Norton, 2000.

Solchanyk, Roman. "The Post-Soviet Transition in Ukraine: Prospects for Stability." In

Contemporary Ukraine: Dynamics of Post-Soviet Transformation. Edited by Taras Kuzio. Armonk: M. E. Sharpe, 1998, pp. 17–40.

Somasundram, M., ed. *Reimagining Sri Lanka: Northern Ireland Insights.* Colombo: International Centre for Ethnic Studies, 1999.

Sondeo de opinión del Observatorio Político Autonómico: 2003. Barcelona: Institut de Ciencies Politiques i Socials, 2004.

Sridharan, E. "Electoral Coalitions in 2004 General Elections: Theory and Evidence." *Economic and Political Weekly,* vol. 39, December 18, 2004, pp. 5418–5425.

———. "The Fragmentation of the Indian Party System, 1952–1999: Seven Competing Explanations." In *Parties and Politics in India.* Edited by Zoya Hasan. Oxford: Oxford University Press, 2002, pp. 475–503.

Srikanth, H., and C. J. Thomas. "Naga Resistance Movement and the Peace Process in Northeast India." *Peace and Democracy in South Asia* 1 (2005), pp. 57–87.

Srinivasan, T. N., ed. *The Future Of Secularism.* Oxford: Oxford University Press, 2007.

Stedman, Stephen. "Spoiler Problems in Peace Processes." *International Security* 22, no. 2 (1997), pp. 5–53.

Steininger, Rolf. "Back to Austria? The Problem of South Tyrol in 1945/46." *European Studies Journal* 7 (Fall 1990), pp. 51–83.

———. "75 Years After: The South Tyrol Conflict Resolved; A Contribution to European Stability and a Model for Settling Conflicts?" In *Austria in the 1950s.* Edited by Gunter Bischof, Anton Pelinka, and Rolf Steininger. New Brunswick, NJ: Transaction Publishers, 1995, pp. 116–137.

Stepan, Alfred. *Arguing Comparative Politics.* New York: Oxford University Press, 2001.

———, ed. *Democracies in Danger.* Baltimore: Johns Hopkins University Press. 2009.

———. "Electorally Generated Veto Players in Unitary and Federal Systems." In *Federalism and Democracy in Latin America.* Edited by Edward L. Gibson. Baltimore: Johns Hopkins University Press, 2004, pp. 323–362.

———. "Federalism and Democracy: Beyond the U.S. Model." *Journal of Democracy* 10 (Fall 1999), pp. 19–34.

———. "Federalism, Multinational Societies, and Negotiating a Democratic 'State Nation': A Theoretical Framework, The Indian Model and a Tamil Case Study." In *Democracies and Diversity: India and the Indian Experience.* Edited by Shankar Bagpai. Oxford: Oxford University Press, 2007, pp. 225–261.

———. "The Multiple Secularisms of Modern Democratic and Non-Democratic Regimes." In *Rethinking Secularism.* Edited by Craig Calhoun and Mark Juergensmeyer. Oxford: Oxford University Press, forthcoming.

———. "Russian Federalism in Comparative Perspective." *Post-Soviet Affairs* 16 (April–June 2000), pp. 133–176.

Stepan, Alfred, and Ezra Suleiman. "The French Fifth Republic: A Model for Import? Reflections on Poland and Brazil." In *Arguing Comparative Politics.* Edited by Alfred Stepan. Oxford: Oxford University Press, 2001, pp. 257–275.

Stern, Jonathan. "The Russian-Ukrainian Gas Crisis of January 2006." Oxford Institute for Energy Studies, 2009.

Sternberger, Dolf. *Verfassungspatriotismus*. Frankfurt am Main: Insel-Verlag, 1990.

Subramanian, Narendra. *Ethnicity and Populist Mobilization: Political Parties, Citizens, and Democracy in South India*. Oxford: Oxford University Press, 1999.

Swamy, M. R. Narayan. *Tigers of Lanka: From Boys to Guerrillas*. Delhi: Konark Publishers, 1994.

Swenden, Wilfried. "Federalism and Second Chambers: Regional Representation in Parliamentary Federalism." D. Phil in the Department of Politics, University of Oxford, 2000.

Swenden, Wilfried, and Marten Theo Jans. "Will It Stay or Will It Go? Federalism and the Sustainability of Belgium." *West European Politics* 29 (2006), pp. 877–894.

Szporluk, Roman. "Reflections on Ukraine after 1994: The Dilemmas of Nationhood." *Harriman Review* 7 (March–May 1994), pp. 1–10.

Tagore, Rabindranath. *Nationalism*. London: MacMillan, 1950.

Tambiah, Stanley J. "Buddhism, Politics, and Violence in Sri Lanka." In *Fundamentalisms and the State: Remaking Politics, Economies, and Militance*. Edited by Martin E. Marty and R. Scott Appleby. Chicago: University of Chicago Press, 1993, pp. 589–619.

———. *Sri Lanka: Ethnic Fratricide and the Dismantling of Democracy*. Chicago: University of Chicago Press, 1986.

Taylor, Charles. "The Politics of Recognition." *Multiculturalism*. Edited by Amy Guttman. Princeton: Princeton University Press, 1994, pp. 25–74.

Thomas, Raju G. C., ed. *Perspectives on Kashmir: The Roots of the Conflict in South Asia*. Boulder, CO: Westview Press, 1992.

Tsbellis, G. "Decision Making in Political Systems: Veto Players in Presidentialism, Parliamentarism, Multicameralism, and Multipartyism." *British Journal of Political Science* 25 (1995), pp. 289–325.

———. *Veto Players: How Political Institutions Work*. Princeton: Princeton University Press, 2002.

Tully, James. *Strange Multiplicity: Constitutionalism in an Age of Diversity*. New York: Cambridge University Press, 1995.

Tyler, Leanne C. "Common Origins, Divergent Outcomes: A Comparative Analysis of India's Nagaland and Mizoram Wars of Secession." Unpublished paper written at the Department of Political Science. Columbia University, May 8, 2009.

The Ukraine List. Created by Dominique Arel. University of Ottawa. Available at www.ukrainianstudies.uottawa.ca/orange.html.

United Nations High Commission for Refugees. *Refworld*. September 4, 2009. Available at www.unhcr.org/cgi-bin/texis/vtx/refworld/rwmain.

United Nations Statistics Division. *UN Demographic Year Book 2006*. New York, 2008.

United States Census Bureau. *State and Country Quickfacts*. April 22, 2010. Available at http://eadiv.state.wy.us/demog_data/pop2000/state00.htm.

United States Department of State. "Report to Congress on Incidents during the Recent Conflict in Sri Lanka." Available at www.state.gov/docuements/organizations/.

United States Government Printing Office. "Acts of Congress Held Unconstitutional in Whole or in Part by the Supreme Court of the United States." Available at www.gpoaccess.gov/constitution/pdf2002/046.pdf.

Vallet, Élisabeth A. "L'Autonomie Corse Face à L'Indivisibilité de la République." *French Politics, Culture, and Society* 22, no. 3 (Fall 2004), pp. 51–75.

Vanhanen, Tatu. *Politics of Ethnic Nepotism.* New Delhi: Sterling Publishers, 1991.

Varadachariar, N. D. *Indian States in the Federation.* Calcutta: Oxford University Press, 1936.

Varshney, Ashutosh. "Contested Meanings: India's National Identity, Hindu National-ism and the Politics of Anxiety." *Daedalus* 122 (Summer 1993), pp. 227–261.

———. *Ethnic Conflict and Civic Life: Hindus and Muslims in India.* New Haven: Yale University Press, 2002.

———. "Will the Stallion Baulk in Mid-Gallop?" *Outlook,* December 30, 2002, avail-able at www.outlookindia.com/article.aspx?218463.

Verba, Sidney, and Norman H. Nie. *Participation in America: Political Democracy and Social Equality.* New York: Harper and Row, 1972.

Volder, Jan de. "Le FN Brade Bruxelles." *Revue Française de Geopolitique,* no. 6 (May 1998).

Walzer, Michael. "Comment." *Multiculturalism.* Edited by Amy Guttman. Prince-ton: Princeton University Press, 1994, pp. 99–104.

Way, Lucan A. "Ukraine's Orange Revolution: Kuchma's Failed Authoritarianism." *Journal of Democracy* 16 (April 2005), pp. 131–145.

Weber, Eugen. *Peasants into Frenchman: The Modernization of Rural France, 1870–1914.* Stanford: Stanford University Press, 1976.

West, John F. *Faroe: The Development of a Nation.* London: Hurst, 1972.

Wheare, Kenneth C. *Federal Government.* Oxford: Oxford University Press, 1963.

Wilkinson, Steven I. *Votes and Violence: Electoral Competition and Ethnic Riots in India.* Cambridge: Cambridge University Press, 2006.

Wilson, Andrew. "Ukraine: Two Presidents and Their Powers." In *Post-Communist Presidents.* Edited by Ray Taras. Cambridge: Cambridge University Press, 1997, pp. 67–105.

Wilson, A. Jeyaratnam. *The Break-up of Sri Lanka: The Sinhalese-Tamil Conflict.* Honolulu: University of Hawaii Press, 1988.

———. *The Gaullist System in Asia: The Constitution of Sri Lanka (1978).* London: Macmillan, 1980.

———. *Politics in Sri Lanka, 1947–79.* London: Palgrave/Macmillan, 1974.

Wolczuk, Kataryna. *The Moulding of Ukraine: The Constitutional Politics of State Formation.* Budapest: Central European University Press, 2001.

World Bank. "Peaceful Pilhada, Dubious Democracy: Ache's Post Conflict Elections and their Implications." *Indonesian Social Development Papers* 11, Jakarta, Novem-ber 2008.

———. *World Development Indicators: 2000, 2006.* Washington, DC: International Bank for Reconstruction and Development/World Bank, 2006.

———. *World Development Indicators: 2008.* Washington, DC: World Bank, 2008.

Wriggins, Howard. *Ceylon: Dilemmas of a New Nation*. Princeton: Princeton University Press, 1960.

Yadav, Yogendra. "The Patterns and Lessons." *Frontline* (India), January 3, 2003, pp. 10–16.

———. "Understanding the Second Democratic Upsurge: Trends of Bahujan Participation in Electoral Politics in the 1990s." In *Transforming India: Social and Political Dynamics of Democracy*. Edited by Francine R. Frankel, Zoya Hasan, Rajeev Bhargava, and Balveer Arora. Delhi: Oxford University Press, 2000, pp. 121–145.

———. "Who Won in Punjab: Of the Real Contest." *Frontline* (India), vol. 10, April 1992, pp. 122–126.

Yadav, Yogendra, and Suhas Palshikar. "Between *Fortuna* and *Virtu*: Explaining the Congress' Ambiguous Victory in 2009." *Economic and Political Weekly*, vol. 44, September 26–October 2, 2009, pp. 33–51.

———. "From Hegemony to Convergence: Party System and Electoral Politics in the Indian States, 1952–2002." *Journal of Indian Institute of Political Economy* 15, nos. 1/2 (January–June 2003).

Young, Iris Marion. *Justice and the Politics of Difference*. Princeton: Princeton University Press, 1990.

Zartman, William I. "The Timing of Peace Initiatives: Hurting Stalemates and Ripe Moments." *Global Review of Ethnopolitics*, no. 1 (2001), pp. 8–18.

Ziblatt, Daniel. *Structuring the State: The Formation of Italy and Germany and the Puzzle of Federalism*. Princeton: Princeton University Press, 2006.

Index

The letter *f* following a page number denotes a figure, and the letter *t* denotes a table.

Abdullah, Sheikh (of Kashmir), 112–13
Aceh: federacy in, 6, 229, 243–52, 255;
  GAM in, 242–52; LOGA in, 251,
  252nn123–24; and MoU treaty, 247–49,
  251, 252n123; Muslims in, 242; and peace
  with Indonesia, xi, 242–53; shari'a law
  in, 250; terrorist camps in, 251; tsunami
  in, 244, 249; vs. the UN, 248
Advani, L. K., 83
Ahtisarri, Martti, 246–48, 252n123
Akali Dal party. *See under* Sikhs
Åland Islands. *See* Finland; Sweden
Ambedkar, B. R., 69, 120–21, 138, 139t
Anderson, Benedict, 116–17
Annadurai, C. N., 118–19, 123, 129–30
Arel, Dominique, 179–80, 183, 183n32, 191
Argentina, viii, 36–38, 38t, 46n16, 58, 58t,
  74, 76t, 264f, 267, 268t
Arunachalam, Ponnambalam, 148
Aspinall, Edward, 245
asymmetrical federalism: collective rights
  and, 18; cultural nationalism and, 21;
  dangers of, 172–73; defined, 18; in democracies, 5; in holding together
  federations, 26, 165; Muslim accommodation and, 61, 111; in nested policy
  grammar, 17–19, 22, 56, 170; robust multinationalism and, 262–63; state-nations
  and, 5–7, 8t, 17–18, 22, 173, 201; vs. unitary states, 17–18, 56, 170t, 203, 232; vs.
  U.S. federalism, 260, 270; veto and, 272t
Atkinson, Anthony B., 273
Australia: amendment process in, 261–
  62n8; as coming together federation,

25–26, 260; democracy in, 36–38,
  46n16, 264f, 272t; inequality of representation in, 260t, 268t; national pride in,
  58t; as nation-state, viii, 3, 36–38, 38t;
  symmetrical federalism in, 260–61,
  264f; trust in institutions of, 38t; U.S.
  federalism and, 258; veto in, 260, 272t
Austria: democracy in, 36–38, 46n16, 264f,
  272t; independence of, 27; inequality of
  representation in, 260t, 268–69t; as irredentist, 229; national pride in, 58t; as
  nation-state, viii, 3, 11, 36–38, 38t; South
  Tyrol and, 229–36, 253; symmetrical
  federalism in, 260–61, 264f; trust in institutions of, 38t, 74f, 76t; U.S. federalism and, 258–61; veto and, 121, 259, 272t;
  Yugoslavia and, 253
authoritarianism, 64–66, 65t, 66t, 70t, 82,
  92, 174n1, 180, 196t, 202, 228–31
Azores. *See* Portugal

Badal, Prakash Singh, 92–94, 98
Baltic states, 25n28, 182, 193n63. *See also*
  Estonia; Latvia; Lithuania
Bandaranaike, S. W. R. D., 150–52, 155–
  58, 158n40
Barnett, Ross, 129–30, 132, 134
Baruah, Sanjib, 106, 108
Basque Country, 2, 27, 30–32, 62, 122–
  23n24, 254, 263
Belgium: asymmetrical federalism in, 5–
  6, 9, 37, 165, 261–63, 264f, 271; democ-
  racy in, 36–38, 46n16, 125, 196t, 264f,
  272t; identities in, 14, 31–36, 60–61;

Belgium (*continued*)
independence parties in, 160; inequality
of representation in, 260t, 268t; national
pride in, 58t; nation-state status and,
25–26, 184; parliamentary system in,
265, 271; political parties in, 81; reintegration in, 35; religion in, 68; as
robustly multinational, 2, 147, 264; as
state-nation, viii, 16, 25, 36–38, 38t, 258;
trust in institutions of, 38t, 74f, 76t; U.S.
federalism and, 258; veto in, 259, 271,
272t. *See also* Flanders; Walloons/Wal-
lonia
Bharatiya Janata Party (BJP). *See* BJP
(Bharatiya Janata Party)
Bhattacharya, Mohit, 120
Bhindranwale, J. S., 93–94, 94n6
Bhutan, 209, 209n4
BJP (Bharatiya Janata Party), 69, 77n55,
81, 83–88, 98, 100, 135, 156n36. *See also*
Congress Party (India)
Bose, Sumantra, 161
Brass, Paul R., 91n1, 93–94
Brazil: authoritarianism and, 65n43, 65t;
democracy in, 36–38, 46n16, 63–65,
65t, 195, 196t, 264f, 272t; inequality of
representation in, 267, 268t; national
pride in, 58; as nation-state, viii, 36–38;
population of, 43; symmetrical federal-
ism in, 264f; trust in institutions of, 38t,
76t
Buddhists. *See* India; Sinhalese; Sri Lan-
kan/Ceylonese Buddhists
Bunce, Valerie, 15n13, 16, 34, 144n1
Bundestreue (loyalty to the federation), 13,
99
Burma, 6, 16–17, 102, 258, 267–70. *See also*
Myanmar

Caminal, Miquel, 12
Canada: asymmetrical federalism in, 5–6,
9, 26, 37, 49, 165, 261–63, 264f, 271; democracy in, 36–38, 46n16, 125, 264f,
272t; French language in, 263; independence parties in, 160; inequality of representation in, 260t, 268t; national pride
in, 58t; nation-state components in, 25;
parliamentary system in, 265, 271; popu-

lation of, 43; as robustly multinational,
2, 49, 264, 264f; as state-nation, viii, 16,
25, 36–38, 38t, 258; trust in institutions
of, 38t, 74f, 76t; veto in, 259, 271, 272t
Casanova, José, 179n21, 182n29
Catalonia: identities in, ix, 27, 30–31, 32t,
35, 135, 137; language issues in, 122–
23n24, 263; multinational federalism in,
12; nationalism in, 30; rights of, 254; as
robustly multinational, 2; vs. Spanish
language, 130n43
Centre for the Study of Developing Societies (CSDS), 57, 60, 63, 73–77, 105,
113
centric-regional parties, 18, 20–21, 81, 130–
33, 135–36, 171t, 265
Ceylon, x, 5, 144n2, 145–57, 166–67. *See
also* Sri Lanka; Sri Lankan/Ceylonese
Buddhists
Chabod, Federico, 233
Chelvanayakam, S. J. V., 150
Chhibber, Pradeep, 43
Chile, 63–65, 65n43, 65t, 74f, 195, 196t
China, xi, 6, 145, 202, 255
Christians. *See* India; Indonesia;
Mizoram; Nagaland
civil war. *See* Aceh; Indonesia; Sri Lanka;
Tamils in Sri Lanka
coming together federations, 25–26, 46,
55, 120–21, 260. *See also* holding together federations
confederations, 11–14, 27, 208, 232
conflictual identities, 16, 34. *See also*
Tamils in India
Congress Party (India): vs. Akali Dal, 92,
94; coalitions in, 81, 86–87; Independence movement led by, 100, 106; in
Jammu and Kashmir, 109, 112–13; minorities protected by, 54; in Mizoram,
101, 104–6; nationalist movement led
by, 52; Sikhs and, 84; in Tamil Nadu,
123–27, 125n29, 130–31, 134, 136, 138;
unity fostered by, 53–55. *See also* BJP
(Bharatiya Janata Party)
constitutional patriotism, 5, 12–13, 62
Corsica. *See* France
CSDS. *See* Centre for the Study of Developing Societies (CSDS)

cultural vs. secessionist nationalism, 18, 21–22, 22n21, 117–19, 125n29, 126–27. *See also* Tamils in India; Tamils in Sri Lanka
Czech Republic, 74f, 198n73, 199

Dahl, Robert, 5n4, 16, 259, 274t
Dalai Lama, 202, 255
Dalits. *See* India: marginal groups in
D'Anieri, Paul, 191
Dasgupta, Jyotirindra, 108
De Gasperi-Gruber Accord, 233–35, 253
democracy: asymmetrical federalism in, 5; defeated by political struggle, 244; federacies and, 202; ideal types of, 8t; Islam and, 41; multinational, 47, 116, 119, 122, 125, 129, 264f; vs. nation-state building, viii–x, 3, 108, 275; vs. oppressive national policies, 23; religiosity and, 66–72, 167, 168f; requirements for, 175–79; SDSA study of, 57n35, 61, 75, 161–64, 167; socioeconomic development and, 41–42; state-nations and, viii, 1of, 14, 16–17, 81, 108–11, 159, 193; vs. U.S. federalism, 275; U.S. federal model of, xi–xii, 257–75; veto in, 272t, 274t. *See also* Indian Hindus; Indian Muslims; robust multinationalism; Sikhs; Sri Lankan/Ceylonese Buddhists
demos-enabling federalism, 120–23
Denmark, 68, 74f, 190n51, 206n2, 219, 258, 272t
Denmark–Faroe Island federacy, xi, 6, 210, 218–25, 220n30, 222n35, 253–54
Denmark-Greenland federacy, xi, 5–6, 202, 210, 225–28, 247, 253–54
Djuli, Nur, 246–47, 246n109, 252n123
DMK (Dravida Munnetra Kazhagam). *See* Tamil Nadu: Dravidians in
Dravidians. *See* Tamil Nadu, Dravidians in

Elazar, Daniel J., 209, 226, 236
Elster, John, 261
England. *See* Great Britain; United Kingdom
Estonia, 11, 181, 181n25, 198n73, 199, 216
ethno-federalism, 10, 15–17, 15n13, 19–21, 21n19, 35, 37, 144, 144n1, 255, 269

European Union (EU), 11, 57, 193n63, 198–99, 217, 249–50, 254

Faroe Islands. *See* Denmark–Faroe Island federacy
federacies: vs. associated states, 208–9, 253; vs. asymmetrical federalism, 208–10, 252–55; characteristics of, 204–9, 212–17, 221–26, 247–49; vs. confederations, 208; democracy and, 202; ideal types of, 201–2, 204–7; identities in, 252–55; irredentism and, 204–9, 252–56; overview of, 201–55; presidentialism and, 208; robust multinationalism and, xi; state-nations and, xi, 8t; unitary states and, 201, 207, 254–55. *See also* Aceh; China; Corsica; Denmark; Finland; France; Italy
federalism: demos-enabling, 120–23; U.S. model of, xi–xii, 257–75. *See also* asymmetrical federalism; coming together federations; ethno-federalism; federacies; holding together federations; symmetrical federalism
federalism defined, 5n4, 16
Finland, 74f, 76t, 190n51, 272t
Finland–Åland Island federacy, xi, 6, 202, 210–18, 246–48, 252n123, 253–55
Firth, Peter, 250
Flanders, 2, 32–33, 33t, 35–36, 135, 137, 263
Forrester, D. B., 128n37, 133
France: Åland Islands and, 212, 216; asymmetrical federalism in, 240; Corsica as possible federacy in, 202, 228–32, 239–41; dual executive system in, 197–98; Italy and, 229–31, 236; Muslims in, 29; as nation builder, 22–23, 25; as nation-state, 2–3, 9, 28, 29, 52, 83, 179, 202, 239; political parties in, 81; religion and, 19, 68–69; trust in institutions of, 74f; veto in, 272t
Franco, Francisco, 23, 30, 62
Freedom House Surveys, 169, 174, 193

GAM (Gerakan Aceh Merdeka), 242–52
Gandhi, Indira, 42, 74n52, 84, 92–94, 99, 113, 131–33
Gandhi, Mahatma, ix, 52–53, 68, 123, 138–39, 139t

Gandhi, Rajiv, 84
Gandhi, Sanjay, 94
Gellner, Ernest, 14n12, 21, 24, 117, 133
Georgia, 191–93
German Democratic Republic, 27
German Federal Republic, 9, 27, 62
Germany: democracy in, 46n16, 264f, 272t;
Denmark and, 219, 258; Finland and, 76t;
Greenland and, 226; inequality of repre-
sentation in, 260t, 268–69t, 269; Italy and,
229–30; national pride in, 58, 58t; as
nation-state, viii, 3, 11, 27, 36–38, 38t; reli-
gion in, 68; residual powers in, 260; sym-
metrical federalism in, 260–61, 264f; trust
in institutions of, 38t, 74f, 76t; U.S. feder-
alism and, 258; veto in, 260, 272t
Gini index, 259, 260t, 272–74, 274t
Golwalkar, M. S., 52
Government of India Act (1935), 54, 101
Great Britain, 74f, 81, 153–54, 167, 212, 216,
219. See also United Kingdom
Greece, 272t
Greenland. See Denmark-Greenland
federacy
Gujarat massacre/elections, 74n52, 76n55,
77n55, 80, 84–86, 86f, 88
Gupta, Das, 122–23

Habermas, Jürgen, 12–13, 62
Hale, Henry E., 188n47, 199–200
Helsinki negotiations, xi, 245–53, 245n104,
252n123
Hindus. See Indian Hindus; Jammu re-
gion; Kashmir; Nagaland; Punjab;
Sikhs; Sri Lanka
holding together federations, 22–28, 34–
35, 46, 55, 120–23, 165, 253, 255, 260. See
also coming together federations
Hooghe, Liesbet, 34–35
Horowitz, Donald L., 145, 157
Hrytsak, Yaroslav, 186
human rights issues, 19, 44, 48n21, 74n52,
95n9, 110n39, 183
Humphreys, Macartan, 251

identities. See conflictual identities;
federacies; multiple vs. complementary
identities

identity and trust in state-nations overview, 28–39, 38t
India: asymmetrical federalism in, ix, 5–6,
9, 37, 49, 126, 165, 170t, 261–63, 264f,
271; authoritarianism and, 64, 65t;
Bhutan and, 209; Buddhists in, 41, 67,
111, 163t; Christians in, 41, 53, 61–62,
67–71, 89, 100; colonialism in, 50–51,
54–55, 117; Communist Parties in, 12n11,
48, 48n20, 92, 135; democracy in, ix, 36–
50, 62–72, 81–83, 115, 167, 168f, 196t,
264f, 272t; federalism in, 26–27, 81;
holding together federalism in, 46, 55,
120–23, 165; human rights issues in,
48n21, 74n52; identities in, ix, 60–62, 82,
94; Independence of, 48, 52–53, 118, 125,
147–48; inequality of representation in,
260t, 268t; languages in, 20–21, 40, 44,
46–47, 55, 60, 60n39, 83, 92–93, 121–22,
126; majoritarianism in, 163, 163t; marginal groups in, x, 47, 59, 59t, 66, 66t,
78, 79t, 80, 80t, 82, 100; multinational
federalism and, 4, 29; nationalism in,
51–56, 59, 61, 101, 122–24; national pride
in, 56–62; nation-state components in,
25, 39, 51–54, 83, 184; parliamentary system in, 20, 55, 85–87, 121, 136, 170t, 265,
271; Partition and, 51, 54, 68, 92, 109;
policy grammar in, 167–69; population
of, 36, 42–43, 43n13; poverty in, 36, 40–
42, 44, 45t, 55, 66t, 78, 79t, 82; religious
diversity in, 39–40, 46, 46n17, 55, 66–
72, 83; robust multinationalism and, ix,
2, 39, 147, 264, 264f; scope values and,
40–44, 114; as secular state, 156–57;
specificity of, 44–50, 54; as state-nation,
viii, 11, 16, 25, 38t, 39–88; trust in institutions of, 38t, 48, 72–77, 166, 167t; vs.
U.S., 46–47, 55, 79–81, 120–21, 257, 261,
264; veto in, 271; voting efficacy in, 77–
81. See also BJP (Bharatiya Janata
Party); Congress Party (India); Kashmir;
Mizoram; Nagaland; National Democratic Alliance (NDA); Pakistan; Punjab; Sikhs; Sri Lanka; Tamils in India
Indian Hindus: affirmative action supported
by, 163, 163t; cultural diversity and, 51–53;
democracy supported by, 69–70, 70t, 71f,

82, 167, 168f; Indian institutions trusted by, 72t, 167t; majoritarianism of, 83, 162–63, 163t; Muslims and, 68–69, 82–83, 156n36; national identity among, 61, 61t; nationalists among, 51–52, 67, 69, 83, 85, 112, 156n36; populations of, ix, 41, 46–47, 67; state support for, 156, 156n36; veto power of, 54; voter turnout among, 80, 80t

Indian Muslims: accommodation of, 61; cultural assimilation and, 24; democracy supported by, ix, 69–70, 70t, 71f, 72t, 80, 82; governmental protection of, 54; Hindus and, 68–69, 82–83, 156n36; as marginal group, ix; massacres of, 74n52, 80, 85; national identity among, 61, 61t; national pride among, 59, 59t; Partition and, 54; population of, 41, 46n17, 67; poverty level of, 45t; on Provincial Council Power, 166t; state institutions supported by, 87; trust in Indian Army among, 167t; veto power of, 54; voting efficacy and, 78, 79t; voting rates among, 72t, 80, 80t

Indian National Election Studies, ix, 63, 70, 78, 108n35, 115n43, 134

Indian Peripheral States, 90t

individual rights and collective recognition, 17–19, 56

Indonesia: Christians in, 242; democracy and, 242–52; federacy and, 6, 229, 243–52; geography of, 49; and Helsinki negotiations, 245–53; military rule in, 75n54, 242–43; MoU treaty in, 246n109, 247–49, 251, 252n123; Muslims in, 242–43; Norwegian peacekeeping mission in, 244–45; and peace with Aceh, xi, 242–53, 250n116; vs. Tamil Tigers, 244; terrorism in, 242; U.S. federal model and, 258

inequality of representation, 259, 260t, 270–75

Inglehart, Ronald, 37n46, 57

Ireland, 5n5, 42, 51n23, 74f, 263n11, 272t

irredentism. See Austria; Denmark–Faroe Island federacy; federacies; Italy; Sweden; Ukraine

Islam. See Muslims

Italy, xi, 74f, 202, 216, 229–37, 253–54, 272t

Jammu and Kashmir, 39n1, 49n22, 90t, 109–15, 209. See also Kashmir

Jammu region, 109n37, 111–12. See also Kashmir

Janata Party. See BJP (Bharatiya Janata Party)

Japan, 2–3, 9, 74f, 146, 272t

Jennings, Ivor, 149

Jones, Sidney, 250, 251n119

Kalla, Jusuf, 245, 245n104, 252

Kashmir: elections in, 77n55, 113, 115n43; Hindus in, 109n37; India and, ix, 48, 61, 109–15, 114t; languages in, 112; location of, 90t; Muslims in, 39n1, 61, 109n37, 111, 113; Nehru and, 109–10; Pakistan and, 39n1, 110, 113–14, 114t, 115n43; political history of, 109–13; populations in, 49n22, 109n37; regional divisions of, 39n1, 109n37; robust multinationalism and, 2, 39n1; separatist insurgency in, x, 39, 39n1, 48, 89–90, 109, 113–14; and trust in Indian institutions, 113–14; UN and, 90, 110. See also Jammu and Kashmir; Jammu region; Ladakh region

Kaviraj, Sudipta, 51

Khalistan independence movement. See Punjab; Sikhs

Khilnani, Sunil, 56, 56n33

Khmelnytskyi, Bohdan, 186

Khrushchev, Nikita, 175

Kogan, Norman, 231

Korea, vii n1, 63–64, 65n43, 65t, 75n54

Kravchuk, Leonid, 177–78, 182, 194

Krawchenko, Bohdan, 182

Kuchma, Leonid, 174n1, 186, 194, 198n73, 199

Ladakh region, 39n1, 109n37, 111–12, 114t. See also Jammu region; Kashmir

Laldenga (Mizo leader), 102–5

Lapidoth, Ruth, 210, 215, 217–18, 220n30, 221–23

Lasala-Blanco, Narayani, 140n55

Latvia, 11, 181, 181n25, 198n73, 199, 216

Law on Governing Aceh (LOGA), 251, 252nn123–24

Lijphart, Arend, 41–42, 45t
Linz, Juan J., ix, xii–xiii, 4, 12–13, 22–23, 57n35, 82–85, 179n21, 180
Lipset, Seymour, 41–42
Lithuania, 11, 176, 199, 199n74
LOGA (Law on Governing Aceh), 251, 252nn123–24
Lokniti Network, ix, xii–xiv
Lutz, Donald, 261
Luxembourg, 6n7, 184, 189, 272t
Luxembourg Income Study, 273

Madras presidency. See South India; Tamil Nadu
malapportionment. See Burma; Gini index; inequality of representation
Manor, James, 151
Marshall, Geoffrey, 206n2, 222n35
Mehta, Ferozeshah, 53
Miley, Thomas Jeffrey, xiii, 31
Mill, John Stuart, 40, 40n5, 133
Mizoram: Assam state and, 101–3; asymmetrical federalism and, 106; Burma and, 101; Christians in, 62, 89; Congress Party in, 101, 104–6; democracy supported in, 105; divisions in, 103–4; Hindus in, 263; identities in, 101, 105–6; independence struggles in, x, 2, 39, 48, 89–90, 100–108, 111; India and, 18, 101–6, 106, 113, 208; Laldenga and, 102–5; languages in, 100; location of, 90f; Mizo National Front in, 102–6; and Mizos in India, 49n22; mutually hurting stalemate in, 103–4, 106; vs. Nagaland, 100–108; non-Mizos in, 105, 261, 263; Pakistan and, 102–3; peace in, 106; Scheduled Tribes in, 100; and trust in Indian institutions, 113; Zoramthanga and, 105
Modeen, Tore, 211, 213
Modi, Narendra, 84, 88
Moldova, 174, 191–93, 193n63
Motyl, Alex, 182
MoU treaty. See Aceh; Indonesia
multiculturalism, 29, 47
multicultural states. See Ceylon; India; Switzerland; United States
multinational democracy. See democracy: multinational

multinational federalism, 12–15, 28–29, 34, 41–43, 266. See also pure multinationalism; robust multinationalism
multiple vs. complementary identities: in Belgium, 31, 33t, 34–35; vs. conflictual identities, 16; in Flanders, 32, 35; in India, ix, 39, 82, 94; national pride and, 7, 14; and separatism, ix; in Spain, 29, 31, 32t, 35; state-nations and, viii, 4, 8t, 18, 22, 57n35. See also Belgium; Flanders; India; Spain; Tamil Nadu
Mumbai terrorist attacks, 87
Muslims. See Aceh; France; Indian Muslims; Indonesia; Kashmir; Ladakh region; Pakistan; Sri Lanka
Mussolini, Benito, 229–32, 236
mutually hurting stalemates, 103–4, 106–8, 244–45
Myanmar, 101, 107. See also Burma

Nadar, Kamaraj, 124–26, 140n54
Nagaland: Assam state and, 101–3, 108, 111; Christians in, 62, 100; Government of India Act and, 101; Hindus in, 100; identities in, 101, 101n15, 108n35; India and, 106–8; insurgencies in, x, 2, 39, 48, 89–90, 100, 105–9; languages in, 100, 107; location of, 90f; Manipur and, 108; vs. Mizoram, 100–108; mutually hurting stalemate and, 107–8; and Naga population in India, 49n22; political leaders in, 102–5, 107–8; vs. Punjab, 96; Scheduled Tribes in, 100; Shillong Accord in, 107
Naicker, Ramaswami. See Periar
Narayan, Jayaprakash, 139t
National Democratic Alliance (NDA), 83–84, 86–87
nationalism. See Basque Country; Catalonia; cultural vs. secessionist nationalism; India; Indian Hindus; pure multinationalism; robust multinationalism; South India; Tamils in India; Tamils in Sri Lanka; Ukraine
nation-states: characteristics of, 8t; creation of, vii, 3–4, 10–11, 14, 24, 275; danger in policies of, 175–79; federalism and, 3, 11, 14, 275; ideal types of, viii, x,

3, 7–9, 8t, 13, 17, 27–28, 37–38, 184; as modern state model, 275; vs. nationalism, xi, 11, 13, 23; vs. state-nations, vii–viii, 1–38, 88, 157–59, 173–74, 184–86, 188–90, 243; superiority claimed for, 38; unitary, x, 3, 26, 207, 210, 212, 237, 255. *See also* Argentina; Australia; Austria; Belgium; Brazil; Ceylon; Denmark; Finland; France; Germany; India; Luxembourg; Spain; Sri Lanka; Switzerland; Ukraine

NDA (National Democratic Alliance), 83–84, 86–87

Nehru, Jaraharwal: death of, 130; inclusionary policies of, ix; Jammu and Kashmir and, 109–10, 112; Kamaraj and, 124; Kashmir and, 109–10, 110n38; multinational tensions managed by, 4; on Nagaland, 101n15; name recognition of, 138, 139t; vs. nationalism, 53; vs. Pakistan, 109–10; as positive symbol, 185n39; Punjab and, 92

Nehru (Motilal) Report (1928), 54–55

nested policy grammar, viii, x, 17–22, 56, 119–23, 167–69, 170t, 197

Netherlands, 74f, 272t

New Zealand, 81, 261–62n8, 272t

"no exit" policies, 48, 96, 127, 127n33

Norris, Pippa, 73

Norway, 11, 73, 74f, 164, 169, 218n24, 244, 272t

Nurdin, A. R., 250n116

Obeyesekere, Gananath, 145, 154

Olcott, Henry Steel, 154–55

Orange Revolution. *See* Ukraine

Pakistan: vs. India, 74–75, 75n54, 90–91, 109–10, 110n39; Jammu and Kashmir and, 109–10; Kashmir and, 39n1, 110, 113–14, 114t, 115n43; Mizoram and, 102–3; Mumbai terrorist attack and, 87; Muslims in, 41, 54; vs. Nehru, 109–10; trust in institutions of, 75n54. *See also* Partition

Pallaver, Günther, 236

Palshikar, Suhas, 87

parliamentary systems, 20, 159, 208, 212,

224, 271, 272t. *See also* Belgium; Canada; India; presidential systems; semi-presidential systems; Spain

Partition, 41, 51, 54, 68, 92, 109, 109n37, 120

Patel, Sardar, 123, 139t

Periar (Naicker, Ramaswami), 118–19, 140n53

Phadnis, Urmila, 155

Poland, 176–77, 199–200, 216

political integration vs. cultural assimilation, 18, 21

polity-wide careers, 20–21, 129–30, 150

polity-wide parties, 18, 20–22, 81, 92, 123–26, 135, 135t, 153

Ponnambalam, G. G., 150

Portugal, 199n74; amendment process in, 261–62n8, 272t; Azore secession from, xi, 228, 237–39; Ceylon and, 153; democracy in, 202; federacy in, 202, 254; as nation-state, 3; semi-presidentialism in, 199–200; trust in institutions of, 74f; veto in, 272t

poverty and veto players, 271–75, 274t

presidential systems, 264–65, 272t. *See also* parliamentary systems; semi-presidential systems

Puerto Rico, 209–10

Punjab: Congress Party in, 96, 98–100; economy of, 91n1; Hindus in, 92; human rights issues in, 95n9; identities in, 51, 62; Khalistan independence movement in, x, 2, 39, 48–49, 89, 91–100, 111; location of, 90f; vs. Nagaland, 96; Nehru and, 92; population of, 49n22; terrorist violence in, 95, 96f; and trust in Indian institutions, 113. *See also* Sikhs

pure multinationalism, viii n3, 9–17, 20, 34–35

Puri, Harish, 93

putting together federalism, 26n30, 220n30

Quebec, 2, 26, 160, 263

Rainwater, Lee, 273

Requejo, Ferran, 12

residual powers, 221–22, 261

Rezvani, David, 209–10

Riker, William, 11, 25n28, 257

robust multinationalism: alternative formulas for, x–xi; asymmetrical federalism and, 262–63; defined, viii; democracy and, xi, 193, 257–58, 262–74; parliamentarism and, 20; state-nations and, 17; vs. Ukraine, 174; in a unitary state, 201; U.S. federalism and, 257–58, 262–75. *See also* Belgium; Canada; Catalonia; India; Italy; Kashmir; multinational federalism; pure multi-nationalism; Spain; Sri Lanka; Tamil Nadu

Romania, 191–92

Roper, Steven, 199n74

Rose, Richard, 176, 180, 194–95

Rudolph, Lloyd I., 118, 125

Russia. *See* Finland–Åland Island federacy; Ukraine; U.S.S.R.

Rustow, Dankwart A., 168, 244

Sardinia, 229, 231–32, 236–37

Savarkar, Vinayak, 138, 139t

SBY (Susilo Bambang Yudhoyono), 244–45, 245n104, 252n123

Scandinavia, 2, 11, 25n28, 190, 202, 210–11, 228, 234. *See also* Denmark; Norway; Sweden

Scheduled Tribes. *See* India: marginal groups in; Nagaland

scope values, xi, 36, 40–44, 114, 202, 228–29

SDSA (State of Democracy in South Asia) study, 57n35, 61, 75, 161–64, 167

secessionism, xi, 3, 8t, 10f, 20–21, 22n21, 131n45, 265. *See also* cultural nationalism; Flanders; Portugal; Punjab; South Tyrol; Tamil Nadu; Tamils in India

secessionist nationalism, 18, 21–22, 22n21, 116–19, 124–27, 127n33, 129–34

semi-presidential systems, 17–21, 56, 159, 169, 170t, 197–200, 199n74, 272t. *See also* parliamentary systems; presidential systems

Senanayake, D. S., 151, 156

Sicily, 229, 231–32, 236–37

Sikhs: Akali Dal party of, 85, 92–95, 95n9, 98, 98n10, 100; democracy supported by, 69–71; economy of, 91n1; extremists among, 48n20, 94; Hindus and, 83–85, 87, 92, 98; India and, 41, 84, 91–92, 94–95, 98n10; Khalistan independence and, 39, 89, 95–97, 97t; massacre of, 74n52, 94–95; national identity among, 61t, 62; and population in India, 41; voter turnout among, 80, 80t

Singh, Bhagat, 139t

Sinhalese: on amnesty, 165, 166t; Buddhists among, x, 150, 155, 157, 161; and civil war with Tamils, x, 144–48, 152–55, 157–61, 161n50, 165, 172; on discrimination, 161–62, 162t; on federalism, 165; language issues of, 21, 150–53, 163–64, 184; as majority, 144n3, 150, 153, 157; nationalism of, 151; nation building by, 161; nation-state policies among, 150, 152–53, 157–58; peace sought by, 164–65, 166t; political leaders and parties of, 150–52, 155–57, 169; population of, 148; Sinhalese Only campaign in, 150–53, 164; on Sri Lankan Army, 165; state policies toward, 184n34. *See also* Sri Lanka

Skach, Cindy, 197

Smeeding, Timothy M., 273

Smith, D. E., 153

Smyrl, Marc, 240

Sørensen, Axel, 226–27

South India, 116–19, 123–24, 130. *See also* Tamil Nadu; Tamils in India

South Tyrol, xi, 229–30, 230n60, 233–36, 241, 253, 256

Soviet Union. *See* U.S.S.R.

Spain: asymmetrical federalism in, 5–6, 9, 37, 49, 165, 254, 261–63, 264f, 271; authoritarianism and, 65t; democracy in, 31, 36–38, 46n16, 63, 125, 196t, 263; federalism in, xii, 11, 49, 165, 257; identities in, 14, 29–31, 32t, 60–61; inequality of representation in, 260t, 268t; multinational components in, 22–23, 29–30, 49; national pride in, 58, 58t; nation-state components in, 25–26, 28, 184; parliamentary system in, 265, 271; population of, 43; residual powers in, 261; as robustly multinational, 2, 147, 264; Spanish Civil War in, 30; as state-nation, viii–ix, 11, 16, 25, 28, 36–38, 38t,

258; trust in institutions of, 38t, 74f; U.S. federalism and, 258; veto in, 260, 271, 272t. *See also* Basque Country; Catalonia

Sri Lanka: asymmetrical federalism in, 6, 165, 170t, 172; career opportunities in, 129, 152–55; ceasefire in, 164–65; civil war in, 5–6, 145–47, 158, 160, 161n53, 165, 169–72, 172n64, 184, 191; colonial religions in, 153–55; democracy in, 5–6, 16–17, 141, 146, 148n14, 149, 167–71; federalism in, 5n5, 6, 170; Great Britain and, 153–54, 167; Hindus in, x, 144, 144–45n3, 147–48, 152–55, 158, 161, 167, 167t, 172; language issues in, 20–21, 150–53, 157, 184, 193; Muslims in, 144–45n3, 162, 162t, 164–65, 166t; nation-state policies in, 5–6, 150, 160, 162, 164, 166, 169, 172; peace in, 145–46, 160, 163–64, 166t, 168–69; policy grammar in, 167–69; political leaders and parties of, 149–53, 155–60; political rights in, 169–72; presidential system in, 158–60; progressive nature of, 145–46; public opinion in, 161–68; robust multinationalism and, 148–49, 169, 174; semi-presidential system in, 170t; territorial divisions in, 147–49; terrorist violence in, 146n11; tsunami in, 244; violence in, 145–47. *See also* Ceylon; Tamils in Sri Lanka

Sri Lankan/Ceylonese Buddhists: vs. affirmative action, 163, 163t; on amnesty, 165; democracy supported by, 162–63, 163t, 168f; on equal rights, 167t; as majority, 144n3, 150, 153, 157, 162, 163t, 167; mobilization of, 151, 155–57; and myths regarding Ceylon, 154; nationalism of, 154–57; population of, 144, 162; state-nation policies of, 162; state policies toward, 184, 184n34; state religion and, 157, 170t; vs. Tamil/Hindus, x, 150, 155, 157–58, 172; and trust in Sri Lankan institutions, 161–63, 163t, 167t

Stalin, Joseph, 186, 186n41

state-nation characteristics, viii, 4, 7–8, 8t, 37–38, 173

state-nation enabling factors, 179–86

state-nation goals, 191

state-nation ideal types, viii, 7, 9, 13, 17, 27–28, 37–38, 138. *See also* Ukraine

state-nation overviews, 1–38, 89–114

state-nations vs. nation states, vii–xvi, 1–38, 8t, 157–59, 173–74, 184–86, 188–90, 254

stateness, 10, 15n13, 109–15, 191, 242–43

State of Democracy in South Asia study. *See* SDSA

Stepan, Alfred: Aceh and, 250n116; and Burmese opposition, 266–67; democracy breakdown studied by, 82–83; Finland–Åland Island federacy and, 246, 252n123; Gujarat model and, 84–85; Hindi language issues and, 129; identity conceptions of, 23; India/Kashmir conflict and, 110n39; Indonesia peace process and, 250n118, 251n119; Linz's collaborations with, xii–xiii, 4, 23, 82–84, 110n39, 180; Mizo National Front (MNF) agreement and, 104n25, 105, 105n27; on SDSA board, 57n35; in Sri Lanka, 184n34; state-nation concept and, 4; Tamil Eelam restoration and, 159–60n46; Tamil principals interviewed by, 161n50, 164n54, 165, 165n56; Ukraine and, 179–80, 179n20, 183n32, 188n47; on veto players, 121. *See also* Arel, Dominique; Djuli, Nur; Hale, Henry E.; Jones, Sidney; Nurdin, A. R.

Sternberger, Dolf, 62

Strachey, John, 50, 51n23

Subramanian, Narendra, 118–19, 129

Suharto (Indonesian president), 242

Susilo Bambang Yudhoyono (SBY), 244–45, 245n104, 252n123

Sutarto, Endriartono, 243, 244n103

Sweden, 3, 11, 74f, 190n51, 210–12, 213n16, 216–17, 253–54, 272t

Switzerland: asymmetrical federalism in, 37; as coming together federation, 25, 260; democracy in, 36–38, 46n16, 264f, 272t; inequality of representation in, 260t, 268t; national pride in, 58, 58n36, 58t; nation-state components in, 184; religion in, 68; as state-nation, viii, 4, 27–28, 38t, 58n36, 258; symmetrical federalism in, 260–61, 264f; territorial mobili-

Switzerland (*continued*)
zation absent in, 2; trust in institutions of, 76t; U.S. federalism and, 258; veto in, 260, 272t
symmetrical federalism, 8t, 17–18, 26, 56, 165, 260–64, 264f. *See also* asymmetrical federalism
Szporluk, Roman, 179n21, 181

Tagore, Rabindranath, 52
Tambiah, S. J., 145, 154–56, 158, 161
Tamil Nadu: asymmetrical federalism in, 126; Brahmin power in, 117–19; castes in, 117–19; centric-regional parties in, 130–33, 135; Congress Party in, 123–27, 130–31, 134, 136, 138; cultural vs. secessionist nationalism in, 117–19; democracy and, 137t, 139t, 141, 142t; Dravidians in, x, 2, 39, 116–19, 122–23, 125n29, 126, 129, 132n36, 136, 170t; elections in, 135, 135t; identities in, 123–25, 127–30, 134–40, 135t, 136t, 139t, 142–43; vs. India, 130; languages in, 117–19, 122, 128–29; location of, 90f; nationalism in, 132–34; nation-state policies in, 159; Northern vs. Southern Hindus and, 117; political integration in, 133–34, 159; political parties of, 132–36; polity-wide parties in, 123–26, 128–33, 135, 135t; robust multinationalism and, 134; secession as nonissue in, 116, 119, 126, 129, 133, 147; trust in central government in, 142–43, 142t. *See also* South India; Tamils in Sri Lanka
Tamils in India: asymmetrical federalism and, 170t; career opportunities for, 127–30; castes among, 125; cultural nationalism among, 124–25, 125n29, 129–34, 171; democracy and, 141, 142t; and Indian Independence, 124; Indian policies toward, 170t; language issues and, 118, 122, 125–26, 128–30, 133–34, 170t; Madras and, 117, 122, 126; political organizations of, 126–27, 129–34; religious recognition for, 170t; robust multinationalism and, 134; secessionist nationalism among, 124–27, 129–34, 145; Sri Lankan Tamils and, 167

Tamils in Sri Lanka: administrative posts held by, 147–48, 153, 158, 165, 184; on amnesty, 165, 166t; asymmetrical federalism and, 170t, 172; vs. Buddhists, x, 150, 155, 157–58, 172; career opportunities for, 129, 152–54; and civil war with Sinhalese, x, 144–48, 152–55, 157–61, 161n50, 165, 172; conflictual identities and, 161; cultural nationalism among, 171; on discrimination, 162, 162t; disenfranchisement of, 149–50, 157, 159–60, 163–65, 184; federalism and, 165, 172; Hindus and, 144–45n3, 147, 155, 165, 172; Indian Tamils and, 167; Jaffna Zone Tamils and, 147, 149, 161; language issues and, 128n37, 150–53, 163–64, 170t, 184; Marxism and, 149–51; overview of, 144–71; peace sought by, 164–65; political leaders and parties of, 149–50, 155, 159–60, 165, 169; on Provincial Council Power, 166t; recognition of, 172; secessionist nationalism among, x, 147–49, 159–61, 161n50, 164, 166; semi-presidential system and, 170t; Sri Lankan policies toward, 170t; territorial divisions of, 147–49; and trust in Sri Lankan institutions, 161–62, 165; and Up-Country Tamils, 147, 149–50, 161, 162t, 164–65, 166t; and violent conflict, 171. *See also* Tamil Nadu
Taylor, Charles, 18–19, 24, 172
Tito, Josip, 16, 229, 231–32
Transnistria, 174, 192
trust in state institutions, viii, 7, 20, 22, 29–30, 36–38, 63
Tsbellis, George, 262, 270–71
Tymoshenko, Yulia, 194

Ukraine: Chernobyl disaster and, 186; citizenship laws of, 181–83; civil liberties in, 193; common symbols in, 185–86; Communist Party of, 177–78, 182; confident democrats in, 194–95, 195t; constitution preamble of, 182–83; democracy and, 174–75, 189, 191–200, 195t; demographics of, 175–76; dual executive system in, 197; elections in, 193; identities in, 174–77, 180–81, 185, 187,

196t; independence of, 175–76, 179n20, 181, 183; language issues in, 174, 176–78, 180, 183–93; minorities in, 176, 183–84, 192, 201; nationalists in, 182–86, 193; nation-state policies and, 6, 6n7; Orange Revolution in, 174n1, 179, 187–89, 193–94, 199; overview of, 173–200; peace in, 191–93; polarization in, 187–88; political freedom in, 193; political rights in, 174n1; religious issues in, 176; requirements for democracy in, 173–79; vs. robust multinationalism, 174; Rukh nationalist party in, 177–78, 182, 182n29; Russian irredentism and, x, 173, 178–79, 190; Russian language in, 188–93; Russians in, 6n7, 175–78, 180–82, 184–87, 191, 194–95, 196t; state building in, 180–87; state-nation factors in, x, 179–86; trust in institutions of, 177, 195; U.S.S.R. and, 174n1, 176–77, 193

unitary states: vs. asymmetrical federalism, 17–18, 56, 170t, 203, 232; federacies and, 201–55; federalism and, 24–26, 25n26, 203, 275; independence from, 203–4; nation-state policies and, x–xi, 3, 5, 8t, 173; separatist conditions in, 203; state-nation policies and, x, 5–6, 8t; veto in, 272t, 274t. See also Belgium; Denmark; federacies; Finland; France; Indonesia; Japan; Luxembourg; Norway; Portugal; Sri Lanka; Sweden; Ukraine

United Kingdom, 5n5, 51n23, 160, 262n11, 272t. See also Great Britain

United Nations, vii, vii n1, 90, 110, 226, 233, 235, 248, 253

United Nations Development Program, xiii, 45t

United States: Åland Islands and, 212; amendment process in, 261, 271; Azores and, 253; as coming together federation, 25–26, 46, 55, 120–21, 260; democracy in, 36–38, 46n16, 264f, 272t; federal model overview, xi–xii, 257–75; Greenland and, 226; House of Representatives, 259, 271; vs. India, 46–47, 55, 79–81, 80t, 120–21, 257, 261, 264; inequality of representation in, xii, 259, 260t, 266, 268t; national identity in, 140, 141t; na-

tional pride in, 58, 58t; as nation-state, viii, 36–38, 38t; political parties in, 81; population of, 43; presidential system in, 262, 264–66, 271; Puerto Rico and, 209; religion in, 19, 46, 68; residual powers in, 261, 261n7; Senate, 259, 261; separation of powers in, 262; Supreme Court of, 262; symmetrical federalism in, 260–62, 264f; territorial mobilization absent in, 2; trust in institutions of, 38t, 74f, 76t; veto in, 121, 259–60, 262, 270–71, 272t; voter turnout in, 79, 80t

Uruguay, 63–65, 65n43, 65t

U.S.S.R. (Soviet Union): disintegration of, 15; ethno-federal states of, 10, 17; Finland and, 212, 216; putting together federalism in, 26n30; Stalin as positive figure in, 183, 186; stateness crisis in, 45, 96. See also Ukraine

Valle d'Aosta, 229–32, 236

Vanhanen, Tatu, 294

Varshney, Ashutosh, xiii, 84–85

Verfassungspatriotismus (commitment to constitution), 12, 27, 62

veto players, 121, 260, 271–73

veto powers, 54, 121, 259–60, 262, 265, 271, 272t, 274t

voter turnout, 79–81, 95n8, 98

Walloons/Wallonia, 33, 33t, 36, 263

Walzer, Michael, 18–19

Way, Lucan, 174n1, 192, 192n56

Weber, Eugen, viii, 24

we-feeling, 5, 7, 11, 13–15, 111, 161, 172, 186

West, John, 218n24

Wheare, Kenneth C., 122n21, 257

Wilson, A. Jeyaratnam, 159–60

Wilson, Andrew, 187n44

Wolczuk, Kataryna, 178, 181

World Values Survey, viii, 37–38, 57–58, 73–75, 77t, 140

Wriggins, Harold, 145–46, 152

Yadav, Yogendra, ix, xii–xiii, 84–85, 87, 134

Yanukovych, Viktor, 176n7, 190, 194

Yeltsin, Boris, 182n30, 198, 198n73
Yudhoyono, Susilo Bambang ("SBY"), 244–45, 245n104, 252n123
Yugoslavia, xii, 9–10, 14–17, 34–35, 45, 96, 144. *See also* Austria; Italy

Yushchenko, Viktor, 187–88, 190, 193–94, 199
Yusuf, Irwandi, 249–51

Zoramthanga (Mizo leader), 105